THE UNEASY PARTNERSHIP

GENE M. LYONS

THE *Uneasy*
PARTNERSHIP
Social Science and the
Federal Government in
the Twentieth Century

RUSSELL SAGE FOUNDATION
NEW YORK, N.Y.   1969

PUBLICATIONS OF RUSSELL SAGE FOUNDATION

Russell Sage Foundation was established in 1907 by Mrs. Russell Sage for the improvement of social and living conditions in the United States. In carrying out its purpose the Foundation conducts research under the direction of members of the staff or in close collaboration with other institutions, and supports programs designed to improve the utilization of social science knowledge. As an integral part of its operations, the Foundation from time to time publishes books or pamphlets resulting from these activities. Publication under the imprint of the Foundation does not necessarily imply agreement by the Foundation, its Trustees, or its staff with the interpretations or conclusions of the authors.

CONTENTS

PREFACE

FOR TWO YEARS, between 1966 and 1968, I had the good fortune to serve as Executive Secretary of the Advisory Committee on Government Programs in the Behavioral Sciences, National Academy of Sciences–National Research Council. The Committee was charged with a broad mandate to examine the use and support of social and behavioral science research by agencies of the federal government. During the course of the Committee's deliberations, the whole area of social science research in the federal government became the subject of increasingly serious attention: bills were introduced in the Congress to establish a National Social Science Foundation and a Council of Social Advisers; the National Academy of Sciences and the Social Science Research Council jointly launched a large-scale Behavioral and Social Science Survey; the National Science Board appointed a Special Commission on the Social Sciences; testimony was offered before congressional committees to set up a National Data Center; and the budgets for social science research in federal agencies were measurably increased.

The response to social science research in government was not entirely positive, however. Project Camelot—that vast but ill-fated program, financed by the Army and designed to study patterns of social change in Latin America—had marked a serious disruption of the work of American scholars in many foreign countries. The Project Camelot affair was but one of several events that began to arouse suspicions about the role of research under government auspices—suspicions between American and foreign social scientists, among American social scientists themselves, and between American social scientists and agencies of the federal government. The idea of a National Data Center brought cries of anguish and fears—principally from journalists and some members of Congress—that the centralized accumulation of information on individual citizens would lead to dangerous invasions of personal privacy. There was also a certain disappointment and cynicism (whether justified or not is another matter) with regard to the "utility" of research when programs of the federal government in which social scientists (and social science findings) were visibly involved seemed to offer no more of an answer to vexing social problems than did less systematic, more intuitive approaches to human affairs.

As the Advisory Committee began its review of social science in the federal government, it seemed useful (and, for that matter, necessary) to take a look backward to the origins of existing research programs and to the experience with earlier efforts to relate social science to the processes of the federal government. As Executive Secretary of the Committee, much of my time was devoted to putting the past record together in order to provide the members of the Committee with a body of information on the programs they were reviewing and with a sense of historical perspective against which the contemporary issues of social science in the federal government could be appraised.

From the very beginning, it was anticipated that the historical record I was accumulating and analyzing might provide the basis for a small book for general distribution. Indeed, the presentation of the material was designed with this prospect in mind. The work on the Committee's report was completed in the spring of 1968 and the report itself, including a series of recommendations on strengthening the use of social science by federal agencies, was published in September.[1] I was then able to turn to the background material I had developed for the Committee and complete the task of preparing a manuscript for publication. The work of the Advisory Committee and my own participation in its

[1] *The Behavioral Sciences and the Federal Government*, Report of the Advisory Committee on Government Programs in the Behavioral Sciences, Publication 1680, National Academy of Sciences–National Research Council (Washington, D.C., 1968).

efforts were supported by grants to the National Academy of Sciences by the Department of Defense and the Russell Sage Foundation. My final work on the manuscript was made possible through the Russell Sage grant to the Academy with the Foundation also agreeing to publish the book. The purpose of this book, like the background papers on which it is based, is to provide an historical record and perspective against which to examine current issues of social science in the federal government.

Throughout this enterprise I have accumulated many debts, too many, I fear, for me ever to feel that I shall be able to make proper repayment. From members of the Advisory Committee I received not only warm support, but also a broad education in the social sciences. I am thus truly grateful to Donald R. Young, Chairman; Herbert A. Simon, Vice Chairman; Frederick N. Cleaveland; A. Hunter Dupree; George M. Foster, Jr.; Albert Garretson; Morris Janowitz; Herbert C. Kelman; Lyle H. Lanier; Wilbert E. Moore; Karl J. Pelzer; Ithiel De Sola Pool; Thomas C. Schelling; Joseph J. Spengler; Alexander Spoehr; and George K. Tanham.

To Donald R. Young I must express a special debt. As Chairman of the Advisory Committee, Dr. Young brought to us all a lifetime of concern and devotion to the strengthening of social science and its application to the problems of society. To me, he was a source of invaluable information, having participated in many of the major developments in social science since the early 1930's. But, more important, he was willing to share with me his insight, his experience, his warmth as a human being. I will always cherish the grand opportunity I had to work with him and the confidence he showed in my own contribution to the effort in which we were engaged.

As a member of the staff of the Division of Behavioral Sciences, National Academy of Sciences–National Research Council, I was able to examine the particular issues of social science from an important vantage point in the politics of national science policies. Within the Division, Dr. Henry David, Executive Secretary, was a constant source of support. Dr. David is a knowledgeable and stimulating man and I could not have hoped for a more valued colleague. My research assistant and secretary was Mrs. Gay

Henderson, who contributed a sense of order and competence to our work that was indispensable. How often I realized my good luck in having Mrs. Henderson to help me! I also enjoyed working with Dr. Alexander Clark, who joined the Division during the last year of my stay. And I am grateful for the kind assistance of Mrs. Marjorie Wilson and Mrs. Sharon Bauer of the Division staff.

Dr. Frederick Seitz, President of the National Academy of Sciences, showed a personal interest in my work that I will always remember. Dr. Orville Brim, President of the Russell Sage Foundation, has encouraged me to carry this book through to completion and shared with me his own deep concern with the issues with which I have dealt. Within the Academy, in the various federal agencies with which I had contact, from universities all over the country, there were friends and colleagues who permitted me to question them, to test out ideas, to talk out my problems. I can do little more than list their names (undoubtedly omitting some names that should be here), hoping that each will understand my debt to him: Gabriel Almond, Ralph Beals, Jeanne Brand, Elisabeth Crawford, Wilton Dillon, Steven Ebbin, Robert Green, Pendleton Herring, Harold Lasswell, Harold Orlans, Luigi Petrullo, Raymond Platig, Don K. Price, Henry Riecken, Gene Sunderlin, Conrad Taeuber, Richard Trumbull, and Stephen Viederman.

Finally, any author bears a special sense of responsibility to his family; so do I to my wife, Micheline, and to my children, Catherine, Daniel, and Mark. They, more than others, I fear, had to suffer because of the struggles with ideas and words that I, like any author, went through before this book was finished. My hope is that they understood (and continue to understand) why my attention was often diverted and why the subject of this book has been so important to me.

But, when all is said and done and all acknowledgements made, let me insist that I, and I alone, am responsible for this book. None of the people or agencies that have helped me can be expected to agree with what I have said. Most especially, the Russell Sage Foundation, as publisher of the book, is free of responsibility for its contents. This is my book, as it must be.

GENE M. LYONS

FOREWORD

As a BEGINNING graduate student in sociology in 1919, and for some years thereafter, I (and others of my generation) never expected more than minor support for research, and most of that from my own university in the form of time free from teaching duties. In the five decades since then, I have seen funds for graduate fellowships, for advanced research, and for the application of research to practical affairs become available in (by 1919 terms) unimaginable amounts from private foundations, business and businessmen, and government. Indeed, in some fields, there are widespread complaints that there are more research funds available than social scientists can effectively and productively manage.

The earliest research support for social scientists in significant amounts was provided by philanthropic foundations. Perhaps the most crucial of the early foundation allocations for research in the social sciences were the sizable grants made by the Laura Spelman Rockefeller Memorial in the 1920s. Administrators of the Memorial felt that "Through the promotion of the social sciences, . . . there would come a greater knowledge as to social conditions, a better understanding of social forces, and a higher objectivity in the development of social policy."[1] Whether or not these broad purposes were achieved (or approached), the Memorial grants first demonstrated to a wide group of academic social scientists the possibilities, advantages, and problems of subsidized research.

---

[1] Final Report of the Laura Spelman Rockefeller Memorial (New York, 1933), p. 10.

Foundation grants of over $4 million were disbursed to the Social Science Research Council in the decade beginning in 1923 by the Memorial, the Rockefeller Foundation, the General Education Board, the Carnegie Corporation of New York, the Rosenwald Fund, the Russell Sage Foundation, and others. Awarded to social scientists all over the country, these funds emphasized the common interests and essential unity of the social sciences. Generally foundation interest in the social sciences then, as today, was based on the potential application of research for the amelioration of the social ills with which the foundations themselves were concerned. However, few foundations then, again as today, based their programs on broad support of research as an essential groundwork for the improvement of knowledge about social behavior.

The interest of business and industry in the social sciences, like that of foundations, mainly has been based on the expectation of practical applications, though understandably with less altruistic objectives in mind. Among social scientists, economists naturally were the first to be recognized by business as an important resource. Not only were economists the first social scientists commonly to be employed by corporations, but the economics-based schools of business also were the first academic enterprises to receive support from business and industrial companies. Only in more recent years has an appreciable number of business and industrial leaders come to understand that all of the social sciences have contributions to make to their professional problems. It still is not common, but it now is not rare, to find anthropologists, social psychologists, and sociologists in the employ of corporations, with some engaged in research and others in advisory or administrative positions. Corporate philanthropy, however, has shown minor interest in the social sciences other than in economics.

There is no need here to make extended comment on the relations of the social sciences and the federal government, for that is the subject of the book for which this foreword is written. Here it only need be said that there is a long history of association between the government and social science and that the federal government now is the overshadowing source of support for advanced study and research and for the practical application of the social sciences as a whole. (It may be added that many social scientists work in state and city governments, but that this confusing mass of experience has been inadequately studied and thus defies general comment.)

The National Science Foundation estimated that $333 million would be expended by the federal government for social science in 1968. This estimate may have been somewhat inflated by the inclusion by departments and agencies of an unknown but considerable number of activities, such as the keeping of simple statistical records, which do not fall within the broadest definition of social science as ordinarily understood. Yet, whatever the proper deduction from this estimate may be, the remainder is enough to dwarf contributions from other sources. Thus, the estimate for social science expenditures just by the Foundation itself and the National Institutes of Health, both agencies which do have an acceptable concept of social science, alone total over $46 million. In the years shortly prior to World War II it was practically impossible to write a text in any social science without relying on findings from research financed by the private foundations. The same must be said today of research financed by government.

The sheer amount of money annually invested in the social sciences by the federal government demands a review of its objectives, a study of the diversified and complex administration of research by a variety of departments and agencies, and an analysis of recommendations made for improvement of the role of research. Furthermore, growing skepticism on the part of many social scientists concerning the practical wisdom and the ethical implications of accepting federal funds for research, particularly from mission-oriented departments such as the Department of Defense and the Department of State, can hardly be viewed in perspective without an examination of the total governmental experience such as Dr. Lyons now has completed. Common fears concerning the possible distorting effects on academic social science of heavy dependence on federal subsidies also now may be considered in the light of the overall situation.

The evaluation of the relations of government and the social sciences provided by Dr. Lyons provides a model for parallel studies of the relations of private philanthropy and of business and business leaders with the social sciences. There are apprehensions on the part of many social scientists concerning these two sources of support, no less than concern about support from the federal government. Private philanthropy has been charged by responsible social scientists and others with exerting financial influence to divert their work away from basic into applied research, into socially irrelevant trivia, and into some specialties and away from others perhaps more important. Private business, of course, most often has been criticized for favoring the *status quo,* if not the *status quo ante,* as well as for emphasizing practical results to the point of unethical concern with profits to the disadvantage of the total society.

Without debating the merits of such critical views, it is vital for social science, indeed for all science and scholarship, that significant support be received from all three sources—from foundations, private business and business men, and government. Support is not likely to be in equal proportions, nor need it be, so long as no one source becomes so large in relation to the others as to be excessively dominant in its influence. Most likely, the contributions to the social sciences from each source will be related to continuing expectation that social research is needed both in the resolution of pressing social questions and as a basis for long-range social planning. It is imperative that support by any one source be so designed that it fully respects and complements the objectives and values not only of the academic community but also of the other sources of research support.

All social scientists and others who have faith in the current and future role of the social sciences in the struggle for social advance are indebted to Dr. Lyons for his analytical and constructive account of the experience, pitfalls, and potential relations between the federal government and social scientists. They should also be grateful that his work has made it plain that, although the federal government has the resources and the growing will to carry the major financial burden for social science support, its dominating position, however understanding and praiseworthy, calls not for withdrawal from the field as some have argued, but for increased positive concern by the private sectors of society.

DONALD R. YOUNG

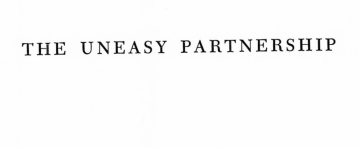

THE UNEASY PARTNERSHIP

CHAPTER I

KNOWLEDGE
AND GOVERNMENT

IT IS STATED in the proceedings of the American Philosophical Society that the great French naturalist, the Comte de Buffon, was among the first foreign scientists to be elected to membership. This honor was bestowed upon Buffon despite his earlier observation that the climate of America was practically unfit for human beings and his consequent pessimism about the future of settlements in the new land. Buffon's disparagement of their country was ignored by the American savants when it came to his election. Perhaps they were impressed by his impartiality; for when Benjamin Franklin sent him evidence to the contrary, Buffon, like the honest scientist he was, modified his earlier speculations. But the possibility that Buffon might have had a point seems to have lingered in the minds of some of his American colleagues. For when the federal government prepared to conduct the second decennial census of population in 1800, the Society petitioned the Congress to include questions that would ascertain "the effect of the soil and climate of the United States on the inhabitants thereof."[1]

The Society's petition was not acted upon, even though the influence of climate on human development and on political and social institutions had been a familiar theme in the writings of philosophers like Montesquieu whose works were well known to

---

[1] Gilbert Chinard, "The American Philosophical Society and the World of Science (1768–1800)," *Proceedings of the American Philosophical Society,* Vol. 87, No. 1 (July 14, 1943), pp. 1–11. See also Henry Steele Commager and Elmo Giordanetti (eds.), *Was America a Mistake?* (New York: Harper Torchbooks, 1967), including the reading from the works of the Comte de Buffon.

many American statesmen. There seems, however, to have been no deep scientific concern about these matters among members of the Society, as there was undoubtedly little political concern among members of the Congress. Those who drew up the petition to enlarge the scope of the 1800 census appear to have been motivated by general curiosity and by a certain chauvinistic desire to find evidence "that under the joint influence of the soil, climate and occupation, the duration of human life in this portion of the earth will be found at least equal to what it is in any other, and that population increases with a rapidity unequalled in all others." What is significant is that the method that the Society encouraged toward this end—the systematic gathering and analysis of facts— was empirical and not doctrinaire.

Much has been written about the scientific spirit that characterized the men who founded and first led the American republic. A. Hunter Dupree has said that "the natural law to which the colonists appealed in 1776 and the faith in reason which they trusted for deliverance from both political and clerical despotism sprang in part from science and established a climate congenial to its growth."[2] And Don K. Price has suggested that the "first effect" of the leadership of Franklin, Thomas Jefferson, and their friends "was to destroy the traditional theory of hereditary sovereignty and to substitute the idea that the people had a right, *by rational and empirical processes,* to build their governmental institutions to suit themselves."[3] To this, Merle Curti has added: "Franklin helped tame the thunderbolt, and by doing so helped foster a more empirical and less fearful attitude toward the world."[4]

The scientific spirit of the Founding Fathers had its roots in the Enlightenment with its emphasis on reason, progress, and earthly salvation. But this spirit was also shaped by a pragmatism and utilitarianism that grew out of the practical demands of settling a new land and that have characterized American society and Amer-

[2] A. Hunter Dupree, *Science and the Federal Government* (Cambridge: Belknap Press of Harvard, 1957), p. 6.

[3] Don K. Price, *Government and Science* (New York: New York University Press, 1954), p. 4 (emphasis added).

[4] Merle Curti, *The Growth of American Thought* (3rd ed.; New York: Harper & Row, 1964), p. 93.

ican science from the beginning. For men like Franklin and Jefferson, science was not an abstraction. Both were eminently practical, little given to theorizing. Their inclination was to put science to work to make the lives of people more productive and to further the development of their country. It might be said that they possessed the technological, rather than the scientific, spirit—no less empirical, but highly utilitarian in emphasis.

The empirical attitude found its way into the Constitution through provision for a census of population once every ten years in order that "Representatives . . . be apportioned among the several States . . . according to their respective numbers." The census, as Price has put it, "thus . . . became the ultimate basis of sovereign power in the United States."[5] Initially, however, it was a sensible and objective way of gaining equality of representation in the House of Representatives by a direct count of voters. Today, two centuries after the election of the Comte de Buffon to membership in the Philosophical Society, it serves many other functions. The census and other statistical programs of the federal government are now important bases for formulating fiscal and monetary policies; for distributing education and welfare funds among states, cities, and counties; and for public planning of school construction, highway systems, airlines routes, and health facilities.

The mountains of empirical data that the government now collects would undoubtedly astonish the scientists who, under Jefferson's leadership, sent the early petition to the national legislature and would bewilder those members of the Sixth Congress who, to all intents and purposes, ignored it. Nowadays, the activities of the federal government require continual and cumulative information about agricultural production, prices, and utilization; industrial capacity and resources; national income and its distribution; transportation facilities; housing; population trends and mobility; educational institutions, expenditures, and enrollments; births, marriages, deaths, and diseases; health and welfare services; employment, earnings, and occupational training; the rate and direction of scientific research and technological development—and the list could go on. Official statistics are not only the

5 Price, *op. cit.*, p. 5.

"ultimate basis of sovereign power"; they also have a heavy influence on how that power will be used.

The information that the federal government requires to conduct public business is a measure not only of the expansion of federal programs, but also of the relevance of social science to public policies. In the years since the turn of the twentieth century, the federal government has had to respond to economic and social changes that have occurred in the wake of two world wars, the Depression, new international commitments, the revolution in science and technology, and new demands for meeting the democratic promise of equal opportunity. The government responds to social and economic change by formulating public policies on various important matters: the allocation of economic resources, the mobilization and deployment of military power, the protection of rights and property, the development of educational facilities, the conservation and protection of the physical environment.

Formulating policy—or, in practice, passing laws or authorizing programs that define policy and put it into effect—is a political matter. It is a complex process that involves empirical analysis, political bargaining, weighing historical precedents, and consulting the experience or intuition of executive officials and legislators. The policy process has been rightly called a "seamless web" with no fixed starting point and with a continual interplay of motives, interests, and influences. The importance of empirical analysis in this "seamless web" was underscored by Wilbur Cohen soon after he was appointed Secretary of the Department of Health, Education, and Welfare in 1968. Having risen to the top in a department in which he had had long experience, he spoke with a certain nostalgia of the dependence of policy-makers like himself on the sources of information and analysis down the line. He placed great value on the work of statisticians, who "ask the questions, gather the facts and write the reports which are used to formulate Federal policies and programs."[6]

The importance of statistics in policy-making is not, however, automatic; much depends on their being accepted as accurate and

---

[6] Reported by Jerry Klutz, "The Federal Diary," *Washington Post*, May 22, 1968, p. A 22.

pertinent. Statistics are a representation of an economic or social condition: the number of births and deaths over a given period of time represents a trend in population rise or fall; the total value of goods and services produced in the nation over one, two, or five years represents the rate of economic growth or decline; the number of children attending school under differing conditions of classroom size, racial distribution, and costs of education per pupil represents the state of educational opportunity. By revealing such conditions or trends in the social system, statistics provide the raw information needed to decide on any government policy or program.

But do statistics *accurately* represent the economic or social state they are intended to picture? And even if they are accurate, what, in the final analysis, is their significance? The popular skepticism about statistics—that statistics can lie, be distorted, or mean all things to all men—is balanced by the equally popular acceptance of the accuracy and honesty of government statistics. The validity of statistical information, however, depends on the methods through which the actions of agencies responsible for collecting data are controlled for accuracy. These methods depend, in turn, on techniques developed in the social sciences, as well as on hard work, patience, care, and common sense. The analysis of statistical information, interpreting its true meaning, depends no less on the social sciences. The purpose of social science is the discovery of knowledge about human behavior and social institutions. It is this knowledge that gives form and shape, order and purpose, to raw information about people, their mobility, their buying habits, their health, their educational opportunities.

Contemporary social science in the United States is a twentieth-century phenomenon. Its origins lie in the growth of scientific methods throughout the nineteenth century and the specialization that by the end of the century began to influence patterns of research in all fields. From the broad studies of law, history, and philosophy, the social sciences emerged at a time when biologists were providing a new understanding of man's evolution, psychologists new concepts of human motivation and emotion, and anthropologists systematic methods for examining human societies and their institutions. The early development of social science, moreover, coincided with a growing complexity in national life produced by widespread industrialization and urbanization. Indeed, these changes in American life brought the social sciences in closer contact with government, at first with city and state governments and later with the federal government.

Early in the nineteenth century, as the elder Arthur M. Schlesinger has written, "the common man [generally a farmer or rural tradesman] agreed with President Jackson that any intelligent citizen could discharge the duties of any governmental office . . . [and thus he] had an abiding suspicion of the theorist or the 'scholar in politics.' "[7] For by this time the spirit of the frontier had, to a considerable extent, superceded that of the Enlightenment as the operating principle of American life, and men in public office had more faith in independent common sense than in information provided by specialists. By the end of the century, however, "as the urban influence became uppermost . . . in a civilization rapidly growing more complex, men began to place a higher value on thoroughly mastering a skill or conquering a particular intellectual domain. . . . Even in public life expert knowledge steadily played a larger part, notably in the administrative services of city, state and nation."[8] For example, some of the major cities established bureaus of municipal research which played an important role in the reform movement and in fostering good government through the scientific management of public affairs.

Early in the twentieth century, social science surveys of crime, corruption, and poverty were as much a part of the reform movement as the journalistic exposés of muckrakers. These surveys advanced systematic research by developing techniques for interviewing large numbers of people, collecting bodies of empirical evidence about economic and social conditions, and examining the often hidden yet crucial workings of economic and social institutions. But they also had political effects; they brought social scientists into the ranks of the reformers. The whole question of reform gave rise to differences and disagreements among social scientists and tended

[7] Arthur M. Schlesinger, *Paths to the Present* (New York: The Macmillan Company, 1959), p. 11.
[8] *Ibid.*, p. 20.

to divide those interested chiefly in the accumulation of knowledge from those impelled to take some form of social action. It also created tensions between social scientists and policy-makers, for the latter resented systematic analysis as a challenge to their own intuition and experience, let alone their vested interests.

These two sets of tensions—among social scientists and between them and politicians—have persisted throughout the history of government–social science relations since the early years of the century. Writing in 1922, Walter Lippmann observed that every "complicated community has sought the assistance of special men," in former times "augurs, priests, elders." In its early stages, "our own democracy . . . sought lawyers to manage its government," and as society grew "furiously and to colossal dimensions by the application of technical knowledge," policy-makers called on new experts in specialized fields. Yet "curiously enough," Lippmann said, the policy-maker "was slow to call in the social scientist." Why?

> The man of affairs, observing that the social scientist knows only from the outside what he knows, in part at least, from the inside, recognizing that the social scientist's hypothesis is not in the nature of things susceptible of laboratory proof, and that verification is possible only in the "real" world, has developed a rather low opinion of social scientists who do not share his views of public policy.[9]

The opinion of the policy-maker, moreover, was reinforced because the social scientist, as Lippmann went on to explain, "shares this estimate of himself." He "has little inner certainty about his own work . . . only half believes in it . . . his data are uncertain, his means of verification lacking." Where does the solution lie?

> The physical scientists achieved their freedom from clericalism by working out a method that produced conclusions of a sort that could not be suppressed or ignored. They convinced themselves and acquired dignity, and knew what they were fighting for. The social scientist will acquire his dignity and his strength when he

9 Walter Lippmann, *Public Opinion* (New York: The Free Press Paperback Edition, 1965), pp. 233–235.

has worked out his method. He will do that by turning into opportunity the need among directing men of the Great Society for
instruments of analysis by which an invisible and most stupen-
dously difficult environment can be made intelligible.[10]

The years since 1922 have been particularly formative years
for the development of the social sciences. Equally aware of
Lippmann's warning, social scientists have been giving increasing
attention to "method" since he wrote and gradually seeking to ac-
quit themselves of the accusation of reformism. Indeed, the Social
Science Research Council, founded in the early 1920's as a source
of intellectual and financial support for social scientists in universities, had as a major objective the encouragement of increasingly
rigorous methods of research. Since then, the greatest advances
have been made in the field of economics, though all fields have
become more empirical and demanding. By the early 1930's, methods of reliably estimating national income had been developed by
the National Bureau of Economic Research, which established an
empirical basis for large-scale economic analysis that has become
increasingly essential to government policy-making. In the 1930's,
as well, experiments in opinion and attitude research provided the
bases for choosing small samples of people whose views and conditions represented those of larger groups, even of the total population. These methods of the sample survey, in turn, permitted
frequent review of demographic and economic changes, providing
up-to-date information without the time, expense, and complexity
of a full census. They have been of critical importance in the expansion of the federal statistical programs and in the use of opin-
ion-polling in business, politics, and education.

During the Second World War, advances in the field of social
psychology were made in doing research on troop morale, psychological warfare, and intelligence analysis. As a new field, social psychology provided a bridge between the study of individual behavior patterns by experimental psychologists and the broader study
of social groups and institutions by sociologists. Anthropologists
contributed concepts about the relations between culture and
personality. After the war, the work of social psychologists and

[10] *Ibid.*, pp. 235–236.

anthropologists served to broaden the study of economic institutions by providing techniques for examining the motives as well as the effects of economic behavior, and also added a whole new behavioral dimension to the study of politics and government. In all of these developments, the emphasis was on finding out *what is* rather than what *should be,* on penetrating to the core of human and social processes, and on basing analysis and judgment on as sound an empirical base as possible.

Despite the developments of the past fifty years, the social sciences are frequently referred to as "young," "immature," or, more optimistically, "emerging," particularly when considering their usefulness to policy-makers. The inference is that these sciences are somehow "incomplete" and that once they are fully "grown," they will be considerably more useful than they are now. Part of the problem lies, it is said, in the lack of an adequate empirical basis for verifying propositions about individual and social behavior. Theories thus remain untested and highly speculative. At the same time, there is a great fragmentation in the institutions of social science, mostly dispersed among various universities and divided into disciplines and sub-disciplines, fields and sub-fields. This high degree of specialization was a response to the demand for increased precision, the need to isolate sets of behavioral phenomena and concentrate on them in depth. It was also a response to the enormous range of the social sciences and the necessity of organizing research on an incremental basis. But the search for certitude went on without strong centralizing forces that could organize material into a relevant synthesis. There has been no equivalent of the large industrial laboratories or medical centers in which all the available data bearing on a particular problem can be accumulated and verified. As a result, there is frequently a lack of comparability in the findings of research on similar problems, little cumulative building of knowledge, and, most important from the point of view of the policy-maker, a limited capacity to predict.

It is the predictive power of the social sciences that is most frequently the stumbling block in applying social science to public policies, since the decisions of policy-makers inevitably affect the future and they understandably want assurances about the results of their actions. Robert K. Merton was quite correct—and his observation has, if anything, been confirmed in the twenty years since he wrote—that "intellectuals concerned with human affairs in general find themselves in a less secure status than the physical and biological scientists who affect public policy." He explained this by pointing out that "there is considerable degree of *indeterminacy* in the social scientist's findings, in so far as they bear upon projected action."[11] This very indeterminacy then leads to tension between the expert and the policy-maker, since the results of research are rarely decisive. The policy-maker must still perform a difficult act of judgment based on his own views and experience; so he may well question the relevance of a social science that, for his purposes, is inconclusive and yet raises questions about the limited basis of his own evaluation.

Knowledge is always tentative, however, subject to continual confirmation, development, or rejection, in all fields of science. What is learned today may be disproved tomorrow, be subsequently assessed as a crucial point of departure for a highly productive line of inquiry, or, more modestly and usually, be valued as part of increasing understanding in a field of study without being decisive. In applying social science findings to a practical problem, any proposition about human behavior at a given point in time may seem so general as to be meaningless for practical purposes, so conditional as to be a weak reed on which to depend, or so particular as to be bound by elements of time, space, or culture that make its wider application doubtful.

There is a misleading but seductive ideal of the research process, borrowed from the physical and biological sciences, in which work proceeds in an orderly, linear, almost deterministic fashion from the discovery of knowledge to the development of a product that men can use—an explosive, a pill, a laser, a serum. The ideal ignores, of course, the countless failures, dead ends, and unexpected applications that researchers or their followers stumble on without premeditation. By analogy, however, research projects on the behavior of infants are expected to lead to effective programs for child development, and research projects on motivation and

---

[11] Robert K. Merton, *Social Theory and Social Structure* (rev. ed.; Glencoe, Illinois: The Free Press, 1957), pp. 210–211.

deviant behavior to effective programs for crime prevention. They may—but they may not.

The tentative nature of knowledge, the level of generality or the level of specificity of propositions about human behavior, and the lack of any assured development from basic concept to usable product—these may seem to be fundamental limitations on the practical utility of social science in government. Or, again, they may not seem so. And this is true of the physical and biological sciences as well as the social sciences. What is involved is the level of expectation. If it is expected that social science will—or should —provide obviously correct answers to complex and vexing social and economic problems, then there is bound to be grave disappointment and even disenchantment. Knowledge is not a way of avoiding decisions.

Yet the limits on the predictive capacity of the social sciences may also rest on an unwillingness to apply what is known—however tentative—so that the validity of knowledge can be tested. By its very nature, social science upsets the preconceptions and notions that give meaning to human experience. Knowledge about human nature tests and challenges taboos, ideologies, loyalties, all the assumptions upon which an individual or a group—a political faction, an administrative agency, or a pressure group—has based his or its case, or even its *raison d'être*. So, understandably, the progress of research and the application of its findings are hampered, particularly in public affairs. Any group, public or private, that has a claim on public resources or an interest in maintaining the *status quo,* is bound to resist the systematic analysis of information that threatens the basis of its position.

It is perhaps important to emphasize that the physical and biological sciences have been subject to similar constraints. Knowledge about nature and its application can be as destructive of established beliefs and order as knowledge about man and society. The examples range from the historic conflicts between science and religion to more recent attacks by the pharmaceutical industry on new knowledge about drugs and the opposition of military factions to new weapons technologies. Such opposition persists, but it tends to lose its force and effectiveness if the problems that society faces prove increasingly unresponsive to conventional remedies and if the society, because of its historical experience, is structurally and psychologically prepared to apply science to its problems. For example, the experience of the Second World War led the United States to recognize the importance of the physical sciences, and afterwards the government supported research on a large scale, particularly in the fields of national defense and space exploration. Since then science has become institutionalized, at least to the extent that both the President and Congress, when dealing with a difficult problem of public policy, can now turn to sources of scientific advice.

The great size and complexity of contemporary public issues —poverty in the ghettos, economic and social changes in the underdeveloped nations, inflation, urban decay—are so overwhelming that there is increasing difficulty and inadequacy in basing decisions on simple axioms that derive from personal experience. Crime prevention measures, for example, are based on some expectation of their deterrent effect. Men *do* respond to fear, and thus a program of crime prevention might be based on this simple truth. But they also respond to affection, to respect, to the promise of prestige, and to financial gain. Presumably these responses, or some combination of them, might serve as an equally reliable basis for public programs. But how? And under what circumstances is one set of motivations more effective than another? And how does the nature of public programs—and the assumptions on which they are based—relate to the larger problems of maintaining justice and order as well as to the immediately pressing problem of crime prevention?

During the last thirty years, the federal government, in order to utilize the contributions of science, has had to develop new forms of administrative management. It has had to create new procedures and agencies, some charged with collecting and verifying the information needed for public programs, some with the task of insuring close cooperation between experts and policy-makers. The growth of government statistical programs is one manifestation of this development, as is the organization of economic advisory systems throughout the federal establishment. Economists have played a progressively larger role in government, particularly since the New Deal. The Employment Act of 1946, by establishing a Council of Economic Advisers advisory to the President and a Joint Economic Committee in the Congress, institution-alized the process of applying expert knowledge to matters of fiscal and monetary policy at the highest levels of government.

The critical importance of research and development in the physical sciences during and after the Second World War also led to organizational innovations in the areas of defense and security. These took several forms: the establishment of government laboratories, administered by federal agencies or under contract to private companies; the extension of the contract method in order to finance research, development, and analysis by industrial or university groups; and the creation of non-profit, government-financed corporations like the RAND Corporation and the Institute of Defense Analyses (IDA). Such innovations in administrative technique have been extended to deal in a systematic and analytical way with problems of military strategy, international stability, and foreign economic and technical assistance, as well as with problems of weapons technology. Organizations like the RAND Corporation and IDA have also been created by government agencies to deal with problems of urban reconstruction and social progress, including the Urban Institute and the Institute for Poverty Research. These semi-autonomous institutions, as well as the university and private research teams that operate under contract, have then served to promote the growth of expert staffs within the federal agencies that make use of their work.

Within the government, as well, new techniques of budgetary planning and program evaluation have tended to create demands for new information and new methods of analyzing economic and social change. These techniques have been formalized in the Planning-Programming-Budgeting System (PPBS). The purpose of the System is to find accurate means of measuring the effects of government programs in order to choose the most effective plan among various alternatives. Using the methods of systematic analysis developed in dealing with highly technological problems, PPBS seeks to apply these to a broader range of social problems and to relate policy decisions to budgetary allocations in a single continuing process. PPBS, however, is only the present result of a long evolution in budget and planning development that began with the creation of a centralized budgetary system in the federal government after the First World War. Further progress was made in the experiments in national planning during the New Deal and, later, in the use of "performance budgets" based on the functions, rather than the agencies, of government in the years after the Second World War.

The need for knowledge and analysis in making government decisions on complex issues is increased by the process of checks and balances inherent in the operations of the American political system. Not only is the government accountable to the general public, but the separation of powers within the government requires that the President and Congress account to each other. The constant tension between the two serves to encourage the application of analytical methods to political decision-making. Indeed, any group, competing with other groups and employing every means of persuasion, has to buttress its position on major policy issues with as much factual information and as strong and logical an argument as possible. Congressional hearings may provide illustrations of this. Congressional committees want "facts"; they frequently seek out the advice of "experts" in order to oppose the recommendations of administration specialists; and they may deliberately commission critical evaluations as a basis for modifying the decisions of the Executive Branch.

Policy-makers in both the Executive and Legislative Branches may come to rely more on objective information and analysis, moreover, in cases where they can exercise their own judgment without the constraints imposed by traditional political interests. Robert Lane has pointed out that:

> the dominant scholarly interpretation of policy-making processes has changed in the direction of emphasizing the greater autonomy of political leaders and legislators; with respect to the role of pressure groups, the power elite, and the electorate. . . . if leaders and other legislators are less bound by the domain of pure politics. . . . they are freer to be guided by the promptings of scientists and findings from the domain of knowledge.[12]

---

[12] Robert Lane, "The Decline of Politics and Ideology in a Knowledgeable Society," *The American Sociological Review*, Vol. 31, No. 5 (October 1966), p. 658.

This does not mean an end to politics; it does mean that knowledge can become a more effective and autonomous force in the formulation of policy than it has in the past.

The size and complexity of the problems with which government has to deal and the system of checks and balances encourage every group—government agencies as well as congressional committees and interest groups—to turn increasingly to factual information and systematic analysis to support their programs. The process is carried further by the increasingly pervasive role of science in public affairs, a role built up most dramatically by the great successes in recent years in the physical and biological sciences. To the extent that advances in communication systems, medical research, and space exploration lead to an expectation of "technical" solutions to grave social problems, however, the results can be dangerous. But to the extent that they give support to a more systematic and rational approach to social issues, they sustain a constructive role for social science in the affairs of government.

A constructive role for social science should not, however, be visualized as transforming the American political process into a pattern of classic problem-solving. Even if presidents and congressmen become less constrained by political interests and more free to seek a basis for legislation in fact and analysis, there will still be sharp and understandable differences in setting well-defined goals for public policy. Policy-making will remain politics —with or without science. Knowledge and analysis, moreover, can serve to influence as well as to clarify the alternatives for political choice, to rationalize old predilections as well as to stimulate new programs for social change. Social scientists themselves—in the research choices they make, the techniques of observation they adopt, and the theoretical approaches they defend—do not remain entirely free of personal prejudices, no matter how rigorous they are in their efforts to gain objectivity.

Yet, for all these complications, the role of social science in the federal government has grown enormously over the years owing to three basic causes. The first is the growth of the federal government itself and the increasing influence of federal policies and programs upon American social and economic life. This growth became evident soon after the First World War, progressed by leaps and bounds under the New Deal, and continued steadily during the Second World War and afterwards in response to the international crises of the war and postwar periods and the internal changes taking place in American society. The second cause is the simultaneous development of social science itself: the emphasis on empirical evidence, on systematic methods for collecting and analyzing information, and on theories of individual and social behavior that can be tested and are not based on limited experience or hasty speculation, or on how we would like people to behave rather than how they actually do behave. Finally, a third cause is to be found in the development of administrative techniques to make government operations more efficient, bureaucrats and political appointees more accountable for their actions, and obdurate economic and social problems more tractable and manageable. These innovations in administration have made it more and more possible for the knowledge and methods of social science to serve as a guide in political choices made by the President and Congress.

These three historical developments—the growth of federal power, social knowledge, and administrative skill—have taken place at the same time in response to the practical challenges and are so interrelated with each other as to form one complex evolutionary pattern. The direction in which they will carry social science in the federal government is neither clear nor inevitable. Political interests and preferences will continue to dictate policy. To these will be added—at different times and different intensities —fears of science: fear of a science without values or goals, fear of a science that can be used to manipulate and maintain the existing system rather than to serve social progress, fear of a science that creates more problems than it can solve. It is these fears and the need for understanding of the role of knowledge in government that impel us to examine the past, to look for a frame of reference and a historical perspective within which to view the growth and problems of social science in the federal government—and that is the purpose of this book.

CHAPTER II

THE SHAPING
OF SOCIAL SCIENCE

LATE IN 1945, Wesley C. Mitchell, the distinguished economist and Director of Research for the National Bureau of Economic Research, appeared before a congressional committee to argue the case for including the social sciences in the proposed National Science Foundation. In the course of his testimony and in response to questions from members of the Senate committee reviewing the legislative proposal, Mitchell recalled the "enormous difficulties" that were encountered in economic mobilization during the First World War because "we didn't know a great many of the basic facts about our resources or about how to combine them." And he noted that the same task had been carried out with much greater success during the Second World War "primarily because the people who were doing it had at their disposal the results of a great deal of careful inquiry, and inquiry of a more thoroughgoing and realistic kind than used to be carried on in the social sciences."[1]

With Mitchell, representing the Social Science Research Council (SSRC), were Robert Yerkes, William Ogburn, Edwin Nourse, and John Gaus. All of these men had seen changes in their own fields like those Mitchell talked about, and they, like Mitchell, had helped to bring some of them about. So had Charles Merriam, who had founded the SSRC and been something of a social-scientist-in-residence in Roosevelt's New Deal. They were all part of a generation, perhaps the first generation of American social

---

[1] *Science Legislation*, Hearings before Subcommittee on War Mobilization, Committee on Military Affairs, U.S. Senate, 79th Congress, 1st Session, 1945, p. 781.

scientists, for whom the Second World War marked the end of one era and the beginning of another. They had seen modern social science and modern government emerge side by side and had spent their lives in making contributions to both—Yerkes in the field of military psychology, Ogburn in relating government planning to social change, Nourse in agricultural economics, Gaus in public administration, and Merriam in dealing with the dilemma of knowledge and power in theory and practice.

Mitchell was in many ways typical of his generation. He entered the first class at the new University of Chicago in 1892, intending to study the classics. He soon came under the influence of John Dewey and Thorstein Veblen, however, and his plans and life changed. From Dewey, whom he called "the first behaviorist," he learned that economics was essentially a study of human behavior; from Veblen he learned to look at economic theories as expressions of the cultures in which they originated.[2] Years later, writing in 1928 to his fellow economist, John Maurice Clark, he showed how strong the influence of Dewey had been.

> I was fascinated by his view of the place which logic holds in human behavior. . . . It explained the economic theorists. . . . It is a misconception to suppose that consumers guide their course by ratiocination—they don't think except under stress. There is no way of deducing from certain principles what they will do, just because their behavior is not itself rational. One has to find out what they do. That is a matter of observation, which the economic theorists had taken all too lightly.[3]

Of Veblen, Mitchell was more critical though he remained warm in his affection for the man. When, in later years, they both lived in New York, Mitchell's wife recalled that "ours was one of the few homes where . . . [Veblen] the silent, the shy . . . felt thoroughly at ease."[4] But Mitchell, early in his career, dedicated even then to the slow laborious work of statistical collection and meas-

---

[2] Lucy Sprague Mitchell, "A Personal Sketch," in Arthur F. Burns (ed.), *Wesley Clair Mitchell, the Economic Scientist* (New York: National Bureau of Economic Research, 1952), pp. 60–61.

[3] Quoted, *ibid.*, p. 95.

[4] *Ibid.*, p. 91.

urement, had asked: "Can't you . . . [agree] that even Veblen's constructive work would have been in closer harmony with his critique of economic method if he were more patient in accumulating and presenting his evidence?"[5] And later, this time to Clark again, he wrote: "[Veblen's] working conceptions of human nature might be a vast improvement; he might have uncanny insights; but he could do no more than make certain conclusions plausible—like the rest. How important were the factors he dealt with and the factors he scamped was never established."[6]

Mitchell's whole life was unremittingly devoted to the careful accumulation of economic and social observations and to the development of theories and concepts of economic behavior based on these observations rather than on ethical or metaphysical speculations. Almost immediately after graduating from Chicago, he spent a year at the still impermanent and ill-staffed Census Office in Washington. There, he complained, "the servility of Washington clerks nauseated me and the feebleness of the official representatives of economics . . . almost frightened me."[7] When he returned to Washington some twenty years later to serve as Chief of the Price Section of the War Industries Board during World War I, he found the government's use of statistics, though improved, nowhere near what was needed or what it should have been. Only by the end of the war could Mitchell say that the government was "in a fair way to develop for the first time a systematic organization of federal statistics."[8]

But for Mitchell, statistics were not an end in themselves. They were data, they were tools, the essential tools of economic and social analysis. They were but a step toward the final goal, toward using the social sciences to give men an alternative to "the savage dependence upon catastrophes for progress." Speaking these words in 1919 as President of the American Statistical Association, Mitchell saw the world as "a very dangerous place . . .

[5] Quoted, *ibid.*, p. 91.
[6] Quoted, *ibid.*, p. 95.
[7] Quoted, *ibid.*, p. 63.
[8] Quoted in Arthur F. Burns, "Wesley Mitchell and the National Bureau," *Twenty-Ninth Annual Report,* National Bureau of Economic Research (New York, 1949), p. 5.

where we could not keep social organization what it is even if we wanted to." But how were men to meet social change if they did not understand it? "In science and industry . . . we do not wait for catastrophes to force new ways upon us . . . We rely . . . upon quantitative analysis to point the way; and we advance because we are constantly improving and applying such analysis." Although Mitchell admitted to being something of a reformer himself, his words were an admonition to those who called for social reform without knowing what was involved. They were also a challenge to his fellow social scientists to apply "all the intelligence and energy" they possessed to their disciplines, which he described as still "immature, speculative, filled with controversies."[9]

In the years between the two world wars, Mitchell, like Merriam, Yerkes, Nourse, Ogburn, and Gaus, participated in many of the important intellectual, institutional, and governmental movements to develop the social sciences and relate them to government programs and policies. Almost until his death, he directed the research work of the National Bureau of Economic Research which, as Kenneth Boulding has observed, provided the empirical basis for the "new economics" that was built on the Keynesian theories of economic growth.[10] In the 1920's he also led three national economic surveys under the auspices of the President's Conference on Unemployment of 1921. The last of these, *Recent Economic Changes in the United States*, published in 1929, contained the following statement: "Research and study, the orderly classification of knowledge, joined to increasing skill, well may make complete control of the economic system a possibility."[11] Though this must have seemed unduly optimistic on the eve of the Depression, the report did foresee a time when economic analysis would be used in making policy and so anticipated the Employment Act of 1946.

Having a broad interest in all the social sciences, Mitchell

[9] Quoted, *ibid.*, pp. 5–6.
[10] Kenneth Boulding, "Contemporary Economic Research," in Donald P. Ray, *Trends in Social Science* (New York: Philosophical Library, 1961), pp. 9–10.
[11] *Recent Economic Changes in the United States*, Report of the Committee on Recent Economic Changes of the President's Conference on Unemployment (New York: McGraw-Hill Book Co., 1929), p. xx.

served on the Social Science Research Council and chaired another committee established by Herbert Hoover, the President's Research Committee on Social Trends. The Committee's report, published as *Recent Social Trends in the United States,* reflected the interests of the SSRC in emphasizing the interdependence of the factors of social change and the importance of the social sciences in national planning.[12] And following the recommendations of *Recent Social Trends,* the first Roosevelt Administration established a National Planning Board on which Mitchell served during its early years. Throughout the 1920's and 1930's he continued to be a constant advocate of an expanded and centralized system of government statistics as an essential prerequisite to scientific analysis and social planning. His work served as a guide for setting up the Central Statistical Board in 1933 and for passage of the Federal Reports Act in 1942, both key points in the development of a government-wide statistical system.

When the National Bureau of Economic Research celebrated its twenty-fifth anniversary in 1946, Mitchell reviewed developents in economics as he saw them.

> We can [now] define our problems more clearly and grasp more firmly their relations to one another; a larger and richer body of objective data is available for our use; the methods of deriving warranted conclusions from these raw materials are more varied and more powerful. [Nevertheless we are envious] of the youngsters now beginning careers of research . . . [who] will learn from our mistakes as well as our successes, and lay plans of their own better than we can formulate.[13]

He ended by inviting his audience back for the fiftieth anniversary of the Bureau in 1970 "for another glance at the past and further planning for the future." Only two years later, however, Mitchell died.

---

12 *Recent Social Trends in the United States,* Report of the President's Research Committee on Social Trends (2 vols.; New York: McGraw-Hill Book Co., 1933).

13 Wesley C. Mitchell, "Empirical Research and the Development of Economic Science," in *Economic Research and the Development of Economic Science and Public Policy* (New York: National Bureau of Economic Research, 1946), pp. 3–20.

Before and During World War I

In the early decades of the twentieth century, the place of social science in the federal government was largely influenced by three forces: the growth of statistical agencies for the collection of information on demographic trends and natural resources, the impetus to social and administrative reform given by the Progressive movement, and the requirements of national mobilization during the First World War. Along with these three trends social science was itself taking form, emerging out of the period of moral philosophy and responding to the more rigorous demands of science.

Louis Wirth has characterized "the developing social science at the turn of the century" as being "significantly shaped by the dominant philosophy of the period with its empirical and pragmatic temper, its consequent emphasis upon the actual problems of the developing American society, its revulsion from doctrinaire metaphysics and armchair speculation, and its accent upon observation and experimentation."[14] For a time after the Civil War, social scientists and social reformers joined forces in the American Social Science Association, but intellectually and institutionally the merger was short-lived. For the two groups were dominated by different purposes and different perspectives; one proposed to analyze society, the other to reconstruct it. By the early 1900's the Association had long since passed its period of strength, and it finally disappeared when its remaining members, mostly dedicated to welfare, formed the National Conference of Social Work.[15] By then those devoted to pure scientific research had already joined various professional associations that had been founded earlier: the American Historical Association (in 1884), the American Economic Association (in 1885), the American Psychological Association (in 1892), the American Anthropological

---

[14] Louis Wirth, "The Social Sciences," in Merle E. Curti (ed.), *American Scholarship in the Twentieth Century* (Cambridge: Harvard University Press, 1953), p. 40.

[15] For a history of the American Social Science Association, see L. L. Bernard and Jessie Bernard, *Origins of American Sociology: The Social Science Movement in the United States* (New York: Russell & Russell, 1965).

Association (in 1902), the American Political Science Association (in 1903), and the American Sociological Society (in 1905). The structure of American social science thus began to take shape; conceived in a period of social change, it was nonetheless differentiated into specialized groups and divorced from the agencies of social action.

The year 1902 marked the establishment of a permanent Bureau of the Census, soon after Wesley Mitchell had had his own rather dismal experience there. It was an event which, A. Hunter Dupree has suggested, "gave demography a stable place in the government, by implication establishing the social sciences as well."[16] For more than a century, the decennial census required under the Constitution had been undertaken by staffs that were hastily assembled, largely inexperienced, and politically appointed, and that were just as hastily disbanded once the basic task was accomplished. There had been some progress, however. As early as 1800, it will be recalled, learned societies had petitioned Congress to use the census as a means of gaining a more meaningful profile of American society than "a mere enumeration of population."[17] Also, from the time of its establishment in 1839, the American Statistical Association had begun its regular critiques of the methods and analysis of the decennial census, a task in which it was later joined by the American Economic Association. In 1870 the Census Office initiated the use of tallying machines in compiling data, and by the 1890 census it was using electrical tabulating systems, thus developing a capacity for dealing with large sets of figures quickly and efficiently.[18] By far the greatest progress in expanding the scope and refining the techniques of data collection took place under Francis A. Walker, who supervised the ninth and tenth censuses in 1870 and 1880. And the censuses of 1890 and 1900, building on the earlier work of

[16] A. Hunter Dupree, *Science in the Federal Government* (Cambridge: Belknap Press of Harvard, 1957), p. 279.

[17] W. Stull Holt, *The Bureau of the Census*, The Institute of Government Research, Service Monographs of the U.S. Government, No. 53 (Washington, D.C.: The Brookings Institution, 1929), p. 5.

[18] *Ibid.*, pp. 13–30. See also Leon E. Truesdell, *The Development of Punch Card Tabulation in the Bureau of the Census, 1890–1940*, Bureau of the Census (Washington, D.C., 1965).

Walker, included more information than had previously been collected. At the same time the Department of Agriculture, the first regulatory commissions, and the conservation agencies were also developing regular statistical surveys in connection with their own program activities.

The establishment of the Bureau of the Census on a permanent basis—first in the Department of the Interior and, a year later, in 1903, in the Department of Commerce and Labor—was the result of various kinds of pressure brought to bear on the government: the recommendations of the supervisor of the 1890 census based on the experience of that census; the appeals of business groups and the continual demands of professional groups through the American Statistical Association and the American Economic Association; popular criticisms of the population returns of the 1890 census which indicated a smaller population growth than anticipated; and international efforts to devise uniform census schedules on a world-wide basis.[19] By 1902 these pressures had their political effect and the Census Bureau was made permanent. But it did not become a central statistical organization, though its functions were, from the first, recognized to be government-wide in application. Not only did the Department of Agriculture develop a separate, though cooperating, staff in its own field, but the Bureau of Labor and other commissions and agencies, supported by interest groups of their own, continued to build up statistical services quite distinct from the Bureau of the Census.

If the establishment of a permanent Census Bureau created a place for the social sciences in government, so did the Progressive movement in the period up to World War I. The professional associations of social scientists developed separately from the broader movements of social workers and the muckrakers and reformers of the time. But the attention of both scientists and reformers was inevitably drawn to the changing character of American society, to the effects of industrialization, immigration, urban-

---

[19] Walter F. Willcox, "The Development of the American Census Office since 1890," *Political Science Quarterly*, Vol. XXIX, No. 1 (March 1914), pp. 438–459.

ization, corporate concentration, and political corruption. For both, the way of progress lay in full exposure of the forces at work in society. Social scientists thus participated in the Progressive movement, with many no doubt as concerned with reform as the reformers themselves. They served as staffs of experts for congressional investigating bodies like the Industrial Commission of 1898, the Immigration Commission of 1907, and the National Monetary Commission of 1908. They developed theories and standards of governmental efficiency, for the major cities in the municipal bureaus of research, and for the federal government in studies such as those undertaken by President Taft's Commission on Economy and Efficiency. And they began to function as expert advisers to political leaders, as in the earliest of "brain trusts" under Governor Robert La Follette in Wisconsin.

This participation of social scientists in the struggle for reform was, in many ways, consistent with the new dimensions of the social sciences themselves. These changes and their relationship to reform have been described by Richard Hofstadter with considerable insight and vigor:

> What the muckrakers and the realistic writers were doing in their fields the speculative thinkers and social scientists were also doing in theirs. As scholars reached out for their own "realistic" categories, the formalistic thought of an earlier and more conservative generation fell under close and often damaging scrutiny. Economists were pondering Veblen's efforts to replace the economic man of the classical school with his wasteful consumer and his predatory captain of industry. Legal realists were supplanting the "pure" jurisprudential agent of earlier legal theorists with the flesh-and-blood image of the corporation lawyer dressed in judicial robes and stuffed with corporation prejudices. Political scientists were losing their old veneration for the state as an abstract repository of something called sovereignty and accepting the views of men like Charles A. Beard and Arthur F. Bentley, who conceived of the state as a concrete instrument that registered the social pressures brought to bear upon it by various interest groups. Historians were beginning to apply the economic interpretation of history. The new discipline of sociology, intimately linked with social settlement work and Christian social reform, was criticizing the older notions of individuality and morality and developing a

new, "realistic" social psychology. John Dewey was attacking formalistic categories in philosophy and trying to develop a more descriptive and operational account of the uses of ideas.[20]

Almost inescapably imbued with the spirit of Progressivism, social scientists often found themselves in a dilemma, torn between the aims of science and those of reform. For some, the solution lay in avoiding public issues and concentrating on the development of an empirical basis for analysis in order to divorce scientific conclusions from everything but the observable facts. For others, it lay in the impartial and honest application of intelligence to public affairs. Still others came to dissociate administration from politics, a trend that characterized the study of public administration for many years, and to assume that pure efficiency was the only purpose of government. But, whatever solution they chose, it was essentially their objective examination of the society in which they lived that led American social scientists to take a political stand. If many took an active part in the reform movement, it was certainly by choice and their activism owed as much to their insights as scientists as to their sense of responsibility as citizens. But for all their engagement in politics, by the time the war broke out they had created a social science that was based on empirical methods of investigation and that rejected folklore and maxims as explanations of human behavior and social institutions.

In retrospect, World War I seems to have been a rehearsal for World War II in its effects on social science as well as on other aspects of the society. In both wars, economists called in to participate in the mobilization of resources found that they needed to deal with the total economy and not only its parts. In both wars, too, there was a need for more numerous and more manageable statistics than yet existed. Indeed, the demand for better statistical services, which had brought about the establishment of a permanent Census Bureau in 1902, was greatly intensified by World War I and continued to grow through the Depression, the Second World War, and the postwar years of increasing government ac-

---

[20] Richard Hofstadter, *The Age of Reform* (New York: Alfred A. Knopf, 1955), pp. 198–199.

tivity. In this continuing development, the two wars were enormously important stimulants. For war is a moment of crisis which compresses time and illuminates needs that less dramatic environments obscure or never force to the surface. War also involves the entire society and gives the central government new powers, for the exercise of which it needs new sources of information and expertise. World War I was shorter, there was less time to organize, but there were important lessons to be learned. Among these was the lesson Mitchell sought to communicate to the professional statisticians in his 1919 presidential address.

> Through all these years we have been mainly a learned society, cherishing our particular subject, criticizing those who neglect or misuse it, occasionally proffering advice, summing up experience, but not participating aggressively in the rough-and-tumble of statistical practice . . . But conditions have changed . . . and if we do our part . . . they may change more.[21]

For one group of social scientists, the psychologists, World War I provided an important place in government for the first time. By then, experimental psychology had had some thirty or forty years of development, dating from the establishment of the first psychological laboratories in Germany and the United States in the late 1870's. By the turn of the century, the first intelligence tests had been invented and work was being carried on in such areas of human behavior as sensation, reaction, learning, memory, and attention.[22] Psychologists had thus accumulated knowledge and techniques directly applicable to the problems of manpower selection and training that confronted the military services. But there remained the task of bringing these to the attention of the military authorities and gaining their confidence in what psychologists had to offer and what they could do. There were, as Robert M. Yerkes pointed out, "common misconceptions and confusions. Psychology meant to the average army officer something wholly intangible, even mysterious. He thought of its methods as

---

21 In Wesley C. Mitchell, *The Backward Art of Spending Money and Other Essays* (New York: McGraw-Hill Book Co., 1937), p. 53.
22 Edwin G. Boring (ed.), *Psychology for the Armed Services* (Washington, D.C.: The Infantry Journal, 1945), pp. 11–12.

akin to those of the spiritualist, the devotee of the psychical research, or those of the 'medium.' "[23]

It happened that psychologists were the only social scientists,
along with anthropologists, that were formally represented in
the National Research Council. The Council was formed in 1916
as an operating arm of the National Academy of Sciences to provide a broader and more effective instrument than the Academy
itself for making scientific resources available to the government.
The limited and honorific membership of the Academy and its
general state of inactivity at the time made it cumbersome and
unequal to the potential needs of war. Enterprising Academy
leaders decided to form the Council in order to overcome these
inadequacies.[24] When the military turned to the Council for assistance in 1917, it found a Psychology Committee organized and acting in cooperation with more than a dozen committees of the
American Psychological Association, each specialized in an area
of psychology applicable to military problems. Consequently, during the war psychologists could operate through committees which
were related to the broader organizational framework of the Council and the Academy. Later the committees were also able to exert
influence on the military services through psychologists who were
directly appointed to military units such as the Office of the Army
Surgeon General and the Office of the Adjutant General. They
thus had enough external authority and internal influence to make
their weight felt. Their major contribution lay in the field of intelligence testing—organizing an extensive program for the controlled testing of military troops, and devising the classic Alpha
and Beta tests, which set a precedent for the wide use of intelligence tests after the war.[25]

Still another development during the war, unrelated to the
work of economists or psychologists, is important for an understanding of the use of social scientists by the government. In the
fall of 1917, President Wilson's confidential adviser, Colonel Edward House, began to recruit a group of experts, mainly from the
universities, to collect the information and other materials that

---

[23] Robert M. Yerkes (ed.), *The New World of Science: Its Development During
the War* (New York: The Century Co., 1920), p. 351.
[24] Dupree, *op. cit.*, pp. 308–315.
[25] Yerkes, *op. cit.*, pp. 351–389.

would eventually be needed at the Peace Conference. This group, given the name "The Inquiry," operated outside the regular channels of the State Department through the Colonel's personal relations with the President. Nominally, The Inquiry was under the direction of Colonel House's brother-in-law, Sidney E. Mezes, President of the College of the City of New York. Actually, much of its work was supervised by Isaiah Bowman, Director of the American Geographical Society, who served as Executive Officer and chief territorial specialist and was able to put the Society's facilities at the disposal of the government. The chief reason given for instituting The Inquiry was the lack of expert knowledge in the regular diplomatic service in dealing with the important "questions of geography, history, ethnology, economics, strategy, etc., that would be the chief considerations at the Peace Conference."[26] Understandably The Inquiry was resented by many in the State Department. So, while the special group of experts was eventually included in the American delegation organized by the Department to support the President in the peace negotiations, the tensions between the two groups never completely abated.[27]

The activities of economists, psychologists, international lawyers, historians, and geographers had demonstrated the relevance of organized knowledge to emergency government in time of war; but little of the wartime structure was retained in the permanent government to reinforce and further develop these relationships once the war was over. In his final report, the Director of the War Industries Board, the financier Bernard Baruch, recommended that an emergency planning body with a skeleton staff be retained, so that any future industrial mobilization could be undertaken on the basis of prior planning, much in the manner of contingency planning worked out by the military.[28] This proposal, had it been adopted, might have led to further plans for the continuous collec-

[26] Sidney Edward Mezes, "Preparations for Peace," in Edward M. House and Charles Seymour, *What Really Happened at Paris: The Story of the Peace Conference, 1918–1919* (New York: Charles Scribner's Sons, 1921), p. 3.

[27] See James T. Shotwell, *At the Peace Conference* (New York: The Macmillan Co., 1937), especially pp. 11–19.

[28] Bernard M. Baruch, *American Industry in the War,* A Report of the War Industries Board (Washington, D.C.: Government Printing Office, 1921), p. 9.

tion of information about the nation's economic resources and their growth or change. No such emergency planning group was established, however. Similarly, by the end of the war, a Central Bureau of Planning and Statistics had been formed as a clearing house for all statistical services and as a base point from which to develop a more permanent centralized system. In 1919, however, the Central Bureau was permitted to expire, not to re-emerge in another form (the Central Statistical Board) until 1933. Finally, any effect that the experience of The Inquiry might have had on the growth of research activities in the State Department was substantially nullified by the Senate's rejection of the League of Nations Covenant and the national retreat into twenty years of isolationism—as well as by lingering resentment in the Department because of the intrusion of outside experts.

In the field of military psychology the situation was somewhat different. Very few of the innovations made by psychologists were lasting or made the military any better prepared to cope with the larger and infinitely more complex mobilization problems of the Second World War. This was largely the result of the low priority given to military preparedness throughout the interwar years. However, the wartime use of intelligence testing set a precedent elsewhere in government and especially in private industry. Indeed, the personnel work that psychologists had performed for the military was called a "war gift to industry"; private companies began to use psychologists, consulting firms were organized, and new techniques were invented.[29] In government, the Civil Service Commission engaged as consultants several of the psychologists who had worked with the Army, and it established for the first time, in 1922, a Research Division for developing methods of personnel testing and selection. Through the years, moreover, research and development came to play a larger part in the Commission's work in the personnel field.[30] These achievements, however, were very limited in scope. In the private sector research was not related

[29] Loren Baritz, *The Servants of Power* (New York: John Wiley & Sons, 1960), pp. 48–49.
[30] Samuel Kavruck, "Thirty-Three Years of Test Research: A Short History of Test Development in the U.S. Civil Service Commission," *The American Psychologist*, Vol. 11, No. 7 (July 1956), pp. 329–333.

to or supported by government programs, and in government the emphasis largely remained on testing rather than on the application of psychology to the broader problems of organization and management.

The 1920's: Institutes for Social Science

Few of the wartime research projects were carried on after 1919. In the government of the 1920's, it was the Department of Agriculture that made by far the most systematic and sustained use of research in the social sciences. Some progress in this direction had already been made before the war, supported by the Progressive movement of the rural Midwest; and agricultural economists and rural sociologists were to carry this work much further under the New Deal. After the war, research in the Department was chiefly focused on the increasingly persistent economic dislocation among farmers, a problem even in the prosperous days before the Depression. Indeed, in 1921, in the midst of a crisis marked by falling farm prices, the Department brought several research units together to form the Bureau of Agricultural Economics, thus providing a stronger and better-coordinated research unit for contending with the economic problems of farmers.

Economic and social research in the Department of Agriculture rested on several foundations. First, almost from its establishment in 1862, the Department created an important place for scientific research in its structure and gave high priority to the dissemination of scientific knowledge to farmers. This research came to include an impressive program of statistical inventories of rural populations and agricultural extension services. It was in land grant schools such as the University of Wisconsin, in addition, that agricultural economics and rural sociology first became subjects of scholarly and scientific interest. Finally, changes in national development in the early part of the twentieth century —the closing of the frontier, the shortage of new lands for settlement, the impact of industrialization and mechanization on farm methods, and the new commercial and marketing practices—presented farmers with difficult economic and social problems of adjustment. All of these conditions were very evident even before the war, when David Houston became Secretary of the Department in 1913 and started the process of building a strong program of economic research. Houston later recalled:

> I knew that [the] main function [of the Department of Agriculture] was to promote more efficient production, to improve the processes of marketing, to create better credit facilities for the farmer, to make rural life more profitable and attractive, and to make more of the benefits of modern science accrue to the rural population. . . . I was aware, too, that the farmers' more acute problems were in the field of economics.[31]

One of the most difficult problems to solve was the lack of any balance between farm production and market demand, an issue that was to become more and more pronounced during the interwar years. Unlike industrial production, farm production did not adjust to fluctuations in market demand. The propensity of individual farmers was to produce as much as possible; and the increase in production, made possible by scientific and technological advances over the years, resulted in falling prices if there was no commensurate increase in demand. This distressing situation was relieved by the mounting requirements for foodstuffs on both the domestic and foreign markets during the First World War. With the end of the war, however, with the reduction of foreign needs, and with the general economic recession in the United States in 1920–1921, farm prices fell sharply. It was during this crisis that the Bureau of Agricultural Economics, formed by consolidating smaller research units, was established.

Through the 1920's, many agricultural economists discussed the idea of production control as the answer to the farm problem, and the Bureau of Agricultural Economics became a focal point of the discussion. Effective production control, however, necessitated much more federal intervention in economic affairs than the Coolidge and Hoover Administrations were prepared to undertake. Who would tell the farmers what to produce? And how would they

---

[31] Quoted in John M. Gaus and Leon Wolcott, *Public Administration and the United States Department of Agriculture* (Chicago: Public Administration Clearing House, 1940), p. 33.

be compensated for unused acreage? Instead, Hoover, when he became President, gave priority to programs that sought to protect American farmers from unfavorable conditions on world markets and to ease rural mortgage and credit facilities; in essence, the Hoover Administration left the central problem to private market mechanisms.

Within the Bureau itself, a series of research and informational services were developed to bring to the farmers a full understanding of the economic problems they faced. These services included studies of efficient methods of farm management, surveys of commodity market conditions, and analyses of the general economic trends, both domestic and international, that affected agriculture. One of these was the important series called "Agricultural Outlook Reports." At the same time, the Bureau expanded its own capacity for research and used its influence to encourage the study of agricultural economics and rural sociology in the universities. Rural sociology became a very important field of study in the Department's Division of Farm Population and Rural Life despite the persistent assumption among many economists that, if economic problems were solved, other social problems would disappear.[32] Under the Purnell Act of 1925, the Department was also authorized to make grants to state agricultural experiment stations for research in the economic and sociological aspects of agriculture. In sum, the chief function of the Bureau was to provide farmers with information, to give them all the facts and figures they might need to try to ease their own economic difficulties without the intervention of government.

The experience of the Bureau of Agricultural Economics demonstrated the growing importance of social science research as a continuous and integrated activity in government. If there were limits to the role of research in agricultural policy, this was a reflection of the limited role of government itself in the economy. From a highly active role during the war, the federal government under Republican Presidents Harding, Coolidge, and Hoover retreated to a posture of caution and restraint. Research, however,

---

[32] See Edmund deS. Brunner, *The Growth of a Science* (New York: Harper & Bros., 1957), p. 5.

was established as a legitimate government function and, within limits, was sustained and supported, especially by Herbert Hoover who was the dominant figure in government in that decade. As an engineer, Hoover had a deep respect for factual information. While still Secretary of Commerce, he gave strong support to statistical programs and other research services that could help the business community. In his memoirs, he wrote that he had stimulated the reform and expansion of statistical services in the hope "that warnings of economic movements, such as production, inventories, and consumption, would help to make business more certain . . . we believed that business judgment as to supply and demand could be strengthened."[33] As in the case of agriculture, the role of government was limited to the collection and distribution of information. In accordance with the prevailing political notions, it was assumed that the private decisions of individual farmers and businessmen, in aggregate, would serve to augment the public good.

Hoover went a step further than statistical programs, however, in order to encourage the private community, particularly the business community, to act so as to stabilize the course of economic growth without direct government intervention. Both as Secretary of Commerce and as President, he chaired general conferences on economic and social issues which brought together business, labor, and agricultural leaders and which were often either preceded or followed by major research projects. A broad survey such as *Recent Economic Changes* under the direction of Wesley Mitchell, for example, originated in the 1921 Conference on Unemployment for which Hoover was largely responsible. He also sought to persuade industry and the philanthropic foundations to support basic scientific research in the universities as an essential underpinning for continued economic development. In all of these ventures he made wide use of groups of experts drawn from among the leading physical and social scientists of the period. His intention was to develop broad channels for cooperative action among influential segments of the society, to support these efforts with scientific

[33] Herbert Hoover, *The Memoirs of Herbert Hoover* (New York: The Macmillan Co., 1952), Vol. II, p. 176.

and economic advice, and, in the process, to avoid the necessity for action by the central government. He also took a certain pride in the fact that the costs of many of the economic and social studies he helped to initiate were more often covered by private foundations than by public agencies.

It is significant that there were research groups already in existence, quite a few of them specializing in economics, to which Hoover could turn, as well as private foundations willing to support them. The 1920's saw the rise of new institutes devoted to social science research that were privately financed, independent of the government, but available to government for advice and consultation. Indeed, two of these, the National Bureau of Economic Research and the Institute for Government Research, became involved in several of the more ambitious government-sponsored projects undertaken during the period. Both of these organizations were originally founded to do work in special fields—the National Bureau in the field of economic statistics and methodology, and the Institute for Government Research in the application of scientific methods to government administration. They also owed their origins to the government's demand for this kind of knowledge during the war and to the availability of private funds, mainly from foundations like the Rockefeller Foundation and the Carnegie Corporation. The importance of these organizations, and of the Social Science Research Council founded in 1923, lay in the new avenues they provided for organizing otherwise specialized and disparate branches of knowledge in order to relate them to the problems of government.

In the social sciences there were no ties between the government and the universities like those that existed through the National Research Council and the National Academy of Sciences. The staff of the Bureau of Agricultural Economics was unusual in being able to maintain relations with their colleagues in the universities through the land grant system. In other fields there were no such links, and the general disciplinary structure of professional associations, which were relatively new and weak, did not conform to the way government agencies confronted public problems. The new research organizations began to fill the gap and provide a more workable basis for cooperation between social scientists and the federal government, whether or not this was their original purpose. The Institute for Government Research (later merged into the Brookings Institution) took care to maintain very close ties with the government. The National Bureau of Economic Research was more occupied with the development of an empirical basis for economic theory. And the SSRC was directly concerned with offering research opportunities that were not available through university sources. But, in encouraging interdisciplinary activities, the SSRC tended to mitigate the effects of the high degree of specialization in the social sciences and to counteract the isolation of much research from the problems of society.

The National Bureau of Economic Research was actually conceived—though not fully launched because of the outbreak of war—with the creation of The Committee on the Distribution of Income in 1917. The founders were Malcolm C. Rorty of the American Telephone and Telegraph Co. and N. I. Stone, former statistician of the U.S. Tariff Board. Rorty and Stone had originally met in connection with unemployment programs and legislation in New York. After several disagreements, they decided to join forces to set up "an organization that devoted itself to fact finding on controversial economic subjects of great public interest." To help them in planning the enterprise, Rorty and Stone first contacted three economists of high reputation yet with somewhat different interests and views: Mitchell, who was by then at Columbia University; Dean Edwin F. Gay of the Harvard Business School; and John R. Commons of the University of Wisconsin, a labor economist who had served as a member of La Follette's brain trust. With their advice, Rorty and Stone proceeded to set up the Committee and to seek private financing to support a research program. Within months, however, the United States entered the war and their plans were set aside. But the war, if anything, intensified their interest in an organization that would be devoted to the full and objective examination of national economic problems, with first priority given to the study of national income. So, as soon as the war was over, Rorty set out to raise the necessary funds and, by the early part of 1920, the National Bureau was established with Mitchell as Director of Research.[34]

Under Mitchell's guidance, the research program of the Bureau was planned on a long-term basis, reflecting his own interest in the development of cumulative studies, in the need for continuing statistical analyses, and in the trial-and-error testing of concepts and theories against ever more reliable empirical data.[35] The early projects of the Bureau concentrated on two major subjects: national income and its distribution, the chief interest of Rorty and Stone, and business cycles, Mitchell's own specialty. Over a period of ten years, members of the Bureau's professional staff, especially Simon Kuznets, developed the theoretical structure for an increasingly complex but manageable system of national income estimates. Moreover, with the Depression, the government's need for just such a system of economic measures became much more acute. So much so that in 1932, by a resolution of the Senate, the methods of estimating national income developed by the Bureau were adopted by the Department of Commerce, so that the series could be continued under government auspices.

While estimates of national income and the study of business cycles were the most important activities of the Bureau, the staff often engaged in short-term analyses as well, usually at the request of government agencies. Such were the several studies undertaken first in connection with the Conference on Unemployment in 1921 and later in response to the continuing interest in problems of unemployment and economic change on the part of Hoover, as Secretary of Commerce and as President, both. Mitchell was anxious to respond to such requests, but was fully conscious of the limits of these activities. As before, he felt that "action based on such knowledge of the facts as competent investigators can gather quickly is likely to be wiser than action based upon

---

[34] N. I. Stone, "The Beginnings of the National Bureau of Economic Research," *Twenty-Fifth Annual Report,* National Bureau of Economic Research (New York, 1945), pp. 5–10.

[35] The following discussion is based on Wesley C. Mitchell, "The National Bureau's First Quarter-Century," *Twenty-Fifth Annual Report,* National Bureau of Economic Research (New York, 1945), pp. 11–40.

'hunches.'" Nevertheless the process could hardly be called research; it involved "raking together the readily available material, analyzing as best we could in the time allowed, and producing a report on the 'dead line.'" Under these conditions, there was little chance to contribute to fundamental knowledge and considerable risk that changing conditions might invalidate research findings. This is undoubtedly what Mitchell had in mind when he later commented: "our experience with *ad hoc* investigations confirms the opinion that they contribute less in the long run to the knowledge men need, and less to the practical treatment of social ills, than systematic studies of broader and more fundamental character."[36]

The Institute for Government Research was founded for much the same reasons as the National Bureau. Rorty and Stone, in setting up the Bureau, were interested in a research organization whose work would be above partisan controversy and would be respected and used by all parties to disagreements on national economic policies. The very objectivity of its studies would thus enable the Bureau to serve as a vital factor in the settlement of differences without becoming a party to a dispute or taking sides. Similarly, the founders of the Institute for Government Research —one of three institutes consolidated into the Brookings Institution in 1928—believed "that there should be a non-partisan, independent institution to consider the problems of public administration, and particularly those of the National Government, for the purposes of making known the most scientific practical principles and procedures that should obtain in the conduct of public affairs."[37] This conviction grew out of both the reform and scientific movements early in the century. The way to better government, it was argued, was through the scientific examination of government procedures and the application of efficient methods of administration to public affairs. Thus the Institute was to be available to both the executive and the legislature as a "technical staff agency."

[36] *Ibid.*, p. 15.
[37] *The Institute for Government Research, Its Organization, Work and Publications* (Washington, D.C.: The Institute for Government Research, March 1922), p. 3.

The original stimulus for founding the Institute had come from the Commission on Economy and Efficiency appointed by President Taft in 1910, largely through the influence of leaders in the movement for scientific administration. Prominent among these was Frederick A. Cleveland, who was director of the New York Bureau of Municipal Research and became chairman and directing head of the Commission. The Commission, with the President's concurrence, was interested in the full range of government administration and in the interrelation of all its parts. In this respect, its work set a precedent for President Roosevelt's Committee on Administrative Management in the late 1930's and for the two Hoover Commissions on government organization after the Second World War. What distinguished the Taft Commission, however, was its exclusive emphasis on the managerial rather than the political role of the President. Also, for the first time, it recommended the use of the budget as a tool of management in government and set the stage for the eventual enactment of the Budget and Accounting Act of 1921. Unfortunately the Commission's initial attempt at budgetary reform, though approved by President Taft, ran into opposition in the Congress, which viewed budgetary reform, at least as conceived and recommended by the Commission, as a threat to its own prerogatives.[38]

The Institute of Government Research was created by the principal participants in the Taft Commission, who were convinced, on the basis of their experience, of the need for the equivalent of a municipal research bureau at the national level. With support from the Rockefeller Foundation, the Institute organized a board chaired by Frank J. Goodnow, then President of the Johns Hopkins University and one of the early advocates of scientific public administration, and a staff directed by William F. Willoughby, one of the leaders in the field of budgetary reform. Consistent with Goodnow's thesis that policy and administration had to be separated, the Institute recognized that "the accomplishment of specific reforms" was "the task of those who are charged

---

[38] *The Institute for Government Research, An Account of Research Activities* (Washington, D.C.: The Brookings Institution, 1956), pp. 3–4; also W. F. Willoughby, *The National Budget System* (Baltimore: The Johns Hopkins Press, 1927), pp. 20–23.

with the responsibility of legislation and administration," i.e., the Congress and the President. Its own role was "to assist, by scientific study and research, in laying a solid foundation of information and experience upon which such reforms may be successfully built."[39] From the beginning, the national budget became the number one priority subject for the Institute even though, with the outbreak of the war, the research staff became engaged in a number of quick organizational studies for government agencies. Thus, while the war disrupted the early program of the Institute, it did help to develop close working relations between the staff and the government. More important, perhaps, the war and the problems of postwar adjustment created a new and sympathetic climate for budgetary reform in which the Institute could make its first major contribution to government affairs.

Unlike the Taft Commission, the Institute worked for budgetary reform largely by exerting influence through Congress. During the war Willoughby had directed several studies on the budget question, including a study of the budgetary systems of several foreign governments and a survey of the movement toward budgetary reform in the states. Information about the Institute's work was also circulated to members of Congress and, shortly after the war ended, a Select Committee on the Budget was established in the House. Willoughby was engaged as principal staff consultant with major responsibility for organizing the Committee's investigation and writing its report; subsequently he performed a similar task for the Senate. The result, the Budget and Accounting Act of 1921, established both a Bureau of the Budget and an independent Office of the Comptroller General. Initially vetoed by President Wilson on the grounds that the provisions for appointment and removal of the Comptroller General were unconstitutional, the Act was later approved by the Harding Administration after being passed by Congress a second time.[40]

After completing its work on budgetary reform, the Institute began to concentrate on other areas of government administration.

---

[39] *The Institute for Government Research, Its Organization, Work, and Publications, op. cit.,* p. 5.
[40] Willoughby, *op. cit.,* pp. 8–9.

Under Willoughby's direction, it produced throughout the next decade a series of service monographs which gave a detailed analysis, bureau by bureau, of the Executive Branch of the government. Several of these monographs became classic studies, most particularly the one on the Bureau of Indian Affairs, which was completed under Lewis Meriam's direction in 1927 and provided a basis for far-reaching reforms in the Indian Service in the early 1930's.[41] In all of these studies, the separation of policy and administration was emphasized as a matter of principle. At the same time, the Institute was not uninterested in the progress of administrative reform and the politics of its accomplishment. Indeed, Willoughby and others found themselves actively campaigning for budgetary reform and even cajoling members of Congress into accepting the new budgetary system.

During the early 1920's, the Institute was continually in financial difficulties and was frequently assisted by the fund-raising activities of Robert S. Brookings, a St. Louis financier who had served on the board from the beginning. In 1922 Brookings also took the initiative in setting up the Institute of Economics with support from the Carnegie Corporation "to do for economic policy what the Institute for Government Research was doing for government administration."[42] Under the direction of Harold Moulton, the Institute of Economics immediately began to study questions of international economic reconstruction and the effects of international policies on commerce, agriculture, industry, and labor. Whereas the National Bureau of Economic Research was primarily concerned with methodology, the Institute of Economics mainly addressed itself to the solution of specific problems, though always demanding the same high scientific standards. At the same time, the Brookings Institute, like the National Bureau, responded to calls for information and staff assistance from various government agencies including Congress. In 1924 Brookings also set up a Graduate School of Economics and Government in Washington, separate from but affiliated with the two Institutes.

[41] Lewis Meriam, *The Problem of Indian Administration* (Baltimore: The Johns Hopkins Press, 1928).
[42] Charles B. Saunders, Jr., *The Brookings Institution: A Fifty Year History* (Washington, D.C.: The Brookings Institution, 1966), p. 27.

By 1928, because of problems in financing the two Institutes and internal differences about the educational purpose of the Graduate School, the three enterprises were consolidated into the Brookings Institution, a move Brookings had contemplated as early as 1924. The Graduate School, abolished as such, was turned into a training division, and the Institutes became operating divisions in the larger entity.[43] By the late 1920's, there thus existed in Washington a broad-based research institution that was devoted both to the development of the social sciences and their application to the problems of government. By then, too, there loomed over the horizon the disrupting effects of the Depression, which were to create a new political environment for relating research to public policies.

The Social Science Research Council

The National Bureau of Economic Research and the Brookings Institution demonstrated the advantages of having centers for the advancement of social science that were outside of the universities. Their emphasis was on research rather than on teaching, and they were able to choose and focus on vast bodies of knowledge. Social science in the universities, in contrast, was apt to be fragmented, narrow, and parochial. Louis Wirth has pointed out that specialization was reinforced by university organization:

> [While this] gave impetus to the maturation of the social sciences, [it also resulted in their becoming] more estranged from one another. The pressure for academic recognition often led to exaggerated and illogical claims, fruitless interdisciplinary rivalry, the stunting of curiosity and imagination in the training of students, and the oversight of the essential unity and mutual interdependence of the social sciences.[44]

It was this trend toward specialization and isolation which led, in the mid-1920's, to the establishment of the Social Science

43 *Ibid.*, pp. 27–40.
44 Wirth, *op. cit.*, p. 77.

Research Council (SSRC) as a countervailing force, its early development thus coinciding with the organization of the National Bureau and the Brookings Institution. Unlike the Bureau and Brookings, the SSRC was not a research organization. Its purpose was not to undertake research but rather to stimulate greater interaction among the various disciplines, to improve the conditions for research, particularly in the universities, and to increase general understanding of the nature of the social sciences. Because it was a council of all of the social sciences, its intellectual base was broader than that of either the Bureau or Brookings. Most especially, the influence of sociology and psychology in the SSRC worked over the years to give it a somewhat different perspective on social problems. Less exclusively concerned with economic analysis than the National Bureau, the SSRC was more inclined to view economic problems in terms of a socio-economic mix; and, in the study of government, it was less wedded to the goals of efficiency and economy than the Institute for Government Research, more disposed to examine the social and psychological determinants of politics and administration.

The SSRC owed its beginnings to the work of Charles E. Merriam. A teacher at the University of Chicago since 1900, Merriam was chiefly interested in the development of a science of politics. His doctoral dissertation at Columbia in 1898 and his last major work in 1945—separated by a span of almost fifty years—were both devoted to the study of "systematic politics." Like Wesley Mitchell, Merriam was a product of the early empiricism of social science and of the drive to replace reform with research. Where Mitchell was excited by Dewey and Veblen, Merriam had rebelled at the historical, legalistic analysis he had found at Columbia. But, like Mitchell, he could never completely shake off the temptations of reform. Consequently he devoted himself to exploring the relationship of scientific knowledge to political power. He, too, was continually engaged in the real world of government and politics, serving with groups such as the City Council of Chicago, President Hoover's Research Committee on Social Trends, and President Roosevelt's National Planning Board, serving on the last two with Mitchell. But he gave no less of his time and energy to strengthening the scientific basis of social science; his major vehicles were his own university and the Social Science Research Council.[45]

As President of the American Political Science Association in 1921, Merriam chaired a committee to review the state and future of the discipline. The committee's report went beyond political science, however, to attack the "over-specialization, too complete departmentalization and isolation" of all of the social sciences and to urge "the establishment of a Social Science Research Council."[46] The reasons for the recommendation were several: to extend the application of empirical and inductive methods to the full range of social science; to elicit greater university support for research in the social sciences; and to found an institution comparable to the National Research Council which represented the physical and biological sciences. Through the next two years Merriam was instrumental in gaining support from the other major social science associations, and in December 1923 the SSRC was formally incorporated. His task was undoubtedly facilitated by the financial support the SSRC received, almost from the beginning, from the Rockefeller funds, particularly in the early years from the Laura Spelman Rockefeller Memorial. In 1922 the Memorial came under the direction of Beardsley Ruml, a Chicago friend of Merriam's who was later to become Dean for the social sciences at the University of Chicago. Under Ruml's guidance the Memorial made the social sciences its chief objective during the seven years of its operation, spending more than $40 million during this period. And the SSRC, the National Bureau of Economic Research, and the Brookings Institution were among its principal beneficiaries.[47]

From the beginning the SSRC was divided in its aims, undecided as to how much emphasis to place on the strengthening of

[45] For a penetrating profile of Merriam, see Barry Karl, *Executive Reorganization and Reform in the New Deal* (Cambridge: Harvard University Press, 1963), pp. 37–81.

[46] *Fifth Annual Report,* The Social Science Research Council, 1928–1929 (New York), Appendix A, "History and Purposes of the Social Science Research Council," pp. 39–48.

[47] Raymond B. Fosdick, *The Story of the Rockefeller Foundation* (New York: Harper & Bros., 1952), pp. 192–202.

the social sciences and how much on the solution of social problems, an internal conflict that was to become more intense in the 1930's. Its program of fellowships and research grants was clearly intended to further the first objective: to increase the number of social scientists, to improve their preparation, and to support their investigations through financial assistance for travel, facilities, and equipment. But the question then was how to go beyond this point: to promote the development of social science as a whole and to encourage advances in theory and methods. This was difficult to achieve. For the field was divided into various specialized disciplines, each in a different state of development and each with its own methods and traditions; and many social scientists were unable or unwilling to look beyond the narrow confines of their own academic departments. Many were also afraid that the SSRC might become a central authority directing every enterprise, controlling the major sources of financial support, and inhibiting research outside of an established pattern.

Early in the game, indeed at the second meeting of the Council in 1923, a committee on the aims and methods of research was established. The committee worked slowly, however, and a definite program of methodological study was not formulated until some three years later. This eventually led to the publication of a case book in the methods of social science, to which a number of prominent social scientists contributed.[48] The "case book" approach went beyond a bibliographic exercise and was intended to clarify and analyze the methods actually used in significant areas of investigation, but to do so without making judgments about particular methodologies. At the same time the Council supported a Committee on Social Statistics which, in the long run, had two major influences on the government statistical system. First the Committee, in cooperation with other professional groups, worked to establish the Central Statistical Board in 1933 and set a precedent by continuing to function as an advisory service to the Board. And it also encouraged the utilization, publication, and analysis of social data collected by the Census Bureau

---

[48] Stuart A. Rice (ed.), *Methods in Social Science: A Case Book* (Chicago: University of Chicago Press, 1931).

and other government statistical agencies but not easily available to social scientists. Thus, the Committee, and those that followed it within the SSRC structure, helped to broaden the data base for social analysis, paralleling the efforts of institutes like the National Bureau of Economic Research in the field of economics.

For all this concern in the SSRC for the development of science, there was also a growing sense of responsibility for social problems. In his annual report as Chairman of the Council in 1926, Merriam spoke of the gap between the inadequacy of "our knowledge of social processes" and what he saw as an "urgent need for the application of the gross results of our inquiries to the problems of the world in which we live." He was also driven "to point out our limitations and the possibilities in the way of more complete and useful data." Merriam seemed to be as annoyed by the timidity of his fellow scientists as he was by "the zeal of the prophets." It was obvious that social decisions and actions would be taken with or without the application of knowledge. In the absence of involvement by social scientists, the direction of social change would be left to "the fanatic, radical, or reactionary whose pattern fits him for propaganda rather than for science." Here Merriam agreed with Mitchell who, while he insisted on the importance of long-term research projects for the development of science, also saw the value of brief studies urgently required for political decisions, however inadequate they might be. Merriam, however, seems to have been more impatient than Mitchell; he described much of social research as "uninventive and infertile" and regretted that social scientists had permitted critics to allege "that the effect of social study is to produce timidity and paralyze initiative."[49]

The Research Committee on Social Trends

In 1929 the opportunity arose for relating social science research to the major issues of American society at the highest level of po-

---

[49] *Annual Report*, The Social Science Research Council, 1926 (New York), pp. 14–15.

litical authority, the presidency. That year President Hoover established the Research Committee on Social Trends, with Mitchell as Chairman, Merriam as Vice Chairman, and William Ogburn, the sociologist from the University of Chicago and a leading figure in the SSRC, as Director of Research. The project was financed by the Rockefeller Foundation with the bookkeeping administered by the SSRC. In sponsoring it, Hoover showed the aims and qualities of his early training as an engineer; he was ready, as President, to employ expert advisers in order to collect all the "facts." But the outlook of these expert advisers was less narrow, less concerned with purely economic matters, reflecting the broader interest in all kinds of social phenomena encouraged by the SSRC, especially by men like Ogburn, who, several years earlier, had published his classic book on social change. The work of the project was undoubtedly also facilitated by Mitchell's relationship with the President since the Unemployment Conference of 1921 and by Merriam's contacts with the private foundations.

The report of the Committee, later published as two thick volumes entitled *Recent Social Trends in the United States*, was presented to President Hoover in the fall of 1932 on the eve of the first Administration of Franklin D. Roosevelt.[50] It included a sweeping but penetrating analysis of almost every aspect of American life with each section written by a leading scholar. Certain aspects of economic change were omitted, but these had been covered in the study of this subject undertaken by Mitchell and his colleagues at the National Bureau for the President's earlier committee. Also missing, however, was any full assessment of the effects of international affairs on national issues, though the Committee briefly discussed the future significance of foreign involvements for American society. The major point stressed in the review of findings, written for the Committee by Ogburn and his staff, was the essential unity of "such problems as those of economics, government, religion, education, in a comprehensive study of social movements and tendencies . . . [and] the importance of balance among the factors of change." The "interrelated changes . . . going forward in such bewildering variety at such varying speeds" pre-

---

[50] *Recent Social Trends in the United States, op. cit.*

sented both "dangers" and "promise." There was thus a need for "conscious control," and "the means of social control" were only to be found in "social discovery and the wider adoption of new knowledge."

The report on social trends openly broached the issue of the role of social science research in government. The nature of social change called for planning at every level of society and for a more active role for government in the national life. What was required was a "willingness and determination to undertake important integral changes in the reorganization of social life . . . [and] recognition of the role science must play in such [a process]." Thus, "while the most recent phase of American development in the social field has been the recognition of the necessity of fact finding agencies and equipment, and their actual establishment, the next phase of advance may find more emphasis upon interpretation and synthesis than the last." The problem now was to increase the "interest of government . . . in the technical problems of social research and prevision and planning." With this end in view, the report suggested that the Social Science Research Council might "prove an instrumentality of great value in the broader view of the complex social problems, in the integration of social knowledge, in the initiative toward social planning on a high level." Beyond this, it expressed a hope "that there might in time emerge a National Advisory Council . . . able to contribute to the consideration of the basic social problems of the nation."

Reading *Recent Social Trends,* one gets a sense of the high expectations that the social scientists must have had in presenting these views to the President and, through him, to their colleagues and to the nation. If their hopes were dashed, it was because the President to whom they spoke was a tired, discouraged man. But the study was not tied to the Hoover Administration; it was the work of a respected and independent authority and called for a posture on the part of the federal government that Hoover had never been willing to support. The goals it envisioned went far beyond an increase of economy and efficiency in administration or an extension of a centralized system of government statistics. It advocated nothing less than the fullest application of knowledge and intelligence to the whole decision-making process in the society. It proposed to apply the very methods that social scientists had employed in writing *Recent Social Trends* to the formulation of public policy: combining qualitative interpretation of trends with quantitative statistical measurements and putting them to work in making major political decisions.[51]

The basic argument in *Recent Social Trends* was for the application of knowledge to social action. While admitting that knowledge was not the sole determinant of decisions, that habit, intuition, and a drive for power would continue to motivate men, the Committee maintained that men need not be the victims of emotion nor drift as if they were the puppets of preordained fate. It did not go so far as to recommend a set of mechanisms to insure the application of knowledge. Instead it urged a new approach to social problems—an approach, however, based on a high estimate of the present and future capacities of social science research and on a conviction that empiricism and experiment were as valid in the social as in the physical sciences. The more cautious might have asked whether social science was ready to assume any such responsibility, whether in the brief period of its formation enough had been learned about social change to make social science a reliable tool for prediction. The more engaged and committed, however, might have looked at the turmoil and distress that faced the nation in 1932 and asked what the alternative was, the alternative, as Mitchell had put it, to "savage dependence upon catastrophes for progress."

[51] See William F. Ogburn, "Social Trends," in Louis Wirth (ed.), *1126—A Decade of Social Science Research* (Chicago: University of Chicago Press, 1940), pp. 64–77.

CHAPTER III

THE NEW DEAL

IN THE FINAL MONTHS of his Administration, Herbert Hoover sent a series of legislative proposals to Congress to try to avert complete collapse of the nation's economy; he asked for a cutback in government expenditures, a sales tax, legislation to avert banking closures and bankruptcy, and authority to ease pressures on mortgage payments. But by then the government was no longer his. A new president had been elected in November and Hoover was a "discredited failure." The outlook in 1932 was grim. National income had fallen from $87.4 billion in 1929 to $41.7 billion. The number of unemployed had risen from 4 million in 1930 to 12 million. Net investments had fallen to minus $5.8 billion. Wage payments had fallen from $50 billion in 1929 to $30 billion. "And, as prices and income fell, the burdens of indebtedness—farm mortgages, railroad bonds, municipal and state debts—became insupportable."[1]

Hoover had never lacked for information about the economy and about the factors of change and possible dislocation. As Secretary of Commerce and as President, he had sponsored scholarly studies, called conferences, enlarged statistical services, and assembled and used a large battery of expert advisers. But all the information and advice had been of little use, since he was convinced that remedial action had to be taken outside the federal government, in the private business sector and in the local communities. During his Administration, the separate parts of the na-

---

[1] Arthur M. Schlesinger, Jr., *The Crisis of the Old Order* (Boston: Houghton Mifflin Co., 1957), p. 248.

tion's economy had been drawn, as never before, into a complex pattern of interdependence. Indeed, the report of his Committee on Recent Economic Changes in early 1929 had qualified an otherwise optimistic survey of developments since the recession of 1920–1921 with a warning of the potential danger from just such interdependence and had stressed the need for equilibrium: "that through ignorance of economic principles, or through selfish greed, or inadequate leadership, the steady balance will be disturbed to our economic detriment."[2] When the Depression came, with all its severity and harshness, Hoover insisted that it was uncontrolled speculation in the securities market that had precipitated the widespread collapse; thus the Depression was caused not by any basic deficiency in the system or any lack of federal leadership, but by the selfish greed of a few.[3]

For Franklin D. Roosevelt, the federal government was as legitimate an instrument of public purpose as state or local governments and much, much more so than the financial and industrial organizations of the private business community. And the presidency was "not merely an administrative office," or "an engineering job"; it was "a place of moral leadership."[4] There was thus anticipation of the immediate exercise of federal power even as he took the oath of office on March 4, 1933. So much so that Eleanor Roosevelt called the inauguration "very, very solemn and a little terrifying"—terrifying "because when Franklin got to that part of his speech when he said it might become necessary for him to assume powers ordinarily granted to a President in war time, he received his biggest demonstration."[5] This was the moment that social scientists like Mitchell and Merriam had foreseen with some concern and had asked themselves about, though often rhetorically and in the abstract. Action, political action, would now be taken on a wide range of social and economic problems. The times and the

[2] *Recent Economic Changes in the United States*, Report of the Committee on Recent Economic Changes of the President's Conference on Unemployment (New York: McGraw-Hill Book Co., 1929), p. xx.

[3] Schlesinger, *op. cit.*, pp. 230 and 474–477.

[4] Quoted as remarks by Roosevelt to Anne O'Hare McCormick during the 1932 campaign, *ibid.*, p. 483.

[5] Quoted in Arthur M. Schlesinger, Jr., *The Coming of the New Deal* (Boston: Houghton Mifflin Co., 1959), p. 1.

need and the leader had converged to make this possible—indeed inevitable. How would knowledge be put to work to guide political decisions? Would it, indeed, be put to work at all?

Programs and Administration

The years of Franklin Roosevelt's first two Administrations were extraordinarily exciting, yet also frustrating and frequently divisive, for social scientists in the federal government. The New Deal made permanent a place for social scientists in government that had been gaining acceptance since the turn of the century. But a place for social scientists in government and a place for social science research were—and are—two quite different matters. Under Roosevelt, many social scientists came to serve as policy advisers and as political appointees, roles traditionally assigned to lawyers and businessmen. As policy advisers, they brought their own accumulation of knowledge to bear on matters of high national importance. They were also more cognizant of the function of research in formulating policies and programs, more apt to sponsor research as an integral part of the organizational structure and policy-making process than other advisers, and more aware of the need to maintain close ties between the government and the sources of new ideas in the research and academic community. But their intentions with regard to research—when they had any—could not always be realized. They had joined a government that was shaped for action, led by a President who was highly pragmatic, who moved quickly from problem to problem —sometimes brilliantly, sometimes erratically, sometimes indecisively—and who had little patience with, or capacity for, abstract thinking. He prized social scientists who brought important qualities of mind and manner to the process of government as he prized others of similar character and ability. But there is little evidence that he prized social science research for its own sake. Nevertheless, by giving a place in government to ideas and action, he created the demand and environment for research.

Within the executive agencies, developments in social science research were thus quite varied and depended on the chance interaction of motives as much as on conscious intent. In two agencies—the Bureau of Indian Affairs and the Department of Agriculture—the combination of earlier research programs, sympathetic administrators, intellectual innovations, and political pressures led to positive provisions for integrating research into the policy-making process—but with different results. In other areas related to economic and social legislation, research was used more in recording program operations than in developing public policy. Generally, statistical agencies were expanded and more systematically coordinated with each other through the Central Statistical Board established in 1933. Greater attention was also given by the Board to the development of effective methods for collecting information through sampling techniques and to the improvement of machine tabulation and staff training.

The research programs of the older welfare agencies, like the Children's Bureau and the Women's Bureau, were given a new stimulus by the general increase in social legislation and by their own added administrative responsibilities. To these, and to the statistical and survey programs already in operation for several decades in the Office of Education, was added a new research program in connection with the passage of social security legislation in 1935. Indeed, administrative planning for the social security program had been carried out with the assistance of a committee of the Social Science Research Council, which subsequently undertook studies of European programs of public relief and insurance for the Social Security Board.[6] At the same time, the internal research staff of the Social Security Administration developed into a large technical unit devoted to three principal kinds of work: the collection and analysis of program data, studies of program administration, and long-range studies concerning social security needs and the adequacy of existing provisions.[7]

The research units in these several agencies, however, were under separate management and were often diverted to operating

[6] Annual Report, Social Science Research Council, 1936–1937 (New York), pp. 32–35; Annual Report, Social Science Research Council, 1937–1938 (New York), p. 4.

[7] Arthur J. Altmeyer, The Formative Years of Social Security (Madison: University of Wisconsin Press, 1966), pp. 55–58.

tasks or handicapped in other ways. In the Office of Education, for example, research was hampered by a dependence on state reporting systems that were notoriously uneven. The Office, moreover, was politically weak and could not develop national reporting standards, since any centralizing procedure was likely to be construed by Congress as federal encroachment on the prerogatives of the states.[8] As for the Work Projects Administration, it set up a number of research and records programs chiefly in order to give employment to white collar workers of limited skills. Some attempts—mostly unsuccessful—were made to give cohesion and direction to these programs and to relate their work to that of operating units in the welfare agencies. A social science advisory committee was set up, and certain projects were coordinated with the Central Statistical Board. But the primary object of these exercises was not to do research but to create jobs. Thus, while vital statistics were collected on demographic questions, and natural resources and historical records were categorized in almost every state, there was little uniformity in procedures and there was not always professional supervision of the work.[9] Only by chance, or because of the care and concern of the research staff, were these multiple efforts used for any specific purpose or organized to provide a cumulative basis for social information.[10]

The Bureau of Indian Affairs and the Bureau of Agricultural Economics took much more positive measures to relate their research to the formulation of policy. In the case of Indian affairs, many different factors helped to launch an ambitious program of social science research. Most important were the accumulation of anthropological studies on American Indians, the devel-

---

[8] See Charles H. Judd, *Research in the United States Office of Education,* Staff Study Number 19, Advisory Committee on Education, Office of Education (Washington, D.C., 1939).

[9] For a review of the WPA program, see "Final Report" (mimeographed), Works Project Administration, The Research and Records Programs of the Division of Service Projects, Washington, D.C., May 5, 1944 (National Archives, Records Group No. 69).

[10] *Research—A National Resource,* Report of the Science Committee to the National Resources Committee (Washington, D.C., 1968), Part 1, "Relation of the Federal Government to Research," pp. 53–55.

opment of an Indian reform movement, the administrative study of the Bureau of Indian Affairs by the Institute for Government Research under Lewis Meriam's direction in 1928, and the appointment of John Collier as Commissioner of the Bureau in 1933. The full development of the Bureau of Agricultural Economics under the New Deal was also a product of various intellectual and political movements: the growth of agricultural economics and rural sociology as important subjects of scholarly attention, the extreme crisis in American agriculture during the Depression, and the pressure of farm interest groups and the farm bloc in Congress for federal programs to counteract the effects of falling farm prices.

Anthropologists had made studies of the Indians for years under the auspices of the Bureau of American Ethnology of the Smithsonian Institution. Founded in 1879 by John Wesley Powell, one of the earliest and most gifted of scientific administrators in government, the Bureau became a center for the systematic recording of Indian life.[11] But the facilities of the Bureau and the insights of the anthropologists working with it were rarely, if ever, used in the official administration of Indian affairs by the government.[12] Starting with legislation first passed in 1887, government policies were largely formulated around the concept of "allotments," whereby Indian lands were subdivided and parceled out among tribal members in order to bring the Indians into the stream of American life as individual land owners and farmers. By the time of the Meriam report in 1928, however, the allotment system had contributed to making paupers of most Indians. Many of them had failed as farmers, had been forced to sell or had otherwise lost their lands, and had been given little if any training and education to permit them to cope with life among the whites. In the process, the economic basis of early tribal organization had all but been destroyed. And this unfortunate situation was made worse by al-

---

11 See Wallace Stegner, *Beyond the Hundredth Meridian: John Wesley Powell and the Second Opening of the West* (Boston: Houghton Mifflin Co., 1954).

12 Edward A. Kennard and Gordon MacGregor, "Applied Anthropology in Government: United States," in A. L. Kroeber (ed.), *Anthropology Today* (Chicago: University of Chicago Press, 1953), p. 832.

most consistently poor administration in the Indian Bureau and, as the Meriam report emphasized, a lack of knowledge about Indian life in the Indian Service.[13]

In 1934 these policies were reversed with the enactment of the Indian Reorganization Act, advocated by Collier with the support of the President and the Secretary of the Interior, Harold Ickes. The Act had roots in a reform movement supported by all those who were concerned about the plight of the Indians and eager to defend their rights against encroachment by unscrupulous white men. Collier himself had served as executive secretary for the American Indian Defense Association. Those who worked on the Meriam report contributed what one student has called the authority of "high-minded scientific accuracy."[14] And, most important, anthropologists provided the whole reform movement with the bases for new policies grounded in concepts of cultural relativity and the relationship of culture to personality. With respect to the Indian problem, the correlation that anthropologists found beween individual development and group stability led to the conclusion that the Indians should be treated on their own terms—that is, as groups with distinct cultural patterns. The Reorganization Act tried to accomplish this in several ways: it made provisions for cooperative programs by the tribes, for the restoration of Indian lands, for Indian participation in the Indian Service, and for public health and education facilities. Its purpose was to improve the lot of the individual by strengthening his relationship with the group, in this case, the tribe. Inevitably, the new policy was criticized for running counter to the accepted "melting pot" theory of American society and for maintaining a tribal structure that would keep Indians from assimilation into American life.

Under Collier's administration, an anthropological research unit was established in the Indian Bureau to undertake studies of Indian organizational patterns as a basis for developing self-governing arrangements. This work was particularly important, since

[13] See Lewis Meriam, *The Problem of Indian Administration* (Baltimore: The Johns Hopkins Press, 1928), pp. 3–51.
[14] Randolph C. Downes, "A Crusade for Indian Reform, 1922–1934," *The Mississippi Valley Historical Review*, Vol. XXXII, No. 3 (December 1945), pp. 331–354.

the Indians were not obliged to participate in the provisions of the Reorganization Act unless they agreed to do so by refereundum and set up working constitutions and councils to carry out its purposes. Unfortunately, the research of the anthropologists had not been completed before new arrangements for tribal affairs had to be made and set into motion; it was thus a case of research being too late to be useful. But there were other difficulties. It has been suggested, for example, that "the anthropologists . . . were more interested in the still functioning Indian patterns and trends of social groupings than the new social values that were developing." This attitude may, in part at least, have led to disagreements between the anthropologists and agents of the Indian Service. Anthropologists engaged in research were also accused of treating "the Indian administration . . . as an agency of American culture directly involved in a clash with Indian cultures, rather than an integral part of the social universe of the Indian on the reservation."[15]

In 1938 the research unit was disbanded, and Collier blamed its end wholly on cuts in appropriations. The last director, the anthropologist Scudder Mekeel, thought otherwise. He was certain that the regular Indian Service had exerted pressure to end it because of the inherent conflict between "the professional administrator with little or no social science training and the 'theorist.' "[16] Whatever the case, the fact is that anthropologists did not participate as much as had been anticipated in the construction of Indian constitutions and councils. But this was not the end of research in the Bureau. In conjunction with the Soil Conservation Service of the Department of Agriculture, Bureau social scientists studied the way land was used by the Indians and the other resources that might be exploited on the reservations. They also served as advisers in the Bureau's education program, particularly in the recording of Indian history and cultural traditions and in solving the problems of learning among Indian children. In 1941

15 Kennard and MacGregor, op. cit., p. 833.
16 Scudder Mekeel, "An Appraisal of the Indian Reorganization Act," American Anthropologist, Vol. 46, No. 2, Part 1 (April–June 1944), pp. 209–217. For Collier's reply to Mekeel, see American Anthropologist, Vol. 46, No. 3 (July–September 1944), pp. 422–426.

the Bureau also sponsored a long-range study of the state of Indian life in selected communities of five tribes in order to review the effects of the Reorganization Act and to lay the foundation for future changes.[17] This last project, on which Collier himself placed great importance, produced a number of tribal monographs and experimented in combining research with training in the social sciences for Indian leaders and Indian Service agents. By the time it was completed, however, Indian policy had shifted to a middle ground between the forced assimilation of the allotment period and the strengthening of tribal structures that Collier had advocated. The new policy provided for the gradual withdrawal of federal control over Indian affairs, scheduled in stages and relative to economic and social developments in different Indian groups.[18] Inaugurated after the war, it was a response to the constant demands in Congress for a "solution" to the Indian problem, as well as to the impact of the war itself on Indian life.

It cannot be denied that Indian policy was heavily influenced by research, by both the Meriam report on the management of the Bureau and anthropologists' demonstrations of the interdependence of culture and personality. These effected a basic shift in policy that, despite changes, has persisted to this day. Yet this was achieved only through a political change. The anthropological research staff of the Bureau, in effect, identified themselves with the Indians and so allied themselves with one of the groups vying for a position of influence in shaping policy. Their research then became subject to political and bureaucratic attack from contending parties and could survive only at the political price that the administrator was willing or able to pay. Its objectivity was politically compromised even where it was scientifically sound. There was no doubt that Collier was fully committed to the use of research. But, like many administrators, he could not convince Congress or his own bureaucracy of its importance.

---

[17] Kennard and MacGregor, op. cit., pp. 833–835. See also Laura Thompson, "Action Research among American Indians," Scientific Monthly, Vol. LXX, January 1950, pp. 34–40.

[18] See John H. Provinse, "The Withdrawal of Federal Supervision of the American Indian," reprinted in Investigation of the Bureau of Indian Affairs, Committee on Interior and Insular Affairs, House Report 2503, House of Representatives, 82nd Congress, 2nd Session, 1958, pp. 179–188.

The case of the Bureau of Indian Affairs illustrates, among other things, the vulnerability of research when it becomes a threat to political and bureaucratic interests. Yet research was used with much more success during these same years in dealing with the farm problem, an issue as complicated by powerful interest groups as almost any other in American life. Farmers, food processors, marketing concerns, distributors, consumers, land grant universities, extension services, all play an organized role in the formulation of farm policy. Traditionally, the farm bloc in Congress had power beyond its size and representation, not only because of the importance of the farm issue, but also because of the key positions many representatives and senators from rural sections held in Congress. Generally certain of re-election and returned to their seats time and time again, they rose under the seniority system to committee posts of power and prestige where their strategic role in the legislative process was of critical concern to the President. In this situation the Department of Agriculture was likely to enjoy the strongest political support or suffer the sharpest political attacks—and the same was true of its research program.

By 1933 the plight of the farmers was so hard that there was almost general consensus among farm groups that intervention by the federal government was essential. At the same time, the idea of production control as a solution had gained increasing political support. In putting this idea into political practice, the work of M. L. Wilson, who had served with the Bureau of Agricultural Economics, was of crucial importance.[19] As the historian Richard S. Kirkendall relates, "Wilson concluded that, to solve the farmer's problems, government needed to do more than conduct educational campaigns in rural America. It needed to employ new means of enabling farmers to adjust production to effective demand as industrialists did." Building on the theories and prescriptions of economists like John Black, John Commons, Howard Tolley, and William J. Spillman, Wilson had devised a plan in the

---

19 The discussion that follows relies heavily on Richard S. Kirkendall, *Social Scientists and Farm Politics in the Age of Roosevelt* (Columbia: University of Missouri Press, 1966). Unless otherwise indicated, quotations are taken from Kirkendall's book.

late 1920's which "involved a tax on farm commodities to be paid by the [food] processors . . . and to be used to finance a system of payments to farmers who agreed to adjust production." He also experimented in Montana with rural programs that would bring farmers into the administration of federal controls and thus make federal intervention a cooperative enterprise rather than an external imposition. By chance he was able to communicate his ideas to Roosevelt during the 1932 presidential campaign, principally through two members of the Democratic candidate's early brain trust, Raymond Moley and Rexford Tugwell. Wilson's influence was particularly evident in a major speech on the farm question given by Roosevelt in Topeka, Kansas, the heart of the farm country, in September. Without adopting all of the details of Wilson's proposal, Roosevelt accepted the principle of production control within a broad context of national planning, particularly in terms of land and resources. The election of Roosevelt and the subsequent appointment as Secretary of Agriculture of Henry A. Wallace, with whom Wilson had been earlier associated, then paved the way for political acceptance of what came to be termed the Agricultural Adjustment Act.

The Act was not passed easily, nor did it have an easy life. Its passage was a great victory for the Roosevelt Administration, then barely a few months old, and was attended by a storm of controversy. Resisted by the food processors and other business groups that were to bear the brunt of the processing tax, denounced as "bolshevistic" by congressional conservatives, the Act was not fully understood even by the farm groups it was supposed to benefit. Once passed, it established the Agricultural Adjustment Administration (AAA) within the Department of Agriculture but with a good deal of authority of its own. The first AAA administrator, George Peek, was less than enthusiastic about extending crop control. While his conservatism was useful for conciliating critics of the Act, his quest for autonomy brought him into frequent conflict with Secretary Wallace. At the same time, the General Counsel for the AAA, Jerome Frank, recruited for his office an unusual group of young lawyers, extremely liberal and hopeful in their estimate of what the Act could accomplish. Thus within the Department of Agriculture and in the larger political arena of which it was a part, the AAA was a seething focus of social experimentation, bureaucratic wrangling, and political maneuvering.[20]

The Bureau of Agricultural Economics was the Department's research unit. It provided support for the AAA and the Resettlement Administration; and it had ties with other agencies as well, since many of the Bureau's staff were transferred to planning positions throughout the Department. For example, Howard Tolley, who had first served with the Bureau in the 1920's, was head of the AAA policy planning division when the Supreme Court declared the processing tax unconstitutional. Working with economists in the Bureau, Tolley came up with the alternative of compensating farmers from general public funds rather than from the special taxes originally authorized by the Act. The Bureau also undertook sociological studies to determine the best means of inducing farmers to participate in the Department's programs under the AAA and the Resettlement Administration; and this led to further provisions for the kind of federal-state-local community cooperation that had been encouraged by the Department of Agriculture since its first connections with the land grant colleges and extension services. These sociological studies were later supplemented by a series of attitude and opinion surveys conducted by a unit especially organized for this work, the Division of Program Survey headed by Rensis Likert, the first such unit to be established in any government agency.[21] The work of the Bureau was continually and systematically related to the formulation of overall policies. John Black has described how this was done: "the Secretary had final responsibility for all the decisions, but in most cases he approved what was recommended by his Agricultural Program Board, and the Program Board approved in the main what had been proposed first by an interbureau coordinating subcommittee set up by the Bureau."[22]

---

[20] See Schlesinger, *The Coming of the New Deal, op. cit.,* pp. 27–84; also Kirkendall, *op. cit.,* pp. 50–69.

[21] Rensis Likert, "Democracy in Agriculture—Why and How?" in *Farmers in a Changing World,* Yearbook of Agriculture (Washington, D.C.: Department of Agriculture, 1940), pp. 994–1002.

[22] John D. Black, "The Bureau of Agricultural Economics—The Years in Between," *The Journal of Farm Economics,* Vol. XXIX, No. 4 (November 1947), Part II, p. 1033.

Social science research in agriculture was thus expanded in depth and breadth, going far beyond the data collection stage which characterized research in most other departments; it was also brought into direct relationship with policy formulation and program operation through a variety of formal and informal arrangements. Finally, in late 1938 the Bureau of Agricultural Economics was formally designated by Secretary Wallace as the policy planning division for the whole Department. This move was part of a general reorganization of the Department in an effort to move beyond the emergency period of the early New Deal and to consolidate various programs both in Washington and in the field.

In their classic study of the administration of the Department of Agriculture, Gaus and Wolcott considered that by 1939 "the Department, as something more than a collection of semiautonomous bureaus, had . . . 'come of age' as a Department."[23] Using the Bureau of Agricultural Economics as a kind of "general staff" was an integral part of this process, the end result of an evolution that had begun under Secretary David Houston. While this placed the research function at a higher level of authority and importance than it had ever enjoyed in government, the ascendency was not without its perils. Indeed, John Black recalled that he took exception to the Gaus-Wolcott thesis that the elevation of the Bureau was a strong administrative move. He doubted "whether the Bureau would really be allowed to function as the Department's general staff" under pressures and objections from "other bureaus and agencies in the Department . . . [and] from the farm organizations and the State extension services."[24] In due course his doubts were to be justified. But, for the moment, the Depression, the political importance of the farm issue, the skill of men like Wilson and Tolley, the support from Wallace, and its own professional strength gave the Bureau powerful political protection. Social science research was thus able to function as a positive tool of agricultural policy.

[23] John M. Gaus and Leon Wolcott, *Public Administration and the United States Department of Agriculture* (Chicago: Public Administration Clearing House, 1940), p. 79.

[24] Black, *op. cit.,* p. 1034.

National Planning

The establishment of the Bureau of Agricultural Economics as a "general staff" for the Department demonstrated how essential research was in any attempt at national planning. The concept of planning went back further, of course, and was, in many respects, a child of the Progressive movement with intellectual roots in the liberal thinking of the early decades of the century. Arthur M. Schlesinger, Jr., has summed up the attitude toward planning on the eve of the New Deal in the following way: "As [earlier traditions of social work and of the Social Gospel] had prepared people for the planning idea, so in the twenties [John] Dewey and [Herbert] Croly instilled specific confidence in the power of man to plan, [Thorstein] Veblen asserted the technical feasibility of a planned economy, [Charles] Beard gave planning the stamp of historic necessity. By the end of the decade, the liberal synthesis was becoming clear."[25]

The idea of institutionalizing planning mechanisms in the federal government was also central to the conclusion of the President's Research Committee on Social Trends that "there might in time emerge a National Advisory Council . . . able to contribute to the consideration of the basic social problems of the nation." Such a council was viewed as a means of rationally relating intelligence to social decisions, not only by the government but throughout the society. At the same time, the Committee on Social Trends acknowledged "the important parts played by habit, intelligence, inertia, indifference, emotions or the raw will to power in various forms." "Conscious intelligence" was thus but one of several factors in arriving at any social decision. The question was how to bring it to bear on the complex processes of decision-making in the most effective way.[26] In the Department of Agriculture the answer was found in the formal integration of research and planning. For the government as a whole the immediate answer when Roosevelt

---

[25] Schlesinger, *The Crisis of the Old Order, op. cit.*, p. 139.
[26] *Recent Social Trends in the United States*, Report of the President's Research Committee on Social Trends (2 vols.; New York: McGraw-Hill Book Co., 1933), Vol. I, pp. lxxiii–lxxiv.

took power in 1933 was a National Planning Board established under the authority of the National Industrial Recovery Act of that year.

The National Planning Board, as such, lasted only one year. In 1934 it was replaced by an interdepartmental committee, the National Resources Committee, with the former Board made into an advisory committee, but still in active charge of its program. In 1939 the advisory group was again transformed, this time into the National Resources Planning Board, and established as part of the new Executive Office of the President. Despite these changes, there was continuity in the activities of the planning group. Frederic A. Delano, uncle of the President and long active in city and regional planning, remained chairman throughout its history. Charles Merriam was a member from beginning to end and became the dominant figure. For the first two years Wesley Mitchell was the third member. And after his resignation he was replaced by Beardsley Ruml, Henry Dennison, and later, Thomas Yantis—the last two were businessmen but were very much in sympathy with the objectives of research. Also, the group had the same executive officer for ten years, Charles W. Eliot II, who had been associated with Delano in earlier planning programs. During the 1930's the Board extended its work throughout the whole country through the organization of state and local planning agencies, which served as sources of information and provided bases for the development of rudimentary nation-wide planning activities. In retrospect, centralized planning was never achieved, nor for that matter was it ever contemplated or attempted. What was achieved was a formidable experiment—in an era of highly intensive social experimentation—in economic and social coordination, particularly with regard to the conservation and development of natural resources.

In the first year of his Administration, Roosevelt became increasingly concerned with the need for long-range planning to give overall direction to the numerous government programs in resource development. "We have been going ahead year after year," he remarked, "with rivers and harbors bills and various other pieces of legislation which were more or less dependent, as we all know, on who could talk the loudest. There had never been any definite planning."[27] For the President, planning was not an intellectual exercise but a practical matter of government and politics. His emphasis on resources was explicit in the name given to the planning group after its first year: the National Resources Committee and then the National Resources Planning Board. For Merriam, Mitchell, and their principal collaborators, however, planning meant much more than the prudent management of natural resources; it was a way of strengthening the role of intelligence in all the operations of government along the lines recommended in *Recent Social Trends*.

In 1934 the National Planning Board issued its report, *A Plan for Planning*, which discussed the creation of an agency more permanent than itself, for the Board was established only under emergency legislation. The proposed planning group was to have three main functions: (1) informational and educational; (2) coordinating and advisory; and (3) initiatory. The "initiatory" function was to include "efforts [which] should make it possible to apprehend more clearly and promptly the emerging trends and problems of the nation." Indeed, it was this function, more than the others, which would enable the planning board to serve as "a general staff gathering and analyzing facts, observing the interrelation and administration of broad policies, proposing from time to time alternative lines of national procedure, based upon thorough inquiry and mature consideration."[28] Again, the object was to apply the methods of empirical analysis and trends evaluation to social change on a continuing basis and to make the research results available to government leaders who had the responsibility for decisions.

The Planning Board also recommended that the more permanent arrangement be established directly under the President, the Board itself having been initially set up as part of the Public Works Administration under Secretary of the Interior Harold Ickes. On Ickes' insistence, however, the new National Resources Committee (NRC) was created as an interdepartmental commit-

---

[27] Quoted in Schlesinger, *The Coming of the New Deal, op. cit.*, p. 350.
[28] *A Plan for Planning*, National Planning Board (Washington, D.C., 1934), pp. 36–37.

tee under his chairmanship, while the former Board constituted an advisory committee with its own working staff.[29] In practice, the advisory committee acted, for all intents and purposes, as the NRC and had direct personal contact with the President through both Delano and Merriam. Delano, as the President's uncle, was family, and Merriam over the years had earned the sobriquet "Uncle Charley" from both Roosevelt and Ickes.[30] Through Merriam, Mitchell, and Ruml, the NRC also kept contact with the private foundations and the outside research community, especially the Social Science Research Council, the National Bureau of Economic Research, and the Public Administration Clearing House that had been established in Chicago. Indeed, it was from these particular research groups that the NRC secretariat and major study panels drew many of their staff members.

The business of planning required "the cooperation of the natural and social sciences," for "scientific discoveries and inventions" were primary instigators of social change. These were the views stated in *Recent Social Trends,* doubtless owing to the influence of William Ogburn. In his own contribution to this study, Ogburn pointed out that the problems of social adjustment to scientific and material changes were matters of cardinal concern for social science.[31] In 1934 *A Plan for Planning* again emphasized the need for cooperation between natural and social scientists; and, on request, the SSRC and the National Academy of Sciences submitted memoranda to support the call for more effective planning. The report explained that "the cooperation of scientists . . . should make possible a wiser and sounder adaptation of technology to economic and social advancement, while the cooperation of the social scientists with their research in the field of human behavior should correspondingly facilitate the making and perfecting of social inventions."[32]

For all these fine words, the relations between the two scientific communities were more competitive than cooperative in

[29] Schlesinger, *The Coming of the New Deal, op. cit.,* p. 350.
[30] Richard Polenberg, *Reorganizing Roosevelt's Government* (Cambridge: Harvard University Press, 1966), p. 16.
[31] *Recent Social Trends in the United States, op. cit.,* pp. 122–166.
[32] *A Plan for Planning, op. cit.,* p. 32.

the work of the planning organization almost from the beginning. Indeed, at the very time that the National Planning Board was established in the summer of 1933, scientists at the National Academy of Sciences were taking steps to create a separate Science Advisory Board.[33] The Chairman of the National Research Council at the time was the geographer, Isaiah Bowman, whose work had been important in The Inquiry during World War I and who, more than most members of the Council and its parent body, the National Academy, was eager to relate scientific developments to programs of the federal government. Responding to requests for scientific advice from Secretary of Agriculture Wallace and Secretary of Commerce Daniel C. Roper, Bowman conceived of a new Science Advisory Board (SAB) that would be organized to respond more quickly and effectively to government requirements than the Academy–NRC machinery. President Roosevelt, in turn, acting on plans developed by Bowman and submitted through Secretary Wallace's office, established the SAB by Executive Order on July 31, 1933.

The SAB immediately caused dissension within the Academy. In the first place, the President had acted somewhat more expeditiously than even Bowman seems to have intended and before the SAB had been fully approved by the Academy. The President of the Academy, W. W. Campbell, had not actively opposed Bowman's action but now felt that the Executive Order did not make it clear that, under its charter, the Academy was the official channel of advice between the government and the scientific community. Officially, at any rate, the SAB could now assume that role. In addition to the question of institutional prestige, there was another and deeper cause of disagreement. Campbell represented an older, more traditional position that looked on government involvement with considerable distrust and skepticism. He undoubt-

---

[33] The discussion of the Science Advisory Board relies heavily on the following: Lewis E. Auerbach, "Scientists in the New Deal," *Minerva*, Vol. III, No. 4 (Summer 1965), pp. 457–482; Carroll W. Pursell, Jr., "The Anatomy of a Failure: the Science Advisory Board, 1933–1935," *Proceedings of the American Philosophical Society*, Vol. 109, No. 6 (December 1965), pp. 342–351; and A. Hunter Dupree, *Science in the Federal Government* (Cambridge: Belknap Press of Harvard, 1957), pp. 350–358.

edly feared that the more aggressive Bowman group might compromise the scientific community if it acted outside the checks and cautious discipline of the Academy system. So strongly did he hold these views that he sought, on several occasions, to have the Academy Council disavow the SAB entirely. Disavowal, however, risked disregarding what was in effect a presidential order and laying bare a serious split in the Academy leadership. In the end these differences were resolved, not so much by Academy action, as by the failure of the SAB to gain government support for a broad program of scientific research, drawn up primarily by the Board Chairman, Karl Compton, then President of the Massachusetts Institute of Technology.

In its brief period of existence, the SAB made a more comprehensive approach to the government scientific establishment than had been made at any time in the Academy's history. In responding to requests for advice from agencies such as the Department of Agriculture, the Coast and Geodetic Survey, the Food and Drug Administration, and the Tennessee Valley Authority, the SAB frequently went further than the limited assignment it was given to inquire into the nature of future scientific advice needed in the agency's work.[34] More ambitiously, Compton in 1934 developed a "National Program for Putting Science to Work for the National Welfare."[35] Projecting preliminary proposals he had made a year earlier, Compton recommended that a scientific advisory body (like the SAB) be established on a permanent basis with members appointed by the President on the nomination of the Academy and with a series of subcommittees to assist in the work of the principal scientific bureaus. In addition, he called for a two-year fund of $1.75 million per year (cut back from a more ambitious request of $15 million a year for five years) to be appropriated to the National Academy of Sciences and to be administered by the National Research Council "in the form of grants-in-aid of research in the natural sciences."

Any program such as Compton's came up against a hard-pressed administration still faced with an emergency situation and

[34] See Report of the Science Advisory Board, July 31, 1933, to September 1, 1934; also Second Report of the Science Advisory Board, September 1, 1934, to August 31, 1935.

[35] Reprinted in Second Report of the Science Advisory Board, *ibid.*, pp. 69–100.

beset by acute budgetary problems. Despite the image of loose New Deal spending, Roosevelt, often to the consternation of some of his advisers, constantly called for tight and balanced budgets. The President and his staff responded to Compton's proposals, submitted in several versions, by insisting that any such expenditure of public funds had to insure increased employment opportunities. Research could be supported at such a rate only if it immediately created jobs. Compton also continued to encounter opposition in the Academy where a highly conservative element reigned. On the SAB itself, only one member refused to endorse the proposals, but for reasons that had nothing to do with the prestige or sanctity of the Academy. By a curious twist of history, the dissenter was John C. Merriam, brother of Charles, a distinguished biologist in his own right, and President of the Carnegie Institution. John Merriam questioned the establishment of a network of scientific advisory groups when the objective, as he saw it, should be to strengthen the scientific capability of the government agencies themselves and not make them too dependent on outside expertise.[36] He also agreed with his brother, Charles, that the natural and social sciences ought to be brought into effective cooperation with each other and saw the Compton proposals as setting them even farther apart. Indeed, in writing to Charles in the early summer of 1935, John questioned whether Compton saw beyond "the practical application of science" or had any "conception of the great opportunity afforded by developments in the social and governmental field through aid of modes of approach which have been used in the natural sciences."[37]

Compton, of course, was aware of the opposition of the social scientists to any plan that proposed support for the natural sciences alone. Early versions of his proposal had been referred by the President to Secretary Ickes and from there to Frederic Delano, chairman of the planning group. Describing a discussion that he had with Delano in late 1934, at which John Merriam was present at Delano's request, Compton wrote: "Mr. Delano expressed the opinion that the problems of the social sciences were

---

[36] John C. Merriam, letter to Karl T. Compton, October 22, 1935 (John C. Merriam Papers, Library of Congress, Box No. 158).

[37] John C. Merriam, letter to Charles E. Merriam, June 22, 1935 (John C. Merriam Papers, Library of Congress, Box No. 122).

more important, and that if a program like ours were considered, the same thing should be done for the social sciences—or else they should be worked out together." Compton also surmised, quite correctly, that Delano looked upon "the whole matter as one for possible future consideration as an element in the plans of the National Resources [Committee]."[38] While Delano spoke, Compton recognized that the words and arguments were highly influenced by Charles Merriam and other social scientists. Indeed, he later speculated that the fate of the SAB might have been strikingly different had the Academy been more involved with the social sciences.

By the time the SAB had submitted its second report in the early months of 1935, its fate was sealed. It was permitted to survive until late that year, when the Academy replaced it with a Committee on Government Relations and Science which completed some of the tasks the SAB had started; then the Committee too was set to rest. By the mid-1930's the Academy and the National Research Council were back to normal after a brief, hectic and, in many ways, experimental plunge into an activist role in government. It was a role, however, that Academy scientists were to play with great skill and efficacy in the not too distant future with the outbreak of war. Meanwhile Bowman, Compton, and their supporters had to beat a retreat. Their plans for federal support for research became a matter of study by the new Science Committee established under the National Resources Committee with representatives from the National Academy, the SSRC, and the American Council on Education—a combination that closely reflected the thinking of the Merriam brothers.

Not long after the Science Committee began to function, Charles Merriam wrote to his brother, John, expressing a cautious hope that unity among scientists might now be on the verge of achievement; but he was also concerned about the attitude of his fellow social scientists:

Unfortunately the attitude of our own social scientists has been more responsible than any other one factor for a certain irresolu-

[38] Karl T. Compton, letter to members of the Science Advisory Board, December 24, 1934 (John C. Merriam Papers, Library of Congress, Box No. 159).

tion and tendency to drift. This was due originally, as you know, to the machinations of Bowman, later to the feeling that since Mitchell and I were on the N.R.C. nothing more need be done, and finally to the negativeness of [Robert] Crane [the general director of the SSRC]. I think, however, that all these obstacles have been overcome and the representation we now have will move forward. Ogburn, who is President of the S.S.R.C. is keenly interested and alert to all the possibilities of united action.[39]

Whatever ambitions the Merriams had for the Science Committee were, however, never fully realized. All three councils continued to be represented throughout the history of the Committee, with the American Council of Learned Societies added later; and the Chairman, Edwin B. Wilson, a statistician from the Harvard School of Public Health, was a happy choice to symbolize cooperation among scientists. But the Committee was essentially a social science undertaking, given its origins and the composition of the planning group to which it reported. The natural scientists had an older and stronger position in the scientific bureaus of the older departments. And, so situated, they were able to branch out, in the later New Deal years, into more comprehensive programs that supported large components of basic research. These programs included the creation of central experiment stations in agricultural science, the establishment of the National Institutes of Health under the Public Health Service, and the expansion of the National Advisory Committee for Aeronautics (NACA) through contractual relations with industry and the universities.[40] Indeed, it was the NACA that provided experience for a broader scientific establishment to support defense activities when the specter of World War II began to appear, though what finally developed went far beyond the NACA model. In hardly any respect was the Science Committee a substitute for the place that scientists had earned for themselves in government for over a century or, for that matter, for the unfulfilled expectations of Compton's Science Advisory Board.

For social scientists, the Science Committee became a public

---

39 Charles E. Merriam, letter to John C. Merriam, Nov. 5, 1935 (John C. Merriam Papers, Library of Congress, Box No. 122).
40 Dupree, *op. cit.*, pp. 361–367.

revelation of their own predicament, illustrating the disagreements in their own ranks and the conflicts in their own minds regarding the role of social science in government. Charles Merriam himself, dedicated both to objective scientific inquiry and to practical political action, represented the point of reconciliation—or the gap—between these two points of view. In its memorandum for the early National Planning Board report in 1934, the SSRC had drawn "a sharp distinction . . . between scientific factfinding on the one hand and the determination and execution of policies on the other."[41] Once the Science Committee began to function, this dictum had to be translated into operational terms, and the question arose whether or not Committee reports should extend beyond surveys and analyses to recommendations. This became a controversial issue in the preparation of most major reports of the Committee: the report on population changes, another on technological trends and national policy (both following up themes first developed in the social trends study), and a third on research in the federal government.

At the time the population study was nearing conclusion, William Ogburn raised the question of recommendations in a meeting of the Science Committee. "I had hoped," he said, "that . . . a good deal of emphasis would be placed on recommendations regarding issues of policy of the government." But all he could find were several references to the need for "additional information" and "increasing the appropriations . . . for research," and these he termed "rather hackneyed." At the time he tried to press the Committee to vote on "whether or not we will have more discussion of policy," but to no avail.[42] As research director for the technological trends study, Ogburn caused considerable consternation among the other members of the SSRC because of the extent to which the report did, in fact, make specific recommendations. What was particularly disturbing to the Director of the SSRC, Robert Crane, was that the first printing of the report did not make it clear whether the recommendations were made by the

[41] "The Aid Which the Social Sciences Have Rendered and Can Render to National Planning," *A Plan for Planning, op. cit.,* p. 55.

[42] Minutes, 4th Meeting, Science Committee, National Resources Committee, May 23–24, 1936, pp. 4 and 9 (National Archives, Record Group No. 187).

research team alone or by the Science Committee as a whole, and whether or to what extent they were supported by the organizations, such as the SSRC, which were represented on the Committee. Indeed, Crane at an earlier stage had written to Charles Eliot, transmitting a resolution passed by the SSRC which insisted on this point: "it shall be made clear that the Council designees assume responsibility only for technical and scientific matters and only those matters to which they have subscribed, and that the Council as a whole does not assume responsibility for the findings and recommendations of its chosen designees."[43] The chief bone of contention in the technological trends report was a recommendation to strengthen and make permanent the institutions for national planning, which many social scientists felt did not follow as a logical consequence of the study and also involved it in political controversy.[44]

Edwin B. Wilson, the Chairman of the Science Committee, was caught in the middle of the controversy among social scientists. Returning from an SSRC meeting at which representation on the Science Committee had been discussed, he wrote to Eliot regarding "a somewhat natural fear . . . that the activities of the Committee will involve . . . the Council itself in embarrassments arising as to the question whether the pronouncements of the Committee are or are not confined to strictly scientific judgments."[45] Under the circumstances, some social scientists were reluctant to sit on the Science Committee. When the report on government research was being brought to completion, the Science Committee again discussed the question of recommendations, presumably hoping to avoid the kind of post-publication problem that had followed the technology report. The minutes of the Committee's eighth meeting in April 1938 declared unambiguously, "it is not the duty of the Science Committee to deter-

---

43 Robert T. Crane, letter to Charles W. Eliot II, October 7, 1935, attached to minutes of 22nd meeting, Advisory Committee, National Resources Committee (National Archives, Record Group No. 187).

44 See Edwin B. Wilson, letter to Charles W. Eliot II, August 3, 1937, in Science Committee Minutes File 106.24, National Resources Committee (National Archives, Record Group No. 187).

45 *Ibid.*

mine policies." Recommendations were still permissible, however, but with this stipulation: "any recommendations which the Committee makes should be in the spirit and on the basis of science as distinguished from policy-making."[46] But even this does not seem to have settled the matter. At the next meeting, two months later, the question again arose and "there was a division of opinion." Some members "were very doubtful about the propriety of making any recommendations other than recommendations about further studies. Others were of the opinion that reports are weak if they do not carry recommendations." The matter was never fully resolved.[47]

Another such debate began with the establishment of the President's Committee on Administrative Management in 1937, with Merriam, Louis Brownlow, and Luther Gulick as members. This Committee was staffed by social scientists, in most cases political scientists, who had also been engaged in the work of the planning group and who comprised the cadre of social scientists on the SSRC Committee on Public Administration, which had been established in the early 1930's with Brownlow as chairman. What distinguished the Committee on Administrative Management was the fact that it served, more clearly than the planning committee, as an instrument of presidential, and thus political, policy. So, from the very beginning, research could not be divorced from policy recommendations, though Merriam and others insisted that this was their intent. The purpose of the study was not only to make government more efficient but also to give the President more control over the executive departments. The Committee's presidential ties became even more apparent when social scientists from the Brookings Institution were engaged to support the staff work of the Senate committee that reviewed the President's recommendations of reorganization. The congressional base from which they operated, as well as the idea of pure administrative efficiency which continued to characterize the Brookings

[46] Minutes, 8th meeting, Science Committee, National Resources Committee, April 9–10, 1938 (National Archives, Record Group No. 187), p. 5.
[47] Minutes, 9th meeting, Science Committee, National Resources Committee, June 4–5, 1938 (National Archives, Record Group No. 187), p. 5.

approach to government, brought the Brookings staff into opposition with the social scientists working on the President's Committee. Thus the authority of social science was invoked by both the President and the Congress in their struggle with each other for political ascendency during Roosevelt's second Administration.[48]

In all of these matters the relationship of research to policy remained a controversial and divisive question among social scientists. What plagued the Science Committee was the lack of any mechanism elsewhere in the government for putting its research findings to use in some practical program and the reluctance of many of its members to go beyond the research stage. Its reports were thus of limited utility, though often of high quality, and this was undoubtedly a source of continual frustration to those members who hoped for political action. Its report, *Research—A National Resource,* succeeded in surveying and analyzing the total research capacity of the government and relating government needs to the nation's intellectual resources at large. But to a practical and harassed administrator like Harry Hopkins, the results were disappointing. "If the report . . . had included as its main subject matter a description of research completed or under way and a discussion of gaps in our knowledge where additional research should be undertaken," he wrote to Frederic Delano, "I would be enthusiastic about it. Instead, this report is concerned with the relatively unimportant matter of the detailed difficulties which are encountered in undertaking research work."[49]

The difficulties of the Science Committee, however, were more largely the difficulties of the National Resources Committee itself. In 1939 a number of the recommendations of the President's Committee on Administrative Management were put into effect, principally the institution of the Executive Office of the President, with the Bureau of the Budget and the renamed National Re-

---

48 For broad and perceptive discussions of the work of the President's Committee on Administrative Management, see Polenberg, *op. cit.,* and Barry Karl, *Executive Reorganization and Reform in the New Deal* (Cambridge: Harvard University Press, 1963).

49 Harry L. Hopkins, letter to Frederic A. Delano, November 25, 1938, attached to minutes of 77th meeting of Advisory Committee, National Resources Committee (National Archives, Record Group No. 187).

sources Planning Board included in this new arm of presidential management. The planning group was thus lifted out of its inter-departmental confines into the position of a central planning agency directly under the President. But even here its relation to policy-making was ill defined. Indeed, the report of the Committee on Administrative Management had stipulated that "the function of the proposed Board is not that of making final decisions upon broad questions of national policy—a responsibility which rests and should rest firmly upon the elected representatives of the people of the United States. Such a Board is useful in proportion as it is detached from immediate political power and responsi-bility."[50] The Board's functions were again conceived—as they had been in *Recent Social Trends* and *A Plan for Planning*—in terms of research. This was, of course, no accident; it reflected Merriam's participation and key role in all three enterprises, his desire to protect the integrity of research while still bringing it into relationship with power, and his fear of provoking conserva-tive and congressional opposition to central planning.

What such a mandate involved, however, was a confusion between planning and research by making them, for all practical purposes, one and the same thing. The Board, as a research agency, was too little involved in the hurly-burly of political bar-gaining to have any influence. In effect, it never really accepted its function as a planning agency. It assumed that it had only to announce its research findings for them to gain acceptance, with-out making efforts to explain and defend them in the process through which policy was formulated. This assumption was hardly justified, especially since a seat on the Board (and on the Com-mittee that was its predecessor) was always a part-time job for the members and since the working staff had no political position. The Board could have affected policy only by exerting influence on the President and only to the extent to which he wished to use up part of his own political capital to support the Board's work. But the President usually responded to short-term pressures, espe-

[50] *Report with Special Studies*, President's Committee on Administrative Man-agement (Washington, D.C., 1937), p. 29.

cially in times of crisis. Long-range planning stood little chance of being accepted unless the Board was prepared to fight for it.

The alternative to political action was to seek as wide a circulation as possible for the planning group's reports and use the informal networks of personal and professional acquaintances to get them read in the right places, both in the White House and elsewhere, by those who had political responsibility. Under these circumstances, some men were understandably tempted to expand research findings into policy recommendations, since they knew that neither the Board itself nor any other group was organized to translate raw reports into political action. Yet this temptation was as often neutralized by the standards of objective research which the Science Committee sought to maintain and by the fear of many of its members that, if they overstepped the bounds of scientific inquiry, the whole research enterprise would be compromised. The hopes expressed in *Recent Social Trends* were superficially realized; research was indeed carried on under the highest political authority. But no provision was made to relate it effectively and consistently to the political process of democratic government, as had been done, in a more limited context, in the Department of Agriculture.

Knowledge for What?

In 1939 Robert S. Lynd published his book, *Knowledge for What?* which called on social scientists to put their knowledge to work in days that were dark with the threat of war. He attacked the tendency toward empiricism for its own sake and issued a warning: "If the social scientist is too bent upon 'waiting until all the data are in' . . . the decisions will be made anyway—without him . . . by the 'practical' man and by the 'hard-headed' politician chivvied by interest pressure-blocs."[51] This was the old familiar cry of Wesley Mitchell and Charles Merriam. But Lynd went farther, farther

---

[51] Robert S. Lynd, *Knowledge for What?* (Princeton: Princeton University Press, 1939), p. 9.

than Mitchell particularly, and continually referred to him as the arch-empiricist without purpose. To Mitchell's axiom that "science itself does not pronounce practical or esthetic or moral judgments," Lynd responded: "If . . . 'science' does not pronounce such judgments, *scientists* can."[52]

Here, in many ways, was the difference. Mitchell, and even Merriam, had insisted that the politician—or the manager or the judge—had to make the decision. The social scientist did not and could not. The task of the social scientist was to accumulate and give order to the knowledge on which the decision was based. They recognized that the social scientist might be appointed to a position in which he made policy. But then he was not acting as a scientist, however much he applied the skills and outlook of a scientist to his work. Indeed, it was this distinction that led Mitchell to emphasize the highly concentrated statistical and methodological approach in the National Bureau of Economic Research and Merriam to give the National Resources Planning Board its emphasis on research even in the climate favorable to decisive political action that surrounded the President. The next step was to relate research to policy without compromising the integrity of the research itself. This was a dilemma for them, and one that they never solved in the years that preceded the outbreak of World War II.

The Science Committee's report, *Research—A National Resource,* was at least a step in this direction, for it viewed research in terms of the total society with the capacity of government, industry, and the universities seen in interrelation. Within a few years the requirements of total war were to make heavy demands on research and demonstrate the accuracy of the Committee's perception. At the same time the war was to create new organizational arrangements which would shape the scientific establishment of the postwar period. The physical sciences would be characterized by a high degree of central organization and the social sciences by increasing proliferation and fragmentation. The Planning Board, ineffectual as a centralizing and strengthening force for social science in the government, would be permitted to expire

52 *Ibid.,* p. 242.

and its institutional effects would be dissipated. But social scientists would resolve their differences, at least temporarily, and devote their energies to the practical economic and social problems of a nation at war. For the moment—but only for the moment—the war provided an answer to the question: knowledge for what?

CHAPTER IV

THE SECOND WORLD WAR

THE SOCIAL SCIENCE that emerged after the Second World War, with its large-scale empirical techniques, interdisciplinary research, and testable theories, was largely an American phenomenon. In his presidential address to the American Sociological Association in 1962, Paul Lazarsfeld raised a basic question about this development; he observed that, while it took place in the United States, it owed a large intellectual debt to European sources. The fields of theoretical investigation to which American researchers most often turned and the empirical methods they employed had their roots, he noted, in the European social sciences that developed in the nineteenth century. Yet why was this work so highly institutionalized and so much more advanced in the United States than in Europe?[1]

One reason for this was certainly the continuity of American scientific development—the persistence of pragmatism and the earlier examples of organized research promoted by the Social Science Research Council and supported by the private foundations. Then, too, there was the migration of European scholars (like Lazarsfeld himself) to the United States in the 1930's and their influence in relating sociological theory to political and eco-

---

[1] Paul F. Lazarsfeld, "The Sociology of Empirical Social Research," *American Sociological Review*, Vol. 27, No. 6 (December 1962), p. 761. See also Paul F. Lazarsfeld, "Observations on the Organization of Empirical Social Research in the United States," *Information*, No. 29 (December 1961), pp. 3–37. For an earlier assessment of research institutes in the social sciences, see Wesley C. Mitchell, *The Backward Art of Spending Money and Other Essays* (New York: McGraw-Hill Book Co., 1937), pp. 58 ff.

nomic studies. But the most important factor in the progress of American social science was undoubtedly the Second World War. Many university centers, for example, were first established by groups that had been brought together for wartime research. The nature of wartime research required joint efforts by teams of social scientists from varous disciplines; it was organized in units devoted to specific problems rather than in formal disciplines; and it provided vast sources of information that could not be wholly absorbed at the time but still revealed the limits of traditional techniques.

After the war the social sciences, like the physical sciences, were returned to the American universities. And their development owed much to the enormous growth in the nation's educational and research facilities—to the expansion of university enrollments, the stimulation of research through the concentration of intellectual resources in academic faculties, and financial support from the foundations and government agencies. These patrons also sponsored research in the problems posed by international instability and social and economic change. None of these conditions existed in postwar Europe. But, above all, it was the war, which exhausted Europe, that gave impetus to American advances in the social as well as the physical sciences and that greatly determined the framework for postwar developments.

The organization of the physical sciences in government after the war was different from that of the social sciences. For during the war the physical sciences were, by and large, centrally organized through the Office of Scientific Research and Development (OSRD). Also, physical scientists, knowing the costs of their wartime achievements and the expensive equipment needed to carry on this work, recognized that science could not grow in the future without heavy financial support from the government.[2] Their centralized organization and their general agreement on the necessity for continued government support made it possi-

2 The acceptance of the need for government support was expressed in the Bush Report in 1945: "For reasons presented in this report we are entering a period when science needs and deserves increased support from public funds." Vannevar Bush, *Science: The Endless Frontier* (Washington, D.C., 1945), p. 7.

ble for them to take a firm political stand in the debate on the establishment of the government's scientific structure when the war was over.

In contrast, social scientists were spread out among many government agencies during the war with no central mechanism for articulating and furthering their interests. They were able to increase their knowledge in depth and breadth. The studies they made of wartime manpower mobilization, intelligence and occupational testing, military and civilian morale, and psychological warfare activities provided them with a greater range of material for observation and analysis than they had ever had before. At the same time, the world-wide commitments of the United States brought them into contact with a wide variety of peoples on which to test their concepts. But all their work during this period was designed to serve as a basis for immediate and effective action under wartime pressures. After the war social scientists needed to consolidate and evaluate the gains that had been made; they also had to train a rising generation of social scientists in the new methods of investigation that had undergone rapid development during the war.

Only one of the social sciences, economics, played an immediate part in the postwar government. The Employment Act of 1946 established a Council of Economic Advisers for the purpose of relating economic analysis to public policy at the highest level of government. Here, too, wartime operations were a prelude to, and indeed a conditioning factor in, the organization of postwar institutions. During the war the demands of production control and economic stabilization required the collection of new and more detailed economic information, as well as continuing analyses of interconnected parts of the economy. Two things became increasingly evident in both Congress and the executive departments: that the character of wartime decisions would have an important effect on postwar reconversion; and that postwar economic policies would require the kind of informational and analytic bases that were set up during the war. There was thus general recognition of the need for a permanent top-level agency to analyze economic trends and guide the formation of national policy. None of the other social sciences achieved such recognition.

Economic Mobilization

In late 1938, at a time when the major New Deal programs had been established and were fully staffed, the Civil Service Commission classified 7,830 government employees as working in the social science fields and designated 5,050 of these as economists. Soon after Pearl Harbor it was conservatively estimated that "the number of social scientists placed in [the first] six months [of 1942] was as great as the number of social science positions in the entire federal service in 1938." It was largely the emergency agencies, like the Office of Price Administration and the War Production Board, that required this new staff, most of whom were economists and statisticians serving in research and advisory positions. Social scientists were also to be found in key administrative posts, where their analytical skills were useful for the difficult and complex problems of managing the the war effort.[3]

In theory, the First World War and the New Deal provided a base on which wartime economic mobilization could build. The preparations for the earlier war, however, had been neither well documented nor reported; nor did they compare in size and complexity with the task of mobilizing the economy for the longer and costlier war that lasted from 1940 to 1945. To insure that the earlier failure would not be repeated, the Bureau of the Budget initiated a program to provide a permanent record of the wartime activities of government agencies. Under the Bureau, a Committee on Records of War Administration was established, with a small staff in the Division of Administrative Management "to stimulate the Federal agencies in the maintenance of adequate records of war administration and to carry on independent studies of the war program on a Government-wide basis."[4] The purpose was not only to furnish a historical account but also to provide a systematic record as a guide in any future national emergency and to prepare case studies in the field of public administration. The

---

3 John McDiarmid, "The Mobilization of Social Scientists," in Leonard D. White (ed.), *Civil Service in Wartime* (Chicago: University of Chicago Press, 1945), pp. 74–80.
4 *The United States at War*, Bureau of the Budget (Washington, D.C., 1946), p. ix.

historical program was largely directed and carried out by social scientists with Pendleton Herring, then Secretary of the Graduate School of Public Administration at Harvard, serving first as executive secretary of the Committee and later as Chairman.

Even where the procedures of the First World War were recorded, however, they were not necessarily followed without question. With respect to economic mobilization, for example, President Roosevelt long resisted the idea of appointing an "economic czar" as President Wilson had eventually done in World War I. It was not until May 1943, halfway through the war, that the President established the Office of War Mobilization (OWM) as a kind of "civilian general staff."[5] Actually, a War Production Board (WPB), set up shortly after Pearl Harbor, had been given centralizing authority that it had never effectively exerted. As a subcommittee of the Senate Committee on Military Affairs reported, prior to the establishment of OWM: "It would appear . . . that most of these powers were delegated to the various agencies which now compete with one another in such a way as to engender conflicts inimical to maximum production."[6] Because the OWM was relieved of operating responsibilities that had burdened the WPB, and because the head of OWM, former Justice James Byrnes, had the ear of the President and so enjoyed considerable power, central planning was more effectively undertaken during the later part of the war. The situation had its parallel in the First World War when, after more than a year of trial and error, Bernard Baruch was appointed Chairman of the War Industries Board in March 1918, with basic authority to establish production priorities under broadly delegated presidential power.[7]

The organization and planning of civilian defense mobilization had actually gone through a number of stages following the

[5] For a full discussion of the Office of War Mobilization and its successor, the Office of War Mobilization and Reconversion, see Herman M. Somers, *Presidential Agency* (Cambridge: Harvard University Press, 1950).

[6] Quoted, *ibid.,* p. 37.

[7] Bernard M. Baruch, *American Industry in the War,* A Report of the War Industries Board (Washington, D.C.: Government Printing Office, 1921), pp. 24–29; also Curtice M. Hitchcock, "The History of the War Industries Board," in Clark, Hamilton, and Moulton (eds.), *Reading in the Economics of War* (Chicago: University of Chicago Press, 1918), pp. 245–253.

eruption of war in Europe. In 1939 work on estimating war production requirements was begun by economists under the direction of Stacy May, Director of the Bureau of Research and Statistics, a unit of the Advisory Committee of the Council of National Defense. The Bureau, later brought into the War Production Board, estimated the level of production that would be necessary to meet defense needs, the limits that would have to be imposed on non-military consumption, and the labor demands that would necessitate fuller use of Negroes, women, the aged, and the young. While the early broad estimates had to be continually revised during the war, they provided a base for setting up operations when presented on December 4, 1941, three days before Pearl Harbor.[8] Much more work, of course, was necessary to carry out the wartime production program.

In the area of production priorities, as in price control and rationing, the collection, sorting, analysis, and projection of new economic information were essential to the formulation of national policies and executive decisions. Despite positive advances in the development of federal statistical services, especially since 1933, the wartime administrators and their economic advisers found enormous gaps in the data base from which they had to operate. After the war David Novick described his experience in the War Production Board:

> attempts of the defense agencies during 1940 and 1941 to find adequate analyses of the methods of meeting emergency problems of World War I and the thirties were largely futile because the available records of those periods were found to be both unmanageable and incomplete. . . . [Also] the search for data on the use of specific quantities of steel, copper, aluminum, and other primary materials for various purposes revealed that up to that time practically no information existed in this field. In allocating these materials to essential uses, the WPB had to establish in great detail the extent to which each of these metals was used in all of the end-items and components being manufactured.[9]

8 *Effective Use of Social Science Research in the Federal Services* (New York: Russell Sage Foundation, 1950), pp. 18–19.
9 David Novick, "Research Opportunities in the War Production Board Records," *American Economic Review*, Vol. XXXVII, May 1947, pp. 690–693.

The war necessitated tighter controls over the civilian economy than had ever been exercised and thus required that the government have available many kinds of economic information that it had not needed before and that may have involved, under normal conditions, an unacceptable intervention into the private sector. The methods of collecting the information were determined by the task at hand and limited by the shortage of time, imperfect working conditions, the lack of adequate staffs, and the general confusion that is the chronic accompaniment of wartime government. In the words of a group of economists who held important positions in the Office of Price Administration (OPA), "the control problems at hand rather than the research use was the guide for the collection and analysis of [economic] information. The work was done in haste and with inadequate personnel, which means that often gaps were not filled, summaries were limited in number, explanations of methods were sketchy or absent, and interpretations were made orally."[10]

For all the difficulties they encountered, economists and statisticians played a vital role in government during the war. In essence, "the mobilization of the nation's resources . . . presented an environment which gave scope for the specific knowledge and analytical traits which are induced in an economist's training."[11] But, in operation, the economist's role was primarily "engineering" in nature; goals were set and the job was to meet them. This is not to say that choices were clear-cut and that alternative possibilities were not frequently available when decisions had to be made. Indeed, when time permitted, price actions by OPA administrators, for example, were supported by "economic briefs which explained the structure of the industry and its prices and the business practices followed."[12] Final decisions, however, were frequently and

---

[10] "Content and Research Uses of Price Control and Rationing Records," Report by Subcommittee on Research Use of OPA Records, Committee on Research, American Economic Association, *American Economic Review*, Vol. XXXVII, May 1947, p. 651.

[11] Paul T. Homan, "Economics in the War Period," *American Economic Review*, Vol. XXXVII, No. 5 (December 1946), p. 870.

[12] "Content and Research Uses of Price Control and Rationing Records," *op. cit.*, pp. 661–662.

legitimately open to dispute. Similarly, the establishment of production priorities, which was also subject to economic analysis, depended not only on choices among competing requirements, but also on variables such as production schedules, plant expansion, raw materials, and manpower availability, which did not always fit squarely into place.[13]

In the development of statistics, war was as crucial a factor as it was in other areas. It was World War I that gave the federal statistical system a more positive thrust forward than any previous event in its history. As Wesley Mitchell put it: "the war led to the use of statistics, not only as a record of what had happened, but also as a vital factor in planning what should be done."[14] At the same time, the development of uncoordinated statistical services in a number of permanent and emergency agencies led in the first war to duplication, confusion, and serious burdens on respondents. Indeed, by the end of the war, in response to complaints and protests from businessmen to their congressmen, a central bureau for statistical information was organized. And, though it was permitted to expire in 1919, it was an important milestone on the way to the establishment of the Central Statistical Board in 1933.[15]

Work in statistics after 1920 was chiefly "concentrated on the collection of banking data and on general economic data suitable for the construction of economic time series." Behind these efforts was the economic view of "the business cycle" as "the great menace" to an integrated economy. What was an exception in the 1920's became a more general trend after 1933, however. In the 1920's a major economic problem that could not be explained by theories of the business cycle was the crisis in agriculture, about which special statistical information was required. As the Depression set in, other economic and social problems demanded special attention; new programs for administering relief, alleviating unemployment, and encouraging industrial development required the formulation of new statistical series. Early in the Second

---

[13] For a full discussion of production problems, see Novick, Anshen, and Truppner, *Wartime Production Controls* (New York: Columbia University Press, 1949).

[14] Mitchell, *op. cit.*, p. 42.

[15] *Ibid.*, pp. 42–47.

World War the mobilization of resources made further demands on the government statistical services. For example, it was noted in late 1941 that "the Bureau of Labor Statistics index number of wholesale prices . . . despite all its recent refinement, does not furnish sufficient data for the establishment of price ceilings." Also, for production purposes, "highly individualized data, frequently plant by plant, are needed, in addition to time series and to statistics descriptive of the economy by major economic segments."[16]

At the beginning of the war, the results of the Sixteenth Decennial Census undertaken in 1940 provided a statistical basis for preliminary economic and manpower planning. But population and industrial shifts to meet war requirements, as well as the more complex needs of mobilization, soon outmoded the available figures and data sources. The Census Bureau was pressed not only to undertake more frequent and varied statistical reporting, but also to develop new systems of sampling, questionnaire design, and machine tabulation. Some of these innovations were tied to the particular problems of the wartime economy; but many were to prove "important to the peacetime . . . requirements of the government, business, industry, and research institutions" and destined to "become part of the regular services of the government."[17]

The war, by its very pervasiveness and by the enormous requirements it placed on the economy over a period of years, forced the government to develop a complex set of economic and social statistics and new methods of economic and social analysis that took into account the whole of the economy, not only as an integrated system but also in detailed terms of its parts. And in 1944, even while the enormous government machinery for statistical collection and economic analysis was still developing, the problems of conversion to a peacetime economy were anticipated. Here the failures of the First World War, while inadequately documented, served as a graphic example, warning of the need for planning. In October 1944 the Office of War Mobilization was re-

[16] Winfield R. Riefler, "Government and the Statistician," *Journal of the American Statistical Association*, Vol. 37, No. 217 (March 1942), especially pp. 5–6.
[17] Philip M. Hauser, "Wartime Developments in Census Statistics," *American Sociological Review*, Vol. 10, No. 2 (April 1945), pp. 160–169.

established as the Office of War Mobilization and Reconversion after a complex legislative process, for it was generally recognized that "intelligent planning for reconversion was dependent to a large extent upon a more effective administrative pattern for waging war."[18] Indeed, the institutional and methodological bases for planning during the war were quite as important as the evolution of economic ideas in laying the groundwork for the enactment of the Employment Act of 1946 and the institution of the Council of Economic Advisers.

The war also compelled economists of the traditional school to question some of their assumptions and reckon with advances in sociology and social psychology. The idea of rational self-interest as a prime economic force was especially doubtful in a period of total war, when administrative decisions largely replaced the free interplay of supply and demand in the market place. Political leaders had to be sure that central decisions did not create more hardship than was necessary and that deprivations were shared by all equally. Many problems had to be solved in establishing production priorities, in allocating scarce raw materials, and in arbitrating labor-management disputes when the normal weapons—strikes on the part of workers and shut-downs on the part of plant owners—could not be tolerated. It was, however, difficult to institute and maintain price controls and food rationing in a society of suspicious and independent-minded citizens. Unpopular decisions frequently had to be made. Indeed, in late 1942 the Office of Price Administration seemed "on the verge of collapse," caught in a cross-fire of farmers' demands for higher prices, workers' demands for higher wages, and congressional interventions in defense of constituents' complaints.[19]

It became increasingly necessary to base stabilization measures that would affect consumers, particularly, on as careful a study of the facts and the probable repercussions as time would permit. For example, in late 1944 when it seemed likely that German resistance would prolong the war, the OPA was faced with

---

[18] Stephen Kemp Bailey, *Congress Makes a Law* (New York: Columbia University Press, 1950), p. 29.
[19] *The United States at War, op. cit.*, pp. 386–387.

the possibility of re-instituting rationing controls that had earlier been relaxed. A new rationing program might easily have failed, since there appeared to be an accumulation of valid ration stamps in the hands of consumers that might nullify restrictions. Any move to invalidate these stamps was bound to be considered an arbitrary act—a complaint that plagued the OPA throughout the war. What it had to do was to find out how many stamps were accumulated, who held them, and how best to justify what would certainly be an unpopular decision. So the research staff of the OPA devised a series of questions to be asked by the Bureau of the Census, utilizing the national sample developed in connection with the Bureau's *Monthly Report on the Labor Force.*

The results of the survey confirmed that there was indeed a backlog of ration coupons held by consumers; that any attempt to restrict purchases of items in short supply by increasing their point value would be a hardship for those who spent their coupons currently; and that, without such restrictions, the commodities in short supply would most likely be bought up by those who had accumulated food coupons, thus causing unequal distribution. The alternative, of course, was to invalidate the accumulated coupons, and that was what the OPA decided to do. The survey not only provided the information needed to reach the decision, but also the basis for explaining it to congressmen, the press, and the public. There were protests, of course, but they were provoked not so much by the decision itself as by the fact that no advance notice was given before it took effect.[20]

The use of survey research by the OPA was but one example of increasing use of opinion and attitudinal studies during the war. Earlier, such work had largely been restricted to the Division of Program Surveys of the Department of Agriculture, organized under the direction of Rensis Likert in 1939. Indeed, since Likert's unit had already had experience in developing and relating surveys to government programs, it undertook assignments for several departments after 1941. Among these were a series of surveys in connection with the war finance program, which set a precedent

---

[20] For a full discussion of this case, see Joseph A. Kershaw and Harry Alpert, "The Invalidation of Food Ration Currency, December 1944," *The Journal of Social Issues,* Vol. III, No. 4 (July 1947), pp. 40–48.

for continued research in economic behavior after the war.[21] Their purpose was to provide those responsible for the sale of war bonds with an understanding of the buying habits and motives of the American people. The voluntary purchase of bonds was not only essential to the financing of the war effort, but was also a means of controlling consumer purchasing power and thus contributing to general economic stability.

The survey group had the advantage, in this instance, of being involved in the program from its inception. In "three and one-half years nine major national studies were conducted and twice as many regional or local ones aimed at solving special problems." The researchers were thus able to build on previous experience and choose the best timing and selling techniques for successive war bond drives. The surveys showed that the problems were different at different times. At first people had to understand why it was important for them to buy bonds; at a later stage they had to be given some idea of how much they ought to invest in bonds; and still later they had to be reassured that the bonds were indeed "liquid" and could be redeemed.

Public opinion and attitude surveys were conducted not only in the price control and rationing fields and in connection with the war bond drives, but also in assessing consumer requirements in relation to war production priorities, in testing the attitudes and habits of civilian workers in war plants and shipyards, and in maintaining civilian morale. However, their effectiveness depended a good deal on how they were used, and here experience varied. As early as October 1941, the President had established an Office of Facts and Figures (OFF) under Archibald MacLeish "for the purpose of facilitating the dissemination of factual information to the citizens of the country on the progress of the defense effort and on the defense policies and activities of the government."[22] The problem was essentially that of keeping civilian morale high, a task dependent on a constant and skillful evaluation of

---

21 The following description is based on Dorwin Cartwright, "Surveys of the War Finance Program," in Churchman, Ackoff, and Wax (eds.), *Measurement of Consumer Interest* (Philadelphia: University of Pennsylvania Press, 1947), pp. 198–209.

22 Harold F. Gosnell and Moyca C. David, "Public Opinion Research in Government," *The American Political Science Review*, Vol. XLIII, 1949, p. 566.

public opinion. Unfortunately the use of opinion surveys here was not as successful as it was in the case of the war bond drives. In OFF there was no close working relationship between researchers and operating officials; and when the operation was absorbed into the Office of War Information (OWI), it met, according to a close observer, the skepticism of the Director, Elmer Davis. Davis, "as a newspaper man, a writer, and a radio commentator . . . preferred methods other than elaborate public opinion surveys . . . [and] felt [moreover] that his agency was not charged with the maintenance of national morale."[23] Thus, while a Surveys Division was maintained in the Domestic Branch of OWI, it did not last through the war and was not, as in some other agencies, integrated into the policy-making process.

Economics and statistics had been well launched on their careers in government before this period, during the First World War and the New Deal. Public opinion surveys and related research in social psychology, however, were largely new fields. In Dorwin Cartwright's words: "Just as the first world war witnessed the establishment of psychological testing as a major field of psychology, it now appears that the second world war has brought to maturity social psychology."[24] But like the economists and statisticians, the psychologists, sociologists, and anthropologists dealing with attitudes and preferences were largely engaged in solving "technological problems rather than strictly scientific ones." Advances were mainly methodological rather than theoretical, as new techniques had to be devised to get the answers administrators needed. Social scientists had to deal with larger and more complex populations than those, usually housed around university campuses, that they had been used to. They also had access to new groups, because the war gave government the privilege of intruding into the private lives of its citizens. But what information they gained had to be used not in formulating and refining theories of human behavior but in solving the problems at hand—changing

23 *Ibid.*, p. 567.
24 Dorwin Cartwright, "Social Psychology in the United States during the Second World War," *Human Relations,* Vol. I, No. 2 (November 1947), pp. 333–352.

food habits in order to adjust to meat shortages, accounting for absenteeism among workers in essential industries, or combatting the disruptive and demoralizing effects of unfounded rumors. And scientists were often concerned about the inadequacy of the theoretical bases for much of their applied research.

Social scientists, moreover, were scattered in an expanding and changing network of civilian agencies. Economists, statisticians, and public administration specialists were largely lodged in the OPA and the WPB, but were also found in the War Labor Board, the War Manpower Commission, and the increased staffs of regular agencies like the Treasury Department, the Bureau of the Census, the Budget Bureau, and the Federal Reserve Board. They were sometimes so conspicuous as to provoke opposition, as in 1943 when Congress passed a provision which barred economists from high administrative posts in the OPA.[25]

Survey research groups were set up, with varying degrees of success, in at least half a dozen agencies: the OPA, the WPB, the OWI, the Department of Agriculture, in connection with the Committee on Food Habits of the National Research Council, and in the Census Bureau. Social scientists in different agencies often had connections with each other; they shared the same facilities or worked on common projects or had had earlier professional associations. Statisticians in the Census Bureau, for example, worked closely with the small survey staffs in the OPA and the Division of Program Surveys. The latter was the only one of these survey units to have been set up before the war, in the Department of Agriculture, and it undertook research projects for other agencies under contract. The establishment of the Office of War Mobilization and Reconversion, as an overall coordinating agency and as an agency for postwar planning, also served to strengthen interdepartmental ties despite the pressures of a heavy and exacting workload. But, by and large, social scientists were spread throughout the government with no significant points of focus and leadership. This was in marked contrast to the environment in which physical scientists operated.

25 Homan, *op. cit.*, p. 868.

Central Scientific Organization

American mobilization for the war, to all intents and purposes, started in 1939. The period between the invasion of Poland by Hitler and the attack on Pearl Harbor gave the government some two years to organize the central agencies it needed, first, to assist the powers allied against the Axis and, then, to support the nation's full involvement after December 1941. Mobilization plans drawn up during the interwar years by the Army and Navy were little more than general statements proposing organizational patterns for industrial mobilization. They were ignored by the President, who began to set up a series of organizations under his direct control that soon were sprawling out throughout the federal system. The National Resources Planning Board played little if any role in mobilization, though its chief task since 1933 had been to map out for future development the industrial and resource base of the economy.[26] Indeed, many of the Board's studies, such as those dealing with industrial locations, natural resources, and transportation systems, turned out to be of use to those first responsible for setting up production and stabilization goals. And many of those involved in Board activities took on important assignments in emergency agencies. But whatever the Board undertook to do in its own name, from the early mobilization period until its dissolution in 1943, was more generally related to planning for postwar economic reconversion and growth. In its report for 1943, for example, the Board described its own work as: "aiding in various phases of the war effort where the special knowledge of the members and staff, or the 'clearing house' activities of the organization can be of service. The Board's primary concern is with those actions taken now which will have an important influence on longer-range developments."[27]

Had the Board played a larger role in the war effort and acted as an overall coordination agency as the Office of War Mobilization and Reconversion did later, it might have exerted some influence on the postwar organization of the government's scientific

[26] John D. Millett, *The Process and Organization of Government Planning* (New York: Columbia University Press, 1947), p. 7.

[27] National Resources Development Report for 1942, National Resources Planning Board (Washington, D.C., January 1942), p. 6.

research establishment. As it was, the Board's final reports contributed to the stream of ideas and proposals that led to the Employment Act of 1946. But its earlier work on scientific research and university support, with its heavy emphasis on the interrelationship of the natural and the social sciences, influenced the postwar discussion only through the individual efforts of men who had participated in its activities. Because it was inactive early in the war and because the President permitted it to die in 1943 when Congress refused funds for its continuance, the Board was not able to follow up the examination of government-supported scientific research that it had begun earlier. And men like Mitchell, Merriam, and Ogburn gave way to new and younger leaders in the social science community soon after the war ended.

At meetings early in 1939 the Board did, in fact, discuss the problems of mobilization for war. Returning from a trip to Germany in 1938, Ogburn wrote to Frederic Delano: "I had never seen such thoroughness in preparation for war as is taking place in Germany. . . . some kind of report or study ought to be made of what mobilization for modern warfare means in [the] . . . fields of civil and social institutions." Delano, in turn, sent Ogburn's letter to the President, who wrote back somewhat ambiguously: "I think some study along this line should be made, but before anything is decided on, will you talk with . . . [Louis] Johnson . . . Hopkins and . . . Morgenthau?"[28] Whether or not Delano had these talks, part of the next meeting of the Board's Advisory Committee was devoted to a discussion of "the possibility and desirability of appointing a commission to inquire into the present interrelations of political, private and military activities, to report to the President what, if anything, should be done to provide more effective organization of the Government for the successful preparation, conduct and demobilization of national defense in any war that may be thrust upon it."[29] No such commission was convened, however. And when the President took the first steps in building a wartime

[28] William F. Ogburn, letter to Frederic A. Delano, November 22, 1938; and President Roosevelt, letter to Frederic A. Delano, December 1, 1938 (National Resources Planning Board Files, National Archives).

[29] Minutes, 79th Meeting, Advisory Committee, National Resources Planning Board, January 7, 1939 (National Resources Planning Board Files, National Archives).

organization in 1940—setting up the Office of Emergency Management, the Advisory Committee to the Council of National Defense, and the National Defense Research Committee—it was without reference to the Planning Board.

In the several reports it prepared during the early war years, the Board studied both the need for long-range economic planning and the more immediate problems of reconversion and manpower demobilization that the nation would face. At the end of one of the last meetings of the Science Committee, in January 1943, the Board's Executive Secretary, Charles Eliot, brought up a subject that the Committee had discussed on several previous occasions: postwar research planning. By the end of the two-day session, the Committee unanimously approved a resolution accepting "the responsibility of formulating policies and programs for the advancement of research after the war, as a contribution to the 'Postwar Agenda.' " It also called "upon the Four Councils to canvass their constituent scientific and professional membership to assist in formulating long-term plans and policies, with illustrative proposals, in the areas or disciplines of their special concern and professional interest."[30] By the fall, however, the Board had been dissolved. And when, in 1945, the President wanted a statement of research goals and needs for the "Postwar Agenda," he turned to Vannevar Bush, the Chairman of the National Defense Research Committee and Director of the Office of Scientific Research and Development.

The end of the Planning Board has been attributed to a number of factors. Charles Merriam, who had been associated with the Board throughout its history, pointed to "Congressional-Executive rivalry, attitudes toward the New Deal, difficulties with the personnel problem, [and] the general fear of planning as an entering wedge to total 'economic planning.' "[31] For ten years the

---

[30] Minutes, 26th Meeting, Science Committee, National Resources Planning Board, January 30–31, 1943 (National Resources Planning Board Files, National Archives). The "four councils" referred to are the National Research Council, the Social Science Research Council, the American Council of Learned Societies, and the American Council on Education.

[31] Charles E. Merriam, "The National Resources Planning Board: A Chapter in American Planning Experience," *The American Political Science Review*, Vol. XXXVIII, No. 6 (December 1944), p. 1084.

Board had publicly demonstrated the need for continued central planning. Its reports were widely read and its members and staff were important figures in New Deal Washington. It was a lively center for the discussion of new concepts even though it never achieved any important success.[32] As a planning agency it had little effect on administration policies; while its members had close connections with the President, they often had to act outside the Board to influence operating programs. As a research agency it failed in its aim, difficult at best, to gain general recognition of the need for cooperation among the sciences and for coordinated research attacks on public problems. And by the time the war broke out the leadership of the Board and its top staff had lost their earlier sense of purpose and innovation. As one report has noted: "board meetings tended to be long, discursive, indecisive, and even acrimonious. They were painful affairs."[33] But by then the Board and those who had participated in its work were contributing to new political and intellectual movements that were then taking shape.

The war led to the development of a central science organization along lines quite different from those the National Resources Planning Board and its Science Committee had conceived. Central organization, as A. Hunter Dupree has suggested, has been both a major goal for many in the community of physical scientists and a major characteristic of science-in-government in times of national crisis. The National Academy of Sciences was established during the Civil War, the National Research Council during the First World War, and the abortive Science Advisory Board during the Depression. World War II brought into being the most powerful and highly centralized organization for the sciences, the Office of Scientific Research and Development (OSRD).[34]

The OSRD emerged out of the experience of scientists close to government as an agency that could more directly relate science to government operations than the detached and relatively passive

32 See Edwin Nourse, *Economics in the Public Service* (New York: Harcourt Brace, 1953), pp. 63–64. For another knowledgeable evaluation of the Board, see also Millett, *op. cit.*

33 Millett, *op. cit.*, p. 145.

34 A. Hunter Dupree, "Central Scientific Organization in the United States Government," *Minerva*, Vol. I, No. 4 (Summer 1963), pp. 453–469.

advisory procedures of the National Academy of Sciences working through the National Research Council.[35] Besides the Academy mechanism, the National Advisory Committee for Aeronautics (NACA), first established in 1915, had provided experience for scientists in the interwar years, especially in cooperating closely with important military agencies. Leadership in working out a wartime organization fell to Vannevar Bush, a former Vice President of the Massachusetts Institute of Technology, who had come to Washington in 1938 as head of the Carnegie Institution and had become Chairman of NACA in 1939. Bush, working closely with scientists in the NACA and the National Academy, worked out a plan in 1940 for the establishment of a National Defense Research Committee (NDRC) "to co-ordinate, supervise, and conduct scientific research on the problems underlying warfare." Approved by the President on June 27, 1940, the NDRC became the central base for the scientific organization that was to develop during the war.

The NDRC was a mechanism for the overall coordination and direction of scientific activities that went on in the operating departments. It was also of immense help to the Army and Navy, for the two services were in desperate straits, suddenly confronted with research and procurement tasks that their sadly understaffed and weak internal systems could not support. As time went on it became more and more evident that there were many research projects that needed to be supported before their operational applications were well defined or before the military realized their potential. But there was no mechanism in the government for making this kind of effort. Thus, again on Bush's recommendation, the President established the Office of Scientific Research and Development (OSRD) in 1941 in his own Executive Office and gave it authority to initiate whatever research projects the scientists who headed the scientific agency regarded as necessary or promising. Bush, serving both as Chairman of NDRC and Director of OSRD, with direct access to the President, and in continual contact with the military and naval chiefs, was thus in a unique and powerful position.

---

[35] The following discussion is largely based on James Phinney Baxter III, *Scientists Against Time* (Boston: Little, Brown and Co., 1946), pp. 11–19.

During the war the OSRD set the pattern for the government organization for science that developed later. Its most spectacular achievement was initiating and carrying out the atomic energy program. Although the program was transferred to the Army's Manhattan Project when it entered its operational phase, it remained under the close scientific supervision of Bush and his immediate colleagues. The OSRD did not confine itself to starting new projects and undertaking an evaluation of their possible value and feasibility, often before operational requirements developed in the military bureaucracies. It also arranged for the work to be carried out by offering government contracts to universities and scientific laboratories, a procedure that has been of prime importance in shaping the American scientific establishment. The contract system preserved the freedom of scientific inquiry but related it directly to practical government needs; it also provided public accountability while leaving internal professional controls in the hands of the scientists themselves.

While the OSRD was almost wholly a creation of the physical scientists, several of its programs involved social scientists. These programs were generally organized by the Division of Anthropology and Psychology of the National Research Council, which represented the only social sciences included in the Academy-Council system. However, the Council's wartime work in social science under OSRD auspices was largely restricted to individual testing problems, though there was some examination of environmental influence on human performance. The wartime experience of OSRD leaders thus brought them in touch with only a small part —and a narrowly focused one at that—of the social science community. For most members of the Council's Division of Anthropology and Psychology were specialists in the physical aspects of these two disciplines, in fields closely connected with biology and medicine. Social psychology and social or cultural anthropology were largely missing in their programs. One possible exception was the series of studies concerning American food habits. But in dealing with the large problems of military manpower, there was a significant contrast between the work sponsored by the National Research Council and the more broadly conceived research done elsewhere in the government.

Under a contract between NDRC-OSRD and the Council, a

Committee on Service Personnel, later designated as the Applied Psychology Panel, was set up early in the war to assist the Army and the Navy in solving problems connected with the selection, training, and assignment of military personnel.[36] The Panel supplemented and often supported the work of psychologists attached directly to the staffs of the War Department's Office of the Adjutant General, the Bureau of Naval Personnel, the Air Surgeon's Office of the Army Air Forces, and other military service agencies. It became involved in a number of projects—developing new personnel testing programs, evaluating criteria for job classification, measuring the effect of environmental factors on effective performance, and designing new weapons to take into account the capacity of the average soldier or sailor.

The work of the Applied Psychology Panel can be traced in a direct line from the research on intelligence testing begun by the Psychology Committee of the National Research Council under Robert M. Yerkes' direction in World War I. The achievements of psychologists during the First World War set a precedent for the wider use of intelligence tests and the increased use of research in this field after 1918, particularly in industry. In World War II, therefore, psychologists had available to them the knowledge accumulated over two decades. However, this work was not without grave limitations and was not yet collected and codified in a readily useful form. Moreover, in 1940 the military services were hardly prepared for the mobilization of the huge forces that were to be needed during the war. This lack of preparedness, together with the rapidity and size of the military expansion and the practical limits of existing research, made the selection and assignment of military personnel a matter of trial and error, especially in the early years of the war.[37]

While there were always problems in applying what had been

---

[36] The work of the Applied Psychology Panel has been summarized in Charles W. Bray, *Psychology and Military Proficiency* (Princeton: Princeton University Press, 1948). See also Baxter, *op. cit.*, chap. XXV, "Selection and Training," pp. 395–403.

[37] For a later evaluation of military manpower policies during World War II, see Eli Ginzberg and associates, *The Ineffective Soldier* (3 vols.; New York: Columbia University Press, 1959).

learned in psychological testing to broad manpower policies, social scientists were often able to apply their knowledge successfully when coping with well-defined and relatively narrow tasks. One such task was the assignment of crew members to posts on a new battleship, the U.S.S. "New Jersey," the largest the Navy had ever built. In this case, the Bureau of Naval Personnel and the Applied Psychology Panel cooperated in a joint program of testing, interviewing, and classifying the 2,600 crew members, only 750 of whom had even been to sea before. Tests involved both general intelligence and physical capacities, hearing, vision, and reaction time, and required a detailed analysis of the posts to be filled. The work was done under pressure and some tests proved ineffective. But, all in all, the Captain of the "New Jersey" concluded that the program "definitely contributed to the apparent extraordinary rapid progress made during the shakedown period by the crew of this vessel."[38]

Psychologists operating through the Research Council and also those in special military units assisted the services in making the best use of manpower for performing a variety of repetitive and routine tasks, some of which, but certainly not all, were peculiar to military life. At other times they had to examine special problems in man-machine relations that changed in kind and intensity with advances in technology. This was the nature of the work they did for the National Research Council's Committee on Selection and Training of Aircraft Pilots, a project originally set up at the request of the Civil Aeronautics Administration in 1939, but expanded to include military as well as civilian aviation in 1940.[39]

In numerous and unrelated manpower and personnel projects involving social scientists, however, there were few opportunities to evaluate the results of new experiments or of new applications of knowledge to human affairs on an unprecedented scale. In the case of manning the "New Jersey," it was at least possible to gauge

---

[38] Quoted in Baxter, op. cit., p. 398.
[39] See The Aircraft Pilot: Five Years of Research, Committee on Selection and Training of Aircraft Pilots, National Research Council (Washington, D.C., 1945).

the effectiveness of the project by the Captain's estimate of how well his crew performed. But often the conditions of war were confused and the pressures enormous, so much so that the orderly exchange of information and the replication of research were impossible. The military establishment at war was a highly fragmented and uncontrolled laboratory with few opportunities to measure effectiveness.

Program Research

It has already been suggested that World War II was largely responsible for great advances made in social psychology and allied fields. If so, these advances were made by scientists working in the fields of morale and psychological warfare, and not by those in the Research Council's Applied Psychology Panel and elsewhere who worked primarily in the area of personnel testing and selection. Research in morale made use of a much wider range of knowledge. Social scientists were able to employ the methods of opinion and attitude research that had been developed since the early 1930's. For example, George Gallup and others had demonstrated the effectiveness of polling in relation to elections, and Likert and his associates in the Department of Agriculture had devised interviewing and sampling techniques of increasing reliability in their studies of rural populations. In addition there were concepts borrowed from anthropology and sociology concerning the relationship of cultural patterns and group structure to individual behavior. Kurt Lewin, who had pioneered in the field of "group dynamics," used many of these methods and ideas in his wartime studies of food habits. He was able to demonstrate that ethnic background was as important as economic status in determining the kinds of food families purchased and that group pressure could be a more effective method of changing food habits than appeals through written circulars or lectures.[40] Both prop-

[40] Kurt Lewin, "Forces behind Food Habits and Methods of Change," in *The Problem of Changing Food Habits*, Report of the Committee on Food Habits 1941–1943, Bulletin 108, National Academy of Sciences–National Research Council (Washington, D.C., 1943), pp. 35–65.

ositions were particularly relevant under wartime conditions of food shortages and consumer rationing.

These large-scale techniques and more complex concepts of human behavior were also used in dealing with military manpower problems by the Research Branch of the Army's Information and Education Division, which operated under the professional direction of Samuel A. Stouffer. Established before Pearl Harbor, the Army research unit conducted a vast number of surveys and experiments from 1941 to 1945 to test the adjustment of Americans to Army life, their effectiveness in combat, and their expectations of the society to which they would return. Collected and analyzed in four volumes published after the war, the work of the Research Branch proved an invaluable case study of social science research in government and provided a rare opportunity to relate a particularly active wartime program of applied research to postwar theoretical and methodological developments.[41] Stouffer, in an introductory chapter to the published analysis of the Army research program, discussed four "streams of influence" which had guided the work of his unit: concepts of psychoanalysis which "shifted emphasis in inquiries about human behavior from the study of man as a rational person to man as a person with drives and wishes who was often unconscious of the 'real reasons' for his behavior"; developments in learning theory leading toward an understanding of the complexity of notions such as "reward and punishment" previously conceived somewhat simplistically; the relation of "variations in human behavior" to "the specific values and folkways of . . . cultural and social environment"; and the importance of "a better understanding of the social system apart from individuals comprising it."[42]

The Army's Research Branch had its origins in the work of the Joint Army and Navy Committee on Welfare and Recreation. The Committee was set up in 1941 through a grant from the Carnegie Corporation of New York to assist the services in their military mobilization operations by enlisting the support of private and

---

[41] Samuel A. Stouffer and associates, *The American Soldier* (4 vols.; Princeton: Princeton University Press, 1949).
[42] *Ibid.*, Vol. I, pp. 30–32.

community groups throughout the country. In "seed money" fashion, funds available to the Committee were then authorized to support experimental welfare and recreation projects in Army camps and naval stations; and it was hoped that these would lead to similar projects undertaken by the services themselves. At the same time, the Army's Intelligence Division, with the encouragement of an advisory group of psychologists chaired by Leonard Carmichael, then Chairman of the Division of Anthropology and Psychology of the National Research Council, was planning a survey of the morale of the combat divisions of the Army. For this purpose a research staff under Stouffer was organized, initially with funds provided under the experimental program of the Joint Committee; and it completed a survey of the state of morale in a single combat division in mid-December 1941.[43]

Authority for this initial survey was granted by the Chief of Staff despite an earlier directive from the Secretary of War, Henry Stimson, prohibiting the use of polls among Army personnel. Stimson had issued his order on these grounds: "Our Army must be a cohesive unit, with a definite purpose shared by all. . . . Anonymous opinion or criticism, good or bad, is destructive in its effect on a military organization where accepted responsibility on the part of every individual is fundamental."[44] While the Stimson directive does not appear to have been formally rescinded, it was not very strictly followed. And the use of surveys by the Army became an organized affair shortly after the first survey was completed. Indeed, in April 1942, the Under Secretary of War, Robert P. Patterson, referred to the first survey as having "provided data helpful to various phases of the Army" and went on to say:

> In the next Planning Survey made by the Branch it would be desirable to interview some Negro troops as well as whites. It is therefore suggested that discreetly-phrased questions be asked of

[43] The early history of the Research Branch is reported, *ibid.*, Vol. I, chap. 1; also in the unpublished "History of the Research Branch, Information and Education Division, War Department Special Staff," available in the Office of the Chief of Military History, Department of the Army (Washington, D.C., February 1, 1946), (hereinafter referred to as "OCMH Unpublished Research Branch History").

[44] Quoted in Stouffer, *op. cit.*, Vol. I, p. 12.

Negro troops in an effort to obtain information helpful in policy formation, particularly with respect to charges of discrimination against Negroes in the Army and the attitude of both Negro and white troops with respect to these matters.[45]

Several studies of race relations were consequently made by the Research Branch, and they contributed substantially to clarifying and deepening the understanding of those in the Army staff who had to deal with this difficult problem under the strains of wartime military organization.[46] However, the issue of race relations, and less explosive issues as well, raised fundamental questions about the proper relationship of scientific research to official Army policies. The extension of research beyond the fields of intelligence testing and human performance brought social scientists into closer touch with sensitive areas of policy. Fortunately the difficulties of operation here were largely overcome due to the efforts of the Director of the Information and Education Division, Major General Frederick H. Osborn. Osborn, a business man who had written two books on social science, was exceptionally well suited to the job. A close friend of President Roosevelt and Secretary Stimson, he had served as a member of the Social Science Research Council, as a trustee of the Carnegie Corporation, and as Chairman of the Joint Committee on Welfare and Recreation, before becoming head of the Army Information and Education Division, a position which he kept throughout the war. He was thus able to offer both political and professional support to the Research Branch and also to maintain continuous relations with the Army staff, especially since he soon gained the confidence of the Chief of Staff, General Marshall.

At an early stage in the history of the Branch, Stouffer, as technical director, wrote a memorandum to Osborn discussing the role of research on the basis of his own experience with the study of research agencies undertaken by the National Resources Planning Board in the late 1930's.

[45] Quoted in "OCMH Unpublished Research Branch History," op. cit., p. 12.
[46] The relation of Research Branch surveys to Army policies is described in Ulysses Lee, The Employment of Negro Troops, Office of the Chief of Military History (Washington, D.C., 1966). For an analysis of the Research Branch's surveys, see Stouffer, op. cit., Vol. I, chap. 10, "Negro Soldiers."

[If research is to be more than] an assembling of miscellaneous facts in which nobody but the research agency is interested . . . the administration and the research direction must be in close and continual touch with respect to administrative policies needing research for clarification or decision. [Also] the research agency must try to anticipate future problems by advance planning, in order that research results can be made available very promptly when needed.[47]

If this kind of approach made research more useful in policy planning, it still did not cope with the problem of the proper relationship of research to policy decisions actually taken. Here, a later memorandum by Stouffer showed his agreement with the position Osborn took in this matter:

I think General Osborn has been entirely right in his cardinal policy of keeping research and operations in separate hands. I think he was right in separating the planning and research divisions; I think he was right in keeping research and information in separate branches; I think he was right in insisting that the research man be close to policy but not make policy. . . . This is not an ivory tower policy of research. It presupposes such mutual executive competence and research competence that research would activate both the beginning and the final evaluation of policies. It would place research in the strongest possible position and protect it both from the mistakes of wishful thinking and from the fears of men like the Secretary of War who have opposed Gallup or Roper polls in the Army.[48]

The way in which the Research Branch contributed to Army policy while remaining uninvolved in the policy that was adopted can be illuminated by referring again to the matter of race relations. In 1943 the Army produced a variety of educational materials for distribution to the armed forces on the role of the Negro soldier. These included a film, *The Negro Soldier*, in the Army orientation series, "Why We Fight," and a pamphlet for officers,

[47] Samuel A. Stouffer, memorandum to Major General Frederick H. Osborn, June 3, 1942, reprinted in Stouffer, *op. cit.*, Vol. I, pp. 14–15.

[48] Samuel A. Stouffer, memorandum to Lieutenant Colonel R. Branch, October 16, 1942, Miscellaneous Papers relating to History of Research Branch (Federal Records Center, Modern Military Records Division, National Archives).

Command of Negro Troops. All the information collected by the Research Branch was put to good use, and its staff was consulted at every stage of the work in progress. The actual preparation of the materials was a responsibility of General Osborn's office and decisions were made by Osborn, with Donald R. Young of the Social Science Research Council and the Joint Army and Navy Committee on Welfare and Recreation serving as consultant and, in several cases, being responsible for the drafting and critique of documentation.[49] Thus, while research was a tool of policy and the research staff was intimately involved in the articulation and clarification of the problems the Army staff faced, the decisions and formal implementation of policies were part of a quite separate operation.

Despite the strength of its position in the Army, the Research Branch was hampered by the same difficulties that plagued other research units. It was constantly working against time, under pressure to provide answers for the military command; its staff was constantly changing and often inadequate; and its research questionnaires never completely satisfied the senior staff. But, again, these were the hardships of war and the consequences of trying to understand human behavior in new ways that lacked well-established theoretical foundations and that had to embrace vast areas of human experience. Yet the work of the Branch contributed significantly to helping resolve such military problems as developing *esprit de corps* in infantry troops, devising an equitable and manageable system of demobilization, evaluating informational activities for maintaining high morale, and coping with the strains of race relations.

The Army Research Branch also illustrated the significant place of the war in the development of the social sciences and in the shaping of the postwar scientific structure in the government. The Branch was reduced to skeleton form almost as soon as the war was over. Stouffer and his colleagues returned to academic life, Stouffer himself to set up the Laboratory in Social Relations at Harvard, one of the major interdisciplinary centers for the growth of social science in the postwar period. For several years

---

[49] Lee, *op. cit.*, pp. 387–392.

the former Army staff concentrated on exploiting the theoretical and methodological aspects of their wartime research. The published results, principally *The American Soldier,* and their teaching activities played an important part in the consolidation and advancement of the field of social psychology. But their wartime work, like that of most economists, statisticians, and social scientists in other fields, had not been carried out within the network of the OSRD. Their contribution to the war was also less dramatic than the technological accomplishments of the physical scientists. They thus had little opportunity to use their experience to influence the direction of postwar scientific planning in government.

As the work of the Army's Research Branch demonstrated, connecting links between research and program administration depended on factors of both organization and personnel. This was especially so during the war, when the speed and pressure of operations greatly affected the role that research could play. If research was placed out of the stream of an organization's major activities, it became, as Stouffer suggested, little more than an accumulation of data and analysis. If it was fully involved in the planning and decision-making process, it risked losing its distinctive and independent function in the organization. Furthermore, the rapport established between the researcher and the policymaker or operator was as critical a factor as the system of organization. The researcher had to help the administrator by identifying and clarifying the alternative courses of action open to him without going so far as to determine what action should be taken—a difficult position to maintain when the need for action was as great as it was in time of war.

These lessons were learned not only by those in the Research Branch but also by social scientists in the Japanese relocation centers set up during the war under the War Relocation Authority (WRA). The forcible evacuation and detention of the minority of Japanese origin was a measure of doubtful necessity taken to allay the fears of sabotage and disloyalty that swept those sections of the country where large groups of Japanese immigrants and Americans of Japanese descent lived. Under the pressures of military security, the order was given to exclude Japanese from designated areas on the West Coast. But many people, including the

President, were afraid that this would set a precedent for further abrogations of civil liberties during the crisis of a major war.[50]

A social science research unit was organized in the first Japanese relocation center set up at Poston, on Indian land in the Colorado River Valley, in March 1942. Under Alexander H. Leighton, a psychiatrist, the Poston unit initially had a dual purpose. The first and most immediate one was "to aid the administration by analyzing the attitudes [and responses] of the evacuees . . . to administrative acts and to draw practical conclusions as to what worked well, what did not work so well and why." Then, thinking ahead to the eventual occupation of Japan, the researchers were "to gather data of a general character that might be of value in the administration of dislocated communities in occupied areas."[51] The experience of the Poston research unit in the summer and fall of 1942, especially in dealing with tense rivalries among the evacuees themselves and outbursts of violence against the Center administrators, led to the establishment of community analysis units in all centers operated by the War Relocation Authority. And a Community Analysis Section was also set up at headquarters in Washington under John Provinse, an anthropologist with experience in the Soil Conservation Service.[52]

The centralized administration of research provided useful support for social scientists working in the camps. The effectiveness of the research, however, was usually dependent on the relations between the research staff and those in immediate charge of the camp operations. For that matter a tri-partite relationship was involved: the researcher, the administrator, and the Japanese evacuees. It was essential, for example, that the research staff gain the confidence of the evacuees whom they interviewed and relied on for information. The Japanese, naturally, were prone to view the administrators as hostile and to suspect the researchers of be-

[50] See *Impounded People*, War Relocation Authority, Department of the Interior (Washington, D.C., 1946), pp. 1–37; also Dorothy S. Thomas and Richard S. Nishimoto, *The Spoilage* (Berkeley: University of California Press, 1946), pp. 1–52.

[51] Alexander H. Leighton, *The Governing Of Men* (Princeton: Princeton University Press, 1945), p. 373.

[52] Edward H. Spicer, "The Use of Social Scientists by the War Relocation Authority," *Applied Anthropology*, Vol. 5, No. 2 (Spring 1946), pp. 17–18.

ing "spies" for the administration. And the researchers, mainly anthropologists, regarded the center as a total social organization of which the administrators were a part and thus subject to as intensive observation as the evacuees. At Poston it became the practice to make reports and analyses available to the administrators, while basic data and field notes remained subject to disposition by the professional research staff.[53] When the Japanese could be made to understand that what they told the interviewer was held in confidence, research was more likely to uncover what they were really thinking.

The administrators of relocation centers worked under constant pressure. In the early months they had to organize the rudiments of life out of almost nothing. They bore the brunt of Japanese resentment during the entire period of internment and had to cope with the internal politics and dissensions within the Japanese community. And they were responsible for the efforts to resettle the evacuees when, in December 1944, orders were given to close the camps. Consequently, as Leighton and his staff found out at Poston, the administrators had little time or inclination to read long reports or to review social analyses of trends in the camp. To make research relevant, Leighton had to take a position somewhat separate from the research group and participate "in the almost daily give and take of planning and decision," injecting into the policy process "fragments of fact and opinion and ultimately a general point of view" based on the work of the research unit. While these practical procedures gave the research staff direct access to the administrators, they provided no more than "a constantly open channel . . . to the top group in the administration." They definitely did not mean "responsibility in operations."[54] In other centers too, the research units acted as "an aid in maintaining communication between a group of administrators and a group of administered people."[55] Their role was not unlike that of the Army Research Branch, which served as a channel between the troops in uniform and the military command. In both cases the

[53] Leighton, op. cit., pp. 392–393.
[54] Ibid., pp. 396–397.
[55] Spicer, op. cit., pp. 35–36.

effectiveness of the researchers depended on their striking a balance between involvement and detachment with regard to the administrators.

Foreign Operations

In all the relocation camps, however, the WRA staff, unlike the Army research staff, was working with people who, while many of them were American citizens, had different habits, different values, and different social patterns than those dominant in the society. Indeed, the Poston experiment gave some idea of the problems that would arise in dealing with peoples of other cultures, and not only the Japanese, at a later stage in the war. The United States was ill-equipped for the scale of foreign operations that the war brought on. In 1939 when war broke out in Europe, for example, the Foreign Service numbered less than one thousand. The function of Foreign Service officers was highly circumscribed and their experience was limited, for the isolationist policies of the United States had permitted little more than passive observation of world events. There were no large groups in the universities with first-hand knowledge of the many parts of the world involved in the war. And government efforts to drum up patriotic spirit tended to encourage the formation of popular stereotypes and monolithic notions of foreign nations and peoples. Even in the relocation camps, administrators frequently made few distinctions among the evacuees despite the differences among Japanese groups in their background, their ties to the United States, and their sense of loyalty.[56]

In foreign operations, social scientists contributed to government programs through both research and teaching: in the collection and distribution of information about foreign areas; in the training of military officers for service in foreign countries; and in the study and assessment of the activities and attitudes of foreign governments and populations, both civilian and military, during the war. While the first two tasks were traditional academic activi-

[56] See *Impounded People, op. cit.*

ties, they exposed the inadequacies of the nation's research and educational facilities in these fields. In an effort to bring together all the available knowledge and scientific expertise, the Ethnogeographic Board was established in the Smithsonian Institution under the joint sponsorship of the Smithsonian, the National Research Council, the Social Science Research Council, and the American Council of Learned Societies. The Board compiled a register of social scientists and others with research or business experience in various parts of the world; it also furnished bibliographies, compilations of existing scientific data on foreign areas, and special reports on problems such as the topography and ethnography of little known areas, particularly in the Pacific region, that were suddenly of strategic importance. During the early stages of the war, before the government agencies had organized their own information-gathering services, the Board proved to be a useful source of advice to the military departments and the intelligence and information agencies. Once this period was over, however, the Board's effectiveness diminished, as it remained modestly staffed, outside the main orbit of government operations, and with no active program of research of its own which might have made it an important center of information.[57]

In the case of foreign area and language training, military-sponsored programs during the war were to contribute to the development of area studies in American colleges and universities after 1945. These area programs differed from traditional academic courses in their interdisciplinary character. In order to be prepared for duty on foreign liaison, intelligence, or occupation service, an officer needed to know a great many things about the people with whom he was to deal—their language, their history and culture, the geography and resources of their country, and their political and economic stake in the current conflict. Few American universities were equipped to offer such "complete coverage," for the academic curriculum offered only highly specialized courses and many faculty members were engaged in other kinds of war work. Moreover, officers could remain in training only a short time

57 Wendell Clark Bennett, *The Ethnogeographic Board*, Miscellaneous Collections, Vol. 107, No. 1, Smithsonian Institution (Washington, D.C., 1947).

before being assigned to an overseas post. Civil affairs training programs were nevertheless set up by universities like Chicago, Harvard, Pittsburgh, and Stanford, and at specially established institutions such as the Army's School of Military Government at the University of Virginia campus at Charlottesville.[58] These short, hurried courses usually contained little more than straightforward descriptive matter. Unless the officer-trainee came with some preparatory work behind him, there was little opportunity to give him an understanding of the new concepts and methods with which social scientists were beginning to study societies and social change.

Social scientists were better able to use their knowledge in a variety of agencies—military, intelligence, and information—engaged in foreign operations. Their approach to problems was much the same as that of the research staff of the Army Research Branch and those who conducted opinion and attitude surveys in connection with civilian mobilization programs. They took into consideration the sources of non-rational behavior, the significance of cultural patterns and mores in behavior, and the impact of the group on the individual, and particularly the primary group to which the individual is most immediately related. Their methods of studying foreign societies were also similar to those used in the Army and economic programs: sample surveys, statistical analyses, and depth interviewing. In many instances, however, the social scientists, unlike the WRA researchers, had no direct access to foreign populations, particularly those behind enemy lines. Here they used the traditional techniques of historical and literary interpretation and sought to make contact with exiled or refugee groups or prisoners of war in lieu of being able to reach more representative segments of the society. Also, using the methods of content analysis, they studied press reports, radio broadcasts, and propaganda materials in order to estimate changes in political and social systems and to predict the actions and reactions of governments and political leaders.

[58] Charles S. Hyneman, "The Army's Civil Affairs Training Program," *The American Political Science Review*, Vol. XXXVIII, No. 2 (April 1944), pp. 342–353.

Social scientists in these fields—intelligence, psychological warfare, propaganda, and so on—found themselves in much the same situation as those in the civilian mobilization and military manpower programs. That is, they worked in many different agencies, which were differently organized and offered different opportunities for effective action.[59] There were two separate agencies, for example, engaged in systematic analysis of enemy propaganda. One was based in the Library of Congress and was headed by Harold D. Lasswell, whose work in this field dated back at least to 1927 when he published a study of propaganda techniques in the First World War.[60] Under Lasswell's direction, the staff of the Wartime Communications Research Project undertook a series of analyses of the press, publications, and other printed material in order to interpret the shifting balance of power during the early war years. The unit was also something of a training center. For Lasswell, too, theoretical advances were always important, even in time of war, especially if they were conducive to greater clarity in analysis. He expressed the importance of content analysis thus: "Words are involved in power, since the indexes of power may be largely verbal (ordering-obeying, proposing-endorsing, and the like). Words are also involved in the readjustment of power—in revolutionary agitation, in constitutional innovation."[61]

Another agency of this kind was the Princeton Listening Center, set up under a grant from the Rockefeller Foundation in November 1939, to prepare reports of short wave broadcasts from major European capitals in order "to understand better the psychology behind Nazi propaganda." In 1941, at the request of the State Department, the Center was moved to Washington and was established as the Foreign Broadcast Monitoring Service under the Federal Communications Commission. Operating throughout the war, the Service provided government agencies with copies of

59 For a broad review of most of these programs, see Charles A. H. Thomson, *Overseas Information Service of the United States Government* (Washington, D.C.: The Brookings Institution, 1948), pp. 17–198.

60 Harold D. Lasswell, *Propaganda Technique in the World War* (New York: Alfred A. Knopf, 1927).

61 Harold D. Lasswell, *et al., Language of Politics* (New York: G. W. Stewart, 1949), p. 18.

propaganda broadcasts as well as special reports. These reports employed the techniques of content analysis in order "to predict Axis moves, both military and political."[62] But even when the Service was right in its predictions, there was little way of knowing if its reports were read conscientiously or if they were taken into account in Allied strategic planning. And the Service was only one of many intelligence agencies with no systematic connection with other units conducting similar studies.

The major civilian intelligence and propaganda organizations grew out of two emergency agencies that were already in existence at the time of the attack on Pearl Harbor: the Office of the Coordinator of Inter-American Affairs (CIAA) and the Coordinator of Information (COI). The Director of CIAA, Nelson Rockefeller, managed to resist repeated attempts to incorporate his agency into a larger one and maintained its autonomous status and its separate research units throughout the war. As for the COI, its Foreign Information Service—as well as the Office of Facts and Figures, concerned with domestic matters—became the nucleus of the Office of War Information (OWI) established in 1942. The rest of COI, engaged in collecting and analyzing intelligence data rather than analyzing radio broadcasts, was reorganized as the Office of Strategic Services (OSS) under Colonel William Donovan. The OWI, with its domestic and overseas branches, the OSS, the CIAA, the Wartime Communications Project, the Foreign Broadcast Monitoring Service, and military intelligence and psychological warfare units in both the Army and the Navy, in Washington and at headquarters in the various theaters of war—all these dispersed and uncoordinated organizations had a hand in the intelligence and propaganda work of the war. In the field all units, whether military or part of the OSS or OWI, were ultimately responsible to the theater commander. At home the only central authority was the President, who did not act as he had done in the matter of economic mobilization—he failed to establish a central

[62] Hadley Cantril, *The Human Dimension: Experiences in Policy Research* (New Brunswick: Rutgers University Press, 1967), pp. 30–34. For an analysis of the techniques of the Service, see Alexander L. George, "Prediction of Political Action by means of Propaganda Analysis," *Public Opinion Quarterly*, Vol. 20, Spring 1960, pp. 334–345.

agency that would eliminate overlapping functions, coordinate the work of the various operating agencies, and settle their rival claims.

Unlike the physical scientists who could turn to the central organization of OSRD, social scientists had to depend on whatever conditions prevailed in their individual operating units. Their efforts were often frustrated, either because there was little receptivity to social science or because the war moved too quickly and drastically for the research process. For example, Leonard Doob, on the research staff of the OWI Overseas Branch, recalled that "policy-makers (usually journalists) found what they frankly called 'hot dope'—such as gossip about a dictator's mistress or an estimate of whether a neutral country would remain neutral—more intriguing and important than an out-of-date appraisal of basic factors affecting a country or its people."[63] And William L. Langer, speaking of the OSS, where conditions were better because academics rather than journalists ruled the roost, still had occasion to complain: "Often we did not learn until too late of real needs, and often we labored hard only to find that our effort was simply duplication. Many of our most solid and valuable reports, I am sure, never reached those people who could have profited most from them."[64]

Even in situations where social scientists were able to function very effectively, their work was often limited by strategic policies that had been decided on with little, if any, reference to systematic research. Their task, again, was technical in essence: how to achieve stated policy goals and how to meet obstructions to those goals encountered on the way. For example, the policy of "unconditional surrender" adopted by the President early in the war for political reasons, both domestic and external, was one that affected researchers at many levels. As Doob reported: "The policy of unconditional surrender for Germany, which may have stiff-

---

63 Leonard W. Doob, "The Utilization of Social Scientists in the Overseas Branch of the Office of War Information," *The American Political Science Review*, Vol. XLI, No. 4 (August 1947), pp. 658–659.

64 William L. Langer, "Scholarship and the Intelligence Problem," *Proceedings of the American Philosophical Society*, Vol. 92, No. 1 (March 8, 1948), p. 44.

ened German resistance, was perhaps . . . wise . . . in the long run, but . . . no research could be carried out in the OWI to estimate its wisdom in advance, and none could be tolerated to ascertain the desirability of publicizing its existence."[65]

Psychological warfare operations in the European theater were also affected by the doctrine of unconditional surrender. The standing directive for psychological warfare against members of the German armed forces, issued in June 1944, stipulated that the Allies did not recognize "any claim of the German Army to be absolved from its full share of responsibility for German aggression . . . [or] the possibility of divorcing the 'fighting war' from the atrocities which the German soldier has committed or condoned."[66] In broadcasts to the German troops or in writing leaflets for distribution behind their lines, the Psychological Warfare Division of SHAEF (Supreme Headquarters Allied Expeditionary Force) could not make any promises to induce them to lay down their arms. Then, too, there was some doubt about what "unconditional surrender" really meant, and attempts to define it were more confusing than clarifying. It was therefore difficult to counteract the work of German propagandists, who interpreted the doctrine as "total slavery" in order to persuade their own people and troops not to surrender.

Some American and British propagandists tried to get around this difficulty by impressing two ideas on the German troops: "(a) the inevitability of Allied Victory and (b) the integrity and decency of the democratic world, in contrast with the corruption and untrustworthiness of the Nazi leaders."[67] Their success, however, was difficult to measure since it was almost impossible, except in isolated cases, to disentangle the effects of propaganda from the pressures of the fighting, the drying up of resources, and the other forces that undermined the morale of the German troops. Analyzing data collected during the war, Edward Shils and Morris Janowitz found that "the solidarity of the German Army was

---

[65] Doob, *op. cit.*, p. 658.

[66] Reprinted in Daniel Lerner, *Sykewar* (New York: G. W. Stewart, 1949), p. 404.

[67] R. H. S. Crossman, "Supplementary Essay," *ibid.*, p. 332.

. . . based only very indirectly and very partially on political convictions or broader ethical beliefs." More important, "where the primary group developed a high degree of cohesion, morale was high and resistance effective . . . regardless in the main of the political attitudes of the soldiers."[68] The doctrine of unconditional surrender was certainly of use as a political weapon and a means of establishing Germany's "national guilt"; but it may also have weakened pressures for troop surrender in so far as it prevented efforts to separate soldiers from their group leaders and organization.

Dealing with the unconditional surrender of Japan proved another and perhaps more difficult problem for research. One of the major research projects on Japan was run by the Foreign Morale Analysis Division (FMAD) of the Office of War Information, set up in 1944 in cooperation with the Military Intelligence Service of the War Department. The Division's staff was headed by Alexander Leighton, who brought with him part of the team that had operated at the relocation center at Poston and employed a number of translators and analysts of Japanese background who had been trained at the camp. They had available to them reports from military intelligence sources, including information collected from Japanese prisoners of war, as well as Japanese publications and records of radio broadcasts collected by civilian agencies. In addition to piecing together, ordering, and analyzing these various sources of information, the Division sponsored special studies, such as the report on Japanese cultural patterns by the anthropologist, Ruth Benedict, which made wide use of historical and literary references.[69]

The FMAD was reasonably successful in obtaining "a better understanding of Japanese social and psychological characteristics as they related to military morale on the battlefront and to civilian

---

[68] Edward A. Shils and Morris Janowitz, "Cohesion and Disintegration in the Wehrmacht in World War II," *Public Opinion Quarterly*, Vol. 12, Summer 1948, pp. 314–315.

[69] The work of the Foreign Morale Analysis Division is described in Alexander H. Leighton, *Human Relations in a Changing World* (New York: E. P. Dutton & Co., 1949). Dr. Ruth Benedict's work was subsequently published in *The Chrysanthemum and the Sword* (Boston: Houghton Mifflin Co., 1946).

morale in Japan."[70] It was less successful in communicating this understanding to political and military planners, most of whom held fast to an image of Japanese fanaticism that shaped their estimate of the price the Japanese were willing to pay before surrendering. The early studies of the Division indicated that strong determination to resist attack was not uniform, either among the troops or at home, and that there was a wide range of personality types among the Japanese, not all of whom could be placed in a single stereotyped category. But these findings were difficult for planners to accept. They brought into question the assumptions on which they based their plans, but gave them no measure of assurance about the level of resistance that might be expected. The findings also raised questions about the applicability of the doctrine of unconditional surrender, especially as it called for the abdication of the Japanese emperor as a condition of surrender. As FMAD reports described how the Japanese determination to fight was being seriously undermined, the Emperor came to the fore as a potential rallying point for those groups that were losing hope and saw nothing but disaster if the war went on.

The surrender of Japan in August came after the dropping of atomic bombs on Hiroshima and Nagasaki. If the Emperor was permitted to remain, this was at least consistent with the studies of the research staff. But the decision to use the A-bomb was based on estimates of continued Japanese resistance that were contrary to the reports being written by the Division. Later these reports were substantially confirmed by the Strategic Bombing Survey, which shortly after the war investigated the effects of strategic bombing on Japan. But at no time did the FMAD staff know about the A-bomb project, one of the best-guarded secrets of the war. Nor is there evidence that any of their reports reached the hands of the military planners who estimated the costs of an invasion of the home islands. In the last analysis, the reports of the FMAD might not have made any difference in the decision that President Truman made, since he was already aware of internal splits in Japan through political sources. But the fact remains that social science research had little or no influence on such

[70] Leighton, *Human Relations in a Changing World, op. cit.*, p. 295.

decisions because there was no central wartime agency responsible for foreign policy and capable of putting research to use. At the same time, there was no central organization of social scientists to promote the use of research studies within the policy-making process of the government.

Major decisions with regard to foreign policy and the strategic and military planning of the war were made in the great wartime conferences by the President and his immediate political advisers; and here the emphasis was put on the military requirements of achieving unconditional surrender of the enemy. A good many agencies were engaged in executing these decisions, all working separately from one another, and all highly intent on taking action and responding to a fast-moving and changing state of affairs. It was an atmosphere in which social science research could operate effectively only on a small scale and only when there was personal confidence between operator and researcher—and often even this was impossible.

As for the agency normally in charge of foreign affairs, the Department of State, it had little to do with strategic planning or overseas military operations and offered little or no leadership to civilian agencies engaged in foreign activities. It too suffered from the general confusion of wartime conditions, the lack of prior planning, and the way the President decided he had to run the government under conditions of total war. Then, almost as a deliberate policy, the Department abdicated its overseas responsibilities to the military as soon as hostilities began. It proved unwilling or incapable of dealing "vigorously and aggressively" with operating and technical day-by-day problems, such as those connected with wartime agreements or psychological warfare, an inability that, it has been judged, "was due largely to the dominance of the foreign service tradition, procedure and tempo."[71]

The efforts of the Department of State in coordinating government-wide activities were instead concerned with planning foreign policy for the postwar period and, in particular, with the construction of new international organizations. Whatever research the Department supported was also directed to this end.

[71] *The United States at War, op. cit.*, pp. 407–408.

As early as the first months of 1941, shortly after President Roosevelt's "Four Freedoms" speech of January 6, the Secretary of State, Cordell Hull, established a special research unit under Leo Pasvolsky of the Brookings Institution to begin studying the problems of postwar international institutions. Pasvolsky's group served as a funnel for all proposals from other departments and outside private groups and also undertook analyses of the full significance, in political and economic terms, of the postwar commitments of the United States. It was this group that was largely responsible for the final drafting of the American proposals on a United Nations Organization presented to the Dumbarton Oaks conference in 1944, and that provided the secretariat for that conference and for the UN Charter Conference held in San Francisco in the spring of 1945.[72]

In make-up and approach the State Department group was quite different from the research units in the intelligence, information, and psychological warfare agencies. Its work had to do with postwar planning rather than wartime operations. Its staff was made up of historians, political scientists, lawyers, and economists, whereas the other agencies, with the possible exception of the OSS, were staffed mostly by psychologists, sociologists, and anthropologists. And its methods were considerably more traditional and orthodox, chiefly those of historical and institutional analysis with a high policy orientation. As described by Harley Notter, a good deal of attention was given to "problem papers," which "began with a statement of the precise practical issue to be faced so far as it could be defined and then proceeded to an analysis of all alternative solutions that might be considered in choosing a course of policy designed to settle the issue or at least to put it on the way toward settlement."[73]

Yet, however different the State Department group may have been, it provided still another place for experts in the wartime government and demonstrated the advantages of systematic re-

---

[72] See Harley A. Notter, *Postwar Foreign Policy Preparation, 1939–1945,* Publication 3580, General Foreign Policy Series 15, Department of State (Washington, D.C., 1949).

[73] *Ibid.,* p. 151.

search in connection with government programs. Moreover, research here was in an unusually advantageous position. Unlike "The Inquiry," which had been established as a private research arm of President Wilson in 1918 outside regular government channels, the Pasvolsky group was organized within the State Department structure. Pasvolsky himself was in contact with Hull as a Special Assistant, and early in the war the Secretary had obtained the President's consent to make the Department a major agency for postwar planning.[74] Besides, the research unit included staff members from research foundations like the Council on Foreign Relations, and was thus connected with private groups that played an influential part in developing a forum of ideas for postwar institutions and encouraging public support for American commitment to international organizations. Within limits here, research did play an effective part in the formulation of policy.

The Demobilization of Social Science

Wartime programs had required new applications of social science theory and new techniques of survey research, interviewing, and laboratory experimentation; and these were to have important effects on postwar intellectual developments. Anthropological concepts derived from the study of primitive cultures had been applied to contemporary societies; biologically-based psychology had been broadened to include developments in social psychology and sociology; and these modes of understanding human behavior had added a new dimension to economic and political analysis. But during the war the emphasis had been on action, the ranks of trained social scientists had been thin, and a good many questions remained to be answered.

How valid were some of the experiments conducted during the war? Would new methods and techniques, often hastily devised to deal with particular problems, prove of general utility? Would new methodologies developed during the war permit the

---

[74] Cordell Hull, *Memoirs* (New York: The Macmillan Co., 1948), Vol. II, pp. 1625–1675.

examination of new theoretical questions? What was the relationship of the behavioral approach of sociologists and psychologists to the more traditional study of political and economic institutions and processes? How should curricula be reorganized to include the behavioral approach? What did such reorganization mean in terms of faculty, in terms of the disciplines, in terms of relating research to education?

In government the new techniques went beyond traditional methods of research and challenged the adequacy of formal documentation and practical experience as a basis for judgment and decision-making. However these innovations were still suspect. Policy-makers understood the need for facts and statistics and for a careful and objective analysis of their significance. But they were less inclined to accept research that went beyond a logical description of observable data and explored human motives that were obscure, difficult to explain, or subject to wide variation because of the complex interactions of culture, group, and individual.

When the war ended almost all the social science research programs were disbanded and, even where they were retained or transformed, they were greatly reduced in size and in vitality. Demobilization and budget restrictions left little room for social science research, and the researchers themselves were anxious to return to the universities. At the same time the war had demonstrated the enormous benefits of government support for the physical sciences. And postwar conditions—the revolution in weapons technology, the emergence of the United States as a dominant world power with wide international commitments—led to the formation and maintenance of a federal scientific establishment substantially different from what had existed during the New Deal. Dominated by physical scientists, this new scientific establishment would soon establish the boundaries and the framework for all of science in the federal government, including social science.

CHAPTER V

THE COMMON DEFENSE

THE COSMOS CLUB in Washington is to much of American science, it has been said, "what Paris cafes are to the existentialists, both the shell and the seed-bed of considerable professional activity." Although membership in the Club remains select, it has increased in recent years, and its composition has reflected the different demands which the federal government has made on science at different times. Thus, "a study made in 1955 of membership trends in a 25-year period that began in 1931 revealed very natural peaks, with economists and other social scientists reaching high levels in the early years of the New Deal and the natural scientists (always the largest group) on the rise in the period after World War II."[1]

The years since 1945 have indeed witnessed the rise of natural scientists in government. A scientist now sits as special assistant to the President for science and technology and oversees an interlocking advisory system of government and university scientists through the President's Science Advisory Committee and the Federal Council for Science and Technology. As Director of the Office of Science and Technology, he heads a small but expert staff to support the work of both the Committee and the Council and carry out special presidential assignments. In major executive departments, programs of science and technology are directed by physicists, chemists, biologists, and engineers serving at the level of Assistant Secretary or equivalent. Scientists also direct the affairs of the National Science Foundation and the National Insti-

---

[1] Elinor Langer, "Science Goes to Lunch," *Science*, Vol. 146, No. 3648 (November 27, 1964), pp. 1145–1149.

tutes of Health; and they are in charge of defense, atomic energy, and space exploration programs which are major sources of support for scientific and medical research throughout the country. All of this is in addition to the previously established and no less influential positions that scientists have held over the years in the National Bureau of Standards, the Weather Bureau, the conservation agencies, and other technical bureaus.

This picture offers a marked contrast with the 1930's, which were years of disappointment, especially for those, like Karl Compton and Isaiah Bowman, who had unsuccessfully promoted the formation of the Science Advisory Board and failed to obtain large-scale support for research. The federal structure for science did not, however, emerge full blown at the end of the war. Indeed, soon after the war was over, scientists themselves began the process of dismantling the influential Office of Scientific Research and Development (OSRD) that Vannevar Bush had headed. It was only by the late 1950's that the kind of central organization for federal scientific activities that the OSRD represented was again established, this time because of the cold war and the competition from the Soviet Union in military technology and space exploration.

As they assumed positions of prominence after the war, natural scientists frequently discovered the price of close proximity to critical points of national policy-making, especially when they became involved in the decision to proceed with the hydrogen bomb, or in controversy over the continental defense system or the use of long-range missiles. As science and technology became more important in determining national security policy, the role of the scientist as researcher, on the one hand, and as adviser to political leaders, on the other, frequently became confused. The place where research ended and judgment began was not always understood or else not accepted in exactly the same way by all parties concerned. The pressures were such that scientists were sometimes tempted to act on the basis of partial scientific evidence or to resort to speculation for lack of adequate data. And there was always the possibility that a scientist's own policy preferences, consciously or not, might affect his interpretation of research evidence.

Even while the OSRD was being broken up, physical scientists were struggling to define the extent of their responsibility for political decisions. They had had little influence in making the decision to use the atomic bomb against Japan. Perhaps because of that very experience, scientists in several laboratories of the wartime Manhattan Project began to organize themselves in order to exert more influence on postwar programs for the use of atomic energy. In two cases their efforts were instrumental in shaping national policy: in the passage of legislation that established an Atomic Energy Commission (AEC) under civilian rather than military control; and in the formulation of a policy for the international control of atomic energy. The General Advisory Committee of the AEC also served scientists as a permanent institutional "presence" in Washington. This was especially important when their proposal for a National Science Foundation foundered after an encouraging start.

Immediately after the war, the primary aim of physical scientists was the establishment of a federal agency to support basic research. The war had taught them that they needed heavy and continual financial support, support that could only come from the federal government. However, they were still wary of political interference and thus sought to devise a system of government support that would operate in accordance with scientific rather than political standards. Their efforts to protect themselves from political control brought delay, delay during which the cause of science became engulfed in the requirements of the common defense.

The National Science Foundation

On July 3, 1946, the Senate voted by 46 to 26, with 24 members not voting, to exclude the social sciences from the support specified under the proposed National Science Foundation. The vote was taken on an amendment by Senator Thomas C. Hart, Republican from Connecticut, to a bill sponsored by Democratic Senator Harley Kilgore of West Virginia. Senator Hart opened the discussion by pointing out that the passage of his amendment would bring the proposed Foundation back to the original plan drawn up by Vannevar Bush. He also explained that he sought to exclude the social sciences because "no agreement has been reached with reference to what social science really means." It may include, the Senator suggested, "philosophy, anthropology, all the racial questions, all kinds of economics, including political economics, literature, perhaps religion, and various kinds of ideology." If that was not enough to frighten any already skeptical legislator, Senator Hart further asserted that the social sciences would be both a political and financial burden to the new agency and that there was "no connection between the social sciences, a very abstract field, and the concrete field which constitutes the other subjects to be dealt with by the proposed science foundation."[2]

Though the debate was short, Senator Hart was answered by Senator Elbert Thomas, Democrat of Utah, who emphasized the needs of government agencies for social science and the inevitable social and economic effects of research in the natural sciences. But Republican Senator Alexander Smith of New Jersey, stating that he spoke as one "much interested in social science," insisted that the bill being discussed was "a bill for research in pure science, not in applied science." His assumption seemed to be that all social science was in fact applied, and he appealed to his colleagues not to confuse the situation by including the social sciences in the program of the proposed Foundation. Before the vote was taken, the sponsor of the bill, Senator Kilgore, informed his colleagues that this very matter had been discussed in committee with "scientific leaders," though none of them were social scientists. And it had then been agreed upon that, while "the natural sciences and the social sciences were linked together," the Foundation would not support work in the social sciences until social scientists had drawn up a program and the Foundation staff and board had approved the program on its "scientific" merits.[3]

The vote in the Senate came just a year after Vannevar Bush presented his report, *Science: the Endless Frontier*, to President Truman, recommending that there be established a "National Re-

[2] *The Congressional Record*, U.S. Senate, July 3, 1946, p. 8231.
[3] *Ibid.*, pp. 8230–8232.

search Foundation" to "assist and encourage research in the public interest."[4] The report was worked out during the first half of 1945 in response to four questions that had been proposed by Bush and his staff in the Office of Scientific Research and Development and been made, at their urging, a matter of official inquiry by the late President Roosevelt the previous November.[5] The first two questions had to do with the declassification of scientific findings amassed during the war and with future support for medicine and related sciences. The last two questions asked, in effect, for recommendations on the overall structure of postwar government-science relations:

> What can the Government do now and in the future to aid research activities by public and private organizations?
> Can an effective program be proposed for discovering and developing scientific talent in American youth so that the continuing future of scientific research in this country may be assured on a level comparable to what has been done during the war?

Bush's report was a synthesis and summary of the studies of four committees of scientists, each having taken responsibility for answering one of the questions. The committee on research was headed by Isaiah Bowman and the committee on scientific talent by Henry Allen Moe, head of the Guggenheim Foundation. It was the Bowman committee that made the recommendation for "a new Federal instrumentality," a Foundation to support "scientific research in educational and nonprofit research institutions," to "establish scholarships and fellowships," to promote the "dissemination of scientific and technical information," and to encourage "international cooperation in science." In what was to lead to the greatest controversy in the next few years, the Bowman group also suggested that the Foundation "be in the hands of a board of trustees . . . appointed by the President . . . from a panel nominated by the National Academy of Sciences."[6]

In transmitting his report to the President, Bush interpreted

---

[4] Vannevar Bush, *Science: the Endless Frontier* (Washington, D.C., 1945).

[5] Daniel S. Greenberg, *The Politics of Pure Science* (New York: North American Library, 1967), p. 105.

[6] Bush, *op. cit.*, p. 69.

his charge as being limited to "the natural sciences, including biology and medicine." He acknowledged that "progress in other fields, such as the social sciences and the humanities, is likewise important; but the program for science presented in my report warrants immediate attention." His arguments in support of establishing a new Foundation were substantially drawn from the experience of the war: that scientific research was "absolutely essential to national security"; that during the war we had "been living on our fat"; and that there was no alternative to government support to insure a renewal and development of scientific resources. If there were any doubts about these points, the Bush report brought together an impressive amount of convincing evidence. Its basic premise was never challenged except by a minority—largely representing industrial companies—that feared that a huge government research establishment would substantially weaken research in the private sector. What was more forcefully challenged was the method of operation that Bush recommended and —to a lesser extent—his exclusion of the social sciences.

It was the Bureau of the Budget that led the opposition to the Bush recommendation that the new Foundation be directed by a group of part-time scientific trustees to whom the agency's administration would be responsible.[7] The argument of the scientists was based on a desire to isolate the research agency from political pressures and bureaucratic controls as much as possible. The Bush report proposed that operating departments of the government—particularly the military services—would continue to support applied research in furtherance of their own missions and that the Foundation would be "an independent agency devoted to the support of scientific research and advanced scientific education alone." In order to insure this independence, Bush asked for a budget that would permit long-range research support for periods up to five years or more and for an administration run by scientists according to criteria of scientific excellence.[8] The Budget Bureau, on the other hand, recommended that the Foun-

[7] See Don K. Price, *Government and Science* (New York: New York University Press, 1954), pp. 48–50.
[8] Bush, *op. cit.*, pp. 25–27.

tion administrator be appointed by the President and be responsible directly to him. Research, it was argued, could best be protected from political pressures by presidential authority. In the words of the Budget Director, Harold D. Smith: "I feel it is my duty to keep the scientists from making a mistake in the field of public administration."[9] Thus, in his message to Congress in early September, President Truman supported the Bush proposal for a new Foundation, but insisted that its head had to be responsible to the President.

The President went beyond administrative matters, however, in recommending that the social sciences also be included in the Foundation. But between the President's message and the Hart amendment the following July, there was no presentation on behalf of the social sciences that was in any way as impressive as the Bush report. Almost from the moment President Roosevelt had agreed to ask Bush to draw up a plan for postwar government support of research, the issue became a topic of discussion among leaders in the social science community. Indeed, the Science Committee for the National Resources Planning Board, which was dominated by social scientists, had considered making a report on postwar research shortly before its demise in 1943. Moreover, social scientists were working at high levels in the Budget Bureau, which was very much involved in postwar planning and responsible for advising the President on legislative proposals. But social scientists lacked the conviction, shared by Bush and the natural scientists, that government support was essential to the future growth of science. Many of them seriously doubted that a system could be devised, whatever safeguards Bush recommended, that would protect university-based research, especially in the social sciences, from public criticism and interference if it were financed by the government.

The Bush report presented the social scientists with a dilemma. To oppose the report might cause a serious split with colleagues in the natural sciences. To approve the report and as-

[9] *Science Legislation,* Hearings before Subcommittee on War Mobilization, Committee on Military Affairs, U.S. Senate, 79th Congress, 1st Session, 1945, Part 1, p. 104.

sist in adopting its provisions might bring about disproportionate support for the natural as against the social sciences in the universities. To establish a separate agency for the social sciences was impossible because of the lack of political support. And to take no stand at all was an abdication of responsibility, a position repugnant to most social scientists in view of their work with the National Resources Planning Board before the war and the place they held in many of the wartime research programs in government. The stand they finally took was chiefly determined by the President's decision to support the Bush proposals but to ask for the inclusion of the social sciences as well as direct presidential appointment of the administrator. Social science leaders were undoubtedly aware of the President's decision in advance because of their close ties with high-ranking staff in the Bureau of the Budget. By September 1945, shortly after the President's message to Congress, the Social Science Research Council had completed a statement on "the federal government and research in the social sciences." And in October Wesley Mitchell and a number of SSRC colleagues presented these views to the Senate Committee hearing testimony on the research bill.[10]

Mitchell acknowledged that the matter had been under consideration by the SSRC for about a year. He also noted that "fears have been voiced in some quarters that the social sciences will come to be subjected to Government control, and in others that in dealing with disputatious issues it may be difficult to hold clearly in sight the line between fact and opinion." But the problems were not new and had been faced by social scientists before. Indeed their experience in "several of the major agencies which have successfully conducted social science research on matters of vital public interest" was clear evidence that "sufficient safeguards against either of these dangers are practicable." The SSRC statement thus sought to remind the legislators that the social sciences had also made significant contributions to the war effort and that most problems faced by government, whether in "national defense

---

10 *Ibid.*, Part 4, pp. 738–786. Mitchell was accompanied by several other social scientists who also testified: John M. Gaus, Father John M. Cooper, Edwin G. Nourse, William F. Ogburn, and Robert Yerkes.

and security," or "national health and welfare," required "collaboration and cooperation among the sciences rather than an intensification of past rivalries and competitions." It was generally a positive statement but without the force and substance of the Bush report; and, presented in this context, it appeared to be a reaction to what the natural scientists had already proposed rather than an initiation of new ideas and projects. Moreover, it acknowledged "that the social sciences . . . [had not] reached a stage comparable to that of some of the other scientific disciplines." While this was offered as "the strongest possible reason for advancing their development by every effective means," it was an argument that gave little promise that the social sciences could contribute to national programs.

Mitchell and his colleagues testified at the end of the Senate hearings. Bowman opened the hearings, as the first witness, and introduced his discussion of the social science question with this remark: "it is well known that so much of human prejudice . . . and social philosophy enter into the study of social phenomena that there is the widest difference of opinion as to what constitutes research in many instances in the social sciences." He did agree that in dealing with many issues, particularly those involving the social effects of science, collaboration with social scientists was necessary. He also thought that the field of statistics should be included under the proposed legislation.[11] Whatever misgivings Bowman and other proponents of the Bush report might have had about the inclusion of the social sciences, the Executive Secretary of the American Association for the Advancement of Science (AAAS) informed the committee that, according to a poll taken by the Association, "a substantial number of physical scientists believe that the social sciences should have an integral place in the program."[12] Also, by the time the SSRC group appeared, Budget Director Smith had defended the inclusion of the social sciences.

However, the arguments advanced in favor of the social sciences did not fully dispel the doubts expressed by even sympa-

11 *Ibid.*, Part 1, p. 23.
12 *Ibid.*, Part 1, p. 92.

thetic interrogators, like Senators Kilgore and J. William Fulbright of Arkansas. Fulbright, for example, spoke of the "difficulty" of translating "into action" what social scientists know, and Kilgore called attention to the difficulty of measuring their knowledge with any kind of exactness.[13] Fulbright also pointed out that "people simply don't appreciate the significance of social sciences, which means your legislators don't, either."[14] In each case Mitchell and his SSRC colleagues responded with clarity and with illustrations. But it must be admitted that they shared the doubts implicit in the Senators' questions; they were aware of the lack of popular understanding of the social sciences and of the fact, as Senator Fulbright put it, that "everybody thinks he is an expert." It was also striking that all of the social scientists who testified were in favor of a single administrator appointed by the President; in this matter they opposed many natural scientists and were especially at odds with those who supported the original Bush proposals.

By late 1945 the issue had divided the natural scientists into two groups. One, led by Bowman, called itself the "Committee Supporting the Bush Report"; and the other, formed by Harold C. Urey and Harlow Shapley, was known as "The Committee for a National Science Foundation" and was ready to accept a compromise on administrative arrangements as well as the inclusion of the social sciences.[15] In the early months of 1946 there seemed to be some chance of agreement, as Bowman and Bush met with members of the Senate and indicated their acceptance of a plan for a strong board to serve as a check on a single administrator appointed by the President. But the Bowman group still opposed the inclusion of the social sciences for fear that congressional suspicion of the social sciences would jeopardize passage of the bill.[16] Bush later agreed to the provision, referred to by Senator Kilgore, that would not make it mandatory for the Foundation to support the social sciences, but would permit it to explore the possibility

13 *Ibid.*, Part 4, pp. 762–763.
14 *Ibid.*, Part 4, p. 780.
15 Howard A. Meyerhoff, "Science Legislation and the Holiday Recess," *Science*, Vol. 103, No. 2663 (January 4, 1946), pp. 10–11.
16 Howard A. Meyerhoff, "S.1720 versus S.1777," *Science*, Vol. 103, No. 2667 (February 8, 1946), pp. 161–162.

for support. He insisted that this seemed the wisest move both because President Roosevelt had not originally "turned to men who are professionally social scientists" and "because no program for the social sciences has been prepared and submitted by the social scientists themselves."[17]

Senator Hart's amendment, voted on in July 1946, corresponded to the Bush position. The amended Senate bill, which included the compromise between the single administrator and a strong Board but excluded specific provision for the social sciences, was then voted on favorably. In the meanwhile an alternative bill, which reverted *in toto* back to the original Bush proposals, was introduced in the House and supported by Bowman and Bush despite their earlier agreement to a compromise. The result was a legislative impasse. Action was stalled in the House and no legislation was passed that year. There was consequently a great deal of bitterness in scientific circles, as exemplified by an editorial in *Science,* entitled "Obituary: National Science Foundation, 1946," in which the Executive Secretary of the AAAS issued a warning to his colleagues: "Only in a reasonable show of unity, achieved by some compromise, can scientists expect political results."[18]

After this setback social scientists began to reappraise their position. Until then they had hoped to gain some specific provision for the social sciences in the Foundation. Now they seemed more or less willing to accept the Bush formula—a "permissive but not mandatory" provision—partly because they were discouraged by the vote on the Hart amendment and partly because they wished to preserve the unity among scientists called for by *Science.* Accordingly, leaders in the SSRC, particularly Robert M. Yerkes and Donald Young, joined in forming the Inter-society Committee for a National Science Foundation at the annual meeting of the AAAS in December.

Throughout 1947 social scientists continued to give support

---

[17] *National Science Foundation Act,* Hearings before Subcommittee of Committee on Interstate and Foreign Commerce, House of Representatives, 79th Congress, 2nd Session, 1946, p. 53.

[18] Howard A. Meyerhoff, "Obituary: National Science Foundation, 1946," *Science,* Vol. 104, No. 2693 (August 2, 1946), pp. 97–98.

to the Inter-society Committee even when the Committee, in an effort to get some action, agreed to a bill, approved by both Houses, which would have left control of the Foundation in the hands of a board. Not unexpectedly, the President vetoed the bill on administrative grounds and there was more delay in the establishment of the Foundation. In trying to analyze the reasons for the conflict, Dael Wolfle, who served as secretary of the Inter-society Committee, gave weight to two factors: the poor strategy the Committee used in approving of a bill that both its members and the President disliked; and "the great weight attached to the advice of a few very prominent scientists" by members of Congress "most directly responsible for science legislation."[19]

Over the next two years there was, as Don K. Price put it, "no great political steam behind the National Science Foundation legislation."[20] With the Atomic Energy Commission now organized and new research programs being funded through the AEC and the military departments, the establishment of a Foundation was neither vital to the physical scientists as a source of support nor sufficiently important to political leaders for them to expend political capital on its behalf. As for the social scientists, they made efforts to promote a better understanding of the social sciences among their colleagues in the natural sciences, in Congress, and in the general public, but they took no political action.

During this period a number of attempts were made to review the achievements of social science in various fields. The SSRC set up a committee to consolidate methodological advances in opinion and attitude survey research that had been undertaken during the war. With the assistance of the Carnegie Corporation, it also sponsored an assessment of the work of the Army's wartime research branch under Samuel Stouffer, published in *The American Soldier*. Stuart Chase received broad cooperation from leading social scientists in preparing his book, *The Proper Study of Mankind*, a readable and fairly comprehensive survey of developments in the

[19] Dael Wolfle, "The Inter-Society Committee for a National Science Foundation: Report for 1947," *Science*, Vol. 106, No. 2762 (December 5, 1947), pp. 529–533.
[20] Price, *op. cit.*, p. 56.

social sciences and their relevance to American society. Under the auspices of the SSRC, Talcott Parsons began a broad study on government and social science, though no public report of his conclusions was issued.

But none of these did for the social sciences what the Bush report had done for the natural sciences. The context in which the discussion of postwar research policies went on had been virtually established by Bush and his colleagues at the end of the war. At this time the nation was also disturbed by the tensions of the cold war and concerned about the scientific and technological needs for new weapons and military hardware. It was a political environment in which physical scientists continued to gain recognition and influence. Thus, when a National Science Foundation was finally established in 1950, with an administrator appointed by the President but with a National Science Board of considerable strength, the social sciences were left with the earlier Bush formula—that Foundation support would be "permissive but not mandatory." For the social sciences, however, as for all the sciences, there was increasing support for research from the military departments, especially when the cold war became intensified with the outbreak of the Korean conflict.

The Military Services

The breakup of the wartime social science research programs in the military services was followed by a period of indecision. The defense establishment was disturbed by the uncertainties of the international situation and by debates over the unification of the armed services. Government support for scientific research and education followed no plan during the five years of debate on the National Science Foundation. In the interim, the Office of Naval Research (ONR) filled the gap for all the sciences, including the social sciences. The ONR program was initiated by naval officers who had been involved in research during the war. They were supported by Secretary of the Navy James Forrestal as well as by Bush and other leading scientists of the wartime OSRD group. The ONR program not only provided the single major source of research funds right after the war, but also established policies that gave support to basic research, established scientific rather than bureaucratic criteria for grants, and recognized the internal structures of the scientific community as a source of strength and accountability. In the absence of a National Science Foundation until 1950, ONR became the chief agency used by scientists to obtain federal support for basic research in the universities.

Within ONR it was the Human Resources Division that first administered the program for social science research. The budget for this program grew from $100,000 in 1946 to more than $1.5 million by 1950 and doubled during the first two years of the Korean conflict. Moreover, program administrators took a broad view of social science research that went beyond narrow military requirements.[21] At an early stage, an Advisory Panel on Human Relations and Morale recommended five areas of study that served as program guidelines: the comparative study of different cultures; the structure and function of groups; the communication of ideas, policies, and values; the nature of leadership; and the growth and development of the individual. At the end of the first five years, many of the principal investigators met in a conference to report on the progress of their work. The conference and the continuing activities of the advisory group and the ONR staff were all part of an effort to contribute to a cumulative social science within the framework of an individual grant program. At the same time, they created a cadre of social scientists in the universities who were concerned with Navy problems even though their research had not been forced into any applied directions.[22] The idea was to do work relevant to both the goals of science and the mission of the Navy.

In the late 1940's, an attempt was made to go beyond ONR and establish a defense-wide social science research program un-

---

21 See "Office of Naval Research: 20 Years Bring Changes," *Science*, Vol. 153, No. 3734 (July 22, 1966), pp. 397–400; also John G. Darley, "Psychology and the Office of Naval Research: A Decade of Development," *The American Psychologist*, Vol. 12, No. 5 (May 1957), pp. 305–323.

22 For the results of the conference and a review of the research supported by the Office of Naval Research during its first five years, see Harold Guetzkow (ed.), *Groups, Leadership and Men* (Pittsburgh: Carnegie Press, 1951).

der the guidance of the Committee on Human Resources of the Defense Research and Development Board. The Board had been set up under the National Security Act of 1947 for three primary purposes: to prepare an integrated research program for the military establishment; to relate trends in scientific research to national security; and to develop a means of coordinating the research programs of the three military departments.[23] The first Chairman of the Board was Vannevar Bush, who was succeeded by Karl Compton and later by Walter Whitman, a chemist from M.I.T. The Board consisted of two members each from the Army, the Navy, and the Air Force, in addition to the Chairman. It operated largely through a series of committees in selected fields of science and engineering, sixteen in number, with the Committee on Human Resources responsible for research in the psychological and social sciences. The civilian members of the Committee were men who had had wartime experience in military research programs: Donald Marquis of the University of Michigan served as chairman; and Samuel Stouffer, by then at Harvard, Carroll Shartle of the Ohio State University, and the psychiatrist William C. Menninger were members.[24]

The Human Resources Committee went further in breaking down research work into a number of specialized panels on subjects such as personnel, human relations and morale, human engineering, manpower, training, and psychological warfare. Each panel was also composed of civilian and military members. And from time to time the Committee authorized special surveys and studies in addition to the regular activities of the more permanent panels.[25] In all, the Committee covered the full range of the social sciences used in the military and brought a large number of academicians into the Defense Department's program. In 1953, the last year that the Research and Development Board was in

---

[23] For a general review and analysis of the Research and Development Board, see Price, *op. cit.*, pp. 144–152.

[24] Lyle H. Lanier, "The Psychological and Social Sciences in the National Military Establishment," *The American Psychologist*, Vol. 4, No. 5 (May 1949), pp. 131–132.

[25] Milton D. Graham, "Federal Utilization of Social Science Research, A Preliminary Paper" (Washington, D.C.: The Brookings Institution, 1954), pp. 89–98.

operation, some two hundred people were involved in the activities of the Committee, from both inside and outside the government, and the defense research budget for the psychological and social sciences had grown with the Korean conflict to $26 million.[26] The broad aims of the Committee, as part of the Board, were never achieved, however. A good deal of encouragement was given to individual departmental programs, but no integrated defense research program was ever developed.

The failure of the Research and Development Board was partly due to the weakness of the civilian leadership in the Defense Department in guiding the research programs of the three services and, indeed, in exerting influence over the military services in general. Despite the National Security Act of 1947 and amendments to it in 1949, the defense establishment remained a loose federation of the military services rather than a unified department. Don K. Price, who served for a time as Deputy Chairman of the Board, found that the committee system of the Board was equipped neither to make innovative changes nor to alter the programs developed at the level of the services. Unlike the wartime organization of the Office of Scientific Research and Development, the Board had no authority or funds to initiate research of its own, was largely in the hands of consultants and committee and panel participants who served on a part-time basis, and was constantly immersed in project details and the problems of a splintered committee structure. Price pointed out the "essential difficulty":

> the control of the research programs was being managed in an aggressive way by the military services, which prepared the plans, let the contracts, and received the appropriations. By comparison with their dynamic management a slow and clumsy system of review by three or four layers of committees could hardly have caught up with the parade, even if all committee members had been eager to do so.[27]

The physical scientists, particularly, wanted a system that gave independent initiative to civilian scientists as OSRD had done during the war. The military resisted giving them a place of

[26] *Ibid.*, p. 91.
[27] Price, *op. cit.*, p. 151.

independent initiative partly because of the rivalry among the services—first, for control of atomic weapons and, later, for ballistic missile programs—and partly because of their legitimate concern that centralized scientific authority could lead to strategies with heavy or even exclusive dependence on single weapons systems. Then, having agreed on a multiple weapons strategy, the military services made *quid pro quo* arrangements among themselves and common cause against civilian encroachment from above. But the scientists, on their side, were convinced that the "conservative approach of a military organization" was an "inherent weakness in the military research and development programming" and that it hindered the development of "radically new weapons and weapons systems."[28]

For the social sciences, the dissolution of the Research and Development Board coincided with the beginnings of an operationally oriented research system in all three services, with a heavy emphasis on studies of individual and group behavior that were relevant to military personnel problems. At this level social scientists, particularly those specializing in military psychology, developed procedures for directly serving military personnel programs. In 1951 a report of a working group sponsored by the Research and Development Board and the Defense Personnel Policy Board had strongly urged that "the consideration of human resources research needs and the implementation of research implications should be integrally related to the determination of personnel policy." The report had also recommended that research units be established "within each of the general staff divisions concerned with personnel, training and operations." It was suggested that such close organizational arrangements were necessary to overcome the differences between social scientists and the military that had developed since the war and, indeed, had existed during the war itself.[29]

---

[28] *Subcommittee Report on Research Activities in the Department of Defense and Defense Related Agencies,* Commission on Organization of the Executive Branch of the Government (Washington, D.C., April 1955), p. 26.

[29] *Report of Working Group on Human Behavior under Conditions of Military Services,* A Joint Project of the Research and Development Board and the Personnel Policy Board in the Office of the Secretary of Defense (Washington, D.C., June 1951), pp. 55–56.

The trend toward purely operational research was evident even in the program of the Office of Naval Research in the early 1950's. Significantly, the responsible ONR unit was renamed the Psychological Sciences Division in 1952 and large scale projects in human relations and morale were generally discontinued. In part, this change was a response to congressional criticism of both government and private foundation support for cross-cultural studies, especially studies that involved research on communist societies. It was also a response to the establishment of the National Science Foundation, which was now responsible for supporting basic research. Research in manpower problems and training that ONR had previously funded were transferred to programs administered under the Bureau of Naval Personnel.[30]

In the Army, the outbreak of the Korean conflict required that research be related even more closely to operations than in the Navy, where the ONR spirit of basic research persisted despite the narrowing of focus. Moreover, Korea seemed to confirm the Army's contention that the era of the ground soldier was not over, but was entering a new phase of responsibility and complexity. Immediately after the Second World War the Army enjoyed great political prestige because Army Generals Marshall, Eisenhower, and MacArthur had played central roles in achieving victory. However, with the rise of the Air Force as a separate entity free from the administrative control of the Army, and with the new destructive power of the atomic bomb, military plans tended to give less emphasis to the conquest and occupation of the land mass and more to the use of airpower. Korea demonstrated the limits of air-atomic power, and the military had to develop new concepts of limited warfare in which ground forces were again of prime importance.

Because of the large numbers of troops sent to Korea, there were new opportunities to study the testing and selection of recruits and the behavior of troops in combat. In 1948 the Army had entered into a contract with the Johns Hopkins University for the establishment of the Operations Research Office (ORO), and in 1951 it began to support the Human Resources Research Office (HumRRO) at the George Washington University. Both

[30] See Darley, *op. cit.*

ORO and HumRRO operated large-scale programs in Korea covering a wide range of military problems. ORO sent some 150 analysts to Korea, many engaged in operational studies of logistics, troop mobility, and the conduct of units under combat.[31] It also launched Project Clear, a study of racial integration in the Army in order to determine the effect of President Truman's order in 1948 abolishing segregation in the armed forces. Project Clear, which was comparable to many of the studies on race relations conducted by the Army Research Branch during the Second World War, was a survey of several thousand servicemen and indicated a greater willingness to accept desegregation among both Negroes and whites than the earlier research had done.[32] HumRRO's work in Korea consisted largely of studies of training, motivation, and leadership. In addition, by the mid-1950's there were psychological research units attached to the Office of the Adjutant General, the Office of the Surgeon General, the Quartermaster Corps, the Ordnance Corps, and other technical branches. These various groups were able to communicate with each other through the coordinating mechanisms of the Office of the Chief of Research and Development. The Chief here also served as Chairman of the Army Personnel and Training Research Advisory Committee. The Committee itself was not composed of social scientists who were able to give professional advice but was made up of senior military officers from the major operational and technical branches of the Army.[33] Throughout the Army the emphasis was on operational "payoff."

The Air Force was established as an independent department by the National Security Act of 1947. From then until 1956 it made a number of complicated institutional experiments in developing a social science research program. Even before 1947 the Air Force had taken the first steps in setting up Project RAND,

---

31 W. L. Whitson, "The Growth of the Operations Research Office in the U.S. Army," *Operations Research,* Vol. 8, No. 6 (November–December 1960), p. 812.

32 Charles C. Moskos, Jr., "Racial Integration in the Armed Forces," *American Journal of Sociology,* Vol. 72, No. 2 (September 1966), pp. 132–148.

33 See *Conference Report, Army Human Engineering Conference,* Chief of Research and Development, Department of the Army (Washington, D.C., 1955), pp. 23–25.

initially through the Douglas Aircraft Company. By 1948, when RAND became a separate non-profit corporation, some provision was made for the social sciences in a program chiefly devoted to mathematics and the physical and engineering sciences. At the urging of the mathematician John Williams, the Air Force agreed to a conference of social scientists which was held in New York in September 1947. An impressive group of social scientists, almost all of whom had had wartime experience with the military, was convened to evaluate a series of broadly conceived research projects. These included studies of aggression and morale, psychological warfare, political psychology, and the economics of preparedness and war.[34] It was this conference that laid the groundwork for establishing the Social Science and Economics Divisions of the RAND Corporation. And it was the early work of the Economics Division that led to wide use of systems analysis in the management of the Defense Department.[35]

The RAND Corporation was organized as a basic research enterprise available to any Air Force Division through a special liaison office established under the Deputy Chief of Staff for Research and Development. It had considerable freedom of operation. It was allowed to undertake projects designed by its own staff members and to refuse or to reformulate requests for research which came from the Air Force. From the beginning, however, it was conceived of as a basic resource for the Air Force with a social science component. While RAND was being developed, three other Air Force social science research units were established. The first two, the Human Resources Research Center and the Human Resources Research Laboratory, were the Air Force's response to the stimulus offered by the Defense Research and Development Board in the fields of testing, selection, and classification of personnel. The third, the Human Resources Research Institute, was established in 1949 with a broader social science mandate under the Air University at Maxwell Air Base in Alabama.

The Institute had the shortest and, in many respects, the

34 "Conference of Social Scientists," R-106, The RAND Corporation (Santa Monica, California, June 1948).

35 Bruce L. R. Smith, The RAND Corporation (Cambridge: Harvard University Press, 1966), pp. 60–65.

most uneven life of the Air Force experiments. During the Korean conflict it joined the other two research units, the Center and the Laboratory, in forming a Far East Research Group to study a broad range of social science problems in the field, including psychological warfare, the behavior of prisoners of war, and the operations of Air Force units under combat conditions. But its largest project was an analysis of the Soviet social system conducted under contract with the Russian Research Center of Harvard and undertaken by a group that included Raymond Bauer, Alex Inkeles, and Clyde Kluckhohn.[36] In 1953, when work was well underway, the Institute came under the sharp scrutiny of Congress. The Soviet project was attacked as part of the general attack on all social science research that dealt with the problems of communism. At this time the Air Force itself began to have doubts about the relationship of Institute-sponsored research to the mission of officer education for which Air University was responsible, doubts which were presumably intensified by a lack of effective rapport between the military command and the research staff.[37] Within a short time the Institute was abolished. Although the Air Force continued to support broad social science research through RAND, it made no more grants for university-based studies until a Behavioral Sciences Division was formed in 1956 under the Air Force Office of Scientific Research (AFOSR).

As separate entities, the Human Resources Research Laboratory and Research Center also disappeared in 1954. In their case, however, the work they were doing was absorbed into that of the Air Force Personnel and Training Research Center established under the Air Research and Development Command (subsequently renamed the Personnel Research Laboratory). Techni-

---

[36] Raymond A. Bauer, Alex Inkeles, and Clyde Kluckhohn, *How the Soviet System Works* (Cambridge: Harvard University Press, 1956).

[37] The full story of the Air Force Human Resources Research Institute has not been fully reported. For some insight, see George W. Croker, "Some Principles Regarding the Utilization of Social Science Research within the Military," in *Case Studies in Bringing Behavioral Sciences into Use* (Stanford: Institute for Communication Research, 1961), pp. 112–125; also Raymond V. Bowers, "The Military Establishment" in Paul F. Lazarsfeld, *et al.* (eds.), *The Uses of Sociology* (New York: Basic Books, 1967), pp. 234–274.

cally, the Institute was also incorporated into the new Research Center, but the broader political and sociological studies that the Institute had previously supported were not part of the mission of the new organization. Its task was somewhat ponderously but comprehensively defined as "research, development, and field tests . . . on devices, methods, procedures, and policies for the selection, classification, assignment, formal and on-the-job training and education, in-training and on-the-job proficiency evaluations, and assessment and control of morale factors, of individuals, teams and organizations for the improvement of operation and maintenance of weapons systems, equipment, and supporting activities of the Air Force."[38] The creation of the new Research Center served to integrate research on personnel and training within the framework of the systems approach the Air Force was applying to its overall research and development program.[39] This integrated structure offered a sharp contrast to the highly decentralized organization of the Army, where programs were only loosely coordinated through the advisory group chaired by the Chief of Research and Development. In both cases, however, research was dominated by the requirements of weapons development and the demands of a changing technological base for military operations.

By 1958 each of the military departments had its own system of social science research. Each system emphasized psychology and was largely shaped by the personnel requirements of its department and the objectives of the military in general. Social scientists worked at many different levels in these programs, but almost always within the limits determined by the military command. There were occasional exceptions. At the Army-sponsored ORO and HumRRO, social scientists participated in annual work programs that, especially in the case of ORO, gave them an opportunity to initiate their own research projects. Their mandate,

38 "History of the Air Force Personnel and Training Center, 1 February–30 June 1954," Air Research and Development Command, Lackland Air Force Base (San Antonio, Texas), p. 6.

39 See Arthur W. Melton, Foreword, in Robert M. Gagne (ed.), *Psychological Principles in System Development* (New York: Holt, Rinehart & Winston, 1962), pp. v–viii.

however, was considerably less permissive than the contract that the Air Force had with RAND. At RAND social scientists, mainly on their own initiative, were exploring the complex implications of the strategy of deterrence, and economists, the practical application of systems analysis to defense management and resource allocation. Although the defense program elsewhere was generally confined to applied research on personnel problems, the size of the research effort in the defense establishment and the commitment to research as a legitimate function gave a certain leeway to research administrators. Thus the ONR program continued to sponsor basic research on group psychology and the Air Force Office of Scientific Research (AFOSR) carried on certain investigations related to psychological warfare after 1956. At the same time, the development of Soviet nuclear capability gave impetus to studies of social disaster and civil defense, especially by RAND and the Disaster Research Group organized under the National Academy of Sciences–National Research Council with military financing.[40]

Despite these efforts, there were essential weaknesses in the defense system for the support of research in the social sciences. In 1955 the second Hoover Commission (Commission on Organization of the Executive Branch of the Government) pointed these out in its criticisms of the Defense Department's research structure. Though these criticisms were specifically leveled at research in the physical sciences and engineering, they applied to all research. The weaknesses mentioned were: the lack of strength and direction in the Office of the Secretary of Defense; the fragmentation of programs, particularly in the Army and the Navy; the structural inhibitions to new approaches; and the failure to make effective use of scientific advisory committees and consultants.[41] The Office of the Secretary of Defense had been granted

---

[40] See Herman J. Sander, "The Uses of Sociology for Military Intelligence, Strategic Planning and Psychological Warfare," paper (mimeographed) prepared for the annual meeting of the American Sociological Association (Washington, D.C., 1962).

[41] *Subcommittee Report on Research Activities in the Department of Defense and Defense Related Agencies, op. cit.*

broader powers under the reorganization plan of 1953, which had created new positions at the level of assistant secretary in functional areas such as supply, manpower, and research and development. But the authority of the assistant secretaries was uncertain, since they could not intervene directly in the work of the military departments. Even the Secretary of Defense still had to negotiate with the military services; he could not order them to do his bidding.

In the fall of 1957, however, the Soviet Union launched the first Sputnik, a sign that it now possessed an inter-continental ballistic missile capability and could threaten the United States directly. President Eisenhower immediately took steps to strengthen and consolidate programs for the development of new weapons and space vehicles. A Special Assistant for Science and Technology and a President's Science Advisory Committee were established in the White House. The role of the Secretary of Defense was then strengthened under the Reorganization Act of 1958, particularly in the area of research and development. Under the Act, the Secretary, and through him his immediate staff, could exercise authority over unified military commands, transfer weapons systems from one service to another, and maintain centralized control over expenditures for research and development.

The Reorganization Act of 1958 made a basic change in the environment for research in the defense establishment, though the change was less perceptible in the social sciences than elsewhere. A social science unit was set up in the new Directorate of Defense Research and Engineering (DDRE). And social scientists, though few in number, sat as members of the Defense Science Board, which was established as the major advisory group to the Secretary of Defense and the Director of DDRE. DDRE and the Board, however, were mainly concerned with advanced weapons technology. The opportunity they afforded for central direction was never effectively exploited in the social sciences. Nevertheless, social science research continued to expand in the military as part of the general growth of defense research. The rising research budget in the military provided a cushion for experimentation that no other department could afford.

The Department of Defense

In the late 1950's social science research sponsored by the military departments still had a high operational orientation and was primarily focused on personnel selection, assignment, and training. The broadly conceived role of the RAND Corporation remained an exception to the regular pattern. RAND staff members were permitted to undertake research on their own initiative and to question the assumptions on which any request for advice was based, even to the extent of refusing to undertake the research involved. In a study of the selection of overseas air bases in the mid-1950's, for example, RAND analysts went far beyond the limited mandate of offering guidance on the most effective ways for acquiring, constructing, and using airbase facilities in foreign countries. Without being asked, they proceeded to examine the vulnerability of aircraft on the ground to surprise atomic attack and to demonstrate that preserving a second strike capability was essential to a policy of deterrence. Their analysis was sent through the Air Force hierarchy and, after a long and complex process of education and persuasion, was finally accepted. The result was a fundamental change in the system in order to provide shelter and mobility for the American nuclear deterrent.[42]

Research was also less confined to immediate operational problems in those agencies established within the Defense Department by the Reorganization Act of 1958. For example, soon after it was established, the Directorate of Defense Research and Engineering (DDRE), acting through a special advisory panel, initiated a series of studies on the state of psychology and the social sciences in the defense establishment. In 1959 these studies, which had already been started, were completed by a research group working through the Smithsonian Institution, with Charles W. Bray as staff director. Bray had had long experience in the field of military psychology, having served with the Applied Psychology Panel of the National Research Council during the war and later as Director of the Air Force Personnel and Training Research Center.

[42] The case of the overseas base study is described in Smith, *op. cit.*, pp. 195–240.

The research group had a steering committee and under it a series of task panels whose members came from a wide range of academic institutions and also had considerable experience in government research, especially with the military. The panels reviewed the state of research in six different fields: the design and use of man-machine systems; the capabilities and limitations of human performance; decision processes in the individual; team functions; the adaptation of complex organizations to changing demands; and persuasion and motivation.[43]

The recommendations of the research group were presented to the Defense Science Board in late 1960. They were essentially concerned with the gap that existed between the operationally oriented research of the personnel laboratories and contract organizations, on the one hand, and individual grant programs for university research run by the Office of Naval Research and the Air Force Office of Scientific Research, on the other. The next step, the group suggested, was to develop long-range support for the systematic study of selected areas of research that were relevant to broadly defined defense requirements and that offered reasonable opportunities for practical results if developed in depth by teams of experienced social scientists. Specifically, the research group recommended that the Defense Department provide support for three major centers of research in human performance: one to emphasize a systems approach and develop simulation techniques for studying man-machine relations; a second to concentrate on the measurement of individual performance, including the processes of human thinking and decision-making; and a third to examine human performance in groups. It also recommended that a research institute be established for the theoretical and comparative study of complex military organizations, and that a small number of centers be organized for the study of both persuasion and motivation and their relation to group activity and cultural differences. It was thought that this system of support would give cohesion and direction to basic research in the defense establish-

---

[43] For a summary of the studies of the Smithsonian Research Group, see Charles W. Bray, "Toward a Technology of Human Behavior for Defense Use," *The American Psychologist*, Vol. 17, No. 8 (August 1962), pp. 527–541.

ment and would also provide a mechanism for channeling research findings into the applied programs of the military.

In 1961 the recommendations of the research group were seconded by the Defense Science Board and passed on to DDRE with a strong statement urging that they be implemented. DDRE, in turn, used the research group's report as the basis for establishing a behavioral sciences program in the Advanced Research Projects Agency (ARPA). This was another agency created by the Reorganization Act of 1958 to undertake support for advanced research that cut across the missions of the three services. During its early years the ARPA program tended to follow the lines of the Smithsonian report. It was more encouraging to basic research than the military personnel laboratories, and its grants were larger and more deliberately integrated than those made by ONR and AFOSR. Also, though there were some changes because of pressing problems in the Defense Department, ARPA continued to do research in the areas recommended by the Smithsonian report: teaching and learning, human performance, human communications, bargaining and negotiation, and social change in developing nations.[44]

However, the ARPA behavioral sciences program did not organize the "centers" that the Smithsonian report had recommended. It was funded at considerably less than had been anticipated and did not ever have the staff to review its basic research projects and relate them to the applied work in testing, selection, and training carried out by the military services. Instead of providing a bridge between basic research and applied programs, ARPA became, in practice, a general agency for the support of research like ONR and AFOSR. ARPA also took responsibility for research in problems of social change, partly channeled through RAND and the Institute of Defense Analyses, to support the counter-insurgency and civic action functions of the Defense Department. In this respect, the ARPA program became a convenient

---

[44] For a description of the Behavioral Science Program of the Advanced Research Projects Agency (ARPA), see the testimony of the ARPA Director in *Military Posture*, Hearings before Committee on Armed Services, House of Representatives, 90th Congress, 1st Session, 1967, pp. 1542–1545.

and flexible instrument with which the Department could respond to *ad hoc* problems. While useful, this function undoubtedly tended to weaken even more the ability of ARPA to achieve the goals of the Smithsonian report.

The difficulties of ARPA in fulfilling the expectations of the Smithsonian report went deeper. Whatever the achievements of its basic research program, they had little effect on the methods of personnel selection and training in the services. These achievements were not negligible. The Director of ARPA, in testimony before the House Armed Services Committee in 1967, stated:

> ARPA-sponsored research in the areas of computer-aided instruction has resulted in systems that promise the instructor very precise control and direction of the learning experience, and the possibility of tailoring this experience differentially to fit each individual trainee's needs as instruction progresses. . . . [Another research project has made] substantial progress toward the development of a new . . . technique [for the measurement of performance] that provides more precise information in a more efficient procedure.[45]

But there was no built-in provision for systematically applying the results of this research to the operating programs of the services where training and testing went on. Indeed, the ONR program in group psychology had much the same problem, although it had been in existence for some twenty years and was closer to the center of military operations.

Moreover, ARPA existed within the structure of DDRE. And, while DDRE was responsible for overseeing the social science research program of the entire defense establishment, it was not able to exercise the same kind of influence in the social sciences as it did in the physical sciences and engineering. The social sciences were represented in DDRE usually by no more than one man and at times by no one at all. More and more deeply involved with weapons development, DDRE was not able to give effective support and direction to the social science program in ARPA or elsewhere in the services.

Much of the long-range research supported by ARPA was applicable to personnel selection and training, and here, too, difficulties arose. This part of their operations the military services made every effort to keep under their own control; it was the last major area in the defense establishment to resist centralization. In the early 1960's the Office of the Secretary of Defense achieved effective control in the areas of financial management, weapons development, and strategic planning by acting through the Office of the Comptroller, DDRE, and the Assistant Secretaries of Defense for International Security Affairs and for Systems Analysis. Also, considerable coordination and uniformity was achieved through centralized agencies like the Defense Supply Agency and the Defense Intelligence Agency, and through the practice of designating individual departments as executive agents for the entire defense establishment in specified areas of operations. However, attempts at centralization through the Office of the Assistant Secretary of Defense for Manpower were less successful, although this branch of the Department, in theory at any rate, would seem to be the logical channel for applying the findings of ARPA-sponsored research to manpower policies in the entire defense establishment.

Personnel recruiting and training programs, however, are the heart of military professionalism. They act to preserve the traditions of the services and instill them into new recruits, to establish the necessary rapport between commander and men, and to develop the loyalty and *esprit de corps* essential to the military character. Within each service, as well, there are special manpower and training requirements based on the different weapons systems employed. The Navy is concerned primarily with the manning of ships at sea, the Air Force with the operation of aircraft and missile systems, and the Army with the actions of combat ground forces. Therefore, from the viewpoint of military leaders, control of these recruiting and training programs had to be kept in the hands of the services. And research had to be closely tied to operational demands and contained within the structure of military-controlled institutions.

The need for changes in military manpower policies was nevertheless recognized when the President and the Department of

Defense made efforts to revise the draft law in 1966 and 1967, efforts which were largely unsuccessful. Congress rejected almost all of the President's recommendations, such as calling the youngest rather than the oldest eligible men first, limiting student exemptions so that college and university enrollment would not provide an inequitable protection against the draft, and providing for a lottery system.[46] In effect, Congress passed legislation that continued the existing system. However, in considering revisions of the draft law, the White House and the Defense Department had found it necessary to review population projections, to examine the relationship of military manpower needs to economic and social trends, and to study the effects of military training on both the specialized skills required in the civilian economy and the problems of unskilled young men in the low-income groups. These studies demonstrated the close connection between military and national manpower policies and forced the Defense Department to consider greater rationalization of the various segments of its personnel recruiting and training program.[47]

In the summer of 1966 Secretary of Defense McNamara also announced a new program that related military training to the broadest kind of social problem. Each year 100,000 men were to be drafted for military service although they were not qualified under existing physical and mental standards. The purpose, as he expressed it, was to use the resources of the Defense Department so "that through the application of advanced educational and medical techniques we can salvage tens of thousands of these men each year, first to productive military careers and later for productive roles in society." The Secretary emphasized the "gigantic spin-off" that the Defense Department has "into the society as a whole," and pointed out that "a very substantial number of civilians currently employed in such skilled occupational fields as electronics, engineering, transportation management, machine-

---

[46] For text of the President's message to Congress, see *The New York Times*, March 7, 1967.

[47] For a review of the relationship of military and national manpower policies, see *Government and Manpower*, National Manpower Council (New York: Columbia University Press, 1964), pp. 364–398.

tool operation, automotive and aircraft maintenance, and the building trades . . . have been trained in the armed forces."[48]

"Project 100,000," as it came to be called, indicated a significant change in the use of manpower in the defense establishment. "Only 14 per cent of the more than three million men in our armed forces fire weapons as their primary duty. A full fifty per cent must be trained in technical skills." Because of this fact, McNamara claimed, the Defense Department could take on the task of Project 100,000 without endangering the combat preparedness of the services. In the regular military training programs, there thus began to be more concern with objectives other than combat preparedness. Project 100,000 was put into execution soon after the Secretary spoke. Although recruits were taken into all three services, the project was centralized in the Office of the Assistant Secretary of Defense for Manpower, where a central file of all participants was set up in order to record and evaluate their progress. At the same time, the Office began its own research program, initially funded at $1.5 million annually, on the special problems of teaching and motivation in Project 100,000. Much of the research was funded through the service laboratories and contract organizations, but a number of contracts were also drawn up with social scientists in the universities.[49]

Project 100,000 offered the Manpower Office of the Defense Department its first chance to take a direct hand in research on personnel selection and training. In a speech before the Air Force Association in early 1967, the Assistant Secretary for Manpower, Thomas D. Morris, emphasized research as one of three main factors in formulating future manpower policies. He prefaced a review of current problems in pay and promotion with a set of principles for "manpower policy making." The first was the need "to constantly listen to the voice of the individual service members." As an example here, he pointed to a survey of naval officers and

48 For excerpts from Secretary McNamara's speech, see *The New York Times,* August 24, 1966.
49 For a list of early research projects in connection with "Project 100,000," see *Department of Defense Appropriations for 1968,* Hearings before Committee on Appropriations, House of Representatives, 90th Congress, 1st Session, 1967, Part 3, pp. 615–617.

seamen that was very similar to the attitude and opinion studies of the Army Research Branch during the Second World War. His second principle was "to do a great deal more thinking and analysis to determine precise objectives in recruiting, training, promoting and retaining people for each occupation." His purpose was to adapt policies and programs to "each occupation" rather than "to over-generalize"; and his views here reflected those of Secretary McNamara regarding the variety of occupational and technical skills needed in defense. Finally, Morris stressed "the pressing need for more [social science] research—and more exchange of ideas between research people and manpower managers—in order to pioneer new and better solutions to our problems."[50]

But more was required than principles. The effective authority and strong staffs mustered in other parts of the Defense Department had to be developed in the Manpower Office. As it was, there were substantial gaps between the *policy* function of the Assistant Secretary for Manpower, the *research* function centered in DDRE, and the *operations* function in the three services. The staff involved in these activities knew of each other's existence; they met and discussed common problems; and they made use of each other's services. This system allowed for the exchange of research information and provided a variety of sources for research support. But these advantages did not compensate for the lack of a unified program in which the process of research was more cumulative and the means of applying it more systematic and deliberate. The conscious translation of research findings to meet policy and program requirements has been more effectively realized in other areas of defense organization where techniques of systems analysis have been applied.

Systems Analysis

Since 1945 fundamental changes have taken place in the organization of the defense establishment. The military services have lost much of their autonomy and been brought increasingly under the

[50] Quoted in *Journal of the Armed Forces*, March 18, 1967, pp. 1 ff.

control of the central staff of the Department of Defense. There were several reasons for this: the failure of military leaders, involved in inter-service rivalries, to agree on comprehensive strategic programs throughout the late 1940's and 1950's; the need for increasing political control over military operations; the importance of civilian expertise in the development and management of major new weapons systems; and the need for centralized budgeting as defense expenditures began to claim a larger share of the total federal budget and to have a greater effect on the national economy, the government's fiscal program, and the broad areas of national resource allocation.

This reorganization took place gradually. The National Security Act of 1947 first created a Secretary of National Defense, who presided over the three military departments and bound them into a kind of loose federation. The Secretary of National Defense had little overall authority, however, and civilian secretaries of the departments little influence over the military chiefs. Following the recommendations of the first Secretary of National Defense, James Forrestal, Congress amended the Act in 1949 by establishing the Department of Defense and giving the Secretary augmented authority and staff, especially in the field of budget management. The reorganization plan of 1953 created new positions at the level of assistant secretary, and the Reorganization Act of 1958 gave the Secretary and his immediate staff authority over unified military commands and control over research and development. Military functions thus came to be directed by a central agency while retaining the traditional roles and the internal structure of the three separate services.

Robert McNamara, appointed Secretary of Defense in 1961, completed the process of centralization. Expanding on the authority granted under the 1958 Act, he instituted new methods of budgeting and programming that were based on the purposes of military operations rather than on the roles played by the individual services on "land, sea and air." Budgets were planned according to the requirements of undertaking general or limited war through unified commands. Also, McNamara further consolidated supportive operations by creating new central systems like the Defense Intelligence Agency and the Defense Supply Agency.

Changes in defense management, especially since 1961, have relied heavily on the techniques of what has come to be called systems analysis. From one point of view, it might be said that systems analysis has been the instrument by which the goals of the Reorganization Act of 1958 have been achieved. But, more broadly, the steps in the defense reorganization—from the National Security Act of 1947 through McNamara's centralized management—were necessitated by certain strategic and political requirements. There were, by and large, three such requirements: to subordinate military plans and operations to the objectives of foreign policy; to insure innovation in, and adaptation to, technological change; and to relate large expenditures of funds to policy objectives. Each step in the reorganization process since 1945 has been directed towards one or another of these aims; and systems analysis, introduced after 1961, provided a kind of internal cement to bind together the accumulated organizational adjustments.

Systems analysis grew out of earlier work in operations research during the war. Operations research deals with short-range, somewhat circumscribed problems, with fairly limited and largely quantifiable variables and identifiable goals. Systems analysis—identified as a "style" as much as a standardized method —deals with more complex problems where the objectives are more ambiguous, the variables more numerous and less susceptible to precise measurement, and the general parameters often murky and sprawling. Indeed, there is some question about how far systems analysis can be applied. In solving very complex problems, systems analysis may produce results that are no more systematic or precise than those obtained by using other more traditional techniques. Such an observation is not meant to diminish the importance of systems analysis but only to suggest that its intellectual heritage is long and honorable.

Herbert Simon has pointed out that operations research and systems analysis hark back to the scientific management of Frederick Taylor early in the century.[51] In its application to problems of government, systems analysis might also be said to be a modern

51 Herbert A. Simon, *The New Science of Management Decision* (New York: Harper & Row, 1960), p. 14.

version, complete with computer, of Goodnow's scientific public administration of the same period. A basic tenet of Goodnow's and those that followed him was the separation of policy and administration. The task of administrators was to develop the most efficient methods possible to achieve the goals decided on by the policy-makers. And when the Institute for Government Research, a predecessor of the Brookings Institution, was first established, it defined its role as "a technical staff agency" available to government. The purpose of systems analysis is somewhat the same: to clarify and, if possible, to expand the "options" open to policy-makers without attempting to influence their decisions. However, any analysis of "options" is bound to have an effect on policy decisions; there is no such thing as a completely "objective" administration, whether it employs systems analysis or the earlier techniques of scientific management.

Another precedent for the use of systems analysis is to be found in the concept of the "policy sciences" articulated shortly after the Second World War by Harold Lasswell and his associates. The field of military affairs is, in essence, multi-disciplinary: it is, if you will, a "problem" or "policy" field, as Lasswell defined it.[52] Physical scientists, engineers, and social scientists were initially called into the defense establishment to bring the expertise of their own disciplines to bear on military problems. However, in making their full contribution, which often went beyond narrowly prescribed operational limits, specialists in any one field had to grasp hold of material in other fields and to develop a capacity to deal with the total military system or policy area. Consequently they shifted back and forth over disciplinary lines. And physical scientists, mathematicians, and engineers made significant contributions in certain areas of social science, particularly those that had to do with the strategic and managerial implications of their work on weapons systems. The techniques they used, by and large, were those of operations research and systems analysis. Among the social scientists, economists added

[52] See Harold Lasswell, *et al.*, *The Policy Sciences* (Stanford: Stanford University Press, 1951).

methods of measuring effectiveness through comparative cost analysis.

Economists played a major role in the application of systems analysis to defense management, especially as defense issues could be reduced to essential budgetary questions. But political analysts also had an effect on the direction of defense reorganization. Their interest in military affairs was based on their growing recognition of the role of force in international politics; it was aroused first by the school of political realism in the 1930's, then by the war itself and by the cold war that began in the late 1940's. The atomic bomb, the decision to develop the hydrogen bomb, the communist victory in China, the Korean War, the establishment of NATO —all these events compelled specialists in international relations to recognize that military institutions were a fundamental factor in shaping foreign policy. By the late 1950's there was quite a literature on the subject. Writers analyzed the role of force in world politics in the nuclear age, pointed out that military functions should be brought into line with political objectives, and called for organizational and managerial changes to make the government more responsive to the new strategic situation.[53]

The National Security Council was established in 1947 in order to insure the alignment of military force with political purposes. The Council, however, was an instrument of presidential power and could be used only at the discretion of the President. The Office of Secretary of National Defense was created under the same act for much the same purpose. The problem of political control over the military became of increasing importance as political analysts began to examine the implications of the policy of deterrence and the nature of limited war. One of the most influential books written in the 1950's was *Nuclear Weapons and Foreign Policy* by Henry A. Kissinger. Kissinger called for "a doctrine which defines the purpose of [weapons systems] and the kind of war in which they are to be employed." He sharply criticized the existing policy and organizational processes and recommended a

53 See Gene M. Lyons and Louis Morton, *Schools for Strategy* (New York: Frederick A. Praeger, 1965), pp. 35–47.

reorganization of the defense establishment along functional lines. It was to be divided into two basic units, "the Strategic Force and the Tactical Force," to reflect "the realities of the strategic situation."[54] What he recommended was in fact accomplished by the adoption of a system of unified commands under the Reorganization Act of 1958 and by the procedures for program planning and budgeting instituted in 1961.

Over the years, defense reorganization has thus been shaped by a variety of intellectual criticisms, as well as by the nature of political and managerial problems. Systems analysis has been the operational tool of reorganization, however. In its present form, it derives most directly from two sources: first, the efforts to increase the effectiveness of offensive and defensive weapons systems during the Second World War; and second, the experience of specialized institutions set up to serve the military in the postwar years by developing ways to adjust to technological changes. The first major American operations research group was organized during the war to study anti-submarine warfare using techniques that had earlier been developed by the British. Working under the direction of the Chief of Naval Operations, analysts devised deployment patterns that gave convoys maximum protection against German submarines. They also worked out operating procedures that reduced the vulnerability of naval vessels to attack from *Kamikaze* planes in the war against Japan. When the war was over, the Navy undertook to keep the researchers together under a contract with the Massachusetts Institute of Technology. The contract established the Operations Evaluation Group (OEG) to carry out operational studies in anti-submarine tactics, anti-aircraft gunnery, guided missiles, radar, and atomic warfare.

While OEG's work was largely concentrated on immediate operational problems, a related Naval Warfare Analysis Group organized in the mid-1950's was concerned with broader problems of a politico-military nature. These included an evaluation of the technological progress of Soviet military forces and a projection of the different kinds of war the Navy would have to fight

54 Henry A. Kissinger, *Nuclear Weapons and Foreign Policy* (New York: Harper & Bros., 1957), p. 403 and pp. 419–420.

in the future. In 1962 both OEG and the Analysis Group, as well as the Institute of Naval Studies established several years earlier, were consolidated into one organization, the Center for Naval Analyses administered for the Navy by the Franklin Institute of Philadelphia. So, what had begun as a limited operations research unit during the war, by the mid-1960's had developed into an agency for long-range naval planning made up of physicists, engineers, economists, and political scientists, and dealing with economic questions of logistics and resource allocation as well as political factors of strategic doctrine.[55]

In the Army there had been no application of operations research during the war. In 1948, however, as part of the Army's reassessment of its research and development organization, it established the Operations Research Office (ORO) under contract with the Johns Hopkins University. While ORO's work was largely concerned with the use of weapons and tactical operations, it was called on to assist the Army on other questions in which "hardware" was not involved. These included studies of the Army's role in foreign assistance programs and psychological warfare, as well as Project Clear, the study of racial integration in the Army during the Korean war. In 1961 the Army broke off the arrangement with Johns Hopkins and set up ORO as a separate non-profit organization with a new name, the Research Analysis Corporation (RAC). In essence, the Army's relations with RAC were similar to those it had had with ORO. The RAC annual work program was subject to review by an Army committee just as ORO's program had been. But where ORO had also been subject to review by a university-wide committee at Johns Hopkins, RAC had a board of trustees made up principally of businessmen, industrialists, and retired military officers which was ultimately responsible for the quality of its work.[56]

The expertise available to the separate military services through non-profit and industrial contractors was one of the elements that put the Office of the Secretary of Defense and the Joint Chiefs of Staff at a disadvantage in deciding on competing

[55] Lyons and Morton, *op. cit.*, pp. 240–243.
[56] *Ibid.*, pp. 243–245.

weapons systems in the late 1940's and early 1950's. There were, of course, other elements of weakness as well: the Secretary's lack of authority; the lack of specialized staff; and the fact that the Chiefs were also heads of their services and so frequently at odds and unable to come to agreement. In late 1948, however, Secretary of Defense Forrestal established the Weapons Systems Evaluation Group (WSEG) under the Joint Chiefs of Staff to review and evaluate service proposals for the development of new weapons systems. And in 1956, acting on the recommendations of the second Hoover Commission, the Institute of Defense Analyses (IDA) was established to give WSEG the same kind of outside technical support that OEG gave the Navy, ORO the Army, and RAND the Air Force. IDA was initially set up as a consortium of universities, including M.I.T., California Institute of Technology, Case Institute of Technology, and Stanford University, which provided members for its board of trustees. And, as in the case of other such contract organizations, IDA's activities soon expanded beyond weapons evaluation to include broad studies of a politico-military and economic nature, not only for WSEG, but also for ARPA, the Office of the Assistant Secretary for International Security Affairs and, once it was established in 1961, the Arms Control and Disarmament Agency.[57]

Of all the military contract organizations, however, the RAND Corporation has taken the broadest approach to military problems, has given its staff the greatest amount of latitude in exploring political and economic issues, and has had the most influence on defense reorganization and strategic planning. The study of overseas air bases begun early in the 1950's demonstrated the capacity of RAND to move from the confines of a limited operational problem to a military issue of the highest national importance. Indeed, it was this study, together with other RAND studies on limited war and civil defense, that created a good deal of intellectual ferment inside and outside the government; for it challenged the doctrine of "massive retaliation" followed by the Eisenhower Administration and prepared the way for the adop-

[57] *Ibid.*, pp. 252–257.

tion of a strategy of graduated deterrence by the Kennedy and Johnson Administrations in the 1960's.[58]

It was in RAND, moreover, that Charles Hitch and his colleagues in the Economics Division developed the system of functional budgets and "cost-effectiveness" that provided McNamara with the instruments that he needed to control the defense establishment when he became Secretary of Defense in 1961. In the study of overseas air bases and other projects, RAND analysts had been one of the major groups working to extend the techniques of operations research more broadly into the study of large "systems." Hitch now sought to extend advanced economic analysis in the same way in order to answer three questions: how much of the national wealth should be allocated to national defense? how should that amount be divided among military functions? and how can one insure the most effective use of the funds allocated? These questions were provoked by the obvious inadequacies of the system that had been in operation since the end of the war. The military budget had essentially been made up by totaling the estimates that came from the three services. These estimates, in turn, had been developed on the basis of the roles and missions of the services as determined by the services themselves. Usually the total neither provided for a comprehensive and integrated strategy nor kept within the budgetary limits which the President felt compelled to set. The process of cutting the service estimates down to size was then a matter of internal bargaining rather than a systematic evaluation against operational objectives.

In trying to remedy this situation, Hitch and his colleagues put forward this argument:

> Strategy, technology, and economy are not three independent considerations to be assigned appropriate weights, but interdependent elements of the same problem. Strategies are *ways* of *using* budgets or resources to achieve military objectives. Technology defines the *possible* strategies. The economic problem is to choose that strategy, including equipment and everything else necessary to implement it, which is most efficient (maximizes the attainment of

[58] *Ibid.*, pp. 246–252; also Smith, *op. cit.*

the objective with the given resources) or economical (minimizes the cost of achieving the given objective)—the strategy which is most efficient also being the most economical.[59]

In 1961, Hitch became Defense Comptroller under McNamara and instituted the Planning-Programming-Budgeting System (PPBS) to establish links between military planning and resource allocation. The new system was organized not along the lines of the traditional roles of the three services, but in terms of military functions, such as general war, limited war, and research and development. It also had a planning cycle of five years, subject to annual review and adjustment in accordance with the congressional requirements for annual appropriations.[60] The purpose of PPBS was not only to relate costs more closely to functions, but also to provide a continual evaluation of alternative choices in achieving any given goal. Thus, proposals for the development of new weapons systems would be reviewed for their contribution to military functions and their relationship to existing systems, and compared with alternative means of gaining similar objectives. The whole process, however, depended on projecting costs that were not only economic but frequently political and social in nature and thus less susceptible to the kind of quantification that was required. Thus PPBS became subject to criticism; the military claimed that "effectiveness" was almost exclusively reduced to "cost" factors and that other factors, including military experience, were neglected. In response, the PPBS analysts insisted that the system was no more than a managerial tool that did not compel policy-makers to choose any one course of action but only gave them a clearer picture of the choices available to them.[61]

In Congress, too, there were suspicions about the "systems" experts, suspicions that their methods could be used for both good and evil and that the commodity—experience—that con-

---

[59] Charles J. Hitch and Roland N. McKean, *The Economics of Defense in the Nuclear Age* (Cambridge: Harvard University Press, 1960), p. 3.

[60] See Charles J. Hitch, "Plans, Programs, and Budgets in the Department of Defense," *Operations Research*, Vol. 11, No. 1 (1963), pp. 1–17.

[61] For Hitch's response to critics, see Charles J. Hitch, *Decision-Making for Defense* (Berkeley, University of California Press, 1965), pp. 65–78.

gressmen, like the military, cherish as a tool of analysis and judgment, would be relegated to a low place in policy-making. This was illustrated by a staff memorandum prepared as a guide for hearings on PPBS held by the Senate Subcommittee on National Security and International Operations in 1967 and 1968.

> in Defense the benefits of the PPB system have been overplayed by its proponents. . . . It is not a statistical litmus paper, scientifically sorting good project from bad. It may be used as easily to rationalize a decision as to make a rational choice. It is no substitute for experience and judgment, though men of experience and judgment may find it helpful.[62]

The application of systems analysis to problems involving critical variables of human behavior is not without its hazards. The approach may often require that, for purposes of analysis and comparison, weights be given to different sets of attitudes or human values. These weights may be reasonable and plausible but nonetheless arbitrary, given a paucity of clear experimental evidence to make them any more authoritative. What is hazardous is the temptation to believe that the arbitrary weight—however reasonable and plausible—is nonetheless valid in and of itself because of the rigorous framework within which it is being analyzed. And, to compound the error, there may be pressure to reject or reinterpret evidence that may suggest the contrary. Thus, in a relationship of deterrence, the "intentions" of a potential enemy—and, in a conflict situation, the effect of bombing on enemy morale—become subjects full of controversy in which new evidence or new views on old evidence has to storm the gates of official position with the analysts standing by to protect their professional reputations, their bureaucratic autonomy and, perhaps, their ideological predilections.

The task, of course, is to capitalize on the potential contribution of systems analysis to policy-making while developing safeguards against these hazards. And, indeed, studies to develop or utilize systems analysis have been extended beyond the research organiza-

---

62 *Planning-Programming-Budgeting,* Subcommittee on National Security and International Operations, Committee on Government Operations, U.S. Senate, 90th Congress, 1st Session, 1967, "Initial Memorandum," p. 3.

tions of the defense establishment into the core of planning and operating functions. Within the services, RAC, the Center for Naval Analyses, and RAND operate in direct relation to military planning staffs. RAND and IDA also deal directly with the planning units of the Joint Chiefs of Staff and the Office of the Assistant Secretary for Defense for International Security Affairs. Systems analysis is also integrated into the work of the Office of the Comptroller to support budgetary operations. And special studies are carried out for the Secretary of Defense by a newly established Office of Assistant Secretary for Systems Analysis. In the process, research too is influenced by systems analysis because so many researchers are concentrated in the military-supported non-profit institutes.

The effect of this integration is to provide linkages between the research, policy, and operations functions, the kinds of linkages that are largely missing in the field of military manpower and training. This is, for that matter, a major contribution of systems analysis to meeting a problem that was emphasized at least as far back as *Recent Social Trends*. Also, in its application to complex operational problems, systems analysis opens up new areas for research. Alain Enthoven, one of the major figures in systems analysis, points out:

> [It] includes the application of modern methods of quantitative analysis, including Economic Theory, Mathematical Statistics, Mathematical Operations Research, and various techniques known as Decision Theory. . . . one of the opportunities that systems analysis offers for creative work is seeking ways of giving valid measurements to things previously thought to be unmeasurable.[63]

In calling for the measurement of the "unmeasurable"—so often the "unmeasurable" behavior of people—systems analysis is a major factor in stimulating both basic and applied social science research in the government. It is also a major factor in stimulating new methods for relating social science research to government programs and policy processes. Systems analysis identifies areas where research is required and provides continuing program

[63] *Ibid.*, Part 2, p. 75.

evaluation to test the application of research results. Its broad significance, moreover, became increasingly evident when, in the summer of 1965, the President ordered that the Planning-Programming-Budgeting System, developed in the Defense Department, be adopted throughout the federal government.

Project Camelot

By the mid-1960's social science research was supported by a complex system of organizations within the defense establishment; and, largely owing to the application of systems analysis, it was used not only to solve limited problems of personnel selection and training but also to investigate basic issues of national security. At this time, too, there was a new set of problems to contend with: the political and military instability in the developing nations of Asia, Africa, and Latin America, progressively dramatized by the crisis in the Congo after the withdrawal of the Belgians, the victory of Castro in Cuba, and the eruption of full-scale fighting in Vietnam.

As a matter of policy the United States was committed to assist the developing nations in their desire for economic and social construction. But many of these nations were weakened by internal struggles; and there was constant danger of a military confrontation of the great powers through their support of competing camps. Even as the cold war between the Soviet Union and the United States changed into the delicate politics of coexistence under the impact of mutual deterrence, their basic disagreement on the future of the international system frequently caused them to take sides in the internal conflicts of the developing nations. But their control over the arenas in which they competed was often challenged by the forces of independent nationalism and, in Asia, by the growing power of communist China, now equipped with nuclear weapons.

In an effort to understand the changes taking place in developing countries, the military sponsored various social science projects. One of these, Project Camelot, provoked a storm of political controversy in 1965. Designed as an unclassified study of social change in South America, it was funded under the Army's broad program of research in the problems of insurgency in developing areas of the world. Perhaps inevitably, the nature of the Project's sponsorship was confused in discussions between American researchers and South American social scientists; and the U.S. embassy in Chile, one of the countries visited by members of the research team, was not fully informed of the Project's purpose and scope. Once the sponsorship of the Project was known, Latin Americans suspected that it was a front for U.S. intelligence activities, and their suspicions were exploited by anti-American factions. Indignation ran high in the Latin American press and among intellectuals in the universities. And the total ignorance of the Project by the U.S. embassy only compounded the confusion. As a result, Project Camelot was cancelled, and the State Department instituted procedures to review all government-sponsored social science research abroad for its possible effects on foreign policy.[64]

Project Camelot raised questions about the fundamental objectives of American foreign policy and, for the social scientist, questions as to how far he was responsible for the uses to which his research was put. Though the Project itself was conceived as a broad study of social change, it was financed by funds assigned to the Army for the purpose of preparing and supporting counterinsurgency operations in Latin America, Africa, and Asia. The assumptions behind the Army mission were several: that insurgency forces were often supported by communist powers; that, in such cases, insurgency was a threat to both internal security and international stability; that the United States might have to intervene, either by giving military assistance to the government in power or by using its own troops; and that it was thus essential to understand the economic, social, and political conditions that could lead to insurgent movements.

Project Camelot provoked a good deal of discussion and dissension in a fairly circumscribed circle of congressmen, govern-

---

[64] For a review of some of the basic documents on Project Camelot and related critical writings, see Irving Louis Horowitz (ed.), *The Rise and Fall of Project Camelot* (Cambridge: The M.I.T. Press, 1967).

ment officials, and academic researchers. But such discussions were part of a broader political debate, a debate on the justification for United States military intervention in the crises of underdeveloped countries. After the Dominican Republican affair in 1965 and the escalation of the war in Vietnam, any such military action was a matter of grave political concern. And what concerned many social scientists was the extent to which they were accepting and supporting the premises of official policy when they undertook military-sponsored research, no matter how basic the investigation and how professional and permissive the conditions of military support.

The problems to which Project Camelot was addressed were fundamental: the nature of social change, the factors of instability, the causes of violence. Moreover, they were problems that American social scientists had found critical for study since the war, as they began to refine their techniques and broaden their range of inquiry to include a variety of cultural settings. In itself, Project Camelot was a highly ambitious undertaking with enormous potential for adding to the understanding of social change. But the political circumstances under which it was launched were an embarrassment, to say the least, and made necessary a serious reassessment of the aims of cross-cultural research and the relations between social scientists and the American government.

CHAPTER VI

FOREIGN AFFAIRS

THE DOCTRINE of "containment" that dominated American foreign policy for some two decades emerged with the Truman Doctrine and the Marshall Plan in 1947. It was based largely on an analysis of Soviet behavior by George Kennan, who emphasized that "the political personality of Soviet power as we know it today is the product of ideology and circumstances." In his famous article on the sources of Soviet conduct, Kennan acknowledged the difficulty of weighing the relative influence of "ideology and circumstances" in Soviet policy-making. He nonetheless insisted on making the attempt, and in doing so employed the traditional tools of historical analysis, experienced insight, and balanced intuition. He concluded that the Soviet Union had to be viewed "as a rival, not a partner."

> Soviet policy is highly flexible, and . . . Soviet society may well contain deficiencies which will eventually weaken its own total potential. . . . [This state of affairs] would of itself warrant the United States entering with reasonable confidence upon a policy of firm containment, designed to confront the Russians with unalterable counter-force at every point where they show signs of encroaching upon the interests of a peaceful and stable world.[1]

While the Kennan thesis was generally accepted as a basis for American policy and proved to be sharply perceptive, it left

---

[1] Republished in George F. Kennan, *American Diplomacy 1900–1950* (Chicago: University of Chicago Press, 1951), Part II. For insight into the role Kennan played in the development of policy, see George F. Kennan, *Memoirs* (New York: Harper & Row, 1968), pp. 313 ff.

many questions unanswered. At a meeting of social scientists sponsored by the RAND Corporation in the fall of 1947, a series of projects was planned for the purpose of testing and following up the assumptions behind Kennan's analysis. These included a study of Soviet diplomatic techniques, an operational analysis of Russian foreign trade, and a comparative study of the reactions of ruling groups to internal pressures in several major countries as well as the Soviet Union. In a summary of the discussion, which was designed to map out a social science program for the RAND Corporation, two fields of investigation were recommended for a better understanding of "decision-making and the social structure in the USSR." The first was "clarifying the motivations of the decisions and policies followed by the Russian political and military elite"; and the second was "analyzing internal weaknesses in the social structure of the USSR." With regard to the second project, it was suggested: "the Kennan policy . . . is justified only if it is correct to assume the existence of internal weaknesses in the USSR which can be exploited for American aims. The task is therefore one of localizing actual and potential tensions within the elite, among rival sub-elites, and between elite and mass."[2]

The approach of the social scientists was highly empirical. What they did was to accept the Kennan thesis, but to recommend that its assumptions be tested through continuing research and analysis, and that a working model of the Soviet system be developed as a guide to strategic and tactical moves. A considerable amount of military-supported research was devoted to this very objective. The RAND program, for example, resulted in the publication over the years of studies such as *The Operational Code of the Politburo* by Nathan Leites, *Smolensk under Soviet Rule* by Merle Fainsod, *Soviet Military Doctrine* by Raymond L. Garthoff, *The Organizational Weapon* by Philip Selznick, and *The Real National Income of Soviet Russia Since 1928* by Abram Bergson.[3] Similarly, a number of studies of the Russian national character were completed under the Office of Naval Research project on

[2] "Conference of Social Scientists," R-106, The RAND Corporation (Santa Monica, California, June 1948), p. x.

[3] Bruce L. R. Smith, *The RAND Corporation* (Cambridge: Harvard University Press, 1966), pp. 108–109.

"culture at a distance," carrying on the work begun by Ruth Benedict in her wartime study of Japan.[4] And at Harvard the Project on the Soviet Social System, organized at the Russian Research Center in the early 1950's and largely financed through the Air Force Human Resources Research Institute, was an effort "to assess the social and psychological strengths and weaknesses of the Soviet system."[5]

In contrast with the traditional political analysis of Kennan, the work at RAND, at the Office of Naval Research, and at Harvard was part of a "new" social science that was more empirical and behavioral in emphasis. In the Harvard project, for example, the major source of information was a series of interviews and questionnaires administered to refugees from the Soviet Union in 1950 and 1951. This source presented the researchers with the problem of compensating for bias and distortion. Their method— vastly different from Kennan's—was to obtain a sufficiently large sample of respondents to be able to identify deviant behavior, to design questions that would test for consistency, and to compare their collection of emigré opinions with other sources in the field of Soviet studies. Their work showed, however, how traditional and empirical methodologies could confirm each other's conclusions about important questions of national policy. The broad interest in Soviet studies through the 1950's has been described by Daniel Bell:

> In the last ten years there has been, presumably, a new sophistication, and an extraordinary amount of research and writing on Soviet society, particularly in the United States. Some of this research has come from Russian defectors; most of it has been done in special institutes set up by universities under government or foundation research grants in an effort to obtain reliable knowledge about Soviet behavior. We have seen, too, the entry of new disciplines—anthropology, sociology, and psychiatry—into the study of political phenomena. In some instances these newer ap-

---

[4] See Margaret Mead and Rhoda Metraux (eds.), *The Study of Culture at a Distance* (Chicago: University of Chicago Press, 1952).

[5] See Raymond A. Bauer, Alex Inkeles, and Clyde Kluckhohn, *How the Soviet System Works* (Cambridge: Harvard University Press, 1956).

proaches have claimed to provide a total understanding of Soviet behavior; in others, to supplement existing explanation.[6]

Like the Kennan analysis, much academic and government-financed research on communism dealt with the complexities of the Soviet system, the stress and strain in the struggle between ideology and national interests, and the economic and psychological pressures on authoritarian leadership. Nonetheless, the language of political rhetoric and, more often than not, of official government policy, remained fixed on notions of a monolithic communist system and an unchanging and unchangeable communist leadership. These notions persisted in government and in society in general despite the death of Stalin, the struggle for leadership in the Kremlin, the uprisings in Eastern Europe, and the emergence of communist China as a rival to the Soviet Union as a center for communist strategy. Research that questioned popular myths about communism often had less direct effect on policy than more polemical writing that stressed the significance of ideology in the communist world, even to the exclusion of all other motives.

Yet it must be admitted that research on communism did not point in one obvious and unambiguous direction and that "soviet-ologists" were no more a "bloc" than the system they were studying. In the mix between "ideology and circumstances," to use Kennan's words, there were no sharp distinctions or reliable guidelines. Even where the force of "circumstances" was given heavy emphasis, ample consideration had to be given to ideology as a motivating factor. For ideology was an important political tool in the hands of communist ideologues. Every action had to be justified in ideological terms no matter what the motives behind it. It was thus often difficult to judge what the communists meant as opposed to what they said, especially when the decision-making processes in Moscow and Peking were shrouded in mystery. It was even more difficult to justify diplomatic and military actions to Congress and the public in terms that seemed at variance with the direct

---

[6] Daniel Bell, *The End of Ideology* (Glencoe, Illinois: The Free Press, 1960), p. 300.

challenge that the communists were throwing down. The power of anti-communism in domestic politics served as an obstacle to the full use of research on communism in the policy process.

A most careful and realistic calculation of communist intentions became increasingly important, however, as the military capacity of the Soviets grew in the late 1950's and the superpowers confronted one another in a relationship of mutual deterrence. Here the work of the "sovietologists" became critically relevant. What was the power position of the Soviet military? What factions in the Kremlin hierarchy could be counted on to support a cautious approach to a military crisis? What would be the impact of internal economic demands on Soviet assistance to developing countries? How far could the Soviet leadership be pushed without losing prestige at home? What, if anything, could be done to insure the greatest rationality in communist decision-making? Each of these questions could be answered by a set of rigid assumptions about the nature of communism, by vague and general impressions about changes in the Soviet Union, or by a systematic and rigorous evaluation of Soviet society and the relations between Moscow and the communist movements in other parts of the world. Social scientists were to attempt such an evaluation. But it was questionable how far their work was to influence the decisions of those who made policy.

Foreign Area Research

The study of communist societies was part of the broader study of social change that went through several distinct stages after the Second World War. The great need during the war had been for information—information about the customs of the peoples of the Pacific islands, the transportation system in Europe, the economic capacity of Japan, the location of religious missions in Southeast Asia. One of the few organized university enterprises that could begin to meet such wartime needs was the Cross-Cultural Survey at Yale (later called the Human Relations Area Files), set up by the anthropologist George P. Murdock in the late 1930's to collect and compare information on the primitive

tribes of the world. The Survey, in cooperation with the Ethnogeographic Board at the Smithsonian Institution and later with
Navy support, was expanded to provide more than anthropological data and to serve as a basic source of information on the Pacific area during the war and during the Navy's postwar administration of Micronesia.[7] It served, more broadly, as a pioneering
prototype for the systematic collection of cross-cultural information.

In colleges and universities during the war, area study programs were instituted which combined language training with
geographic and historical studies for prospective civil affairs officers. Before this time such programs had largely been limited to
the study of ancient cultures and civilizations that had little relevance to the contemporary scene. They were usually conducted
by anthropologists and archaeologists, with occasional collaboration from historians and professors of literature. Few sociologists, psychologists, or political scientists were involved. What
distinguished the wartime area study programs was their emphasis
on contemporary political, economic, and social factors in conjunction with cultural and language studies. Japanese and European
programs were organized in anticipation of occupation duties in
those areas. And, in recognition of the new power position of the
Soviet Union, centers for research on Russia and communism were
set up after the war with both private foundation and government support.

The area programs continued to expand throughout the postwar period, as the private foundations became more concerned
about international affairs and more willing to advance funds for
their study. In this way Middle East study centers were established in the wake of the crisis in that area in the late 1940's; Asian
study programs were added to the older centers of sinology as the
communist victory in China created problems for American policy; similarly the granting of independence to nations in Africa in
the 1950's forced scholars to shift their attention from ancient

[7] Wendell Clark Bennett, *The Ethnogeographic Board*, Miscellaneous Collections, Vol. 107, No. 1, Smithsonian Institution (Washington, D.C., 1947),
pp. 6–7.

tribal customs to contemporary developments; and, finally, the success and machinations of Fidel Castro in Cuba reawakened the historic but sporadic interest of Americans in the problems of Latin America.[8]

In 1958 the National Defense Education Act gave added support to area and language programs and, indeed, implanted them more deeply into the educational system by granting funds for the teaching of foreign languages and cultures in secondary schools. By then, however, social scientists were already beginning to concentrate less on particular geographic areas and to examine a wider range of social phenomena, chiefly by means of comparative studies. This intellectual shift was observable in the development of comparative political studies carried on under the auspices of the Social Science Research Council. The older tradition of comparative government was highly institutional in approach and largely concentrated on the United States and Europe. In the early 1950's political scientists and sociologists, many working through the Research Council's committees, began to enlarge the scope of their studies: to include not only "government" but also "politics," not only Europe but also other parts of the world, and to employ not only the time-honored methods of library research but also the new techniques of survey research and depth interviewing.[9] This broader outlook gave new impetus to the empirical and theoretical approaches in social science that were developed after the war and, in particular, to the expansion of direct field investigations.

Scholars interested in field work were able to obtain funds through government-sponsored exchange programs under the Fulbright-Hayes Act and, later, the National Defense Education Act, and the foundation-sponsored Foreign Area Fellowship Program. The social scientists of this generation were thus freed from

<hr />

8 See K. H. Silvert, "Development and International Politics," in Gene M. Lyons (ed.), *America: Purpose and Power* (Chicago: Quadrangle Books, 1965), pp. 244–254.

9 For the development of the Council's study and publication program, see the *Annual Reports*, Social Science Research Council (New York), onwards from 1954, the year when the Committee on Comparative Politics was established.

the confines of the library and given the opportunity to undertake empirical research abroad. They were also politically free to circulate in many parts of the world during the 1950's. With the death of Stalin and the instituting of educational and cultural exchanges between the United States and the Soviet Union, travel into Russia and Eastern Europe, while restricted, was at last possible. The way was open for a small number of scholars to add personal observation to the information gathered from secondary sources such as official statistics and pronouncements or from visitors, refugees, and others who had travelled beyond the "iron curtain."

In Asia and Africa, American social scientists found unusual opportunities in that moment of transition between empire and independence, between the loosening of colonial rule and the hardening of indigenous nationalism. Nationalism was rife and American scholarship provided an instrument through which the struggle for independence against colonial powers could be chronicled and explained to the world. Budding young politicians exposed themselves to the prying questionnaires and surveys of American social scientists with unusual frankness and became more cautious only later, after they assumed the power and responsibility of public office. The Camelot affair marked a change in the reception given to American social scientists abroad and also, to some degree, a change in their relationship to government programs.

One of the complicating elements in the case of Project Camelot was its sponsorship by the Department of the Army. However broadly conceived the project was in terms of the study of social change, its military auspices related it to military purposes rather than to the broader purposes of foreign policy or the growth of social science. During the congressional investigation of Camelot, Congressman Peter Frelinghuysen observed:

> we have never had a clear picture of how and why the Defense Department gets so much money and how it is spent. I would think, if the State Department is going to exercise its responsibilities more vigorously, that it would really need to be in charge of this money, rather than the military. . . . the military services should be allowed to develop reasonable programs of social science research related to military needs. But this research would

seem in many cases not to have any direct military significance, but very considerable foreign policy implications.[10]

The fact is that Project Camelot did have "military significance," though how direct it was may be a matter of opinion. The Army was involved in a number of military assistance programs in Latin America; it supported military civic action programs, and it was engaged in joint training ventures with Latin American military units through the Organization of American States as well as through bilateral arrangements. The management of these enterprises certainly required an understanding of various national histories and cultures. Mr. Frelinghuysen, however, correctly pointed out that such research had "very considerable foreign policy implications" and that it was equally relevant to the activities of civilian foreign affairs agencies, including the Department of State. He raised his point, moreover, during the testimony of Secretary of State Dean Rusk, who had already acknowledged the validity of the committee's earlier observation that "the bulk of Government research in foreign affairs is not controlled or directed by the people who conduct U.S. foreign policy."[11]

Secretary Rusk also took pains to emphasize the problem of political sensitivity in connection with research overseas. He contrasted, for example, "research in such fields as demography and economics, in such fields as trade, where the situation is relaxed" to "subjects that are sensitive, particularly those matters which have to do with the political structure and political forces of a particular country." Although these sensitive matters were "most central in concern to us," he concluded that any examination of them would "have to occur within our own Government on a classified basis."[12] The sensitivity of "political" issues needed no elaboration; it was difficult to understand, however, why questions

---

10 *Behavioral Sciences and the National Security,* Report of and Hearings before Subcommittee on International Organizations and Movements, Committee on Foreign Affairs, House of Representatives, 89th Congress, 2nd Session, 1966, pp. 116–117.

11 *Ibid.,* p. 108.

12 *Ibid.,* p. 112.

of "demography" (population control?) and "economics" were less "sensitive" or, for that matter, less "political."

The Secretary here was guided not only by his personal judgment but also by the Department's experience in the use of research over the years. Research in the State Department centered on policy-oriented political analysis and the collection and evaluation of intelligence data by departmental officers in Washington and in American embassies abroad. This emphasis was explained by Thomas Hughes, the Director of the Department's Bureau of Intelligence and Research (INR), while testifying before a Senate committee in 1967.

> though many . . . departments and agencies invest a good deal more money in social science research than does the Department of State, it remains true that the Department did inherit and does have a substantial and experienced in-house capability for social science research and analysis. [This should be compared with other departments and agencies, notably the military, that] chose not to develop their own in-house research bureaus but rather to contract either with established private individuals and centers or with non-profit institutions set up specifically to serve the research needs of the agency.[13]

The difference, of course, was much more than a matter of "choice"; it was a matter of operating traditions, organizational developments, and staffing patterns.

The Department of Defense originally supported research in international affairs by outside experts so that the military could play an independent role in strategic planning. Those involved in defense reorganization encouraged this practice at the end of the war to insure that foreign policy be brought into line with military capability. It was part of a more general movement that also led to the establishment of the National Security Council, the use of foreign policy advisers in the Office of the Secretary of Defense, and the teaching of international relations in the National

---

[13] *National Foundation for the Social Sciences,* Hearings before Subcommittee on Government Research, Committee on Government Operations, U.S. Senate, 90th Congress, 1st Session, 1967, Part 1, p. 123.

War College and the senior educational institutions of the three military services. Within the defense establishment, research in connection with strategic doctrine was also sponsored by the individual services as one means of supporting their own roles and missions in a changing political and technological environment.

The military also found a use for social science research in contingency planning and, especially, in extending operations research and systems analysis to the whole process of military programming. Since military men lacked the knowledge and professional training required for this work, they had to rely on outside civilian expertise. And, to obtain it, they made use of the contract system that grew out of the weapons development program of the Second World War. The contract system gave them access to larger sections of the intellectual community than would have been the case had they set up internal research units exclusively. The establishment of non-profit research institutes, as an extension of the contract system, provided them with interdisciplinary teams to devote *continuing* attention to important problems and to look for the relevance of research findings to policy purposes. Finally, social scientists in the defense establishment shared some of the benefits of its enormous political power and profited from the high value accorded to the whole enterprise of scientific research. In turn, the military agencies benefited by this association, for they were introduced to the new trends in social science. Research in the State Department—and in the other civilian foreign affairs agencies—went through a quite different development.

The Department of State

The postwar research program in the State Department's Bureau of Intelligence and Research (INR) grew out of the wartime research and analysis group of the Office of Strategic Services and went through two phases. At first, and for a very brief period, special research units were attached to the geographic bureaus that made up the central core of the State Department's operating system. In the second phase, which has lasted from the late 1940's to the present, research was separated from operations by placing it in an autonomous Bureau. This separation was a recognition, as George Denney, the Deputy Director of INR, put it, of "two major approaches to the problems of foreign affairs": the "analytic, reflective, and speculative approach that balances all factors, tries to see all sides and sets forth the trends in the situation"; and "the action approach that seeks to impose some new pattern on the situation, that makes a decision and drives ahead." While separation thus freed researchers "from the immediate authority of the action user," some means had to be found that would insure close working relations between them and the geographic bureaus.[14]

Various linking mechanisms, both formal and informal, were devised for this purpose; and they are still in use today. At regular meetings conducted by the Secretary of State with his principal staff assistants, the Director of INR is responsible for briefing the top staff of the Department on the most recent intelligence information relating to the problems of American foreign policy. Indeed, INR is the Department's connection with the overall intelligence community, including the Central Intelligence Agency and the Defense Intelligence Agency, and it has to compare intelligence data from all sources to the information received every day from overseas embassies and consulates. Since much of this information is highly confidential, work in INR is often forced into classified and policy-oriented channels. These staff briefings are then augmented by written communications on special problems, by *ad hoc* analyses requested by the geographic bureaus, and by longer and more comprehensive analyses submitted regularly by INR staff.[15] The extent to which these studies serve to supplement operating analyses developed in the geographic bureaus greatly

---

[14] Statement by George C. Denney, Jr., Deputy Director of the Bureau of Intelligence and Research, in *Federal Research and Development Programs,* Hearings before Select Committee on Government Research, House of Representatives, 88th Congress, 1st Session, 1963, Part 1, pp. 185–188.

[15] Allan Evans, *Research in Action,* Publication 7964, Department and Foreign Service Series 133, Department of State (Washington, D.C., September 1966).

varies, however, and is highly dependent on informal relations between researchers and operators, as well as on the authority stamped on INR reports by the Secretary and his top staff.

The operating procedures and style of INR do much to explain the development of research as an internal function in the Department of State. Hughes's testimony throws light on this:

These research papers and informal responses [of the INR] meet conditions that are impossible to reconcile with the use of outside academic research facilities. It may be need for speed of response, or diplomatic sensitivity—nearly all these papers are classified —or the need for professional researchers who through daily association with policy officers understand the elements of their problems without extensive guidance.[16]

Early in the Kennedy Administration, however, INR began to contract for policy studies with scholars in universities and independent research organizations. Roger Hilsman, then Director of INR, led reorganization moves designed to make the Bureau more responsive to policy requirements or, as he put it, to get "just the right kind of crisp, taut, to-the-point analyses that were needed."[17] It was one of the changes made by the Kennedy Administration in a general attempt to eliminate the complex mechanisms of planning and follow-up attached to the National Security Council during the Eisenhower years, and to place more direct responsibility for the formulation and execution of foreign policy in the State Department. Hilsman's object was to make the maximum contribution to this move through INR and to bring into the process some of the best minds in the academic community.

The policy studies sponsored by INR have been funded at only about $125,000 a year and have run a gamut of issues from political development in individual countries to the future of regionalism in various parts of the world.[18] At least one former De-

---

16 *National Foundation for the Social Sciences, op. cit.,* p. 124.

17 Roger Hilsman, *To Move a Nation* (New York: Doubleday & Company, 1967), p. 72.

18 For a list of the studies during the first three years of the program, see *Government and Science: Review of the National Science Foundation,* Hearings before Subcommittee on Science, Research and Development, Committee on Science and Astronautics, House of Representatives, 89th Congress, 1st Session, 1965, Vol. II, No. 6, pp. 1291–1294.

partment officer has estimated that they generally have been of limited value to policy makers and operators and, because of their high policy orientation, were never intended to be contributions to the social sciences. They thus "failed to meet the standards and the needs of the Government or the academy."[19] Less harshly, Hughes has noted that "although . . . few of our contract studies have overfulfilled our hopes, none have been totally without value."[20] For Hilsman, the studies were a method of introducing the analytic approach from the outside research community into the Department through the INR. This task required a certain amount of aggressive leadership, for it affected the policy process at a number of sensitive points both within and outside the State Department. Normally INR has functioned only as a supporting agency operating within an approved routine, though with sufficient flexibility to work informally throughout the system and serve as a prod for more probing and comprehensive analysis. The policy-making function, to which Hilsman sought to contribute, is more formally centered in the Policy Planning Council, which may look to INR for support in the same way as the geographic bureaus do.

The Policy Planning Council (originally called the Policy Plannning Staff) was set up in 1947 by Secretary George C. Marshall to provide the long-range view in foreign affairs. The Council, however, has often been distracted from its primary purpose. "Planning staffs," as one observer has noted, "represent a flexible organizational resource."[21] In the case of the State Department, the Council has frequently been used in the management of crises, to support current but particularly important negotiations, and for whatever other immediate duties the Secretary has assigned to it. The amount of genuine planning done by members of the Council has thus depended on the value and support given to the planning

19 William J. Nagle, "Reflections after 3 years in the Foreign Affairs Contract Research World," in *International Education: Past, Present, Problems and Prospects,* Task Force on International Education, Committee on Education and Labor, House Document No. 527, House of Representatives, 89th Congress, 2nd Session, 1966, pp. 315–317.
20 *National Foundation for the Social Sciences, op. cit.,* p. 127.
21 Burton M. Sapin, *The Making of United States Foreign Policy* (Washington, D.C.: The Brookings Institution, 1966), p. 320.

process by the Secretary and on his willingness to insulate it from short-range projects. Robert Bowie, who served as planning head, has suggested that the Council faces a dilemma in deciding how much attention to give to long-range projections and basic concepts, on the one hand, and how much to current operations, on the other. But the fact is that, "for better or for worse, foreign policy becomes operative largely in specific decisions."[22] And there is no alternative to the Council's being heavily involved in operating problems, though its role is essentially different from that of the operating bureaus in viewing and evaluating individual issues in the global context of American foreign policy.

In the Policy Planning Council, as in INR and elsewhere in the State Department, relations with the outside research community are maintained through staffing and consultant arrangements rather than through sponsoring research. Members of both the Policy Planning Council and INR have frequently come from academic posts, usually in the fields of political science and international relations, and academicians have also served in various capacities as consultants to the Department. The INR External Research Office also seeks to maintain ties with the outside research community, principally through the collection and distribution of information on private and government-sponsored research on foreign affairs. Indeed, the External Research Office has become one of the major clearing houses for foreign affairs research information in the country, and its staff can identify those scholars whose research is relevant to any problem with which operating bureaus are dealing. However, it can do little more than make referrals and try to persuade operating and policy groups to make use of research. And this is no easy task, for there is little sympathy with the aims of research in the key Foreign Service corps that makes up the central staff of the Department.

The Foreign Service has always favored the "generalist" as opposed to the specialist and placed a high value on practical experience as opposed to study and analysis. This is not, of course,

---

[22] Robert R. Bowie, "The Secretary and the Development and Coordination of Policy," in Don K. Price (ed.), The Secretary of State (Englewood Cliffs, N.J.: Prentice-Hall, 1960), p. 70.

simply an American peculiarity—it is characteristic of most professional diplomatic services—nor does it mean that specialization, study, and analysis are completely rejected in the value system of the State Department and the Foreign Service. Indeed, the Foreign Service Act of 1946 gave considerable emphasis to the need for specialists and provided for internal study programs by the establishment of the Foreign Service Institute. But progress has been slow, so slow that in 1962 a Committee on Foreign Affairs Personnel, chaired by former Secretary of State Christian Herter, reiterated that "the problem of specialization has been acute in the Foreign Service . . . for many years" and called attention to the growing need for several kinds of experts, including "economists" and "social scientists . . . equipped to deal with problems of social and political development in the newer nations."[23] Important staff changes along these lines might go far in creating a more receptive climate for research in the State Department than exists today. But if the experience of twenty years is any guide, such changes are apt to be modest at best, as witness the description of the typical Foreign Service Officer's operating style given in a study prepared for the Herter Committee: "His style for analyzing information tends to be impressionistic and intuitive rather than formal, methodical, and statistical."[24]   ·

The intellectual perspective of the State Department stands in sharp contrast to the empirical and theoretical orientations that have developed in the social sciences since the Second World War. This may be because the present State Department staff is of an older generation, trained in the more historical and instituitional approaches to international affairs. In congressional testimony in 1966, the political scientist Gabriel Almond characterized the State Department as "a conservative, humanistic institution, dominated by a foreign service which is trained largely in the law, in history, in the humanistic disciplines." He also wished that the "Department of State was more familiar, more receptive

---

[23] *Personnel for the New Diplomacy,* Report of the Committee on Foreign Affairs Personnel (Washington, D.C., December 1962), pp. 54–55.
[24] Regis Walther, *Orientations and Behavioral Styles of Foreign Service Officer* (New York: Carnegie Endowment for International Peace, 1965), p. 16.

to some of the possibilities of the social sciences than it now is."[25] The Department's conservatism may change with the appointment of a new crop of officers and top planners who have been brought up in the new school of social science, for changes in official attitudes depend on prior changes in university education. But changes will also depend on a more precise notion than is presently shared by scientists and practitioners on exactly what these "possibilities of the social sciences" are.

It may be relevant to recall earlier changes in the teaching of international relations and their influence on State Department planning processes in the late 1940's and early 1950's. These changes were manifest in the school of "political realism" that had its roots in the writings of men like the theologian Reinhold Niebuhr, the historian E. H. Carr, the geopolitician Nicholas J. Spykman, and the political theorist Hans J. Morgenthau. They deliberately sought to combine theory and practice, and what they had to say was thus of direct relevance to policy-makers. In large measure, history was the laboratory to which they turned for observation, and here they found that the legalism and moralism that had dominated American foreign policy were inconsistent with the realities of international politics. Among the realists, Morgenthau substituted for legalism and moralism a defense of the national interest in a world of competitive power. While the definition of national interest remained open to controversy, it offered "a broad intellectual category or a way of approaching foreign policy."[26]

Within the State Department the concepts of the school of political realism were articulated and developed as guidelines for policy by the first Policy Planning Council working under the direction of George Kennan. Kenneth Thompson has suggested that the staff sought to evolve a "theoretical foundation to underpin the conduct of our external relations." This rested on several common elements: among them, "the proposition that there are few if

---

[25] *Federal Support of International Social Science and Behavioral Research*, Hearings before Subcommittee on Government Research, Committee on Government Operations, U.S. Senate, 89th Congress, 2nd Session, 1966, p. 114.

[26] Kenneth W. Thompson, *Political Realism and the Crisis of World Politics* (Princeton: Princeton University Press, 1960), pp. 3–38.

any absolutes in international politics"; dissatisfaction with the idea that "power politics and the balance of power [are] the simple evils from which wars emerged"; a rejection of "any belief in human perfectibility" as an unrealistic basis for formulating policy goals; and a "passion for history."[27]

Political realism answered the needs of its time. Based as it was on the history of world politics in the nineteenth and twentieth centuries, it offered at least a partial explanation for current conditions and soon became the dominant intellectual perspective among teachers of international relations and among their students, many of whom brought it from the classroom into the Foreign Service which they entered later. More than that, it offered a kind of grim consolation to a generation that had witnessed two major wars, depressions, and dictatorships, and now faced the prospect of an interminable "cold war." As one observer commented on the writings of Reinhold Niebuhr: "[His] analyses make the impact they do upon modern minds because they 'ring true.' . . . We are attracted to his analysis because it confirms what history and our personal experience confirm."[28] To those actually engaged in formulating foreign policy, political realism provided a large conceptual framework that gave order to the many complex and seemingly unique events with which they had to deal. This was especially necessary at a time when the United States was beginning to play a much larger role in international affairs with little operating tradition, when the Truman Doctrine and the Marshall Plan called for a whole reassessment of foreign policy, and when the American-Soviet conflict created new problems daily. As interpreted by the Policy Planning Council, political realism fortified the doctrine of containment.

Yet, in many ways, the ideas of the political realists were highly speculative. Their notions of human behavior were based not on rigorously analyzed empirical evidence but rather on logical reasoning and on broad generalizations derived from a study of history. Morgenthau's concepts of the nature of power and the

---

[27] For a review of the ideas of the Policy Planning Council that included Paul Nitze, Louis Halle, Dorothy Fosdick, and C. B. Marshall, see *ibid.*, pp. 50–61.

[28] *Ibid.*, p. 23.

national interest, for example, were very ambiguous; and later he had to make continual efforts to explain and elaborate his concept of power, as it came to be interpreted almost exclusively in military terms. The new "possibilities of the social sciences" discussed by Almond come from quite a different source. They are based mainly on quantitative and behavioral approaches in international relations and on cross-cultural studies that employ the methods of survey research, interviewing, and statistical correlation.

Nevertheless, the Foreign Service today leans almost exclusively on the traditional historical and institutional analyses favored by the political realists, when it does not proceed simply on the basis of intuition and practical experience. The conservative attitude of the State Department, its recruitment policies, its emphasis on short-term goals, and its limited research system—all tend to discourage acquaintance with recent trends in social science. The issue is not, however, one of choosing between traditional and contemporary approaches, as is often and erroneously contended. The issue is one of broadening the Department's research system in order to incorporate new ways through which social scientists are seeking to explain events that are important in American foreign policy. A new "paradigm" in the study of international relations is not likely to emerge in the near future. However, it would seem important that those techniques and concepts that are chipping away at the old "paradigm" be reflected in the Department's work.

The Military Operators

One of the conspicuous features of contemporary American foreign affairs is its highly operational nature. Before the Second World War, American diplomacy was largely a matter of traditional political representation. Since then the diplomat has had to share his role with the operators—the soldier, the economic expert, the educational consultant, the cultural affairs officer. Officially, the Secretary of State is the President's principal adviser on foreign policy; and the operating departments—the Defense Department, the United States Information Agency, the Central Intelligence Agency, the Agency for International Development—are subject to the policy guidance of the Secretary in Washington and the Ambassador in the overseas missions. However, the attempt of the State Department to maintain a dominant position among these rivals has not always been successful. At the highest levels, the Department's role depends on a whole set of personal relationships, particularly the relationship between the President and the Secretary. Similarly, at overseas posts, the Ambassador has the task of keeping abreast of the full range of American programs in the country. At both levels, there is a close correlation between policy and operations; if, in theory, policy determines the direction for operations, operations can be equally decisive in shaping the alternatives for policy.

Research in foreign affairs, too, varies in its aim depending on who supports it, the AID, USIA, CIA, the Department of State, or the defense establishment, as Project Camelot clearly showed. Project Camelot exposed the inadequate amount of research in foreign affairs done by civilian agencies and the disproportionate amount undertaken by the military. For example, in 1966 the $10 million that the Defense Department allocated to foreign area studies offered a sharp contrast to the $5 million of AID, the $500,000 of USIA, and the $100,000 of the Department of State. Following the Camelot episode, a Foreign Affairs Research Council was set up by the Department of State under presidential orders to review government-sponsored research projects overseas for their foreign policy implications. Again the dominant position of the military was evident. During the first year 300 projects were evaluated. Of these, 210 originated in the Department of Defense, as compared with 32 in USIA, 22 in AID, 13 in the Arms Control and Disarmament Agency, and 3 in the State Department.[29] Several factors must be considered in explaining the dominant position of the military: the operational nature of military activities, the military habit of seeking expert advice, and the large scientific research structure and budget into which social science projects could easily be absorbed without

29 *Foreign Area Research: A Conference Report,* National Academy of Sciences —National Research Council (Washington, D.C., January 1967), p. 39.

raising pointed questions—internally or in Congress—about their purpose or utility.

Research sponsored by the military, though at first chiefly devoted to problems of technological change, soon began to include problems of international political strategy. When pressed to justify research budgets, arguments were found both in the nature of military operations and the requirements of bureaucratic survival. For example, in 1959 the Navy sponsored Project Michelson to determine what kind of seaborne weapons systems would be required to succeed the nuclear-powered missile-carrying Polaris submarine system. Although justified on the basis of future "hardware" needs, the Project supported a good deal of sociopolitical research, including background studies on the nature of deterrence and strategic forecasting studies that related defense requirements to arms control arrangements. Here empirical and experimental methods were applied to the study of international politics. But this work was viewed with skepticism by congressional committees, particularly those studies that related deterrence to arms control, for they seemed to extend the Navy's research program beyond the limits set by its primary mission. The Project was slowly dissolved but only after the Navy's chief scientist had explained that "the effectiveness of a deterrence system cannot be measured exclusively in terms of the damage which it will inflict." Other factors had to be taken into consideration, including "the credibility that it will be used; the degree of assurance that its use cannot be stopped." And the Chief of Naval Research also emphasized that studies like those undertaken by Project Michelson enabled the Navy to take an independent position on the government's arms control policies, a position the Admiral considered to be of some importance for the Navy's future role.[30]

At the time of Project Camelot, defense agencies engaged in foreign affairs research largely justified their activities as part of the counter-insurgency mission that was specifically assigned to

---

[30] *Department of Defense Appropriations for 1966,* Hearings before Subcommittee of Committee on Appropriations, House of Representatives, 89th Congress, 1st Session, 1965, Part 5, pp. 508–521.

the military by the Kennedy Administration in the early 1960's. The military interest in learning about the political, social, and economic affairs of developing nations goes back to the Korean war, however, and to the military supervision of the political and economic reconstruction of South Korea that followed the end of hostilities. Indeed, the role played by the military in Korea had precedents in the occupation of Germany and Japan after the Second World War. The occupation brought the military into contact with every aspect of civilian life and, in Japan especially, contributed to important changes in the nature of society. Military officials on occupation duty had civilian advisers available to them, either political officers on assignment from the State Department or experts in marketing, transportation, or constitutional reform on loan from other government departments or on leave from universities.[31] The military therefore had the experience of dealing with a wide range of social and economic problems in times of transition and in taking responsibility for such operations.

With the Korean war, changes in American policy required increasing numbers of military units to be stationed overseas, even as the occupation governments established after World War II were being dissolved. During the Korean conflict, and especially after the Eisenhower Administration came to power in 1953, the United States entered into a series of mutual security treaties with the nations that encircled the powers of the communist bloc. These alliances required a variety of military operations such as the staffing of regional defense organizations like the North Atlantic Treaty Organization, the transfer of military equipment, the training of foreign military both in their own countries and in American military installations, and the posting of American military advisory groups in countries throughout the world. At the same time, the American economic aid program was reorganized with an increased emphasis on military support, with the object of helping local governments to build up their own defense establishments.

---

[31] For an analysis of the role of the military in Korea, see Gene M. Lyons, *Military Policy and Economic Aid* (Columbus: Ohio State University Press, 1960).

In 1959 a presidential committee under William H. Draper, Jr., conducted a study of the American aid program in response to congressional criticism of the shift to heavy military assistance. In its conclusions, the Draper committee saw nothing wrong with the balance between military and economic assistance. On the contrary, it asserted, "the Military Assistance Program has provided the mortar giving cohesion, strength and credibility to our collective security arrangements." It thus related the program to the policy of deterrence: "Our accepted strategy of collective security has been, and is dependent on effective local deterrent forces as well as on the global deterrent provided by our nuclear strategic forces."[32]

The Draper report also emphasized how military involvement, both American and foreign, was linked to the larger set of developments that went beyond the requirements of the policy of deterrence. It pointed out that the military training program, then involving "more than 10,000 foreign nationals a year . . . [could] do far more than merely teach recipients to use military equipment and materials." The program could be broadened to meet the "serious shortage of trained people with the broad range of skills which are needed," and would be especially effective because, "in some of the less developed countries, a large proportion of the managerial and executive skills that exist are in [the] armed forces." The report also pointed to the historical role of the Army in making "significant contributions to civilian progress" through "its early surveys, mapping, railroad construction and waterways projects." Finally, it suggested, "the military forces of many of today's less developed countries can contribute to their countries' economic progress" through a varied program of public works.[33]

The direction in which the Draper Committee pointed became increasingly clear in the 1960's, even though there were

[32] *Conclusions Concerning the Mutual Security Program*, Final Report, The President's Committee to Study the United States Military Assistance Program (Washington, D.C., August 17, 1959), p. 17.
[33] *Ibid.*, pp. 42–43.

some shifts in policy. Soon after President Kennedy took office in 1961, the aid programs were evaluated in the periodic review of affairs that occurs with every new administration. And certain organizational changes were made in an effort to consolidate various programs; greater emphasis was placed on long-range economic projects; and aid was given more often in the form of loans rather than outright grants.[34] These changes tended to play down the scope of American military assistance, at least more so than had the earlier Eisenhower policies. Nevertheless, by 1967 the United States had military assistance programs in thirty-nine countries, supported the programs conducted by local military forces in twenty-seven others, and was undertaking the training of 16,800 foreign military personnel.[35] During this period military regimes were established in a number of developing nations, illustrating the important role played by military elites and the significant influence that military assistance could have on the development process.

These military assistance and training programs became more a responsibility of the Army than the Navy or the Air Force. For one thing, the Army had a larger number of bases overseas and larger numbers of personnel to maintain them; so it became more involved with local political authorities and economic conditions. At the same time, it was the local armies that comprised the major military contingents in most developing countries and that took responsibility for both security and public works. In 1956, to support its overseas operations, the Army had set up the Special Operations Research Office (SORO) under arrangements with the American University. In the beginning the work of SORO was limited to preparing handbooks and manuals for troops overseas and materials for the instruction of units being trained for overseas duty. With the development of the counter-insurgency mission in the early 1960's, however, the SORO program was ex-

---

34 David A. Baldwin, *Foreign Aid and American Foreign Policy* (New York: Frederick A. Praeger, 1966), pp. 20–44.
35 Testimony of Deputy Director of Defense Research and Engineering, *National Foundation for the Social Sciences, op. cit.*, Part 1, p. 228.

panded to include studies of insurrection, instructions in guerilla warfare for the newly organized U.S. Special Forces, and broadly conceived studies of social change such as Project Camelot.[36]

It was in the early 1960's, as well, that the Defense Science Board recommended starting a behavioral science research program under the Advanced Research Projects Agency (ARPA). Based on the work of the Bray research group, the program was almost wholly concentrated on the manpower and organizational problems of the defense establishment, except for those aspects of studies of persuasion and motivation that related to propaganda and psychological operations. Accordingly, another study group was established in 1961 under the chairmanship of Ithiel de Sola Pool of M.I.T. Its purpose, as Pool put it, was to examine that "domain of problems . . . roughly characterized as the operations of the Defense Department in relation to the external world."[37] Included in the studies sponsored by the group were analyses of the role of social science research with regard to internal war, military development in the new countries, and population issues, particularly in the underdeveloped areas of the world.

Unlike the Bray report, the Pool group made no recommendations for a broad research program. Instead, its report consisted of a series of papers on selected areas of national security; the authors reviewed the state of social science research in the field and suggested the kind of work that they thought should be supported. In his introduction, Pool summarized some of the problems involved in relating social science research to defense, but noted that "a major step forward in the development of a body of knowledge of security relevance can be achieved by the defense establishment if it chooses to put an adequate level of consistent

---

[36] For a discussion of the expanding Army research program in the early 1960's, see E. K. Karcher, Jr., "Army Social Science Program and Plans," in *The U.S. Army's Limited-War Mission and Social Science Research*, Special Operations Research Office, The American University (Washington, D.C., June 1962), pp. 344–359.

[37] Ithiel de Sola Pool, *et al.*, "Social Science Research and National Security," a report (mimeographed) prepared by the Research Group in Psychology and the Social Sciences, Smithsonian Institution (Washington, D.C., March 5, 1963), p. 2.

and long-term support behind such social researchers as are willing to turn their attention to its problems."[38] Pool, in effect, called for a research organization that, in the areas of strategic and cross-cultural studies, was not unlike the system recommended by the Bray report for matters falling within the internal structure of the military. It was to fill the gap between the operationally oriented "handbook" type of research carried on by SORO and (except for arrangements like those for RAND) the somewhat diffuse system in which the ideas of social science were introduced into strategic thinking and policy planning from both internal and external sources, through both administrative and political channels, by the often fortuitous confluence of people, times, and events.

Although no immediate action was taken on the report of the Pool group, its efforts were of help in setting up still another subcommittee of the Defense Science Board in 1964 to "conduct a study of research and development programs and findings related to ethnic and other motivational factors involved in the causation and conduct of small wars."[39] The subcommittee reviewed the existing program in the defense establishment and came to the following conclusions:

> [There are] serious deficiencies that are not offset by an adequate research effort on the part of universities and other civilian organizations. . . . there is very incomplete knowledge and understanding in depth of the internal cultural, economic, and political conditions that generate conflict between national groups . . . [and], since very little research in existing programs—either civilian or military—is being conducted overseas, there is slight prospect of substantial improvement in this situation until a significant increase in the overall level of research effort is achieved. . . . [Other inadequacies in the program are] the lack of data quantification and statistical analyses in many areas where such methods would be appropriate and feasible . . . the failure to design studies so as to permit drawing sound inferences from their results . . . the failure to organize appropriate multidisciplinary programs and to use the techniques of such related fields as operations research.

38 *Ibid.*, p. 15.
39 *Behavioral Sciences and the National Security*, *op. cit.*, p. 72.

As a remedy, the subcommittee called for a larger and more integrated research program in the fields of limited and internal conflict and social development.[40]

In March 1965 the Director of Defense Research and Engineering directed ARPA and the military departments to initiate programs along lines recommended by the Defense Science Board subcommittee. The Army was assigned the task of establishing, "in the Washington, D.C., area, a centrally coordinated applied research effort" in the behavioral and social sciences on the problems of counter-insurgency. And ARPA was to support large-scale research on similar problems in the universities in order to achieve the "significant increase in the . . . level of research effort" that the subcommittee had recommended.[41] Within months after the directive for the new program was issued, however, Project Camelot was a matter of public debate, and it was an inauspicious moment to ask for an increase in foreign area research by the military. The Project also exposed a growing obstacle to field research abroad; about this time American social scientists found it more and more difficult to gain access to foreign countries and peoples.

No doubt it was largely Project Camelot, especially in Latin America, that raised suspicions about the role and intentions of American social scientists, no matter what the source of their financial support or their institutional affiliations. But there were other more complex causes that contributed to this result: general apprehensions about the direction of American foreign policy; nationalistic hostility to outsiders of any description; the reluctance of foreigners to be the subjects of American researchers; and the feeling of many foreign social scientists that they were not being treated as equals by their American peers.

Immediately following the dissolution of Project Camelot, military research was thus concentrated on the applied program of SORO (renamed the Center for Research in Social Systems, CRESS, in 1966) and on the immediate issues facing the defense establishment in Southeast Asia. Other projects were started, in-

40 *Ibid.*, pp. 72–74.
41 *Ibid.*, pp. 73–74.

cluding studies of Latin American development by the RAND Corporation and limited university-based research on the process of modernization financed by the Office of Naval Research and the Air Force Office of Scientific Research. But these did not amount to much considering what the Defense Science Board had recommended. In many ways the CRESS program reverted to the operational projects that it had begun with. As the Army Chief of Research and Development explained to a congressional committee, "We have cut out the type of study that we think would be subjected to the kind of criticism that [Project Camelot was] subjected to."[42] Nevertheless, the CRESS program continued to be funded at about $2 million per year for work undertaken by two sub-units, the Social Science Research Institute carrying out specific research assignments and the Cultural Information Analysis Center serving as an information clearing house for the Army and for other agencies of the government.

In Southeast Asia a good deal of the social and behavioral science research program was devoted to the immediate problems of the war in Vietnam and to conditions in Thailand, where part of the American force was based. Here the Defense Department's Project Agile, conducted through ARPA, provided a mechanism for relating research in military technology, operations research, and the behavioral sciences to the problems of counter-insurgency. In this respect, Project Agile was an experiment in the application of the systems approach to the conduct of the war and was an extension of earlier research on the "hardware" components used in guerilla warfare. In effect, it gave support to the military command in Vietnam and conducted short-range studies of Vietcong motivation, the attitudes of Vietnamese villagers, and communication patterns among South Vietnamese troops.[43] These projects became controversial in their own right as they became part of the information and analytical base for estimating the effectiveness of military operations. But they were also part of a

42 *Department of Defense Appropriations for 1968,* Hearings before Subcommittee of the Committee on Appropriations, House of Representatives, 90th Congress, 1st Session, 1967, Part 3, p. 234.
43 *Ibid.,* pp. 157–175.

more general program, the chief object of which was to understand and control guerilla activity.

In Thailand, Project Agile prepared a long-range comprehensive plan in cooperation with the Thai government. The plan had several objectives:

> [to] gather and collate critical information on the local geography, the way of life of the local people, and on their attitudes toward the Government; . . . set up and help maintain current files on insurgent incidents and operations, and on the many Government programs and activities undertaken for counterinsurgency purposes in the northeast; and . . . provide assistance in analyzing the effectiveness of various counterinsurgency programs, as well as helping, through analytical techniques to plan further CI programs.[44]

Project Agile demonstrated the close connection between operational requirements and research that could be achieved in the defense establishment. Though not typical of all defense research projects, it did show how military operations could support social science research in fairly fundamental areas, especially when compared with the limited use made of it by the civilian foreign affairs agencies. In none of the civilian agencies was there the built-in drive and momentum that was generated in the military, the ability to mobilize resources and develop an operational base for supporting research. It was this concentration on operations, bolstered by a "systems" approach, that made the military the most substantial supporter of foreign area research in the federal government.

From a political viewpoint, however, military sponsorship involved social scientists in especially vexing problems of intervention in the affairs of developing countries. For the newly emerging nations, the end of empire meant the end of intervention in their internal affairs by the Western powers. When intervening in local affairs, particularly with direct or indirect military assistance, the United States ran the risk of opposing an indigenous nationalistic movement and supporting only the local *status quo*. And, unless it was able to influence the organization and programs of the

[44] *Ibid.*, p. 176.

local government, it also ran the risk of failure and political attack from all sides.

The Vietnam conflict has provoked serious national debate concerning the role of American power in the world and, most particularly, the nature of American intervention in the developing countries. Behind the debate on the conduct of the war itself lies the feeling that the United States has to begin to limit its role in world politics, to define more sharply and more precisely than it had its areas of vital interest, and to restrict its activities to these. It is a mistake for the United States to assume any commitments, in the name either of anti-communism or an ideal of world order, when it can not reasonably control the forces for change and successfully achieve its objectives.

But what are these areas of vital interest? How broadly or narrowly are they to be defined? Defined too broadly, they may, even without reference to abstract goals, lead the United States into the role of world policeman; defined too narrowly, they may lead to a kind of neo-isolationism. Answers to questions such as these require leadership, insight, patience, the greatest amount of knowledge about conditions in developing countries that can be obtained, and the most effective use of it in formulating policy. It was this kind of knowledge—about the nature and process of social change—that Project Camelot had set out to obtain. But the Project was cancelled even before the field research started and the reasons were as much political as they were intellectual. More broadly and ironically, the end of Project Camelot led to a general decline in government support for the very kind of research that was needed to deal with development policy.

The Civilian Operators

Congressional review of social science research, especially in the field of foreign affairs, is frequently harsh and unsympathetic, a fact that the State Department has continually pointed to in explanation of its own low research budget. The hearings on Project Camelot before a subcommittee of the House Foreign Affairs Committee were conducted in a very different atmosphere. Most subcommittee members were dismayed by the way the Project had been handled and concerned about the lack of research in civilian agencies, principally the Department of State. Instead of questioning the need or utility of social science, the subcommittee report urged more and better research, as well as a general "civilianization" of social science support through a National Social Science Foundation, a White House Conference on the Social Sciences, and a Presidential Special Assistant for the Social Sciences.[45]

Elsewhere in the Congress, there has been less support for social science research, particularly in appropriations committees. The military has been as sharply questioned as other agencies, as the history of the Navy's Project Michelson bears witness. There are several reasons for congressional skepticism. For one thing, the social sciences have less mystery about them than the other sciences and it is always possible to raise questions on the basis of common sense. Congressmen and senators demand that research in the social sciences be justified, in full confidence that they can make reasonable judgments about the issues involved. They approach problems of human behavior with considerable and justifiable pride in the understanding of human whims and desires that they have gained from engaging in practical politics. They are thus impatient with jargon or broad and bland generalizations. They expect results. Also, in the field of foreign affairs, they are apt to feel frustrated and resentful because of the increasingly passive role that Congress has played in shaping foreign policy.

The attitude of Congress toward research in foreign affairs is thus mixed. It is left to the executive departments and agencies to state the case for research and each generally speaks only for itself. In this respect the defense agencies have enjoyed greater congressional support and operated in a broader bureaucratic and financial framework; so they have been able to justify research more easily or compensate for budget reductions when they were imposed. With an agency like the Arms Control and Disarmament Agency (ACDA), in contrast, congressional approval is less certain and the framework is much smaller and weaker. Established

---

[45] *Behavioral Sciences and the National Security, op. cit.*, pp. 8r–9r.

in 1961, ACDA developed a research program to provide analytic support for negotiations in arms control matters and to explore new and experimental arrangements for extending arms control. But new ideas in this field are few; progress is slow under the best of conditions and is subject to political agreement even if good ideas emerge from research. Congressmen have grown impatient, even those who are sympathetic to the goals of arms control and aware of the need for research.[46] The ACDA program, particularly its work in the social and behavioral sciences assigned to university and private research institutes, has thus been periodically subjected to severe limitations by Congress.

Congressional restrictions have likewise been imposed on research in the field of social change and development, the object of Project Camelot. In addition to the State Department and the defense agencies, the Peace Corps, the United States Information Agency, the Agency for International Development, and the Central Intelligence Agency support research activities in the developing countries, as well as research in the United States on the problems of development. Each program, however, has to justify itself in contending for funds and support both in the Executive Branch and in Congress. The Peace Corps research program, for example, has generally been concerned with the problems of choosing Peace Corps volunteers, training them, and assigning them overseas. Most of the volunteers are young people, eager to serve, but many are unprepared for the physical and emotional problems they may encounter. A number of research projects have been launched to assist in devising selection procedures, in developing training methods, and, most important perhaps, in evaluating the performance of volunteers overseas. The primary purpose of the evaluation studies is to analyze the demands made on volunteers, to determine the qualities and approaches that offer greatest chance for success, and thus to provide a better basis for selection and training. Evaluation studies are also used to measure the effect

---

[46] See, for example, the questions and comments of Senator Pell and Senator Aiken in *To Amend the Arms Control and Disarmament Act*, Hearings before Committee on Foreign Relations, U.S. Senate, 89th Congress, 1st Session, 1965.

of Peace Corps projects on social change, but they are usually too short-term and uncoordinated make a significant contribution to the broader problems of development.[47]

The United States Information Agency (USIA) has had more experience in employing social science research in its operating programs. The Agency has gone through a long and often torturous evolution that began with the Office of War Information at the time of the Second World War.[48] It has frequently suffered harsh criticism in Congress, especially when American policy and Americans have been unpopular in the world. The style of its programs has varied between a straight, unadulterated account of the facts to a presentation with more ideological overtones. It has two purposes: to interpret foreign attitudes and opinion for executive agencies operating abroad; and, through a variety of communication media, to explain the policies and actions of the United States to foreign audiences. In carrying out both parts of its mission, it has made constant use of survey research in order to learn what others are thinking and to discover what impact its own programs have made. However, activities like those of USIA are carried on by a number of other agencies under both public and private auspices. USIA surveys of foreign opinion, for example, can be compared with many others, including competing polls, editorial comments, and the news carried over sensitive international grapevines. And USIA radio broadcasts, films, and book centers make up but a very small part of the barrage of information about American life that is sent out into the world by privately run television, radio, movie, and publishing companies. The effect of USIA programs is thus very difficult to measure and is lost among the countless impressions of American life given by other sources.[49]

At an early stage in the history of the agency as an independ-

---

[47] For a listing of Peace Corps research projects during its first years, see *Amendment to Peace Corps Act*, Hearings before Committee on Foreign Relations, U.S. Senate, 89th Congress, 1st Session, April 1965, pp. 75–81.

[48] For the early history of the information program during and immediately following the war, see Charles A. H. Thomson, *Overseas Information Service of the U.S. Government* (Washington, D.C.: The Brookings Institution, 1948).

[49] For a discussion of the role of the United States Information Agency and communications in foreign policy, see *Modern Communications and Foreign Policy*, Report No. 5, Subcommittee on International Organizations and Movements, Committee on Foreign Affairs, House of Representatives, 90th Congress, 1st Session, 1967.

ent organization, separated from the State Department, a committee chaired by Wilbur Schramm recommended a program of research and evaluation as "an essential part of [the] operation." The purpose of this research was to obtain "a set of valid assumptions regarding the process of international communication . . . a clear and adequate knowledge of the groups to which the program is directed . . . [and] an objective and continuing audit of its own performance."[50] Soon afterwards the agency began its program of public opinion surveys, usually contracting for the work with local research organizations in the countries being studied. For the most part, these surveys have been attempts to assess foreign reactions to particular events, although from time to time periodic surveys have been made to record trends in foreign attitudes toward American policy and various aspects of American life.

Unfortunately, these periodic studies have usually been discontinued after several years. Indeed, research operations have generally been highly erratic and have included little in the way of methodological advances or analyses in depth of foreign societies, as the Schramm committee recommended. For these reasons, the USIA advisory commission has continually been critical of the research program. In 1964, for example, the committee complained that "little progress has been reported on the commission's recommendations to increase funds for research and for the better use of research in the planning, conduct and evaluation of specific USIA programs and operations."[51] And in 1966 the committee stated more strongly: "USIA managers are not disposed to organize and develop their programs and their budgets around facts as established by research. . . . The use of research has been seriously neglected in USIA to the detriment of the program."[52]

The failure of USIA to develop a better research program may

---

50 "A Program of Research and Evaluation for the International Information Administration," (mimeographed), Recommendations of a Special Committee to the Administrator, United States Information Agency (Washington, D.C., June 15, 1953).

51 *The Nineteenth Report of the United States Advisory Commission on Information*, United States Information Agency (Washington, D.C., February 1966), p. 24.

52 *The Twenty-First Report of the United States Advisory Commission on Information*, United States Information Agency (Washington, D.C., January 1964), p. 24.

be attributed to two major causes. First, its own top administrators have given very uneven support to research; for journalists, radio commentators, and television specialists prefer to rely on their own experience rather than on research as a basis for programming. Then, foreign opinion studies may have political consequences at home, for they serve as a popular barometer of the success or failure of an administration's foreign policy. This was apparent in the 1960 presidential elections, when the Democratic candidate, John F. Kennedy, was able to point to a series of USIA polls to support his contention that American prestige abroad had diminished during the Republican Administration of Dwight D. Eisenhower.[53] Trend analysis, so important to programming, may force the agency to sacrifice research for political survival.

In the Agency for International Development the career of social science research has been no less erratic. Until the early 1960's there was, in fact, no social science research program to guide American foreign aid operations. The need for such a program was first discussed in the report of the Development Assistance Panel, organized by the President's Science Advisory Committee in late 1960.[54] By the time the Panel was ready to submit its recommendations the following spring, the aid program had been reorganized by the new Democratic Administration and it was a propitious moment to suggest that some provision be made for research as part of the "new look." The Chairman of the Panel was Walsh McDermott, Professor of Public Health from Cornell University, and its members included men from the health, agricultural, and engineering fields, as well as the physical and social sciences. Among the social scientists were the anthropologist Allan Holmberg, the economist Max Millikan, and John W. Gardner, a psychologist, then president of the Carnegie Corporation.

The Panel began its report by noting that the chief recipients of American foreign aid were no longer the industrialized nations of western Europe but rather the developing nations of Asia, Africa, and Latin America. These developing nations had "special problems which the industrialized nations, in their evolution into

[53] Theodore Sorenson, *Kennedy* (New York: Harper & Row, 1965), p. 322.
[54] "Research and Development in the New Development Assistance Program," (mimeographed), Report of the Development Advisory Panel, President's Science Advisory Committee (Washington, D.C., May 24, 1961).

modern societies, were never called upon to face." To understand these problems was an essential prerequisite to effective assistance. Before any action was taken, the "organization of skilled inquiry" was necessary in order to define the needs of developing nations and to establish the "framework within which . . . knowledge can be applied." Therefore the Panel urged that a "research and development unit" be established as an integral and essential component of the aid agency. Its work was to consist in the "identification of needs and wants" of developing nations, the "generation of knowledge and techniques" about the development process, the "conduct of experiments" in the recipient countries, and continuing evaluation of its own activities as part of the process of research and experimentation. Most particularly the Panel pointed out:

> it is clear that some long-term basic research in the social sciences will be necessary if the development assistance program is to move forward with assurance. . . . [for] development is far more than the generation of a body of technology and its application to the enjoyment of natural resources; it is also an intricate complex of social and political attitudes, of values, of judgments, and even of faiths.

The Foreign Assistance Act of 1961 followed the suggestion of the McDermott Panel by making provision for a research program in the renamed and reconstituted Agency for International Development (AID). The Panel had recommended a research budget of $50 million for the first year, with increases that would raise it to $95 million in four or five years. In reality the research program for all fields, including social science, never approached this level of expenditure; at first it was given a ceiling of $6 million a year, later raised to $12 million a year, and then cut back again. Also, from the beginning, the program suffered from bureaucratic coolness and congressional criticism. Confronted with the task of reorganizing and staffing the aid program, the first Administrator, Fowler Hamilton, did not consider research to be, as one observer put it, "a priority No. 1 problem."[55] Hamilton's attitude was reinforced by that of much of the AID staff, who were accustomed to

---

55 John Walsh, "AID: Almost Everyone Favors Research on Development Problems but Going Has Not been Smooth," *Science*, Vol. CXL, No. 3568 (May 17, 1963), p. 793.

a tempo of operations that did not allow time for research and who proceeded on the assumption that economic aid and technical assistance would automatically lead to political and social goals compatible with the aims of American foreign policy.

During the first year of the research program a series of unfortunate management decisions were made (involving technical and engineering rather than social science projects), which caused Congress to review the procedures for awarding research contracts and cut the research budget down to $6 million.[56] In response to what was generally acknowledged to be an inadequate screening process, a Research Advisory Committee was set up late in 1962 by the new head of AID, David Bell, with Walsh McDermott again serving as Chairman. The task of rebuilding the research program was begun but it was only moderately successful, for there was still a considerable lack of interest on the part of regional bureau chiefs who were in charge of program operations.[57] As the research program evolved, moreover, it generally consisted of individual projects, many unsolicited, that were grouped together in functional categories—like agriculture, industrial development, and education—but subject to no broad comprehensive plan. By 1967, under the prodding of the Research Advisory Committee, steps were being taken to correct this fragmentation when, with reorganization, the central research staff was broken up and the program divided between the operating and planning bureaus.

In many ways, the difficulties encountered by the research program here were those of AID itself. This Agency and its predecessors have always had to proceed under the assumption that foreign assistance was a temporary affair. In the eyes of Congress,

---

[56] The issue involved questionable contract provisions arrived at in haste at the end of the fiscal year. See *Agency for International Development Contract Operations: Office of Research, Evaluation and Planning Assistance Staff,* Hearings before Committee on Government Operations, U.S. Senate, 87th Congress, 2nd Session, 1962, Parts 1 and 2.

[57] Eugene B. Skolnikoff, "Birth and Death of an Idea: Research in AID," *Bulletin of the Atomic Scientists,* September 1967, pp. 38–40. Skolnikoff was Executive Secretary of the early PSAC Panel on Development and later was a member of the Research Advisory Committee of the Agency for International Development.

particularly, the job of any foreign assistance program was to work itself out of business. Since Europe had needed assistance for only a brief period, reasonable advancement was expected of the newly emerging nations where the problems of development were more complex and necessarily took much longer to solve. Every administration had a hard time defending budgets for foreign aid unless it could point to positive "pay offs" in terms of foreign policy objectives. The words of David Bell illustrate the prevailing political attitude. While he was still AID Administrator, he testified on the International Education Act of 1966, designed to establish a program of institutional grants to colleges and universities for teaching and research in international affairs. Bell explained why it was preferable that the new program be administered by the Department of Health, Education, and Welfare rather than AID.

> [AID is] a good illustration of an agency of Government which needs to draw upon the strength of American universities, but we do it for specific purposes and on a temporary time scale. . . . The purpose of the foreign aid program . . . is self-terminating. We are trying to get other countries on their own feet and get ourselves out of the aid business.[58]

American universities have been co-opted in technical assistance programs from the beginning. In 1964 John W. Gardner prepared a report for Bell, *AID and the Universities,* which explored the role of American universities in developing countries.[59] At that time seventy-two universities were working on some hundred and thirty technical assistance missions for AID. In its recommendations the report stressed the importance of research and its relationship to the universities.

> Research should address itself not only to the discovery of new knowledge [about the processes of modernization], but to devising, designing, and testing of new procedures and materials in

---

58 *International Education,* Hearings before Task Force on International Education, Committee on Education and Labor, House of Representatives, 89th Congress, 2nd Session, 1966, p. 47.

59 John W. Gardner, *AID and the Universities,* Report to the Administrator of the Agency for International Development (Washington, D.C., April 1964).

technical cooperation and to the analytical study—for purposes of improved decision-making—of development assistance activities and their consequences. . . . [Therefore the report recommended a] strong in-house research and analysis unit . . . [and] a research component in many of its university contracts for technical assistance.

The Research Advisory Committee supported the Gardner proposals; and, in subsequent testimony before the House Foreign Affairs Committee, Bell spoke of putting them "into effect."[60] But what was lacking here was a central research program that would give direction and coherence to research that might be carried out through the various university-based technical assistance projects.

There is still another cause for the organizational and political weakness of the AID research program. There has been, as Robert A. Packenham put it, a "gap between purpose and policy."[61] In terms of stated American foreign policy, the purpose of foreign assistance must be related to the political development of the emerging nations. The aid program, however, has generally limited itself to furthering their economic development, as if economic development could be dissociated from other social processes. The notion prevailed for many years that economic and technical assistance could be "non-political"; whereas most social scientists recognized that such assistance necessarily had political effects and that the whole process of modernization had to be viewed in a larger political and social context. Even when, under Title IX of the Foreign Assistance Act, the aim of supporting "grass roots" organizations in order to foster democratic institutions was built into legislation, it was implemented with caution. For one thing, the concern with political development is a long-term matter that runs counter to the operating styles and attitudes of an agency dedicated to short-term goals. But, from an immediate practical point of view, emphasis on political development only puts a spotlight on the "interventionist" nature of any kind of

60 Bill to Amend Further the Foreign Assistance Act of 1961, Committee on Foreign Affairs, House of Representatives, 89th Congress, 1st Session, 1965, p. 6.
61 Robert A. Packenham, "Political-Development Doctrines in the American Foreign Aid Program," *World Politics,* Vol. XVIII, No. 2 (January 1966), p. 229.

great power assistance, an emphasis that could understandably complicate the effectiveness of aid administrators in the field.

In addition to the restrictions placed on social science research in foreign affairs—present in various forms in all agencies —there are thus precautions required in dealing with the "sensitive" issues discussed by Secretary of State Rusk during the Camelot hearings. The sensitivity of foreigners to American researchers is complicated by the relationship of research to intelligence and the suspicion that inevitably surrounds intelligence activities. The Central Intelligence Agency (CIA) is one very large and elaborate mechanism for the collection and analysis of information. By all reliable estimates, most of this information is gathered from open sources and only a small part of it obtained through clandestine channels.[62] It is in analyzing this information, rather than collecting it, that the techniques of social science are most applicable. Intelligence information obtained from the CIA and the Defense and State Departments is regularly summed up in the National Intelligence Estimates, which serve as basic background for the President and members of the National Security Council. The problems of assessing the significance and the adequacy of what is known—about trends in developing countries, elite groups, potential conflicts—are highly amenable to the methods of the social sciences. Roger Hilsman once estimated that the social sciences promised to be of the greatest help to government in the area of intelligence.[63] The extent to which they have actually been used in the CIA remains obscured by the general secrecy that governs the Agency's procedures. One knowledgable estimate, however, is that "social research [in fields other than economics] has never become a recognized portion of the program of intelligence agencies such as the CIA and is relatively trivial in quantity."[64]

Whatever the internal mechanisms of the CIA may be, its

---

[62] See Harry H. Ransom, *Central Intelligence and National Security* (Cambridge: Harvard University Press, 1958); also Allen Dulles, *The Craft of Intelligence* (New York: Harper & Row, 1963).

[63] Roger Hilsman, *Strategic Intelligence and National Decisions* (Glencoe, Illinois: The Free Press, 1956), p. 7.

[64] Ithiel de Sola Pool, "Content Analysis and the Intelligence Function" (mimeographed, n.d.), p. 28.

external operations have created difficult problems for social scientists working abroad, no matter what their sources of support. For example, in 1967 it was revealed that the CIA had furnished undercover support for overseas educational and cultural activities for a period of some fifteen years. Presumably the motive was to provide funds, not available through other sources, to permit American scholars, students, and opinion leaders to develop educational and cultural programs overseas that would counteract communist propaganda. In most cases there was little evidence that those who received support knew its source to be the CIA or that their activities had been directly influenced by CIA operators. But these revelations did becloud the atmosphere of candor and openness that American social science researchers needed in their work with colleagues and informants in foreign countries. The very nature of empirical research, a probing into human motives and attitudes, is likely to provoke distrust. Especially so when the researchers are Americans and the objects of their study are foreign peoples who, because of their history and tradition, suspect that research may be used for sinister political purposes and that any information imparted in confidence may find its way into political dossiers. These suspicions were exacerbated by the exposure of the CIA, as well as by the earlier Camelot affair.

Direction and Coordination

The problems that confront social science research in foreign affairs, diffuse and complex as they are, hardly seem ready for a single grand panacea. They are wrapped up in the real problems of American foreign policy and so cannot easily be resolved. But one deficiency stands out as a matter largely conditioned by internal rather than external pressures and is thus more readily dealt with than some others. There is no government-wide apparatus for relating social science research to American foreign policy. Research is an extension of agency operations, employed only to the extent that individual staff members are willing to promote it and can get support for it in the bargaining that goes on in budgetary and congressional reviews. There is no official support for sustained research either inside or outside of the departments and agencies.

At present there are two mechanisms that help, in quite different but inadequate ways, to coordinate research programs in foreign affairs, and that could muster bureaucratic and political support for research. The first is the Foreign Affairs Research Council of the State Department. The Council was organized in the wake of Project Camelot to review the sensitivity of foreign policy to the projects funded by mission agencies for research overseas. In making this review, the Council is able to keep the State Department continually apprized of the full scope of foreign area research being financed by the government. Its function, however, is negative rather than positive; it decides what research should *not*, rather than what should, be sponsored by the government. The second is the Foreign Area Research Coordination Group (FAR), originally established in 1964 to provide "the systematic coordination of government-sponsored foreign area and cross-cultural research in the social sciences."[65] Staffed by the State Department, FAR operates through a series of working committees organized both on a regional and functional basis.

But FAR has no authority over operating programs. The departments and agencies that participate in its work do so voluntarily because of the advantages it offers them. It provides for the continual exchange of information. It helps research directors in their efforts to defend and further research in their own agencies. And, under its auspices, joint projects requiring the cooperation of several agencies can be initiated. However, the ability of FAR to draw up an overall plan for research in foreign affairs is dependent on the leadership of the Department of State. And the Department is not likely to play an aggressive role here, given

---

[65] *Second Annual Report,* Foreign Area Research Coordination Group, September 1966, reprinted in *Foreign Area Research: A Conference Report, op. cit.,* p. 29.

the limits of its own research program, the narrow perspective of its staff, the lack of any mandate to assume such responsibility, and the general tendency of government departments to avoid as scrupulously as possible any intervention in each other's affairs.

However, there is a third force now in operation that may prove more effective in coordinating research work: the administrative attempt to incorporate the Planning-Programming-Budgeting System (PPBS) into the field of foreign affairs. The System originated in the Department of Defense and, according to a presidential directive issued in 1965, it was to serve as a model for the revision of budgeting procedures throughout every part of the government. Still in its early years, PPBS is clearly experimental and its application often requires a completely new informational and analytical base. In foreign affairs, a series of difficult conceptual and organizational problems have to be solved. These problems occur not only within the several departments and agencies that operate overseas, but also in the affiliations that exist among them and in the role of the State Department as the "first among equals."

First, PPBS requires a definition of policy goals, and this definition must be precise enough to serve as a standard in evaluating operating programs. Foreign policy goals are frequently abstract and vague, however, because of the uncertainties of international politics. Second, PPBS requires criteria for program evaluation in order to determine how effectively resources are used. Social change, however, is difficult to measure. It is a slow process; knowledge about it is limited; and in developing countries the effects of American efforts cannot easily be isolated from those of countless variables over which there is little or no control. Finally, PPBS makes it necessary to review the programs of other agencies that have similar or related policy goals. In foreign affairs, these programs are administered by the Agency for International Development, the Defense Department, the United States Information Agency, and the Peace Corps, for which the Secretary of State has "policy" but not "operating" responsibility. PPBS thus forces the issue of the State Department's control over foreign operations to a head. Despite the support of several presidents, the control of the Secretary of State

—or the ambassador in the field—over the foreign operations of other agencies remains an objective still to be achieved.[66]

The full effect of these new managerial techniques on foreign policy planning is thus highly uncertain. While the Department of State can use PPBS to control foreign affairs effectively, most of its policy and operating staff are accustomed to a different way of asking questions and are somewhat cynical in their attitude toward the central information system and the quantification and empirical analysis that are required. If a central information system is installed, the danger is either that it will not be used by the right people in the right places at the right time and its vast store of information will simply accumulate to no purpose or, conversely, that it will have an overpowering effect on decision-making without the accompanying influence of qualitative and experienced judgment. To be useful, PPBS requires an analytical capability rooted in the methods of empirical social science and a resolution to *direct* foreign policy and not merely to oversee it. In the Department of State neither of these as yet exists.

The role of social science research in shaping American foreign policy thus depends on organizational changes in the government and on a new and better use of research in many departments, notably the State Department. But is the research community itself prepared to respond to new demands that may be made upon it? The answer here lies outside the confines of government—in the colleges, universities, and private research institutes. In the field of international studies there are several streams of thought which have not yet converged, and these differences of approach have prevented social science from having its full effect on the operations of government. One stream has grown out of the study of international affairs and been highly influenced by the school of political realism; a second has followed the lead of area study programs that stress the multi-disciplinary approach to geographic regions; and a

66 See the testimony of the Director of the Bureau of the Budget in *Planning-Programming-Budgeting*, Hearings before Subcommittee on National Security and International Operations, Committee on Government Operations, U.S. Senate, 90th Congress, 1st Session, 1967, Part 1, pp. 28–32. See also the memorandum by Thomas C. Schelling, *PPBS and Foreign Affairs*, prepared for the Subcommittee, 1968.

third has its origins in comparative studies and cross-cultural analyses of human behavior. To these is now added the application of systems analysis to foreign affairs. These streams may meet and cross but they maintain their identity as separate intellectual trends, each with its own internal consistency and support. This greatly complicates the task of using social science in government policies and programs. Competing "schools" and approaches and different research vocabularies tend to disturb the already difficult relations between researcher and policy-maker.[67]

Research in the problems of developing nations also demands international collaboration. American scholars cannot very well study foreign societies without the help of scholars in those countries. Yet one foreign social scientist has accused Americans of doing what he calls "safari" research. They arrive in a foreign country equipped with funds, canned goods, and "with a methodological armory of well-prepared forms, questionnaires, sampling and interviewing instructions"; they hire "native guides" to carry out their instructions and then return to the United States to complete their analysis and publish their findings.[68] This description, no doubt exaggerated for emphasis, has a point. Foreign scientists have come to resent American "academic imperialism" and have asserted their right to be included in research programs carried out in their own countries. But there are other obstacles in the way of international collaboration: the scarcity of social scientists in many parts of the world, the lack of training in modern methods of investigation, and the paucity of organized facilities to carry on research. Yet, without collaboration, American social scientists will find it increasingly difficult to gain access to the information they need and to comprehend the cultural environment in which they are working.

Both the present state of international studies and the problems of international collaboration must be considered in

---

[67] For a useful discussion of the state of international studies, see E. Raymond Platig, *International Relations Research* (Santa Barbara, California: Clio Press, 1967).

[68] Alexander Szailai, "The Multinational Comparative Time Budget Research Project: A Venture in International Research Cooperation," *American Behavioral Scientist*, Vol. 10, No. 4 (December 1966), p. 2.

framing some system for a more effective use of social science than exists today. In many ways, they only complicate what is already a very complicated matter, the very nature of foreign affairs. The difficulties were expressed by Thomas C. Schelling in analyzing the application of PPBS to foreign policy:

> Foreign affairs is a complicated and disorderly business, full of surprises, demanding hard choices that must often be based on judgment rather than analysis, involving relations with more than a hundred countries diverse in their traditions and political institutions—all taking place in a world that changes so rapidly that memory and experience are quickly out of date. *Coordination, integration,* and *rational management* are surely desirable; but whether it is humanly possible to meet anything more than the barest minimum standards is a question to which an optimistic answer can be based only on faith.[69]

Granted—but who can say how "bare" or "minimum" these standards need be?

[69] Schelling, *op. cit.,* p. 1.

CHAPTER VII

SOCIAL CHANGE

IN HIS STUDY of modern capitalism, Andrew Shonfield poses a question that goes to the heart of American politics:

> [It is a] paradox . . . that the Americans who, in the 1930's, acted as the precursors of the new capitalism, seemed to stall in their course just when the system was coming to fruition in the Western world—showing its full powers to provide the great gifts of economic growth, full employment, and social welfare. . . . Why was the original momentum of the New Deal halted?

Shonfield defines the new capitalism in terms of planning mechanisms that bring the public and private sectors of the economy into working relations in order to move toward the realization of accepted goals and values. In response to his own question, he attributes the "stalling" of the New Deal experiment to a "view of the natural predominance of private enterprise . . . and the subordinate role of public initiative," "the competitive theory of administration inside the government," and "the extraordinary propensity to fragment authority at the very centre of the life of the nation."[1]

Federalism, the separation of powers between the executive and the legislature, and pragmatism have all played a part in limiting the development of national planning in the United States. But, in the postwar years, so have steadily rising federal budgets, heavy with defense expenditures, and international and technological stimulants to economic growth. Economic

---

[1] Andrew Shonfield, *Modern Capitalism* (New York: Oxford University Press, 1965), p. 309.

growth, however, was the basis for social developments that took place without government intervention. Personal income increased, educational opportunities expanded, new technologies began to change the patterns of work and leisure. So rapid were these changes that by the 1960's disparities of wealth and poverty, glaringly evident, became incompatible with the promise of American life. The anomaly of poverty in the midst of affluence gave new stimulus to planning. And, since poverty dominated the lives of an expanding urbanized Negro population, race relations as well as poverty became a national and not just a Southern issue, and thus a target for federal programs.

The Civil Rights Act of 1964, protecting equal legal rights for Negroes, ended a long ten-year struggle that began with the Supreme Court decision in the Brown case in 1954. But the granting of legal rights was a hollow gesture in the absence of decent housing, jobs, and educational opportunities. The Civil Rights Act was accompanied by a series of legislative acts providing new authority for the federal government in education, in the stimulation of economic development in depressed areas, and in the reconstruction of the large cities of the North. Negro expectations aroused by the new legislation were disappointed, however, owing to the resistance of large segments of American society and the slow progress made by government at all levels in giving the new programs substance and momentum. And during the long, hot summers of 1965, 1966, and 1967, large-scale riots broke out in the black urban ghettos.

If the enormous economic growth of the United States left a core of poverty unattended, it also created new problems for the well-to-do and the middle class. Postwar economic growth was, as in few other periods of history, a product of rapid and devastating technological change; and with technological change came social change. Technological change has brought "better working conditions . . . the shortening of working hours and the increase in leisure . . . [and] a growing abundance of goods and a continuous flow of improved and new products." But as the National Commission on Technology, Automation, and Economic Progress also pointed out, it has brought "air and water pollution, inadequate water supply, unsatisfactory solid waste disposal, urban congestion and blight, deterioration of natural beauty, and the rapid depletion of natural resources," as well. And for many individuals, it has meant "rootlessness, anonymity, insecurity, monotony and mental disorder."[2]

As government programs have been created to meet the needs of cities, the poor, and the nation's educational system, questions have been raised about priorities, about what needs to be done first, about the best methods of training and education, about the way social groups can be given cohesion and a sense of participation in society, about the prospects of forecasting the social and psychological, as well as the economic, effects of technological change. All of these are questions that fall within the scope of social science. But, except in the case of economics, the social sciences still play a modest role in shaping government policies and programs. Moreover, programs are usually established in response to political and social pressures, and only after they have been set up is there a search for knowledge, concepts, and expertise to make them work. Now that the government has begun to concern itself not only with economic problems but also with the more complex problems of social change, there is new incentive to find some means of giving social science an effective role in the formulation of policy.

This is not simply a matter of "engineering" rationality in policy-making, of bringing social research up to a point of high predictive capacity and subsequently presenting policy-makers with such clear assessments of program consequences that they can weigh the alternatives and arrive at a rational decision. Government decisions are almost always arrived at through a process of political bargaining among various interested parties: the President, Congress, the many agencies and committees of the executive and legislative branches, and various pressure groups with access to the decision-making process. The demands of rationality—a precise statement of the goals of social progress and the measures necessary to achieve them—are as likely to be

---

[2] *Technology and the American Economy,* Report of the National Commission on Technology, Automation, and Economic Progress (Washington, D.C., January 1966), Vol. I, pp. xi–xii.

frustrated by political compromises as by untested propositions about cause-and-effect in social relations. However, so far as political groups seek to justify their own positions by appealing to reason, by bringing forth evidence, and by invoking the authority of science, ideas may have a substantial effect on political decisions. But how valid are these ideas? Is it possible to measure results against premises?

Economic Policies

Paul Samuelson has written that "economics is fortunate among the social sciences in that many of its findings are directly applicable to public policy." Economics, however, owes its position to the "great advances [that] have been made in our factual knowledge about the financial system and in our understanding of how that system works and can be made to work."[3] Economics is unique in its capacity for dealing with aggregate data that reflect the total economy, a capacity characterized not only by an existent informational base but also by well developed methods of handling large quantities of information. In a sense, these advances in economics were facilitated by the course of economic growth. Business firms, industrial and financial corporations, and government agencies all had to accumulate records of their financial operations. These records provided a broad data base for economic analysis, especially as economic operations became national in scope. And, to insure general stability, economists tried to ascertain the major trends within the whole system and to isolate key indicators that would serve as a warning of possible changes and dangers.

As a result, economic advisers became exceptionally useful to the government, and a Council of Economic Advisers was formed after the war. Memories of the Depression and the wartime mobilization, as well as fears of a postwar recession, also created a

---

[3] Paul A. Samuelson, "What Economists Know," in Daniel Lerner (ed.), *The Human Meaning of the Social Sciences* (New York: Meridian Books, 1959), pp. 183–213.

political climate favorable to the formation of the Council. Before the Council was formed, however, the Bureau of Agricultural Economics was the most active and experienced agency in applying social science to government planning. Nowadays, as the federal government begins to undertake new social programs, the early programs of the Department of Agriculture provide organizational precedents to which other departments increasingly refer. Educational leaders speak of establishing new regional laboratories for educational development along the lines of agricultural extention services, and urban planners of creating a network of university-based urban research centers on the pattern of the land grant college system. Also, the participation of farmers in planning and implementing agricultural programs and the use of survey research to learn the views of farmers are precedents for current attempts to bring the poor into the operation of the poverty program. Some understanding of the end of the Bureau of Agricultural Economics, as well as the beginning of the Council of Economic Advisers, is therefore necessary in considering the contemporary problems of applying research to economic and social problems.

Late in 1938 the Bureau of Agricultural Economics was empowered to serve as a general planning staff for the entire Department of Agriculture. And from that year until 1946 Howard Tolley served as its Director. One of the pioneers in agricultural economics, Tolley was devoted to applying the social sciences to the practical problems of the farmer, a devotion that was shared by men like M. L. Wilson, Carl Taylor, Mordecai Ezekial, and others who played such important parts in the work of the Department during Roosevelt's first two terms. By 1939 they had achieved considerable success in dealing with the farm problem, one of the most difficult economic and political problems in American public life. Farm production was increasing and farm markets were more stable than they had been before.

Conditions changed, however, shortly after the Bureau assumed its planning function. The Secretary, Henry A. Wallace, left the Department of Agriculture to become Roosevelt's running mate in the presidential election of 1940, and Tolley lost the top-level support that his task required. At the same time, the war became the all-absorbing preoccupation of the nation's leaders and the farm problem a less critical issue in the Administration's agenda than it had been early in the New Deal. Tolley and his Bureau had to suffer attacks from several directions without much political protection: from competing agricultural bureaucracies, in Washington and in the field, whose programs were affected by general planning; from powerful farm interest groups that now feared that the bases of their political support would be threatened by the Bureau's research; and from members of the farm bloc in Congress, who were responsive to the pressures of interest groups and conservative in outlook. Indeed, during the war the Bureau was like a lightning rod in attracting the complaints and resentments of farm groups against the decisions of wartime agencies exercising emergency powers in price control and rationing.[4] Though the job of the Bureau, as one congressman put it, was to work "for the benefit of agriculture and of the farmer . . . too much of its effort has been devoted to an attempt to prove that the condition of the farmer is satisfactory and that he is being accorded a fair deal in comparison with other classes."[5]

The Department of Agriculture, like the Departments of Labor and Commerce, is a constituent-based department. Its attention is focused both on a particular national problem and a particular part of the population; indeed, the two are indistinguishable. For many years the farmer was in such hard straits that the energies of the Department had to be directed—as a matter of national as well as constituent concern—toward remedies that would improve his condition. If research helped to accomplish this, then he had had no real objection (though others might have). But during the war, farmers, like others, were subject to administrative decisions from Washington that sought to reconcile competing interests with the compelling needs of defense. Farmers looked to the Department of Agriculture to protect their

4 See Richard S. Kirkendall, *Social Scientists and Farm Politics in the Age of Roosevelt* (Columbia: University of Missouri Press, 1966), pp. 195–238. See also Charles M. Hardin, "The Bureau of Agricultural Economics Under Fire," *Journal of Farm Economics*, Vol. XXVIII, No. 3 (August 1946), pp. 635–668.
5 Quoted in Hardin, *op. cit.*, p. 650.

interests as much as they looked to their elected representatives. Under these circumstances, the Bureau was under unusual pressure, especially since its statistical and analytical services were a major source of information for the emergency agencies. Even when the war was over and the federal government turned to the broad economic problems of reconversion, the Department of Agriculture and the research it supported were still under political pressure to serve the farm interest in the pattern of economic relations that was being developed.

In addition to the inherent problems of undertaking social science research in a constituent-based Department, the Bureau encountered new problems when its research began to irritate certain sectors of American rural society. In 1944, for example, the Bureau initiated a series of socio-economic studies of some seventy counties as a continuation of the sociological work it had been encouraging for some years and as a basis, it was hoped, for postwar agricultural planning.[6] In one study completed in late 1945, the researcher, a sociologist, observed that the institutions and activities of rural life in a county in Mississippi were dominated by "the plantation system of farming" and "white supremacy and racial segregation."[7] When his findings became known to Mississippi congressmen, they used all their political power to aggravate the existing congressional resentment against the Bureau. The director of the sociological studies project, Carl Taylor, had tried earlier to explain that a social scientist in government had two roles to play, "one as a scientist and the other as a member of a policy-making group."[8] And Tolley himself now sought to explain the difference between what the Bureau learned through its research and what it contributed to departmental planning. But the political heat was so intense that the recently appointed Secretary, Clinton Anderson, himself a former congressman, proceeded to cut back the Bureau's budget, to restrict it to economic research and the collection of statistics, and to relieve it of program planning responsibilities.[9]

---

[6] *Ibid.*, pp. 652–655; also Kirkendall, *op. cit.*, pp. 234–238.
[7] Kirkendall, *op. cit.*, p. 235.
[8] Quoted, *ibid.*, p. 237.
[9] *Ibid.*, p. 238.

The subsequent resignation of Tolley in May 1946 marked the end of a difficult period in the history of the Bureau of Agriculture Economics. In retrospect, it is hard to decide what the source of difficulty really was. The economist, John Black, who had close relations with the Bureau, was willing to concede that "if Wallace had remained Secretary of Agriculture . . . and the war had not intervened, the role assigned to the Bureau [might] have been increasingly realized."[10] But the powerful farm interest groups and the strategically placed farm bloc congressmen were formidable opponents under any circumstances. Their opposition was undoubtedly intensified by the liberal orientation of Bureau leadership, and Southern congressmen were enraged when the issue of race relations was raised in the Mississippi study. Finally, the Bureau's responsibility for planning may have put it in a more vulnerable position than if it had restricted its activities to research only. Certainly Black had this in mind when he said, "the Department of Agriculture needs a strong general staff, *but . . . the Bureau should not be that general staff.*"[11]

The Secretary's decision in 1946 was only the first step in a series of actions that, by 1953, led to the breakup of the Bureau into four separate services and their dispersal into separate problem-oriented units. To Tolley, by then occupied with world agricultural problems for the Ford Foundation, the "dismemberment" of the Bureau came as a "shock"; and he expressed his opposition to the arrangements that replaced it:

> Why are economic information, research, and analysis being subordinated to and intermingled with engineering and soils on the production side, and with marketing services, regulatory activities and food distribution activities on the marketing side? . . . [Evidently] the present administration . . . feels that the economic problems of agriculture have been receiving unwarranted prominence in recent years . . . [and] does not recognize Agricultural Economics as an established science and profession.[12]

[10] John D. Black, "The Bureau of Agricultural Economics—the Years in Between," *Journal of Farm Economics,* Vol. XXIX, No. 4 (November 1947), Part II, p. 1035.

[11] *Ibid.*

[12] Howard R. Tolley, "Dismemberment of the BAE," *Journal of Farm Economics,* Vol. XXXVI, No. 1 (February 1954), pp. 14–16.

Although Tolley's opinion was shared by most of his former colleagues, his successor as head of the Bureau, O. V. Wells, thought otherwise. He approved of the decision to organize research "around main problem areas rather than around academic disciplines" because it would create new opportunities for work without the loss of objectivity that sometimes comes "from being too closely associated with action programs."[13]

From an administrative point of view, Paul H. Appleby, who had served as Secretary Wallace's special assistant for a number of years, concluded that the dissolution of the Bureau would weaken research in agriculture and make the Department "a place much less attractive to first-rate economists." The original idea to make the Bureau a planning as well as research unit, he recalled, was based on the concept of "social research and program planning as inextricably intertwined and as constituting a continuum—or two continua." In practice, the Bureau continued to undertake its "strictly economic studies." At the same time, it provided "new stimulation and orientation for the operating bureaus," and "informally . . . achieved . . . greater coordination of programs in the counties." Nevertheless, Appleby thought, the Bureau "did not prove as useful to the Secretary's Office as we had hoped." For here, at the highest level in the Department, the critical problems involved reconciling often conflicting differences. In Appleby's words, "institutional social and political wisdom are not synonymous with 'expert knowledge' but result from the interaction of facts and functions, experts and non-experts."[14]

By an interesting historical coincidence, the declining years of the Bureau of Agricultural Economics coincided with the formative years of the Council of Economic Advisers. Through the Council, economic analysis was deliberately integrated into the governmental process at the very highest level of decision-making. Almost from the beginning, however, there were disagreements within the Council over the matter of dissociating its

13 O. V. Wells, "Agricultural Economics under the USDA Reorganization of November 2, 1953," *Journal of Farm Economics*, Vol. XXXVI, No. 1 (February 1954), pp. 1–5.
14 Paul H. Appleby, "An Administrative View," *Journal of Farm Economics*, Vol. XXXVI, No. 1 (February 1954), pp. 8–12.

scientific advice from the President's political choices. The first Council Chairman, Edwin G. Nourse, refused to testify before congressional committees or to become, in effect, an advocate of presidential policy. Advocacy, he considered, was contrary to his own conception of the Council as "a purely advisory agency of the highest professional competence and political detachment." On the other hand, Leon H. Keyserling, the Vice Chairman, thought that the Council was obligated to advise the President and that, at this level particularly, an adviser, no matter how expert, ought to resign if he could not accept the broad lines of presidential policy.[15] Whatever their differences, both Nourse and Keyserling acknowledged that economic analysis provided by the Council was a major but not the exclusive determinant of policy. Political factors also affected the President's decisions. But Nourse wanted to have nothing to do with these; while Keyserling, more aggressive and pragmatic, felt that political factors neither could nor should be ignored by those who were both experts and advisers and had to reconcile these two roles realistically.

The Council of Economic Advisers was itself a product of politics. It was created by the Employment Act of 1946, after a good deal of controversy among opposing factions. The Act was drawn up in response to various conditions, both political and intellectual, that had been developing ever since the First World War.[16] On the intellectual side, there were both the theoretical and institutional developments in economics. As Wesley Mitchell pointed out, while there had been quantitative work on economic problems earlier, the demonstrated need for aggregate data led, in the 1920's and the 1930's, to new methods for collecting statistics and new efforts "to discover what they really meant." Making "mass observations of economic activities" replaced the earlier practice of "setting up imaginary conditions and reasoning about how men would act if they knew and pursued their

15 See Corinne Silverman, *The President's Economic Advisers,* The Inter-University Case Program, #48 (Tuscaloosa: University of Alabama Press, 1949).
16 Unless otherwise noted, the following discussion relies heavily on Stephen Kemp Bailey, *Congress Makes a Law* (New York: Columbia University Press, 1950).

economic interests."[17] This ability to deal with aggregates, with total economies, both methodologically and theoretically, came, as we have seen, into full play in World War II. The growth of economics as a science and an instrument of policy was a necessary precondition for the Employment Act, as was the influence of the theories of John Maynard Keynes regarding the role of government in shaping the economic environment.

The Employment Act, however, was essentially the result of politics and not necessarily the result of Keynesian thinking. There was little of Keynes, for example, in the New Deal, except as its programs became cases in point and could subsequently be analyzed as object lessons. Pragmatism was also the rule in the governmental activities of the National Resources Planning Board and in the privately financed activities of the National Planning Association and the Committee for Economic Development, both founded by progressive business leaders. If policy-makers recognized the need for economic advice, this was largely owing to their memories of the Depression and the widespread, persistent unemployment that only the war had been able to relieve. Both the President and Congress were eager to prevent any postwar recession. And, during the war, they had created the Office of War Mobilization and Reconversion, charged, *inter alia*, with economic planning for the demobilization period. The Employment Act was framed for the same purpose, to provide a means of extending planning into the postwar period.

Other agencies in operation at this time also set a precedent for using economc advice at high levels of government. The Bureau of Agricultural Economics was but one of these. The independent and regulatory commissions, like the Federal Reserve Board, by the nature of their functions, required economic and statistical staffs. So did the Departments of Commerce and Labor, the Treasury Department, and the Bureau of the Budget. And in Congress, large-scale investigations, such as the one carried out by the Temporary National Economic Committee in the late 1930's, provided practical experience with the use of eco-

[17] Wesley Mitchell, "Economic Research and the Needs of the Times," in *Twenty-Fourth Annual Report,* National Bureau of Economic Research (New York, 1944), p. 10.

nomics in political decision-making. Finally, the war itself created a multitude of emergency agencies that were dominated by professional economists.[18]

It must be emphasized, however, that the first proposals for the Employment Act did not provide for a professional body of advisers like the Council.[19] They merely required the President to prepare what was originally called a "national employment and production budget." At first it was thought to assign this task to the Bureau of the Budget, but this was not done for fear that other agencies would object to the increased authority and prestige this would give the Bureau. Consequently it was left to the President, in consultation with his Cabinet and other top advisers, to establish such special advisory mechanisms as he thought necessary.

In the meanwhile, many congressmen, as well as other government officials, began to see dangerous implications in this proposal. They thought that the "national budget," or economic report, should be prepared by a group of men who could be identified and whose professional analysis could be made available to the joint congressional committee also to be set up under the legislation. Any declaration of employment and production goals, in order to be more than hortatory, had to be followed by government programs and expenditures. The authors of the economic report, therefore, would be laying the foundations for future government activity, yet would, in the words of one congressional witness, be "men unknown to the public, whose appointment has not been confirmed by Congress, and who have no formal public responsibility."[20]

Consequently the formation of a Council of Economic Advisers was suggested. Interestingly enough, one of the chief supporters of this proposal was Representative William Whittington of the 3rd Congressional District in Mississippi who, along with

---

18 See Edwin G. Nourse, *Economics in the Public Service* (New York: Harcourt Brace, 1953), pp. 76–93.

19 Bailey, *op. cit.*, pp. 167–171.

20 Testimony of George Terborgh, representing the Machinery and Allied Products Institute, before Committee on Expenditures in the Executive Departments, House of Representatives, quoted, *ibid.*, p. 169.

his other congressional colleagues, had objected to the sociological research of the Bureau of Agricultural Economics. But it was Whittington who advocated "a permanent board, agency, or commission, to give to the President of the United States the best available expert advice of the leading economists, the leading thinkers, the soundest planners of the country, that will enable them to make sound recommendations to the Executive and then to Congress."[21] And in the final version of the Act, which became law on February 20, 1946, the President was to appoint three Council members and these appointments were subject to confirmation by the Senate. The Act carefully specified all that a member had to be:

> a person who, as a result of his training, experience, and attainments, is exceptionally qualified to analyze and interpret economic developments, to appraise programs and activities of the government in the light of the policy declared [in this Act], and to formulate and recommend national economic policy to promote employment, production, and purchasing power under free competitive enterprise.

The Employment Act was a landmark in acknowledging the necessity of systematic and continuing social science research for the formulation of public policy. The members of the first Council, Nourse, Keyserling, and John D. Clark, were certainly aware of the responsibility they faced in maintaining standards of objectivity that met both the intentions of the legislation and the scrutiny of their professional colleagues. Moreover, if they disagreed among themselves on how to meet this responsibility, it was a matter of degree only. Nourse, as has been pointed out, refused to become a public advocate of policy. But, in the first report of the Council as a whole, the members took pains to explain their relation toward politics: "the Employment Act is an endeavor in political science no less than in economics. . . . the raw materials which we have to process and synthesize in formulating 'national economic policies' must pay attention to all three of

---

[21] Quoted, *ibid.*, p. 169. For Whittington's part in the criticism of the Bureau of Agricultural Economics, see Kirkendall, *op. cit.*, p. 237.

these words and not only to the word 'economic.' "[22] As advisers to the President, they were acutely aware of the political framework in which they operated.

They were also aware of the developing nature of their own discipline, as their report showed.

> Economics is a social science, not a natural science. While a few of its basic laws are of a somewhat mechanistic character, they express themselves through the inadequately informed, whimsical, and perverse behavior of millions of human individuals. . . . [Psychologists may] some day give us much-needed light on the real springs of human action—both logical and whimsical. . . . [Meanwhile] economic analysis and statistical records should give us a better understanding of these phenomena [as they can be observed from the outside].[23]

The Council soon served to stimulate the development of new statistical series that would more accurately record the workings of the economic system and experiments with analytical methods that would give greater clarity and meaning to accumulating information. Most particularly they called upon their colleagues in the economics profession to give increasing attention "to the problems of relationships among production, capacity, investment, and consumption for the economy as a whole and for specific branches."

In the field of statistics, the Council of Economic Advisers sought to encourage at least two postwar developments: the coordination of statistical services on a government-wide basis, and the use of statistical analysis as opposed to simple data collection. In 1942 an Office of Statistical Standards had been established in the Bureau of the Budget under the Federal Reports

---

22 "The Environment within which the Council Operates," in *The Economic Report of the President*, January 1948, reprinted in *History of Employment and Manpower Policy in the United States*, Subcommittee on Employment and Manpower, Committee on Labor and Public Welfare, U.S. Senate, 89th Congress, 2nd Session, 1966, Vol. 7, Part I of Selected Readings in Employment and Manpower (hereinafter referred to as "Senate Readings in Employment and Manpower Policy"), p. 137.

23 *Ibid.*, pp. 137–141.

Act as a central clearing house on forms and procedures. Both during and after the war, however, it was greatly handicapped in coordinating the various statistical collection and distribution services, which proliferated with the multiplication of government programs. The Council, together with the congressional Joint Economic Committee that reviewed its report, were two major forces for coordination. For the most part, both relied heavily on existing statistical agencies for basic data and used the information they obtained for large general purposes. Also, they concentrated on estimating the effects of future actions rather than recording the results of current programs. They thus helped to initiate new approaches to statistical collection and new methods for the rapid assembly of material. In its early years, for example, the Council was instrumental in bringing about the early release of quarterly national income estimates and the presentation of more meaningful data on changes in income distribution than had heretofore been available.[24]

In the years since 1946 the Council of Economic Advisers has become a permanent institution of increasing influence both politically and professionally. Its permanency and its influence were not always assured, however. At the very end of the Truman Administration, for example, Congress did not appropriate a full year's budget to support the Council's activities, so uncertain was its future under the incoming Eisenhower Administration. In point of fact, the Council was strengthened under Arthur F. Burns who served as Chairman from 1953 to 1956. Nevertheless, at one time in the 1950's a member of the Council is quoted as having called his position the "highest paid fellowship in the profession."[25] By the 1960's, however, there were few doubts that the Council was here to stay. Its usefulness to the President and Congress was unquestioned. And the need for government to play an

---

[24] Bertram M. Gross and John P. Lewis, "The President's Economic Staff during the Truman Administration," reprinted in "Senate Readings in Employment and Manpower Policy," *op. cit.*, p. 261, footnote 23. See also Fredrick C. Mills and Clarence D. Long, *The Statistical Agencies of the Federal Government* (New York: National Bureau of Economic Research, 1949), p. 93.

[25] Quoted in Walter W. Heller, *New Dimensions of Political Economy* (Cambridge: Harvard University Press, 1966), p. 15.

active role in economic affairs was generally recognized. The end of *laissez-faire* was perhaps best indicated by Walter W. Heller's remark: "When Milton Friedman, the chief guardian of the *laissez-faire* tradition in American economics, said . . . 'We are all Keynesians now,' the profession said 'Amen.' "[26] And Friedman's words were significant because of his influence not only among conservative economists but among conservative politicians as well.

Throughout its history the Council has had difficulties in reconciling professional standards with political requirements. The Nourse position—that the Council should be a scientific agency detached from political affairs—proved unworkable. Politics is the business of government and at the level of the presidency there is no escape. Under Eisenhower, Arthur Burns took a position somewhat between Nourse and Keyserling. He assumed that the Council had to be able to support presidential policies, though the first function of its members was to serve as professional economists. He was thus prepared to testify before Congress in specific instances. While he disagreed with the rigidity of Nourse's position, he later acknowledged that "if there had only been the type of Council that Keyserling envisaged, I never would have accepted the appointment . . . because there had been a Nourse my job was possible."[27]

The Council was able to reconcile professional standards and political requirements for several reasons. In the first place, the Council's very existence is based on its possession of expert knowledge. Since its membership is subject to senatorial confirmation, the professional capability of nominees must be proved in public. The President is thus under pressure to appoint men who have been judged by their own peers to be eminent in their profession. It is his prior defense against possible charges that he is not fulfilling his own responsibilities under the Employment Act. The President's political position is thus related to the standards of the economic profession. Congress, too, has an interest in insuring high professional standards in the Council. Although the Council

26 *Ibid.*, p. 9.
27 Silverman, *op. cit.*, p. 17.

is essentially an arm of presidential policy, a fact confirmed at the very beginning when the proposal to establish an independent commission was defeated, Congress, and particularly the Joint Economic Committee, is dependent on the Council's analysis of economic changes to perform its own role under the Act. Moreover, the membership and staff of the Committee have developed a high degree of expertise in dealing with the Council's reports and with economic matters in general. Under this system, political aims are served while high professional standards are maintained.

Each successive Council has had its own orientation which, of necessity, has reflected the orientation of the administration it has served. Each Council has also engaged in the bargaining carried on within the Executive Branch and, increasingly, in the business of advocating measures in public discussion. But, as a student of the Council noted, "Advocacy has served as a complement to, not a substitute for, analysis."[28] Advocacy, moreover, is a responsibility of the Council because it is not a research organization in essence. Its purpose is to give advice on policy and the task of its members is to relate knowledge and systematic analysis to problems of political importance.

There is, however, a certain protection in the level of analysis at which the Council operates. So long as it deals primarily in macro-economics, in general advice on policy, it avoids, as Heller puts it, "[diverting] energies and efforts from the Council's central purpose and competence . . . [and getting] entangled in the conflicts and cross fire of special interest groups."[29] In the various departments, research on policy, no matter how general, is still specialized in comparison to the Council reports, or at least focused on the primary concerns of the department. Moreover, in a constituent-based department like the Department of Agriculture, research is scrutinized by various pressure groups for any effect it may have on their interests. Indeed, as research is applied closer to the point where public programs are administered, it becomes more vulnerable to political pressure.

---

[28] Edward S. Flash, Jr., *Economic Advice and Presidential Leadership* (New York: Columbia University Press, 1965), p. 292.
[29] Heller, *op. cit.*, p. 56.

Social Programs

In its annual report submitted in January 1967, the Council of Economic Advisers estimated that "if the American economy continues to grow at 4 percent a year, output will double in 18 years, triple in 28, quadruple in 35." More difficult than predicting the rate of economic growth is speculating about the uses to which this new wealth will be put. For the uses of national wealth depend on the priorities the nation establishes, and these priorities in turn depend on the values of the society and the way the political system operates to give these values life. While "billions of private and public decisions determine the distribution of the growing gross national product," the Council states, "these decisions are inevitably affected by public policies." On the one hand, "monetary and credit policies and changes in tax rates and tax incentives restrain or encourage consumer and business outlays and influence their composition." On the other, "the budget-making process at Federal, State, and local levels determines the share of output used to meet public needs." The kinds of decisions and policies that are made become increasingly significant since, as the Council also pointed out, "the increased wealth of the United States permits us to face directly the problems of poverty, lack of education, ill health, and urban decay as national issues requiring a coordinated policy effort."[30]

In the early 1960's a series of legislative and organizational measures were taken to prepare the ground for dealing with the very problems the Council pointed to. Earlier programs, in essence, had been an expression or an extension of the New Deal, particularly the development of social security, the strengthening of workers' rights and benefits, and the development of mechanisms, largely advisory like the Council of Economic Advisers, to permit the federal government to exercise influence on the rate of economic growth. The new legislation was primarily directed to the problems of redistributing income, providing for those whom the older laws had neglected or who were unable to claim a share

[30] *The Economic Report of the President,* together with the *Annual Report,* Council of Economic Advisers (Washington, D.C., 1967), p. 135–137.

in the growing gross national product, and facilitating social adjustment to new technological advances. It included the Manpower Development and Training Act of 1962, the Civil Rights Act of 1964, the establishment of Medicare, the Elementary and Secondary Education Act of 1965, the Public Works and Economic Development Act of 1965, the setting up of the poverty program under an independent Office of Economic Opportunity (OEO), and the organization of the Department of Housing and Urban Development (HUD). In almost every expanded or new program, provision was made for social science research. And by the mid-1960's research in domestic programs began to outstrip research in the defense field. For the fiscal year 1967, for example, almost $100 million was budgeted for social science research in the Office of Education, $35 million in the poverty program through OEO, and $12 million in the Department of Labor, as compared with $28 million in the more established program of the Department of Agriculture and $27.6 million in the defense establishment.[31]

Research in the Department of Agriculture continued to grow, given the political importance of agricultural policy, despite the decline in rural population to less than ten percent of the total population. In 1961 social science research was again unified in the Department under a Director of Agricultural Economics and was carried out primarily in three agencies: the Statistical Reporting Service, the Economic Research Service, and the Farmer Cooperative Service. The contributions of research to departmental policymaking were facilitated by the Director of Agricultural Economics, who took part in the planning activities of the Secretary's office, while the three Services were formally separate from the policy process. This system was quite different from the one that existed in the days of the Bureau of Agricultural Economics under Tolley. But it did serve to make research in agriculture independent "of agencies . . . oriented toward research in the physical sciences and

---

[31] *The Use of Social Research in Federal Domestic Programs,* Staff Study for the Research and Technical Programs Subcommittee, Committee on Government Operations, House of Representatives, 90th Congress, 1st Session, 1967, Part I, pp. 26–28.

in marketing." And, in the opinion of the new administration, it "restored the opportunity to carry out research on the economic and social aspects of overall agricultural problems." Also, research in the Department rested, as it had in the past, mainly in the hands of the internal staff, though they maintained relations with researchers in the state universities, experiment stations, and other institutions.[32] And still, today, it is the activity of a strong internal research staff, developed over the years, that distinguishes the Department's work from that of most of the newer programs. The lack of an internal research staff is, for that matter, a pressing problem in many agencies of the government.

In the Department of Health, Education, and Welfare, social science research is supported in several different agencies and at several different levels. The National Institute of Mental Health (NIMH) has become a major source of financing for fundamental research in the social sciences. The NIMH, and indeed the other National Institutes of Health, are in a very special position. There are no clear lines to relate the research supported by the Institutes to the issues and problems of federal agencies—a situation which has both advantages and disadvantages. From the Institutes' point of view, there are no pressures for skewing research in one direction or another and there is considerable political and adminstrative freedom. The linkage between research and program, therefore, largely depends on the normal flow of research through scholarly and professional communication networks. In this respect the NIMH operates very much like the National Science Foundation and quite differently from other agencies within the Department in which it is established, especially as those agencies have come to operate in recent years.

In the Social Security and Welfare Administrations and in the Office of Education, older research programs were augmented in the late 1950's by cooperative research programs that provided grants to universities and non-profit research institutes to under-

32 *National Foundation for the Social Sciences,* Hearings before Subcommittee on Government Research, Committee on Government Operations, U.S. Senate, 90th Congress, 1st Session, 1967, Part I, pp. 241–244.

take both research and demonstration projects.[33] Under the Elementary and Secondary Education Act of 1965, the program in education was considerably expanded; it provided for the establishment of research and development centers in specialized fields of education, in regionally based educational laboratories, and in information clearing houses. Research and demonstration grants from all three agencies were generally awarded to those who submitted unsolicited proposals after review by both agency specialists and advisory panels. More recently, the Social Security and Welfare Administrations have started to develop programs of *directed* research in order to relate research more closely to agency programs. And in the larger education program there have been several changes tending in the same direction.

The Education Act of 1965 has been called the "greatest landmark in the history of federal aid to education."[34] It was passed after a decade of controversy about the American educational system, first provoked by the self-study stimulated by the Soviet Sputnik and later by the problems of educational opportunity for Negroes and the urban and rural poor. The passage of the Act overcame the obstacles, as Stephen K. Bailey calls them, of "Red, Religion, and Race": that is, "fear of federal control of the educational system"; "the prickly issue of Church-State Relations"; and "fear . . . that federal aid would be used as a club to enforce school integration."[35] Title IV of the Act, which provided a new and expanded basis for educational research, also changed its direction somewhat. Whereas earlier research had been limited to small and unrelated projects for the most part, the new financing allowed for large and sustained projects, particularly in the research and development centers and laboratories of the universi-

---

[33] For discussions of the early welfare and social security programs, see Ida C. Merriam, "Cooperative Research and Demonstration Grant Program of the Social Security Administration," *Social Security Bulletin*, Vol. 24, No. 9 (September 1961), pp. 20–28; also Lee G. Burchinal, "Cooperative Research and Demonstration Grants Program," *Welfare in Review*, Vol. 2, No. 8 (August 1964), pp. 8–19.

[34] Stephen Kemp Bailey, *The Office of Education and the Education Act of 1965*, Inter-University Case Program, #100 (New York: The Bobbs-Merrill Co., 1966), p. 1.

[35] *Ibid.*, p. 4.

ties. In fact, research was now substantially shifted from schools and state departments of education, where it had been almost exclusively concentrated, to groups of social scientists in universities and to non-profit and profit organizations.[36]

Social science research was also expanded in the Department of Commerce with the creation of the Economic Development Administration. Traditionally, the Commerce Department has maintained a program of economic and statistical analysis, largely as a service to the business community. Much of the Department's work is still regularly published in the monthly magazine, *Survey of Current Business,* and the biennial publication, *Business Statistics.* The Department is also responsible for the preparation of national income and product data and has supported the development of an econometric model of the United States.[37] Under the Public Works and Economic Development Act of 1965, the Department's Economic Development Administration (EDA) was charged with the task of undertaking research to "assist in determining the causes of unemployment, underemployment, underdevelopment and chronic depression in the various regions of the Nation" and in formulating programs to meet these conditions.[38] The program was organized around "policy-oriented study groups," through which "specific projects undertaken by . . . staff members, contractors or grantees" are related to a structured research plan in one of several areas: operational analyses, urban analyses, program evaluation, and studies of the national economic environment.[39]

Similarly, in the Department of Labor, a traditional research program in the Bureau of Labor Statistics was augmented by a broader program of research in manpower problems under the Manpower Development and Training Act of 1962. Over the years,

36 See Francis A. J. Ianni, "The Emerging Role of the Bureau of Research," reprinted in *The Use of Social Research in Federal Domestic Programs, op. cit.,* Part II, pp. 165–170.

37 *Annual Report,* Secretary of Commerce, Fiscal Year 1966, Office of Business Economics (Washington, D.C.), p. 17.

38 Anthony H. Pascal, "Research for Economic Development," *The Research Review,* June 1967, Economic Development Administration, Department of Commerce (Washington, D.C.), p. 1.

39 *Ibid.,* pp. 2–3.

the data collection system of the Bureau of Labor Statistics complemented the work of the Department of Commerce, supplying the essential data on the labor force and unemployment. The Manpower Act of 1962 specifically provided for research that would deal more broadly with the effects of automation, the conditions of labor mobility, the training and improvement of the labor force, and the determinants of future manpower needs.[40] Initially, the manpower research program was almost entirely made up of contractual arrangements for specific investigations of short-range manpower problems. Later, two grant programs were instituted, one to support graduate students and the second to provide institutional grants to universities. The purpose of these grants is to increase the number of social scientists working in the manpower field and to arouse more interest in the subject in the universities.[41] The research program is conducted within the Department's Office of Manpower Policy, Evaluation and Research, which has responsibility for the promotion of experimental projects and the evaluation of government labor and employment programs, activities which, in conjunction with research, can contribute to the accumulation of knowledge on manpower problems.

In all of these agencies with new or expanded research—the Welfare and Social Security Administrations, the Office of Education, and the Departments of Labor and Commerce—there had been earlier social science research programs. These programs, however, had either been largely statistical in nature or had consisted of small, usually unrelated, and even unsolicited projects that had little more than an informational purpose. They were products of the *laissez-faire* policy of the federal government and its passive role in the fields of education and social

---

40 See testimony of Secretary of Labor Willard Wirtz, *National Foundation for the Social Sciences, op. cit.,* pp. 16–18; also Howard Rosen, "Research Tools for Solving Manpower Problems," *Business and Government Review,* March–April 1967 (Columbia: University of Missouri), pp. 18–25.

41 See *Manpower Research Projects,* sponsored by the Manpower Administration through June 30, 1966, Department of Labor (Washington, D.C., November 1966).

welfare. The changed attitude of the government was described by a former research director for the Office of Education in 1965:

> Five years ago, we were satisfied with the idea of supporting research if and when a good research idea was presented to us. Today, we are convinced that this laissez-faire attitude must be supplemented by a thorough and responsible evaluation of the needs of education. . . . we should then be willing to look for and deliberately ask for needed research, without waiting for it to come to us.[42]

The new programs mark an effort to be more cohesive, to develop a broad base of support in the social sciences, and to build a cumulative store of knowledge and information that is relevant to agency operations. At least this is the intention and the direction of organizational changes in all of the programs that have been noted, as well as in the Office of Economic Opportunity (OEO) and the Department of Housing and Urban Development (HUD). In OEO, research is administered by an Assistant Director who is also responsible for program planning and evaluation. Research, planning, and evaluation are also bound together in units attached to the special Headstart, Job Corps, and Community Action programs. In the Headstart program, for example, the continual evaluation of special pre-school courses for poor children is an important element in this unusually large social and educational experiment. A set of evaluation centers continually studies the progress of Headstart children; and, as a result of some of their early studies, there were demands for improvements in public school teaching to maintain the eagerness and receptivity to learning that Headstart had stimulated. OEO has also financed the development of new statistical series by the Census Bureau to identify more accurately the characteristics of poverty, as well as the establishment of an Institute for Poverty Research at the University of Wisconsin for the study of new methods and concepts. The Institute has brought together a group of scholars concerned with the prob-

---

[42] Francis A. J. Ianni, *op. cit.*, p. 166.

lems of poverty to whom the OEO staff can turn for advice and counsel.[43]

The Wisconsin Institute is, in some ways, a "RAND Corporation" for the poverty program. The similarity is not accidental, for RAND has served as a model for many domestic programs, particularly those that deal with city planning. Here RAND has set a precedent not only in its organization but also in its methods. Systems analysis has proved increasingly useful in dealing with interconnections among the variables of urban technological and social change. In the initial period after its establishment in 1965, the Department of Housing and Urban Development was engaged in launching new programs of support for cities with little time or funds to organize a meaningful program of research and evaluation. However, in consequence of an early presidential proposal calling for a central agency for research in urban affairs, the Urban Institute was founded in 1968. At the same time, Under Secretary Robert C. Wood spoke of "a comprehensive R & D budget" and of "a positive approach within the department . . . to specify [to universities and to the research-oriented companies] what it is we are after."[44] In 1968 the Department also sought the assistance of the National Research Council in setting up two interlocking advisory groups, one in the social sciences and one in engineering, to assist its staff in planning a long-range and coherent research strategy.

The emerging federal system for social science research reflects recognition of the need for planning and for the close relationship of knowledge to the formulation and execution of social programs. In almost every case there is an attempt to make research relevant to public policies and to develop cumulative knowledge in the field of departmental interest. The methods used to accomplish this are different in different agencies. But in all cases success depends on the ability of departmental research staffs to make long-term plans for research. Strong staff

---

[43] See testimony of Robert A. Levine, Assistant Director, Office of Economic Opportunity, *National Foundation for the Social Sciences, op. cit.,* pp. 23–53.

[44] Quoted in an interview republished in *The Use of Social Research in Federal Domestic Programs, op. cit.,* Part II, p. 567.

guidance is necessary to give direction and purpose to the growing number of investigations that are being carried on. Without it, there would be a return to *laissez-faire* in fact if not in intention. In any social program there are underlying assumptions that what is being done will lead to results—that housing programs will lead to better living conditions for low-income families, that educational programs will lead to new economic and social opportunities for disadvantaged children. The validity of these assumptions is rarely tested. Government programs are the product of political choices that come out of the confrontation of political interests. What research provides is an instrument for examining how well they achieve the political purposes they are designed to fulfill. In the process, research also serves as a tool for reshaping programs and for clarifying the goals of social legislation. But this is possible only if research activities are sustained and cumulative and closely linked with program operations. The process is not without its hazards and pitfalls.

The case of the Moynihan report on the Negro family illustrates some of the problems in relating research to political purposes in the context of the new social legislation.[45] As Assistant Secretary of Labor, Daniel P. Moynihan had, in 1965, completed a confidential report which called for a national effort directed to "the establishment of a stable Negro family structure."[46] Moynihan's contention was that the Civil Rights Act of 1964 had to be followed by economic and social programs of dramatic proportions if the achievements of that legislation were to be given full meaning. The Negro family structure, he claimed, was a critical factor in the ability of Negroes to take advantage of the opportunity for jobs, education, and housing which the Civil Rights Act had been passed to protect. He proposed no specific programs, but instead urged "one general strategy" to rebuild the structure of Negro family life. He sought, in effect, to articulate a working hypothesis against which to test and measure social

---

45 The following discussion relies heavily on the analysis of the Moynihan report and its history in Lee Rainwater and William L. Yancey, *The Moynihan Report and the Politics of Controversy* (Cambridge: The M.I.T. Press, 1967).

46 *The Negro Family: the Case for National Action,* Office of Policy Planning and Research, Department of Labor (Washington, D.C., March 1965).

and economic programs for bringing the Negro poor into the mainstream of American prosperity.

The Moynihan report became the basis for a speech by President Johnson at Howard University in early June. In remarks that were enthusiastically applauded, the President pledged his administration to "the next and more profound stage of the battle for civil rights . . . to give 20 million Negroes the same chance as every other American to learn and grow, to work and share in society, to develop their abilities." And like the Moynihan report, the President's address emphasized the "breakdown of the Negro family structure" as "perhaps most important of all the burdens that Negroes carried." Indeed, he went so far as to say that "unless we work to strengthen the family, to create conditions under which most parents will stay together—all the rest: schools, playgrounds, public assistance and private concern, will never be enough to cut completely the circle of despair and deprivation."[47]

Lee Rainwater and William L. Yancey have noted that "the Moynihan report is not basically a research report or a technical document; it is a polemic which makes use of social science techniques and findings to convince others."[48] In the months that followed, the report came under increasingly severe attack, ironically, from two major sources that would have profited from the call to action that Moynihan sounded: the professional welfare community and civil rights advocates. Civil rights advocates feared that the Moynihan report, by its emphasis on the Negro family, attributed the condition of the Negroes to inherent deficiencies rather than to the ill-treatment they suffered in American society. And the welfare community resented the report's sharp criticism of programs such as the Aid for Dependent Children Program, which worked to disrupt family life by making assistance dependent on the continued absence of the male head of the family. With regard to the first objection, Moynihan had made it clear that the breakdown of the Negro family was a result of the subjugation of the Negro and other oppressive social conditions.

[47] Reprinted in Rainwater and Yancey, *op. cit.*, pp. 125–132.
[48] *Ibid.*, p. 297.

His critics, however, insisted that his emphasis on Negro family life would contribute to the arguments of the racists. In the protests of the welfare community, the facts mentioned in the report were not really disputed. They were facts, however, that had been ignored because of the practice of not differentiating between whites and non-whites in welfare reporting. The Moynihan report thus exposed the failure of the current system to provide adequate information about social problems.

However, some criticisms of the report went deeper than merely factual or political issues. Social scientists, especially, questioned whether Moynihan's whole thesis could be proved. This raises the question, of course, of what is meant by "proof" and, indeed, whether research can establish absolute "proof" of the causes of social dislocation. There is no doubt that Moynihan accumulated and synthesized a considerable amount of statistical and scholarly evidence to support his case. But other evidence might be mustered to demonstrate that disruptive family conditions need not be crippling, that Negro kinship relations provide a wide protective network beyond the immediate family household, and that the middle-class standards of stable family life are not necessarily the most relevant criteria for assessing the contemporary problems of American Negroes.[49] Moreover, the statistical evidence and theoretical concepts available in so complex a matter as Negro poverty and discrimination are still insufficient to determine the underlying causes.

When all is said and done, the Moynihan report was the product of a policy-maker intent, as Rainwater and Yancey have emphasized, on persuading the government to take action. He sought to base his recommendations not on hunches, intuition, or accepted trends, but on a careful and skillful interpretation of the knowledge available to him. But he was forced to act as researcher, interpreter, and persuader all in one. And he presumably intended to include, in the large-scale government program that he recommended, various provisions for research that would test

---

[49] For a summary of some of these points, see the critical but not unsympathetic review of the Moynihan Report by Herbert J. Gans, reprinted, *ibid.*, pp. 445–457.

his original propositions and subject them to continual modification. The attacks on the report produced sufficient political opposition to halt any such plans. Indeed, regardless of the validity of Moynihan's thesis, his report was politically vulnerable because of the precision with which it defined the social and economic goals of programs to assist the Negro. But Moynihan seems to have decided that only by pointing to a clear and precise goal could the government be roused to act responsibly and effectively. As part of his responsibility, a policy-maker has to decide not only *what* action to recommend but also *how* to convince the President and Congress of the necessity of it. And rarely, if ever, will he have enough evidence to make his case incontrovertible.

The Moynihan report, despite the difficulties it encountered, was an indication of the expanding scope of social science research in government, both in the scale of the measures it recommended and the range of subjects it covered. Government agencies now support research in areas that were once forbidden, not because these areas are now less politically controversial, but because it is generally expected that the federal government will concern itself with a broader range of social problems. The new social science research programs function in a political atmosphere that is considerably different from the atmosphere that prevailed twenty years ago, when social studies of Southern agricultural patterns brought about the fall of the Bureau of Agricultural Economics. Undoubtedly certain taboos still exist, especially in constituent-based departments that feel the pressure of interest groups; but these taboos are now less stringent. For example, for years the labor movement was sensitive to any mention of the practice of racial discrimination in apprenticeship training programs. Yet a number of projects sponsored under the Manpower Act have dealt with the issue of discrimination in employment. And these have included a ten-city study of the place of the Negro worker in apprenticeship programs and a study, covering forty business firms, of the "adjustment by employers, unions and workers to the employment of Negro workers in new jobs."[50]

The expansion of government-sponsored research on the

---

[50] See *Manpower Research Projects, op. cit.*

racial question is even more evident in the study of segregated education conducted under the direction of the Johns Hopkins sociologist, James Coleman, for the Office of Education. The study was called for under the Civil Rights Act of 1964 which stipulated that "the Commissioner [of Education] shall conduct a survey and make a report to the President and the Congress . . . concerning the lack of availability of equal educational opportunities for individuals by reason of race, color, religion, or national origin in public educational institutions." The survey that was carried out went on to pursue questions beyond the simple counting of students in segregated and non-segregated schools, however. It also sought to obtain information on "whether the schools offer equal educational opportunities in terms of other criteria which are regarded as good indicators of educational quality," on "how much the students learn as measured by their performance on standardized achievement tests," and on "possible relationships between students' achievement, on the one hand, and the kinds of schools they attend on the other."[51]

The use of sociological evidence in dealing with the problem of segregated education goes back at least as far as the Brown case in 1954. There the Supreme Court accepted sociological evidence prepared by social scientists working with the NAACP legal staff as an indication that segregated schooling was sociologically and psychologically injurious to Negro children. Whatever precedent there was for the use of psychiatrists and psychologists as expert witnesses in legal disputes, the famous "sociological footnote" in the Supreme Court's decision in the Brown case was an event of historic significance. It established the *legal acceptance* of social science findings. By the same token, it might be asserted that the survey called for under the Civil Rights Act established the *political acceptance* of social science findings in the controversial area of race relations. This, despite the estimate by Coleman that "the Congressional intent . . . is somewhat unclear" and that Congress probably considered research only "as a means of finding areas of continued intentional

---

51 James S. Coleman, *et al.*, *Equality of Educational Opportunity*, Office of Education (Washington, D.C., 1966), pp. iii–14.

discrimination." But, as Coleman also pointed out, "the intent later became less punitive-oriented and more future-oriented: i.e., to provide a basis for public policy at the local, state, and national levels, which might overcome inequalities of educational opportunity."[52]

The Coleman report was also remarkable for its scope. It involved some 600,000 children and 60,000 teachers in 4,000 schools and focused on five racial and ethnic minorities: Negroes, Puerto Ricans, Mexican Americans, American Indians, and Oriental Americans. It was thus an unusual example of "big social science." Indeed, the survey provided social scientists with so much data that they were occupied with analysis for some time. For the Office of Education, the survey provided essential information for the development of procedures for desegregating school systems. But the report had to go beyond this; it had to consider not only the schools that were the primary focus of research but also the total social environment of which they were a part, as Coleman subsequently pointed out.

> Altogether, the sources of inequality of educational opportunity appear to lie first in the home itself and the cultural influences immediately surrounding the home; then they lie in the schools' ineffectiveness to free achievement from the impact of the home, and in the schools' cultural homogeneity which perpetuates the social influence of the home and its environs.[53]

Clearly, any study of the problems of Negro education has to concern itself with the family, to which the Moynihan report directed attention, with housing patterns, with white middle-class flights to the suburbs, with the whole interlocking complex of social, psychological, economic, and political factors that influence community life.

The demand for social science research to provide a basis of knowledge for public policies extends from one problem to another. In 1967 the President's Commission on Law Enforcement

---

[52] James S. Coleman, "Equal Schools or Equal Students?" *The Public Interest*, No. 4, Summer 1966, p. 70.
[53] *Ibid.*, pp. 73–74.

and Administration of Justice baldly reported, "There is virtually no subject connected with crime or criminal justice into which further research is unnecessary." This assertion, moreover, followed the Commission's statement that "society has relied primarily on traditional answers and has looked almost exclusively to common sense and hunch for needed changes." But now, even in cases where "research cannot, in itself, provide final answers, it can provide data crucial to making informed policy judgments."[54] The breadth of the Commission's recommendation is symptomatic of the general change in attitude. There are also significant signs of changing times in the establishment of regional educational laboratories, in the EDA research on depressed areas, in the manpower studies of the Labor Department, and in the poverty program's experimental projects in education, training, and community action.

Despite all these signs of progress, it is difficult to say what the future holds. The system of social science research that develops in the federal government—like the system of economic research—will certainly depend on the growth of both intellectual and political support. However, there are current factors at work that may have a substantial influence on future arrangements. First of all, there are the demands for new statistical series that emphasize social rather than economic data and the pressures for more centralized and coordinated depositories for economic and social information. Secondly, there is the new work in social indicators and social accounting designed to give both the President and Congress better means of anticipating social change and planning political measures to cope with it. And, in the third place, there is the application of the Planning-Programming-Budgeting System (PPBS) throughout the federal government, which makes necessary a more precise definition of social objectives and criteria for program evaluation. Whatever happens, social science and politics are bound to become more closely involved than they ever have been.

---

54 *The Challenge of Crime in a Free Society*, A Report by the President's Commission on Law Enforcement and Administration of Justice (Washington, D.C., February 1967), p. 273.

Tools of Analysis

The federal government needs facts. It is a prodigious consumer and manufacturer of information about the society and the economy. Every new social program that has been launched has required new kinds of information and new statistical series to support and evaluate its work. In consequence, many new statistical programs have been added to the number already in existence. And the present federal system of separate, disorganized, and still proliferating groups and agencies devoted to statistical work now urgently requires coordination and centralization. For centralization may have important consequences for advanced research on the processes of social change.

Economists have been fortunate in having at their command a great body of information, constantly accumulated from a variety of sources, against which they were able to test their theories. Social scientists in other fields have not had this advantage. For one thing, there were few agencies in the society which, in the course of their regular operations, collected and collated cumulative social data. The records of public and private social agencies were generally dispersed and decentralized, and even the activities of the Bureau of the Census and the Bureau of Labor Statistics remained limited to gross demographic and economic data that reflected the interest of government in economic rather than social change. In addition, the enactment of the federal reserve system as far back as 1913, served to develop the uniform reporting of banking operations on a national scale.[55] And other coordinated and manageable systems of economic accounting grew out of the consolidation of industrial corporations and the statistical requirements of dealing, likewise on a national scale, with the Depression and the production and allocation problems of the Second World War.

Theories of large-scale social change have thus remained more highly speculative for lack of reliable and consistent aggregate data. Also, economic behavior is but one small aspect of so-

---

[55] See *All-Bank Statistics United States, 1896–1955,* Board of Governors of the Federal Reserve System (Washington, D.C., 1959).

cial behavior, which is a much more complex phenomenon. The first Council of Economic Advisers recognized that even the "basic laws" of economics were only "somewhat mechanistic" and were based on "the inadequately informed, whimsical, and perverse behavior of millions of human individuals." And in dealing with many special economic problems, researchers have had to supplement the traditional methods of economic analysis and resort to modern psychology, especially since the Second World War. During the war, attitude surveys in connection with the war bond drives exposed the variety of motives behind public buying habits. And surveys of consumer finances and attitudes, especially those conducted by the Survey Research Center at the University of Michigan, have provided both government and industry with increasingly important socio-psychological information to supplement the purely economic basis for evaluating and predicting economic changes.

New and expanding sources of economic and social information thus offer significant new opportunities for the study of social change. And research carried on under the new social programs—such as the poverty program and the urban development program—is constantly adding new statistical information to that which has already been accumulated. However, if this information is to be useful for further research, much depends on how it is collected, maintained, and analyzed. The coordination of procedures for data collection and analysis and the consolidation of information relating to any particular problem are therefore of critical importance to the progress of social science and the workings of government.

The consolidation of the statistical services of the federal government has been an issue of debate for some time, one might say from the time the Bureau of the Census was established as a permanent agency in 1902. It will be recalled that efforts to establish a coordinating statistical bureau after the First World War were never realized, and not until 1933 was a Central Statistical Board established. By 1939 the Board was transferred to the Bureau of the Budget, as part of the development of the Executive Office of the President, and renamed the Office of Statistical Standards. In 1942, moreover, the functions of the Office were defined in the Federal Reports Act, which established a legislative basis for the Office. The purpose of the Act was not so much to rationalize the statistical services as to minimize the burden placed on the public as a result of the growing information needs of government agencies.[56]

The Office of Statistical Standards has concentrated on the review and evaluation of statistical forms and questionnaires, though subsequent executive orders have given it responsibility for "the improved gathering, compiling, analyzing, publishing, and disseminating of statistical information by Federal agencies." Within the statistical system as a whole, the Office thus serves as a central coordinating point. Some of the work of coordination is also done by general purpose statistical agencies like the Bureau of the Census and the Bureau of Labor Statistics, which have assigned tasks but which make their regular reports and their organized data collection facilities available to all agencies of the government.[57] Despite these efforts, for the past twenty years there has been general agreement (as expressed by a review body in 1966) that "the high degree of decentralization . . . of the present statistical system has . . . been . . . a major obstacle in the way of its effective functioning."[58]

Recommendations for improving the federal statistical system over the years have generally had three major aims: to increase the accuracy of existing statistical series; to expand statistical programs, particularly in the area of social statistics; and to devise mechanisms through which to relate government statistics from all sources. More recently, the objective of retaining information in its original form has been added. The first major review

[56] Stuart A. Rice, "The Federal Reports Act," *The American Sociologist*, Vol. II, No. II (May 1967), pp. 73–75.

[57] For a survey of the government statistical system, see *Statistical Services of the United States Government*, Bureau of the Budget (rev. ed.; Washington, D.C., 1963).

[58] "Report of the Task Force on the Storage of and Access to Government Statistics," Bureau of the Budget (Washington, D.C., October 1966), (hereinafter referred to as the "Kaysen Committee Report"), in *The Coordination and Integration of Government Statistical Programs*, Subcommittee on Economic Statistics, Joint Economic Committee, 90th Congress, 1st Session, 1967, p. 196.

of the statistical system after World War II was conducted by Frederick C. Mills and Clarence D. Long in 1948 for the first Hoover Commission, one of a series of studies on the organization of the Executive Branch of the federal government.[59]

Anticipating later criticisms, Mills and Long listed a series of problems and deficiencies, including incomplete coordination, overlapping and uncertain jurisdiction among statistical agencies, and a lack of comparability among statistical series. As a remedy they suggested the establishment of an independent Office of Statistical Standards and Services in the Executive Office of the President. In effect, the new office would have pulled the existing Office of Statistical Standards out of the Bureau of the Budget and given it authority to take more positive measures for insuring coordination within the statistical system. These recommendations were based on something more than a desire for statistical and administrative tidiness. In general, the federal statistical system had evolved in response to many different problems and interests, either of government agencies or segments of the private community. In the postwar period, Mills and Long pointed out, the establishment of an agency like the Council of Economic Advisers marked a shift in the attitude of government, a recognition that all parts of the national economy were interrelated and that policy decisions had to be based on an analysis of all the factors involved. This new orientation required an integrated system of statistics rather than the continued accumulation of unrelated groups of data.[60]

No central organization besides the existing Office of Statistical Standards was established following the Mills-Long report, however. Throughout the 1950's and into the 1960's, existing statistical programs continued to expand in response to government needs, as they had since the years of the New Deal, and new programs, especially those that collected social statistics, were progressively added.[61] For example, between 1948 (the year of the

[59] Mills and Long, *op. cit.*
[60] *Ibid.*, pp. 91–93 and 126–139.
[61] The following discussion borrows from Raymond T. Bowman, "Crossroad Choices for Future Development of the Federal Statistical System," *Statistical Reporter*, No. 68–7, January 1968, pp. 113–121.

Mills-Long report) and 1957, the total cost of the principal statistical programs rose from $30.7 million to $52.7 million. By 1967 this figure had risen to $134.4 million. Part of this increase was owing to statistical series developed by the new National Centers for Educational and Health Statistics. The National Center for Health Statistics, for example, assumed responsibility for records on vital statistics—births, deaths, etc.—which had long been maintained by the Census Bureau; but the Center also inaugurated regular sample surveys in the late 1950's on health conditions and services that had not earlier been recorded. A good deal of the increase, however, was in the traditional agencies. From 1948 to 1967 budgets for the Census Bureau rose from $7.4 million to $16.4 million, for the statistical services of the Department of Agriculture from $4.9 million to $17.5 million, and for the Bureau of Labor Statistics from $4.3 million to $20.6 million. These increases, however, greatly reflected statistical collection and processing that these offices, particularly the Census Bureau and the Bureau of Labor Statistics, undertook for agencies like the Office of Economic Opportunity and the Department of Housing and Urban Development, established to carry out the new social programs.

These new programs required not only a greater amount of statistical work but also work of greater complexity, involving the use of new procedures and new forms of data accumulation, analysis, and presentation. And by the 1960's there were new demands for coordination originating outside the government, especially after the publication in 1965 of the report of a committee of the Social Science Research Council on the "preservation and use of economic data."[62] Headed by Professor Richard Ruggles, an economist from Yale, the SSRC committee was formed at the urging of economists and others who wanted access to the original information—the "microdata"—that provided the basis for the aggregated statistics published by government agencies. The original information, often obscured in aggregated form, was

---

[62] For the text of the report, see *The Computer and Invasion of Privacy*, Special Subcommittee on Invasion of Privacy, Committee on Government Operations, House of Representatives, 89th Congress, 2nd Session, 1966, pp. 195–253.

often needed in order to generate and test new hypotheses about economic and social behavior.

The Ruggles committee worked closely with university and government groups from 1962 through 1964 and included in its study an evaluation of the effect of new computer technology on the federal statistical system. The computer, by providing a capacity for more effective and rapid data collection and analysis, exposed more clearly than ever the inadequacies and the lack of comparability among related statistical series that had been emphasized in the Mills-Long report. The computer also made possible a federal data center in which statistical information from all government sources could be stored and made available in its original state for the purpose of research and analysis. Such a data center, the committee report also stated, would have to have some means of keeping certain information confidential or some central organization that would screen private researchers who requested to use the system.

The recommendations of the Ruggles committee were endorsed and carried further by study groups sponsored by the Bureau of the Budget, always with the proviso that the source of information was to be protected, as it had been for years in the periodic census and economic surveys. Most important, a task force headed by Carl Kaysen, Director of the Institute for Advanced Study, in 1966 outlined a plan for reorganization of the federal statistical system that would substantially strengthen methods of centralization while allowing for the preservation of original information. The task force proposed that the Office of Statistical Services be transferred out of the Bureau of the Budget to serve as a staff unit for a Director of the Federal Statistical System, appointed by the President. The Director would have direct authority over a national data center and the Bureau of the Census (transferred from the Department of Commerce) and would be assisted by two advisory groups, a Federal Statistical Council and a Public Advisory Council. Except for the Census Bureau, other statistical agencies would remain where they were, though it "would be the major responsibility of the Director of the Federal Statistical System to see that the proper division of labor, coordination of information, and utilization of the Data Center were made by the constituent agencies in the System."[63]

The Ruggles and Kaysen committee reports may be viewed simply as suggestions for the improvement of statistical methods, as part of a process that has gone on for several decades. But they are more than that; they are concerned with the pressing contemporary needs of both government and social science research. Social scientists have been exploring the nature of social change with increasingly rigorous methods of analysis and seeking to enlarge the range of their observations. The availability of large sources of information is thus of critical importance to them. It has also become a necessity of government as new social programs are mounted to attack the problems of poverty, the ills of congested cities, and the inadequacies of the educational system, especially since statistical information collected for one program may be relevant for another if the original data can be re-analyzed. There is thus a convergence of three forces: new social programs of the federal government; statistical improvements to provide a broader and more manageable base of economic and social information; and research developments to provide more effective theories about the nature of social change, particularly through the identification of key indicators of change and methods of accounting for the effects of deliberate intervention into social processes.[64]

The convergence of these forces has, moreover, come at two levels of the federal government. At one level they meet in a package of proposals for the establishment of a Council of Social Advisers, an annual social report by the President, and a Joint Committee to review the social report in Congress. At another level, they find their way into the application of the Planning-

---

63 "Kaysen Committee Report," *op. cit.*, p. 203.

64 For a discussion of the movement to develop social indicators and systems of social accounting, see Raymond M. Bauer (ed.), *Social Indicators* (Cambridge: The M.I.T. Press, 1966); also "Social Goals and Indicators for American Society," in two issues of *The Annals*, American Academy of Political and Social Science, Vols. 371 and 373, May 1967 and September 1967; and Eleanor Bernert Sheldon and Wilbert E. Moore, *Indicators of Social Change* (New York: Russell Sage Foundation, 1968).

Programming-Budgeting System throughout the government and resultant requirements for new methods of observation and analysis as bases for evaluating how well government programs are achieving their goals.

The proposal for a Council of Social Advisers is modeled on the Employment Act of 1946, which established the Council of Economic Advisers. But there are sound reasons for the proposal aside from precedent. From a practical point of view, social programs developed since 1960 increasingly require a coherent framework within which they can be formulated by the President and defended in Congress, especially as larger sums of money are involved and as agencies assume responsibilities in overlapping areas of jurisdiction. A presidential social report would provide both an incentive and a requirement for developing such a framework, a requirement that would be further strengthened by its review before a joint congressional committee. The task of preparing an annual social report would demand, in turn, some organizational arrangement in the Executive Office of the President. Setting up a small professional staff in a Council of Social Advisers would not only serve this legislative purpose, but it would also institutionalize the process of developing more effective systems of social indicators and social accounting. Like the Council of Economic Advisers, a Council of Social Advisers could serve to stimulate research, in government and outside it, on the nature of social change. It could thus strengthen the entire government structure for applying knowledge to the development of social policies and programs.

However reasonable the argument, there are two equally reasonable objections to it. The proposal might raise difficult political issues; and the proposed system might raise unjustified expectations about the predictive power of social science research. The purpose of the Employment Act of 1946, it will be recalled, was to achieve certain economic goals for which considerable consensus had developed by the end of the war. These goals were the control of unemployment and the continuance of economic growth; and to achieve them the federal government had to play a more positive role in economic affairs. The stimulus to consensus was the memory of the Depression years and the fear that the end of the war might lead to a period of recession. How these goals were to be achieved was left an open question and was often a controversial matter.

Is there a similar consensus of opinion on social goals? Certainly the passage of legislation since 1960 authorizing new social programs suggests a growing political concern about the problems of poverty, urban reconstruction, and educational opportunity. But this concern is not quite the same thing as political agreement on a set of general but quite clear national goals. For one thing, there are questions about the nature of the federal government's role in social programs from both liberals and conservatives. While conservatives maintain a traditional fear of central government, liberals increasingly insist that central administration is not only cumbersome but also inhibits individual and local group participation in carrying programs out. There is thus a growing tendency to set up social programs so that the responsibility for administering them rests with the state governments or local communities. Moreover, the possible methods of achieving the goal of redistributing income—by more jobs, better education and training, social insurance, family allowances, or guaranteed annual income—are highly disputed. The goal (to the extent it is accepted) cannot be conveniently disengaged from the lack of consensus about the means of achieving it. In 1946 there was no question that it was the federal government—and not state or city governments—that had to assume responsibility for economic stability and growth. Under the conditions that then existed, whether the federal government sought to achieve these goals by public expenditures or tax policies or a combination of both (while open to debate) did not prevent agreement on the goals *per se,* at least as a basis for setting up the Council of Economic Advisers.

Political differences aside, many social scientists doubt that social science research is as yet sufficiently developed to be able to predict the consequences of social action—which is a task that could be expected of a Council of Social Advisers. As Otis Dudley Duncan has put it:

> Policies and programs involve a means-end calculus predicated on dependable knowledge of cause-and-effect relationships. We are

familiar with this pattern of connections between knowledge and action in the strictly economic sphere, as when monetary, fiscal, and tax measures are calculated in the light of theories and measurements predicting their effects on employment and price. It hardly needs to be argued that present theory and measurement practices are not adequate for such calculation in the realm of social opportunities.[65]

These doubts are shared by those who are among the most ardent advocates of establishing a Council of Social Advisers, Bertram Gross, for example:

> let us be perfectly clear that the analogy with economic indicators and goals should not be carried too far. In the noneconomic aspects of social measurement and social policy . . . we have lagged far behind the progress made in measuring economic change and ordering economic information. With broader social measures, the complexities are still greater and the dangers of oversimplification still more threatening.[66]

Gross, however, sees the proposal for the establishment of a Council of Social Advisers and an annual social report as providing a legislative mandate for full and energetic research and experimentation to develop reliable systems of social indicators and social accounting. Against this, Wilbert Moore and Eleanor Sheldon of the Russell Sage Foundation, "fear . . . that a Council, if established, would be expected to give immediate and short-run advice, without the appropriateness or capacity to do so."[67] That is, a Council would understandably have to respond to political pressures for advice rather than professional pressures for scientific development. According to this point of view, the immediate task at hand is not to set up a Council prematurely, but to

65 Otis Dudley Duncan, "Discrimination against Negroes," *The Annals,* American Academy of Political and Social Science, Vol. 371, May 1967, p. 94.

66 Bertram Gross, "A New Orientation in American Government," *The Annals,* American Academy of Political and Social Science, Vol. 371, May 1967, p. 18.

67 Moore and Sheldon, Statement prepared for Subcommittee on Government Research, in *Full Opportunity and Social Accounting Act,* Hearings before Subcommittee on Government Research, Committee on Government Operations, U.S. Senate, 90th Congress, 1st Session, 1967, p. 403.

build up the infrastructure of social research that would make a Council effective. This would involve, essentially, the development of an adequate statistical base to test theories of large-scale social change and institutional methods to encourage a cumulative growth of knowledge. Such caution, undoubtedly sound, still brings to mind Robert Lynd's complaints in *Knowledge for What?*: that social scientists are abdicating responsibility for using what knowledge they have until they are sure that "all the evidence is in." Views about a Council of Social Advisers, however, may not be the best basis for judging whether any such complaint is justified. The idea of a Council remains something for the future at best. More immediate are the needs for substantive knowledge to support the evaluation of current programs at a level below the full complexity of large-scale social change. Moreover, there is greater opportunity for bringing social science research to bear on the process of evaluation owing to the analytical requirements of the Planning-Programming-Budgeting System (PPBS).

Based on experience in the Defense Department, PPBS was extended throughout the federal establishment under executive orders issued in August 1965. Speaking to cabinet members and agency heads, the President defined the aims of PPBS in these terms:

1. Identify our national goals with precision and on a continuing basis;
2. Choose among those goals the ones that are most urgent;
3. Search for alternative means of reaching those goals most effectively at the least cost;
4. Inform ourselves not merely on next year's costs, but on the second and third, and subsequent years' costs of our programs;
5. Measure the performance of our programs to insure a dollar's worth of service for each dollar spent.[68]

---

[68] Statement by the President to Cabinet Members and Agency Heads on the New Government-Wide Planning and Budgeting System, August 25, 1965. This Statement and other official documents identified below, can be found in *Planning-Programming-Budgeting*, Subcommittee on National Security and International Operations, Committee on Government Operations, U.S. Senate, 90th Congress, 1st Session, 1967, "Official Documents."

It has already been emphasized that PPBS did not burst forth full grown. Its history can be traced through a series of budgetary and management practices starting with the reform movement at the turn of the century, as well as through the development of economic theory and systems analysis.[69] The intended effect of PPBS is to compel agencies to relate program choices to budgetary decisions (and thus compel them to take planning and evaluation seriously) and, by requiring multi-year projections of costs, to encourage long-range planning. When applied to social programs, however, PPBS confronts problems similar to those that complicate the establishment of a Council of Social Advisers: the difficulty of articulating meaningful goals against which to measure program results; the lack of adequate information for program evaluation; and the lack of reliable theories to provide criteria for measuring the effects of social programs. The scale and level of analysis that is required is different, however.

The application of PPBS has been carried out on a step-by-step basis. It is, for that matter, a continuous process. Some two years after the President's order, the Director of the Budget Bureau acknowledged "not surprisingly, the application of PPB to 21 agencies so far (36 agencies ultimately) dealing with a variety of national problems, has resulted in great differences in technique and result." Disparities were "due in part to differences in the extent to which agencies have worked out means of adapting and using PPB, and in part to the difficulty of the substantive questions involved."[70] Seen in its broadest perspective, PPBS is an effort to bring rationality into government policy-making by relating planning directly to budget decisions. Within this broad aim, it need only be recognized that while the task is not easy, reasoned calculation may be preferable to guesswork as an operating basis for public programs.

Legislative authority for social programs is most usually

---

[69] See the discussion of the development of PPBS in the Department of Defense in Chapter V of this book. For an excellent summary of the relation of PPBS to earlier efforts at budget reform, see Allen Schick, "The Road to PPB: the Stages of Budget Reform," *Public Administration Review*, Vol. XXVI, No. 4 (December 1966), pp. 243–258.

[70] *Planning-Programming-Budgeting, op. cit.,* Part 1, p. 25.

couched in general language, admittedly, and subject to differences of interpretation. This is the price of political consensus. But the general language of legislative intention must be reduced to more precise terms in order to offer guidance and direction for administrative action. At the program level, general goals are reduced to tangible objectives, with or without PPBS. A national goal such as "providing better living conditions in the cities," for example, may be translated into a program to build so many low-cost housing units over such a period of time in so many communities, a bill to "increase opportunities for educational advancement" into special programs of compensatory education for Negro children in urban ghettoes. In each case, it is necessarily assumed that the programs will serve to bring the society closer to the broad legislative goals. The more precise program objectives, however, provide a base point against which to test these assumptions through systematic evaluation of what actually happens when low-cost housing is provided or when new educational programs, like Headstart, are carried out. Are urban living conditions better? Are educational opportunities increased?

PPBS, however, like any administrative device, becomes shallow and mechanistic without a supporting structure of substantive knowledge within which to operate. It is in this sense that PPBS provides a means of relating social science research to government and that research becomes a critical element in government decision-making. The analytical requirements of PPBS, in effect, provide a basis for establishing the relevance of social science research. For example, important information gaps were detected in an early PPBS study on child health programs carried out in the Department of Health, Education, and Welfare. On investigation, analysts could find no records of the effectiveness of former child health programs. Records of moneys that had been spent and medical care administered were not followed up by records of what difference they had made in improving the health of children. The analysts therefore included a recommendation that future programs provide for systematic and independent evaluation. Specifically, they proposed to consider child health programs as experiments based on tentative assumptions about their effects; to observe the programs in operation; to record their effects on improving the health of children;

and, over time, to determine how far the results served the general aim of the program. For the Department of Health, Education, and Welfare, this process would permit periodic adjustments of the level and scope of the program by providing an increasingly valid evaluation of its results. For social scientists, moreover, program information and analyses might prove to be important contributions to a better understanding of what the analysts described as "the interrelationships among the effects of environment, education and medical care."[71]

In this way the program evaluation and planning processes of PPBS provide continuing linkages between research activities and agency policy-making. In the interaction of planning, programming, evaluation, and research, the scope of social science research is continually enlarged and its relevance more clearly defined. The Deputy Under Secretary of Housing and Urban Development found an added advantage in being able to explain to Congress exactly why research was necessary:

> The thing that I find most encouraging about the situation is that the kind of analysis we are doing [under PPBS] also helps to highlight the needs for research and the data we need. Thus, we can explain to the Congress when we ask for research and studies what we hope to gain in the way of helping the Congress as well as ourselves make better decisions on the allocation of housing resources and Federal resources against these needs.[72]

PPBS thus plays an important part in the effort to build coherent programs of social science research in departments and agencies. At the same time, systematic program evaluation promises to make the record of government programs available for the broader study of social change. None of this, however, will happen of itself. It will happen only if there is understanding about the new role for social science in government and if this understanding is expressed in institutional responsibility—so that it cannot be forgotten and permitted to lapse.

---

[71] The child health study is reprinted in *The Planning-Programming-Budgeting System: Progress and Potentials,* Hearings before Subcommittee on Economy in Government, Joint Economic Committee, 90th Congress, 1st Session, 1967, pp. 10–45.

[72] *Ibid.,* p. 76.

Central Organization

These three forces—improvements in statistical methods, experiments in social indicators and social accounting, and the application of PPBS—combine to provide an important opportunity for establishing the relevance of social science research to the federal government and for developing the theoretical and empirical bases for better understanding the nature of large-scale social change. The critical and strategic points in the whole complex process lie in the reform of the statistical services and the social science requirements of program evaluation.[73] Progress in both fields, however, has to be viewed against the broadest perspective of a role for knowledge in government. This is a perspective that cannot be expected to come from individual departments and agencies. Here the focus is, of necessity, on operating programs and on the requirements of research and methodology as instruments of administration. What is needed as a balance rod is a centralizing force to relate the development of statistical services and program evaluation to broader research purposes and to the continued growth of social science.

In the 1930's the Science Committee of the National Resources Planning Board (NRPB) had provided a basis for such a centralizing force, but during a period when there was little substantive social science research in government. In 1938, at the time of the Science Committee report, *Research—A National Resource*, the Bureau of Agricultural Economics was an exception in its use of research for planning and programming. By the late 1960's the Bureau had come to serve as a model for a number of economic and social programs in the federal government. But the Science Committee was replaced by other institutions designed for the same purpose—to encourage the development of science and its application to the problems of society—but different in their origins and outlook.

The Science Committee of the NRPB, like the Board itself

---

[73] For an important analysis of the research requirements of program evaluation, see Edward Suchman, *Evaluative Research* (New York: Russell Sage Foundation, 1967).

and its predecessor, the National Resources Committee, had grown out of the idea of a National Advisory Council originally recommended in *Recent Social Trends*. The function of such a Council was to "consider . . . fundamental questions of the social order, economic, governmental, educational, technical, cultural, always in their inter-relation and in the light of the trends and possibilities of modern science."[74] The idea had its origins in the interdisciplinary, problem-oriented social science of men like Charles Merriam. The governmental mechanisms set up under the New Deal were worked out in the course of meeting and adjusting to the severe economic repercussions of the Depression. Unemployment was the first order of business; an active role for the federal government in society was just beginning to find acceptance; and social science was torn between the inner tug of scientific development and outward pull of social responsibility.

Some thirty years later, American society and American government had changed in the face of new and more complex national problems. The old planning function that the NRPB had been organized to carry out was now entrusted to a number of much more effective agencies in the Executive Office of the President: the Council of Economic Advisers formulated broad economic policies; the National Security Council coordinated foreign and defense policies; and in early 1969 the Council of Urban Affairs was established to coordinate social policies. The task of fostering scientific research to support federal programs, a task plagued with frustration in the Science Committee of the NRPB in the earlier period, was now the responsibility of a new set of scientific agencies centered in the Office of the President's Special Assistant for Science and Technology. These new agencies, in contrast to the NRPB, were dominated by physical and biological scientists, having been initially established in response to the international challenges of space exploration and the arms race. However, since their scope was as broad as the scientific enterprise itself, these agencies provide a central focus for science policies,

---

[74] *Recent Social Trends in the United States,* Report of the President's Research Committee on Social Trends (2 vols.; New York: McGraw-Hill Book Co., 1933), Vol. I, p. lxxiii.

and an examination of their structure and development is thus essential to any discussion of the problems of strengthening the role of social science in the federal government.

CHAPTER VIII

FEDERAL POLICY
FOR SOCIAL SCIENCE

IT MAY BE STATED at the outset that there is no such thing as *a national policy for science*, that it is extremely unlikely that out of the American political process there could emerge a single, all-embracing policy for the use and support of science by the federal government, and that, even if there *could*, there is serious doubt that there *should*. What has evolved since the Second World War is a complex of federal policies that reflect both political and scientific goals. These policies have given rise to a federal organization for science that provides links between the government and scientific communities. They have developed in response to pressing national needs for technological development and, at the same time, to the need of scientists for a steady flow of federal funds to support basic research, education, and the continued growth of the entire scientific enterprise. The system, however, is principally concerned with the physical and biological sciences, and only indirectly with the social sciences.

Scientists have been instrumental in the building of this federal organization for science. They have been effective because of their willingness to respond to political demands, though they have tried to keep their response within the limits of professional and ethical standards. What these limits are has often been a matter of controversy, especially when questions have been raised that involved classified research, security clearances, and the strategic implications of weapons technology. Nevertheless, their willingness to respond to political missions has given scientists the opportunity (and the political backing) to create sources of broad, continuing federal support for basic research. Physical scientists, for example, have been vital to the progress of technological programs in the Atomic Energy Commission, the Department of Defense, and the National Aeronautics and Space Administration. Within these programs, they have persuasively argued for general support for basic research and graduate training, as well as the larger amount of directed and applied research and development. While general support has been substantial, it is dependent on the size of the defense and space budgets and thus may be reduced in times of financial pinch.

In fact, by the mid-1960's the defense and space budgets for research and development tended to reach a plateau and become subject to increasingly sharp scrutiny as a result of congressional pressures for budget ceilings and competing programs of social welfare and urban rebuilding at home. Because of the high dependence of the physical sciences on continued growth in the defense and space programs, some scientists began to speak of a "crisis in the physical sciences." A study group of the National Academy of Sciences defined the problem in 1965: "As the handmaiden mostly of mission-oriented agencies such as the Atomic Energy Commission, the Department of Defense, and the National Aeronautics and Space Administration, whose missions are not likely to expand in the immediate future, [the physical] sciences are caught in a squeeze." It therefore recommended that mission-oriented agencies, "at times . . . when budgets are . . . stationary, should devote a larger fraction of their budgets to basic research," and that the National Science Foundation (NSF) should "become the 'balance wheel,' or even the main 'umbrella' for the support of basic research."[1]

In trying to establish a steady source of federal support for basic research—a primary purpose of scientists in formulating the original plans for the NSF—the physical scientists undoubtedly look with envy at the support given to the biomedical sciences by the National Institutes of Health (NIH). The NIH has a broad mission—the maintenance of general health—that is not

---

[1] *Basic Research and National Goals*, A Report to the Committee on Science and Astronautics by the National Academy of Sciences (Washington, D.C., March 1965), pp. 23–24.

related to any specific federal program, and it is therefore in a more independent financial position. Also NIH programs have not involved scientists in agonizing questions, often with political and ethical overtones, concerning the political use of scientific knowledge, as have programs in the field of national defense, especially. The development of new knowledge—basic research—is as much an NIH mission as the dissemination of knowledge to medical and teaching institutions throughout the country. Potential conflict between political and scientific objectives has thus been generally minimized. However, the growth of NIH—its budget had risen to over $1 billion by the mid-1960's—has also been dependent on its willingness to adjust to political winds. Reviewing the administration of the NIH in 1965, a presidentially appointed Study Committee noted that:

In 1956 no informed person could have quarreled with an assertion that the fraction of national effort devoted to medical research was much too low, in view of the probable benefits of this kind of activity to all our citizenry. Because of this extensive inadequacy of health-related research, the best guiding principle for the National Institutes of Health was also the simplest one: take advantage of any reasonable opportunity that presented itself to employ government funds to increase the amount of high quality health-related research. If social and political developments made it easier to obtain funding for one kind of medical research rather than for another, there was no compelling reason not to adapt the NIH emphases accordingly; when there were so many vacuums to be rapidly attended to, the order of their filling was hardly critical.[2]

Within the NIH a constant debate goes on between those who would support unstructured basic research and those who would direct research programs toward particular health fields in which there is both need and potential for the application of research findings. Again, when the rate of budgetary growth is limited and contending factions cannot agree on how much money is to be spent on basic research and how much on medical

[2] *Biomedical Science and Its Administration,* A Study of the National Institutes of Health, The White House (Washington, D.C., February 1965), p. 10.

application, the argument is often decisively settled by influential members of Congress. In the summer of 1966, moreover, the advocates of basic research received a possible taste of the future when, after years of expanding and unquestioned funding, the President closed a meeting of the directors of the NIH by pointing to the large amounts of tax dollars going into biomedical research and expressing his keen desire "to learn not only what knowledge this buys but what are the payoffs in terms of healthy lives for our citizens."

The policies that govern federal support for the physical sciences, on the one hand, and the biological sciences, on the other, are both similar and different. They are similar in that both sets of policies emphasize pluralistic sources of support and seek to achieve a balance—continually shifting—between problem-oriented research and basic research. They are thus consistent with the general opposition of scientists to a centralized Department of Science and their preference for a looser system that permits political maneuverability and minimizes the dangers of centralized direction of research efforts.

They are different, however, in that the physical sciences have found major sources of support in agencies with operating missions, principally military and space agencies, that primarily serve political purposes rather than the needs of science. The biological sciences, in contrast, have had major support from a complex of health-oriented agencies whose primary purpose is to encourage basic scientific research. As a result, the physical scientists, while meeting the demands of applied programs, have sought to build up the National Science Foundation because of its basic research objective, whereas the biological scientists have had to give increasing emphasis to application—to "payoff"—in order to justify the growth of basic research in the NIH. In both cases, however, there have been institutional arrangements through which scientists could exert political pressure for a dependable system of research support. The physical scientists have been able to work through the Office of Science and Technology and the President's Science Advisory Committee, and the biological scientists through the directorships of the National Institutes of Health and various important congressional committees.

The need for a central base from which to construct coherent policies for the social sciences became increasingly evident in the debate that followed Project Camelot. The immediate issues in the debate were two: the problems of conducting social science research in foreign areas, and the heavy concentration of government-sponsored foreign area research in military agencies. Congressional inquiries about the project went beyond these issues, however, and led to legislative proposals to establish a National Social Science Foundation and an Office of Social Science Adviser to the President, and to organize a White House Conference on the Social and Behavioral Sciences. The initial purpose of these proposals was to provide greater support for social science research outside mission-oriented agencies in order to avoid the problems encountered in the Project Camelot affair. But the scope of the proposals and their potential effects, it soon became clear, were much broader.

They involved the nature and needs of the social sciences, the relation of the universities to the federal government, the staffing of government research bureaus, the utilization of research for programs and policies, the relation of the social to the natural sciences—all the problems that social science had struggled with for more than half a century. The fundamental problem still remained—to relate knowledge to action in the process of democratic government and to finance the growth of knowledge on its own terms. A federal scientific structure now existed to support these two purposes for the natural sciences. In comparison, the position of the social sciences within the federal government was considerably more precarious.

The Growth of Support

During the debate over the National Science Foundation (NSF) between 1945 and 1950, the issue of federal support for basic research was complicated by the insistence of scientists that such support be given on the basis of scientific rather than political criteria. The compromise that was accepted made the Director of the Foundation a direct presidential appointee, but subject to broad policy guidance by a group of scientists serving on the National Science Board. In the years since 1950, "the success of the director," as Don K. Price observed, has depended "on a delicate balance between his loyalties to [the National Science Board] representing the scientific community, and to the President."[3] Indeed, so well did the scientists succeed that this "delicate balance" made it difficult, or even impossible, for the Foundation to serve as an arm of the presidency in the development of national science policy. Formulating science policy was a responsibility the Foundation assumed in the original legislation but one that it never undertook to fulfill and, for that matter, might well have failed in if it had. By its organization and objective, its lines of strength and influence ran to the scientific community, not to the government bureaucracies where it had little influence. This propensity to keep itself politically unencumbered undoubtedly also affected the attitude of the Foundation toward the social sciences, which operated within the "permissive but not mandatory" provision suggested by Vannevar Bush during the NSF hearings.

Its caution with respect to the social sciences, however, was due not only to a fear of becoming politically vulnerable but also to financial constraints. The NSF came into being at the moment the Korean war broke out. The defense budget took an immediate leap upward, endangering new programs whose relationship to national security could not be directly identified. At the same time, a good deal of science was already being funded through the military services and the Atomic Energy Commission. Thus, in reviewing the Foundation's budget request for its first year of full operation, 1951–1952, the House Committee on Appropriations practically wiped out the program for basic research and scientific training because "their early aid in the present emergency is not very tangible."[4]

Partial but still extremely modest funds were eventually re-

[3] Don K. Price, The Scientific Estate (Cambridge: Harvard University Press, 1965), p. 240.

[4] Quoted in Supplemental Appropriations for 1952, Hearings before Committee on Appropriations, U.S. Senate, 82nd Congress, 1st Session, 1951, p. 1106.

stored after Foundation officers and other scientists made force-ful presentations to the Senate Appropriations Committee on the need to take a long-range view of scientific research and its ef-fect on defense capabilities. As Chairman of the National Science Board, James B. Conant emphasized that "we are in for a long drawn out struggle . . . [and] in the process of arming the free world, science and technology play an enormous role."[5] Using the prestige he had earned for his work on the atomic bomb proj-ect, J. Robert Oppenheimer sought to illustrate the significance of taking the long view: "The name attached to one of the vital com-ponents of the first atomic bomb was the name of a young man who took his degree with me at the time of Pearl Harbor. That kind of thing will happen over and over again."[6] Despite such arguments, the early NSF budgets were far less than originally envisaged; only planning money was appropriated the first year and less than $4 million the second, as contrasted with earlier estimates that $100 million to $200 million would be necessary.

Under the circumstances, it is not surprising that it was not until the winter of 1953 that the Foundation undertook its first formal review on how the social sciences might be supported under the "permissive but not mandatory" clause. By far the most important motive for the review was the legislative history of the National Science Foundation Act and the support that social scientists had given to its passage. But, in addition, the Founda-tion realized that social science research was getting more support from the private foundations and, with the rearmament that fol-lowed the Korean conflict, from the rising research budgets of the defense agencies.[7] At the same time, one edge of the social sci-ences, the "hard" edge of experimental psychology, was already represented as a designated program area within the field of the biological sciences with an advisory group of its own. Finally, there were undoubtedly habits of experience operating; the core of

[5] *Ibid.*, p. 1104.
[6] *Ibid.*, p. 1163.
[7] Harry Alpert, "The Social Sciences and the National Science Foundation: 1945–1955," *American Sociological Review*, Vol. 20, No. 6 (December 1955), p. 655.

administrative leadership in the NSF came, in large measure, from the Office of Naval Research where the support for basic scientific research had included a substantial program in psychology, broadly conceived in several cases to encompass social psychology and other social sciences.[8]

The review which began in 1953 was the beginning of a process which, by the end of 1958, saw the establishment of a unified social science program in the Foundation carried forward by an Office of Social Sciences. Within a year, moreover, the "Office" was given the status of a "Division," thus offering the unit equal status, in name at any rate, with other sections of the organization. The process went through several well-defined stages, under the guidance of the program director, Harry Alpert, a sociologist who had come to Washington during the war and had later remained with the Office of Statistical Standards in the Bureau of the Budget. Each stage was carefully gauged to emphasize the scientific component of the social sciences and the unity of the scientific endeavor, to dispel apprehensions among natural scientists and members of Congress about any reformist spirit among social scientists, and to take advantage of a broadening acceptance of the social sciences as it developed.

Thus, the first projects of social science support were limited to areas of so-called "convergence" between the social and natural sciences. In the Biological and Medical Sciences Division, for example, a program was established in anthropological and related sciences, such as functional archaeology, human ecology, demography, psycho-linguistics, and experimental and quantitative social psychology. Similarly, in the Mathematical, Physical, and Engineering Sciences Division, there was a program in socio-physical sciences which included interdisciplinary research in such areas as mathematical social science, human geography, economic engineering, and statistical design. At Alpert's urging, this Division

---

[8] See John G. Darley, "Psychology and the Office of Naval Research: A Decade of Development," *The American Psychologist*, Vol. 12, 1957. These included the Foundation's Director, Alan T. Waterman, the Deputy Director, C. E. Sunderlin, and John T. Wilson, the latter a psychologist himself.

also soon came to include work in the history, philosophy, and sociology of science. And by 1956 the Foundation's fellowship program began to offer limited opportunities for social scientists in similar areas of "convergence."[9]

Under the "permissive, but not mandatory" clause, the development of the social sciences in the NSF depended, to a large extent, on the attitude of the Director and the members of the National Science Board. The Director, Alan T. Waterman, a physicist, had formerly been Deputy Chief and Chief Scientist of the Office of Naval Research and it was his appointment, especially, that stamped the Foundation with the ONR operating style during its formative years. He proceeded with caution, emphasized the importance of basic research, relied heavily on panels of professional advisers to test all projects for their scientific validity, and agreed with the Bush position that scientists had to maintain control over Foundation activities. The early "convergent" programs brought advisory panels of social scientists into the Foundation system. Their functions, however, were largely limited to the evaluation of proposals for support and did not extend into the higher levels of Foundation policy. Under the planning process that began in 1953 and especially with the establishment of a consolidated social science program in 1958 and a separate Division by late 1959, an overall advisory panel was organized that could look at the social sciences more broadly and support the director of the program in his recommendations to the Board.

On the National Science Board itself, the social sciences were represented only indirectly by individuals from educational institutions and private foundations. For example, the first Board included Charles Dollard, a sociologist who was also president of the Carnegie Corporation of New York, and Frederick A. Middlebush, a political scientist who was president of the University of Missouri. To a great extent, this kind of indirect representation continued. As late as 1965 when the Foundation's work was being reviewed by a House committee, the President of the Social Sci-

---

[9] *Fifth Annual Report*, National Science Foundation (Washington, D.C., 1955).

ence Research Council, Pendleton Herring, who had himself served on the social science advisory panel, noted that the situation on the Board had not appreciably changed.

> When it comes to the Board of the National Science Foundation, it seems to me that, if the Science Foundation is to continue, as it presumably will, with supporting the social sciences, there should be social scientists on that Board. When I say social scientists, I don't mean a college president, I don't mean someone who was a dean in the past or someone who had some indirect interest, I mean someone who is a leader in one of the disciplines.[10]

The Foundation's first unified social science research program was funded in the fiscal year 1958 and its budget totaled slightly over $750,000, as compared with research program budgets amounting to $8.9 million for the biological sciences and $9.5 million for the physical sciences. Over half of the social science program was in anthropology with less than $200,000 earmarked for sociology and modest sums for economics and the history and philosophy of science.[11] By 1960 expenditures for social science research had grown to over $2 million, a figure that increased fivefold to $10 million by 1965.[12] This growth reflected the increasing commitment of the Foundation to the social sciences and the confidence that had developed as a result of the caution and care with which the early program was conceived and carried forward. But it was also part of the general growth of Foundation activities that brought a tenfold increase in the total budget, from less than $50 million in 1958 to almost $500 million in 1965.

This growth of the NSF was part of the larger effort to support science and technology through federal programs that fol-

---

[10] *Review of the National Science Foundation,* Subcommittee on Science, Research, and Development, Committee on Science and Astronautics, House of Representatives, 89th Congress, 1st Session, 1965, Vol. I, p. 438. The appointment in 1968 of James G. March, Dean of Social Science, University of California, at Irvine may be more what Herring had in mind than earlier appointments.

[11] *Eighth Annual Report,* National Science Foundation (Washington, D.C., 1958), p. 47.

[12] For comparative figures, see *Review of the National Science Foundation, op. cit.,* pp. 38–42.

lowed the announcement of the first Soviet space vehicle in the fall of 1957. The response to Sputnik went beyond huge budgetary increases, as we have seen. Almost immediately President Eisenhower elevated science advisory mechanisms in his Executive Office to the level of a President's Science Advisory Committee (PSAC) and appointed James Killian, President of the Massachusetts Institute of Technology, as its Chairman and his Special Assistant for Science and Technology. Research and development on long-range missiles and space satellites was consolidated and given new visibility and support in a National Aeronautics and Space Administration. In the defense establishment, the Directorate of Defense Research and Engineering was established with operational authority over the research programs of the military departments and direct responsibility for the development of advanced weapons systems through an Advanced Research Projects Agency. While all of these efforts were primarily directed towards meeting the military threat that the Soviet Sputnik presented, they had the effect of placing scientists in dominant roles in the federal policy-making system, something that had not happened since the breakup of the Office of Scientific Research and Development after the war.

Through their new positions of influence the scientists sought to direct federal support for science beyond the immediate critical tasks at hand and to strengthen the country's scientific foundations, particularly in the universities and large research laboratories. This was illustrated by an early report by PSAC called *Strengthening American Science*. Endorsed by the President, the report pointed out: "Not only the nation's security but its long-term health and economic welfare, the excellence of its scientific life, and the quality of American higher education are now fatefully bound up with the care and thoughtfulness with which the Government supports research."[13] These were the views that Conant and Oppenheimer had sought to convey in the early 1950's; it was not until the late 1950's, however, that the scientists had enough influence to earn them political support.

---

[13] *Strengthening American Science*, A Report of the President's Science Advisory Committee (Washington, D.C., December 1958), p. 2.

The expansion of federal support for the natural sciences extended to the social sciences as well. Within the defense establishment, basic research was supported as a secondary effect of work in applied research and through grant programs administered through the Air Force Office of Scientific Research, the Office of Naval Research, and, later, the Advanced Research Projects Agency. In addition to the defense establishment and the NSF, the National Institutes of Health and particularly the National Institute of Mental Health (NIMH) began to emerge in the late 1950's as a principal source of support for social science research. While the NIMH program was initially medical in emphasis, it was easily expanded to include research on the problems of mental health in their broadest social environment.[14] In 1952 the NIMH research grant program totaled some $5 million. By 1963 grants made outside the large-scale research program undertaken within NIMH itself came to more than $35 million; and thirty-five percent of this was for studies on the psychological, social, and cultural bases of behavior, compared with twenty-four percent for research on the biological bases of behavior.[15]

By the 1960's the social sciences were being supported by the federal government under the broad rubrics of defense and health in the wave of support for science and education that followed the launching of Sputnik. The base of support, moreover, became broadened with the passage of new legislation in the fields of manpower planning, education, social welfare, and regional economic development, and with the provisions for social science research within these programs. It became increasingly clear that the federal government was replacing the private foundations as the major source of support for the social sciences. And in the debate that began with Project Camelot in 1965, a national foundation for the social sciences was proposed, and studies were

---

[14] See John A. Clausen, "Social Science Research in the National Mental Health Program," *American Sociological Review*, Vol. 15, No. 3 (June 1950), pp. 402–409.

[15] Jeanne L. Brand and Philip Sapir (eds.), "An Historical Perspective on the National Institute of Mental Health," (mimeographed), National Institute of Mental Health, Department of Health, Education, and Welfare (Washington, D.C., February 1964), pp. 30–31.

sponsored by the National Academy of Sciences and the National Science Board on the effective use of social science research. All of these efforts pointed to the need for a coherent set of federal policies for social science. By the mid-1960's, moreover, social scientists were at the point of consensus on the issue of federal support that natural scientists had reached right after the war. They agreed that scientific developments depended on federal support and could no longer be sustained by university and private foundation support alone. There was less agreement on what the shape of federal organization for social science should be.

The Quest for Recognition

The need for federal financing was the result of both the growing requirements of social science research and trends in the policies of the major private foundations. Support for the social sciences by the private foundations has followed a tradition that began with the Russell Sage Foundation's sponsorship of social surveys early in the century. Other foundations followed suit. In the 1920's and 1930's the Laura Spelman Rockefeller Memorial and the Rockefeller Foundation made large grants to the Social Science Research Council; later the Carnegie Corporation of New York supported such monumental projects as Gunnar Myrdal's study of the American Negro in *An American Dilemma* and Samuel Stouffer's analysis of the Army's wartime social research in *The American Soldier*. Foundation concern for the social sciences, however, has more often been a by-product of their interest in the solution of national and social problems than in the development of the disciplines. Indeed, it is this interest which, legally, is at the heart of American philanthropy. The tax-exempt status of the foundations rests on the contribution they make to the national welfare. Thus, while foundations have been among the most important consumers of social science research, they have been less consistent in financing the development of social science itself.

In the early 1950's the private foundations were sharply criticized by investigating committees of the House of Representatives with their support of the social sciences as a principal target.

In 1952 one committee, the so-called Cox Committee, tried to discover whether the foundations had supported projects that tended "to weaken or discredit the capitalistic system in the United States and to favor Marxist socialism." The chief object of attack was the foundation funding of research centers in Russian and communist affairs at major universities like Harvard and Columbia. By the time the hearings ended, the committee's views were moderated and it generally judged "the record of the foundations" to be "good."[16] In 1954, however, a second committee, this one chaired by Congressman Carrol Reece of Tennessee, used the investigating platform to denounce what they called the "socialism" of the social sciences and the "scientism" of the behavioral approach.[17] The Reece Committee report was repudiated by the minority Democratic members, who went so far as to call the proceeding "an ugly stain on the majestic record of the . . . House of Representatives."[18] As it turned out, the Committee's report and its accusations had no perceptible effect on foundation policies. Whatever impact they had was more attributable to the general anti-communist hysteria and anti-intellectualism of which they were a part.

Indeed, it was in the early 1950's that the expanded program of the Ford Foundation included heavy support for social science, for both its application to social problems and its scientific development. Originally founded in the 1930's as a close family trust, the Ford Foundation became the giant among philanthropies in 1950 when it announced a reorganization and a new program. Following the recommendations of a study undertaken by a committee chaired by H. Rowan Gaither, Jr., a San Francisco lawyer, the Foundation planned to operate in five areas.[19] In traditional foundation style, the first four areas consisted of large

---

16 Quoted in F. Emerson Andrews, *Philanthropic Foundations* (New York: Russell Sage Foundation, 1956), p. 344.

17 *Tax-Exempt Foundations,* Report of the Special Committee to Investigate Tax-Exempt Foundations and Comparable Organizations, House Report No. 2681, House of Representatives, 83rd Congress, 2nd Session, 1954.

18 *Ibid.,* p. 421.

19 *Report of the Study for the Ford Foundation on Policy and Program,* Ford Foundation (November 1949).

sets of national problems: maintaining world order, strengthening democracy, strengthening the economy, and improving education. The fifth program area, however, consisted of research in individual behavior and human relations and was to be devoted to the "advancement of the scientific study of man." The study committee not only emphasized the importance of this area as essential for progress in its more action-oriented programs, but also pointed to "its relative neglect by other financial sources." On the advice of a group of social scientists, the committee specified various criteria for supporting work in what were now labeled the "behavioral sciences"—a term used before but given common currency for the first time by the Ford program. These criteria were intended to insure that the work in some way contributed to basic theory, methodology, interdisciplinary ties, or cross-cultural studies.

The "behavioral sciences" came to mean psychology, sociology, and anthropology, principally, and those parts of economics and political science concerned with individual and group behavior rather than with institutions and processes. The emphasis, however, was on the rigor of research methods, on demonstrating that the study of social phenomena could be "scientific" by concentrating on quantitative analysis and testable theories. It was an effort to support trends in the social sciences that had started in the interwar years and had been advanced in many of the wartime research programs. And the use of the term, "behavioral sciences," was part of an effort to dispel those notions of vagueness and reformism which so many laymen, including members of Congress, associated with the "social sciences."

The Ford behavioral science division was carried on as a separate Foundation program from 1951 through 1956 under the direction of the sociologist Bernard Berelson. During these years, the division sought to increase the number of behavioral scientists, to give greater rigor and unity to the study of human behavior, and to strengthen educational and research institutions in the field.[20] The Foundation made the first of a series of grants to ma-

20 The following discussion is largely based on the behavioral sciences section in the *Annual Reports* of the Ford Foundation for the years 1952–1957.

jor universities to enable them to improve the conditions and facilities for research in the behavioral sciences. This was followed
by a major undertaking that has been of prime importance for the
postwar development of the behavioral sciences: the establishment of the Center for Advanced Study in the Behavioral Sciences in Palo Alto, California, as an independent Ford-launched
enterprise. Opened in 1954 under the direction of Ralph W. Tyler, the Center was designed as a research center for specialists
in the behavioral sciences whatever their disciplinary origin—for
sociologists, psychologists, anthropologists, economists, or political scientists, as well as mathematicians and biologists whose work
was related either to methods of analyzing data on human behavior or to the physiological bases of behavior. In Tyler's words, the
Center provided "an opportunity for a selected number of university faculty members concerned with the study of human behavior to come together in one place in order to help one another gain
new skills and insights and to work upon common problems in
addition to their individual specialties."[21] Less solemnly, the Center was dubbed "the think tank" and described as a contributor
to "the leisure of the theory class."

While the behavioral science program was primarily devoted
to the development of research capability, in both men and
means, this development always had to be considered in terms of
its eventual usefulness in research applied directly to social problems. Indeed, one branch of applied research that grew in importance in the division was a study of mental health, similar in
many respects to the program at the National Institute of Mental
Health. But where the NIMH program grew out of its base in the
medical sciences, the Ford program was set up to deal with the
social and environmental problems of mental health from the very
first. The division also sought to stimulate an examination of the
problems involved in the utilization of the behavioral sciences. In
1954 the director asked Wilbur Schramm of Stanford University to
undertake a planning review in this field. Schramm's general objectives for Foundation support were in two categories: more effective relationships between the producers and consumers of be-

---

[21] Quoted in *Annual Report,* Ford Foundation, 1954, p. 51.

havioral science knowledge, and better understanding of the social process of applying knowledge to action.[22]

The objectives that Schramm proposed were of great importance, but the division had scarcely begun to work on them when it was abolished. In 1955 a large grant was made to the Russell Sage Foundation (which operates on a much smaller endowment) to continue and expand its work on the application of the social sciences to the practicing professions; a smaller grant was made to Schramm to establish a clearing house on utilization at Stanford.[23] In 1956, however, the Ford Foundation trustees decided to relate behavioral science research directly to action programs and to discontinue the separate division. The decision coincided with Gaither's stepping down as president and a general reshuffling of the leadership. But, on reviewing the program that had involved grants of some $38.5 million in five years, it was indicated that "many aspects of the study of human behavior will continue to receive consideration in other Foundation programs."[24]

Though brief, the Ford program gave considerable visibility to the social sciences, and especially to the behavioral approach. The university grants and the Center at Palo Alto also helped to arouse interest in behavioral science and give it greater cohesion. There were, however, other centers of development for the behavioral sciences. Some of them were older than the Ford program and dated back to the war; several of them had benefited from Ford's beneficence; and many of them were in communication with each other through the participation of their leading members in the activities of the Center at Palo Alto and other foundation-supported programs. They included the Laboratory in Social Relations under Stouffer at Harvard, the Research Center for Group Dynamics first founded at M.I.T. by the late Kurt Lewin and later moved to the University of Michigan, the Institute for Social Research under Rensis Likert at the University of Michigan,

---

22 "Utilization of the Behavioral Sciences," report (mineographed) of a planning review for the Behavioral Sciences Division, Ford Foundation (September 1, 1954).

23 See *Studies in the Utilization of Behavioral Science*, Institute for Communication Research (Stanford: Stanford University Press, 1961), Vol. I.

24 *Annual Report*, Ford Foundation, 1957, p. 13.

the Mental Health Research Institute also at Michigan, and the Bureau of Applied Research under Robert Merton and Paul Lazarsfeld at Columbia University. The end of the Ford program, however, meant the end of a very substantial source of support for basic research.

By coincidence, this happened at a time when the social science program of the National Science Foundation was being developed. In 1957 many of the principal advocates were brought together to seek recognition for the behavioral sciences from the federal government. Here, too, the impact of Sputnik seems to have played an important role. Presumably acting on his own initiative, Vice President Richard Nixon arranged a meeting with James G. Miller, Director of the Mental Health Research Institute at Michigan, and expressed his opinion that the expanding federal programs for the support of science ought to give greater recognition to the social sciences. Miller, for some years, had been developing a concept of the behavioral sciences that included those aspects of both the social and biological sciences that might contribute to the development of "an empirically testable general theory of behavior."[25] He was thus in full agreement with Nixon and, at the Vice President's urging, he organized a group to draw up a case for increased federal support.

The Miller group was brought together on an *ad hoc* basis late in 1957 and in February 1958 issued a statement, "National Support for Behavioral Science."[26] The group included Stouffer and Clyde Kluckhohn from Harvard, Merton from Columbia, Donald Marquis from Michigan who, with Hans Speier of RAND, had been a major consultant on the early Ford program, Ralph Tyler, and Max Millikan, Director of the Center for International Studies at M.I.T. The statement defined "behavioral science" in terms of Miller's earlier work as "the combined endeavor of many fields investigating all aspects of behavior," ranging from anthropology and economics to neurology, physiology, sociology, and zoology. It emphasized the application of behavioral science to

---

[25] See James G. Miller, "Toward a General Theory for the Behavioral Sciences," *The American Psychologist*, Vol. 10, No. 9 (September 1955), pp. 513–531.

[26] The statement was republished in "National Support for Behavioral Science," *Behavioral Science*, Vol. 3, No. 3 (July 1958), pp. 217–227.

almost every aspect of organized society and called for increased funds for research, training, and facilities from the National Science Foundation and other federal agencies. It also argued for the "formation of an advisory panel of behavioral scientists to work closely with the Special Assistant to the President for Science and Technology." Once the report was written, the group was disbanded, though Miller himself was invited to present his views to the President's Science Advisory Committee.

Despite such high level representation, there was no immediate response to the Miller group's report. Indirectly, however, it led to the establishment of a special behavioral science panel by the President's Science Advisory Committee in 1961. This came about through a complicated train of events, or rather, two of them. The first of these involved the National Academy of Science and its affiliate, the National Research Council. Only months after the Miller group issued its statement, the President of the Academy and the Council, Detlev Bronk, established a Committee on Behavioral Science in the Research Council's Division of Anthropology and Psychology. The charge to the Committee was to examine what the Council was doing in the area of behavioral science and what more it might do.

Bronk was presumably apprized of all these events since he was concurrently Chairman of the National Science Board and a member of PSAC, as well as President of the Academy. Moreover, the special Committee of the Research Council included several members of the Miller group, including Miller himself. Also, at the annual meeting of the Research Council in March 1959, Clyde Kluckhohn and Donald Marquis, both of whom were members of the original Miller group and the special Committee, led a discussion on "The Place of Behavioral Science in the National Research Council."[27] The Committee issued no public report of its own, only an interim report to the President in 1960. The Academy, occupied with expanding responsibility in its traditional fields of interest, took no immediate action. Bronk, however, put the Miller

27 *Annual Report*, National Academy of Sciences–National Research Council, Fiscal Year 1958–1959 (Washington, D.C.), pp. 4 and 33; *Annual Report*, National Academy of Sciences–National Research Council, Fiscal Year 1959–1960 (Washington, D.C.), p. 32.

effort into a semi-official channel and also undoubtedly began to communicate new developments in the social sciences to an important segment of the community of physical and biological scientists.

The second train of events began with the election of John F. Kennedy as President in the fall of 1960 and the appointment of Jerome Wiesner of M.I.T. as his Science Adviser. Before his appointment, Wiesner had been in a particularly strategic position to meet with social and behavioral scientists and to know what they were thinking. He was, of course, close to Killian, who had met with the Miller group and who had then returned to M.I.T. when he left the White House. But Wiesner himself had become very much involved in the intellectual environment of Harvard and M.I.T. and in organized meetings of physical scientists, engineers, and social scientists on the issues of defense strategy and arms control. He was thus cognizant of the problems of support that social scientists faced.

Some years later Wiesner explained that the PSAC panel report on the behavioral sciences had been prepared at his request. The work had been undertaken, he said, after a "number of behavioral scientists" had talked with him "about the difficulties the field was encountering both in finding adequate support and an agency of the Federal Government that had the responsibility . . . for this area."[28] At the same time, the Kennedy Administration had brought into the federal government a sizable group of academics, attracted by the opportunities for innovation that the new President offered. Though they were largely concerned with national security affairs, they represented a potentially strong influence for support of the social sciences. Thus it seemed like a propitious time to make a case for social science. There was, however, a certain irony in the contrast with the situation some thirty years earlier, when other intellectuals had entered the government under Roosevelt's New Deal. Then it was a group of natural sci-

---

[28] Quoted in *The Use of Social Research in Federal Domestic Programs,* Staff Study for the Research and Technical Programs Subcommittee, Committee on Government Operations, House of Representatives, 90th Congress, 1st Session, 1967, Part I, p. 8.

entists who sought government support for research, and their proposals were reviewed through a structure in which social scientists like Charles Merriam and Wesley Mitchell were close to high authority. Now the situation was reversed—though this was probably far from Wiesner's mind, if he remembered it at all.

The statement of the behavioral sciences group set up under PSAC auspices was issued on April 20, 1962, under the title, *Strengthening the Behavioral Sciences.*[29] The chairman of the subpanel was Neal E. Miller, an experimental psychologist, then of Yale, who had been chairman of the National Research Council's Division of Anthropology and Psychology and was aware of the earlier efforts to make the problems of the behavioral sciences an issue of national concern. The membership was heavily weighted on the side of experimental and social psychology; there was no economist and only Herbert A. Simon represented political science, though in recent years Simon's work has been mainly in the fields of organization theory and computer technology.

Nevertheless, the PSAC panel report defined the behavioral sciences as "psychology, anthropology, sociology, economics, political science, linguistics" and emphasized the wide range of its concerns, from experiments on the brain to the study of social institutions and cultures. The relationship of the traditional social sciences to the new concept of behavioral sciences was explained by the statement that "the scholarly disciplines from which behavioral sciences sprang were in most cases able to carry out their studies without the appurtenances of the empirical sciences." In this respect, the definition of the behavioral sciences was more limited than that which the James Miller group had made. The emphasis in the report, however, was on the scientific study of individual and group behavior and on the methods common to all sciences: "observation, instrumentation, field and laboratory experiments, statistical analysis of data, construction of models and theories, and good, hard thinking." By implication,

---

[29] *Strengthening the Behavioral Sciences,* Statement by the Behavioral Sciences Subpanel, The Life Sciences Panel, President's Science Advisory Committee (Washington, D.C., 1962).

this definition excluded from the behavioral sciences those social science investigations in which more qualitative and historical approaches were employed—unless they were included under "good, hard thinking."

Opportunities for scientific development were cogently illustrated in selected areas, including the study of communications, mechanisms of personality change, the study of cultures and societies, and studies of thinking processes. In these cases, and others as well, it was argued that the process of objective study in the behavioral sciences was as valid as in the physical and biological sciences, but that future advances were dependent on large-scale research and training and on broadly conceived and systematic methods of collecting and analyzing basic behavioral data. The main purpose of the report was to establish the need for major federal funding for fundamental research of this kind.

The recommendations of the subpanel were both general and specific in nature. In general terms, the report called for greater support for training and facilities, re-examination by government agencies and the scientific community of systems of data collection for use in both the United States and foreign societies, and provision for large units of behavioral study. In specific terms, it recommended that the Social Science Research Council be asked to monitor systems for gathering information about non-economic aspects of behavior in American society, that the disciplinary structure of the National Academy of Sciences–National Research Council be broadened, that a study group of public and private agencies be commissioned to examine the systematic collection of cross-cultural data, and that government agencies review their internal mechanisms for making greater use of behavioral science research in their programs.

The immediate effects of the PSAC panel report were minimal. The group had been organized as a subpanel of PSAC's Life Sciences Panel, but its report was published without special endorsement by PSAC or provision for implementing its recommendations. While the procedure was not unusual for PSAC reports, it left things in the air. Only one suggestion of the panel was immediately followed. A few months later the National Research Council expanded its Division of Anthropology and Psychology into a Division of Behavioral Sciences and, with the addition of new representation, began to increase its capacity to advise the government. But there were no forces in the government that could take advantage of the latent authority that the panel's report could muster.

In 1964 a quite separate interagency committee on behavioral sciences did meet under the auspices of the Federal Council for Science and Technology to evaluate government research programs and suggest steps to strengthen the role of behavioral science in the federal departments and agencies.[30] The Council was an instrument of interagency coordination, and the President's Science Adviser served as its Chairman. It was thus an appropriate mechanism to take the recommendations of the PSAC panel report on internal research programs beyond the point of suggestion.

The efforts of the Council committee, however, met with little success. Problems of definition and differences of reporting and organization made it virtually impossible to arrive at a realistic and informative assessment of social and behavioral science research in government. Even within a single agency, it was frequently difficult to obtain all the information or pinpoint responsibility for research support and utilization. The committee was thus dismissed with the disappointing conclusion that "it has proved somewhat difficult to use the disciplines of the behavioral sciences as an effective approach to the solution of governmental problems, and thought is being given to viewing the behavioral sciences in the context of specific problems rather than in the context of the disciplines themselves."[31]

To a certain extent, the conclusion of the Federal Council committee was a step backward from the PSAC panel report. The problems the committee faced were problems of definition and of gathering evidence that considerable research was in fact now being supported. The committee had sought to identify research that was defined as such and that conformed to the same

[30] *The Role of the Federal Council for Science and Technology*, Report for 1963 and 1964, Office of Science and Technology, Executive Office of the President (Washington, D.C.), pp. 37–38.
[31] *Ibid.*, p. 38.

standards in all agencies, but found that it was impossible to do so. It concluded that there were serious gaps in the research programs but could not specify what these were. And the alternative of "viewing the behavioral sciences in the context of specific problems" was not further explored.

The PSAC panel report had been a meaningful (though summary) synthesis and presentation of developments in the social and behavioral sciences in the almost twenty-year period since World War II. It had sought to gain federal support for the behavioral sciences on the same basis that it was granted to the other sciences. But its potential impact was lost at a time when expanding government programs in the domestic fields of economic growth, poverty, urban planning, and crime prevention began to generate demands for the kind of information and analysis that the panel report had pointed to. Programs of foreign aid and defense support in the international field also depended on research. But the political forces behind these demands were dispersed and disorganized, as was the social science community itself. There was neither political nor scientific support that could be effectively mobilized to bring the questions back to the central focus the PSAC panel report had given them and begin to develop an overall strategy for research support and utilization. The report, for all intents and purposes, was a dead letter, except as part of an evolutionary and learning process. One major problem was that, within the office of the President's Science Adviser, there was no clear notion of where the responsibility lay for supporting behavioral science research. Thus, while the office had initiated the study that led to the report, there was no way for it to follow up on the report's proposals. There were no social or behavioral scientists on PSAC; no member of the staff of the Office of Science and Technology had responsibility in the area of social and behavioral science research; and the Federal Council, which had entered the picture, responded to the diverging views of the operating departments rather than the centralizing perspective of government policy.

By the mid-1960's federal support for the social sciences was, in effect, highly decentralized and scattered through a variety of agencies, having developed in response to operating needs and a general growth in research funding. Research expenditures now totaled more than $300 million. There had been changes in the pattern of spending with the government's increasing interest in domestic affairs such as health, education, and welfare and a general leveling off in the areas of defense and national security. The pluralism of the system was not unlike the pluralism in the system of support for research in the physical and biological sciences. There were, however, several critical differences. The level of support was significantly lower in the social sciences. And the social science programs were not linked together by a network of consultative mechanisms, by agencies for central review like those institutionalized in the office of the President's Science Adviser, or by built-in congressional interests that had emerged in other fields of science, most notably the biomedical sciences.

A Foundation for the Social Sciences

In 1965, however, Project Camelot exploded. And the inquiry that it provoked clearly exposed the predicament of the social sciences in the federal establishment and led to the proposal to establish a National Social Science Foundation. The proposal was examined in depth in a series of hearings held in 1966 and 1967 by the Subcommittee on Government Research of the Senate Committee on Government Operations. The hearings had originally been called to examine the problems of foreign area research raised by Project Camelot. As the Committee report later suggested, the hearings broadened into a study of "the needs and promises of the social sciences in general" and consequently "the inquiry was expanded to include domestic social science problems as well."[32] The proposal for a separate foundation was actively promoted soon after the hearings began by the Subcommittee Chairman, Senator Fred Harris, Democrat of Oklahoma, and largely developed by his staff director, Steven Ebbin, a political scientist with earlier experience in the State Department.

[32] *Establishment of a National Foundation for the Social Sciences,* Report of Committee on Government Operations, U.S. Senate, 90th Congress, 2nd Session, 1968, p. 6.

The proposal for a foundation for social science thus took shape through congressional initiative. Unlike the early Bush Plan for the NSF, it did not stem from a study conducted by scientists themselves. Indeed, in the various propositions worked out by social scientists to encourage federal support, there is little evidence of serious thought being given to a separate foundation for the social sciences. Certainly the absence of any earlier proposal showed that social scientists were aware of the political realities. They had produced no military weapon, no space vehicle, no successful vaccine that would permit them to stake a major claim for public support. Nor, apparently, did they wish to call into question the increasing funds they were receiving from the National Science Foundation and the National Institutes of Health. Moreover, by making common cause with the other scientists, they protected themselves from those who expected instant wisdom from social analysis and from those who had little understanding or esteem for the role of social science in meeting social problems.

Senator Harris' sponsorship of the social science bill was one of several ventures through which he came to be known as the "senator for science." It was possible for him to play this role in the Senate because of the lack of focus in the upper house for issues of science policy. The Atomic Energy Act of 1946 had led to the creation of a Joint Committee on Atomic Energy in 1946 as a device to consolidate congressional resources and influence in a new and complex area of public policy. Other and more general scientific issues were subject to congressional review and deliberation through regular standing and appropriations committees in their review of executive departments, particularly the military departments and the Department of Health, Education, and Welfare. Here the emphasis was on the departmental mission and not on science policy.

Following the Soviet Sputnik, however, a new standing committee was established in each house of Congress, primarily to deal with matters of space. Significantly, while the Senate Committee was designated the Committee on Aeronautical and Space Sciences, the House Committee was more broadly conceived as the Committee on Science and Astronautics. In practice, moreover, the House Committee took a wider range of scientific issues under its jurisdiction than the Senate Committee. For example, during the 89th session of Congress, in 1965 and 1966, the House Committee, in addition to authorization hearings on the program of the National Aeronautics and Space Administration, conducted, through a Subcommittee on Science, Research and Development, a broad review and assessment of the first fifteen years of the National Science Foundation. The House Committee also established permanent panels of scientists and engineers from academic institutions and private industry to give advice on matters of national science policy. There was no standing committee in the Senate authorized to deal with general problems of national science policy.

Under these conditions, Senator Harris was able to examine a number of issues in science policy under the conveniently broad mandate that the Committee on Government Operations enjoys. As Chairman of its Subcommittee on Government Research, he proceeded to hold hearings and exploratory seminars between 1966 and 1968 on the geographic distribution of federal research and development contracts and grants, on the current state and future development of the biomedical sciences, on the proposal for the establishment of a Council of Social Advisers, as well as on the proposition to create a National Social Science Foundation. He also took a leading role in the Senate in defending the expenditures of the National Science Foundation against the budgetary cutbacks that Congress had to make in 1967 and 1968 as a result of the mounting costs of the Vietnam conflict. His interest in the social sciences, moreover, seems to have been intensified by his membership in the presidentially appointed National Advisory Commission on Civil Disorders, which was set up following the summer riots in 1967 and whose report emphasized the need for an understanding of the dynamics of social behavior as a basis for government programs.

For Harris, a separate foundation would "give the recognition, status, visibility, and prestige the social sciences need." Some of the elder statesmen of social science might, and did, dispute this "need," mindful as they were of the earlier congressional suspicion of the social sciences and not convinced that it had yet disappeared. But Harris' point was that social science was now being supported by many agencies, that it needed to be advanced in order to be of greater use to government, but that there were risks (as Project Camelot had demonstrated) in depending too heavily on mission-oriented agencies for support. Also, the National Science Foundation would, of necessity, continue to be dominated by physical scientists, who understandably would put their own needs first and thus limit the scope and level of support for social science. Finally, the precedent for a separate foundation had been established with the creation of the National Foundation for the Humanities and the Arts with two endowments, one in the arts and the other in the humanities. Under the humanities endowment, moreover, there was provision for support for social science projects that followed an historical or humanistic approach. Thus, Harris insisted that a separate foundation did not necessarily mean that the NSF would not continue to provide limited support for social science as it had in the past.[33]

In 1967 Senator Harris proceeded to build a legislative record on the proposal for a separate social science foundation, having held preliminary hearings a year before actually submitting the proposal as a recommended bill.[34] In February he called for testimony from a number of government agencies and met with a variety of opinions, indicating that there was no general position in the Administration. The Director of the National Science Foundation opposed a separate foundation and outlined the basis for an expanded social science program in the NSF; representatives for the Department of Defense and the Office of Economic Opportunity thought it would probably be unwise to set up a separate foundation; others, like the Secretary of Labor, had no definite view on the proposal, but emphasized the need to strengthen social science research in their own departments; and still others, like representatives of the Department of State and the Peace Corps, agreed that a new foundation would indeed give the social sciences a substantial boost in the federal government.[35]

[33] See Fred R. Harris, "The Case for a National Social Science Foundation," *Science*, Vol. 157, No. 3788 (August 4, 1967), pp. 507–509.

[34] *National Foundation for the Social Sciences*, Hearings before Subcommittee on Government Research, Committee on Government Operations, U.S. Senate, 90th Congress, 1st Session, 1967, Parts 1–3.

[35] *Ibid.*, Part 1.

Later that year Harris called on social scientists to testify; and, again, opinions varied and fell into no perceptible pattern. From Kingsley Davis, an eminent demographer from the University of California in Berkeley and the first sociologist to be elected to the National Academy of Sciences, there was strong support for the Harris bill. Davis insisted:

> the ambivalence toward social science makes its public support and encouragement more precarious than that given to the natural and physical disciplines . . . [and thus warrants] every means that can be found to strengthen [the fields of social inquiry] against obstacles to scientific objectivity.[36]

There was also support from Warren Miller, director of the Inter-University Consortium for Political Research at the University of Michigan, but his reasons were different. Miller argued that only a federal foundation run by social scientists could be expected to fight for the level of support and general infrastructure needed to exploit new developments in social science, such as his own institute's work in political behavior.[37]

The most direct opposition to the Harris proposal came from Herbert Simon, political scientist and psychologist from Carnegie-Mellon University and, like Davis, one of the few social scientists to be a member of the National Academy. Simon made it clear that he did not believe that it would be a catastrophe to create a separate foundation. But, unlike Davis, he emphasized the scientific and political necessity for maintaining a single science organization, the NSF. He argued that the place to seek recognition for social science was not in a separate foundation but in the agencies in which national science policies were formulated, principally the President's Science Advisory Committee and the Office of Science and Technology.[38] Somewhere between the positions taken by Davis and Simon, Don K. Price of Harvard was ready to see a separate foundation created but preferred to establish some sort of coordinating mechanism to insure coherent

---

36 *Ibid.*, Part 2, p. 265.
37 *Ibid.*, pp. 326–342.
38 *Ibid.*, pp. 391–409. It should be noted that the next year, 1968, Simon became the first social scientist to be appointed to the President's Science Advisory Committee.

federal support for basic research and higher education in all the sciences and in the humanities as well.[39]

Harris himself read the testimony before his Subcommittee as general support for a separate foundation and proceeded to report his bill out of Subcommittee with a favorable recommendation in the middle of 1968. However, no companion bill had come up for hearings in the House. Instead, the House Committee on Science and Astronautics had proposed a bill to amend the National Science Foundation legislation, which by then had been passed and signed by the President. The bill specified the social sciences for support by the NSF, making regular the indirect authority that the Foundation had exercised for years under the "permissive but not mandatory" clause. Thus, while Harris could count on substantial support, though no assured majority, for his bill in the Senate, it was unlikely that the measure would even begin to move through the House during the current congressional session. At the same time, severe restrictions were being imposed on all federal spending, primarily as the price the President had to pay for passage of a tax increase and the maintenance of high costs in continuing the Vietnam war. There seemed to be no point in pushing a proposal that had little chance of immediate political success or of immediate funding even if authorizing legislation were passed.

The Harris bill, however, had forced social scientists to confront the problem of their relations with the government seriously and systematically. It was an important element in the general reassessment of the role of the social sciences in the federal government that had started with Project Camelot. Late in 1968 three social science groups were busy studying what these relations should be. The first to complete its work was the Advisory Committee on Government Programs in the Behavioral Sciences, set up by the National Academy of Sciences–National Research Council right after the Project Camelot affair had occurred. The second was a joint project sponsored by the Academy and the Social Science Research Council to survey the state and future needs of the social sciences: the Behavioral and Social Science

[39] *Ibid.*, pp. 414–423.

Survey. Finally, during the hearings on the Harris bill, the NSF announced the creation of a Special Commission on the Social Sciences to explore ways to strengthen the social sciences and make them more responsive to the needs of society. Throughout the Harris hearings—and before, during the Project Camelot debate—the social science community (admittedly an abstraction, at best) was marked by a singular lack of cohesion and leadership. It remained to be seen whether the three study groups would provide a focus that would unite social scientists in support of a federal policy for social science.

The Report of the National Academy of Sciences

The report of the National Academy's Advisory Committee on Government Programs in the Behavioral Sciences, issued in September 1968, provided both continuity with past assessments of the role of social science in the federal government and a point for new departures.[40] There was continuity, first of all, in the series of events which led to the establishment of the Committee. It will be recalled that the one recommendation of the 1962 PSAC panel report on the behavioral sciences that was acted upon immediately, was that the National Academy of Sciences–National Research Council broaden its representation to include all the behavioral sciences. Shortly thereafter, the Division of Anthropology and Psychology in the Research Council structure became the Division of Behavioral Sciences, and a few social scientists were accepted as Academy members. Kingsley Davis was elected to membership in 1966, Herbert Simon in 1967, and Kenneth Arrow, an economist, and Robert K. Merton, a sociologist, in 1968.

Within the new Division in the Research Council, the major social science disciplines were represented—anthropology, economics, political science, psychology, and sociology—and history, geography, linguistics, and psychiatry were added later. In 1964

40 *The Behavioral Sciences and the Federal Government,* Report of the Advisory Committee on Government Programs in the Behavioral Sciences, Publication 1680, National Academy of Sciences–National Research Council (Washington, D.C., 1968).

and early 1965 there were discussions in the Division, and in the Academy in general, on the need for an overall review of social science programs in the federal agencies in order to determine what broader role with respect to these sciences the Academy might play in the future. While these highly informal discussions were taking place, the Defense Department approached the Academy, proposing that a study group be established to examine the implications of the Project Camelot affair. The request was quite natural, for the Academy had been greatly involved in defense research activities since the Second World War, and at this time the President of the Academy, Frederick Seitz, was Chairman of the Defense Science Board.

At the suggestion of the then chairman of the Division of Behavioral Sciences, G. P. Murdock, the anthropologist, Seitz called in for consultation Donald R. Young, former head of the Social Science Research Council and retired president of the Russell Sage Foundation. A sociologist who had done pioneering work on racial and minority questions, Young had been a principal consultant to the Army Research Branch during the war and, while president of Russell Sage, had sponsored major efforts in relating social science research to social problems, including social science training for the practicing professions. Young agreed to chair the proposed Academy Committee after general agreement that any committee that was set up would be granted an open mandate by the Council and not be limited to the Camelot case. It was also agreed that the Committee would need substantial support, both within the government and outside it, if its work was to be "creditable." Therefore the presidents of most of the major social science associations were invited to serve as members of the committee, and the Russell Sage Foundation approved a grant to support its work, in addition to the original grant made to the Academy by the Department of Defense.

The Advisory Committee, despite its broad charter, necessarily devoted the greatest amount of its attention during the first year to the problems of foreign area research that had been exposed by Project Camelot. In the fall of 1966, moreover, the Committee had a chance to serve as a point of contact between the government and academic research communities on the overseas research issue and also to establish close working relations with the Department of State. The Behavioral Science Subcommittee of the Foreign Area Research Coordination Group (FAR), the interagency coordinating unit staffed by the Department of State, asked the Advisory Committee to sponsor a conference on foreign area research that would bring together government research administrators and academic social scientists. The agenda for the conference, developed jointly by the staffs of the group and the Advisory Committee, included three subjects: planning and supporting foreign area research, the conduct of research overseas, and the uses of foreign area research.[41]

The immediate purpose of the conference was, in many respects, therapeutic. The Project Camelot affair and the subsequent revelations about CIA subvention of educational activities overseas had been followed by a widening of the breach between the government agencies and university scholars. One aim of the conference was to keep a dialogue going and, if possible, to find measures that would dispel the suspicion and, in some cases, the antagonism that existed. The conference itself made no recommendations. But the conference report, summarizing the discussion, became the starting point for a subsequent review within FAR and the individual government agencies of all government policies with regard to research overseas. And out of this review, in late 1967, came the statement of guiding principles for foreign area research confirmed by all the FAR agencies. These principles were: that government support of contract research should always be acknowledged; that classification of such research should be kept at a minimum; that agencies should encourage open publication of research results; and that the advancement of knowledge should be a factor in designing even action-oriented research projects.[42] Within limits, the principles sought to reconcile the operational requirements of the government with the professional requirements of effective social science research abroad. They did

[41] *Foreign Area Research: A Conference Report*, Advisory Committee on Government Programs in the Behavioral Sciences, National Academy of Sciences–National Research Council (Washington, D.C., January 1967).

[42] See *FAR Horizons*, Foreign Area Research Coordination Group, Department of State (Washington, D.C., January 1968), Vol. 1, No. 1.

nothing, however, to change the relations among government programs or to promote the more effective use of research within agencies.

For the Academy Advisory Committee, the foreign area research conference was but one step in a process of exploration; it then began to consider the domestic programs in which social science research was supported and which, by now, were beginning to exceed the defense and foreign affairs programs. The fact is that there were problems that plagued all social science research in both foreign and domestic programs. These included the organization of research activities in federal agencies, the recruitment of social scientists, social science materials in government training programs, and the translation of research findings for the formulation of public policies. Of course, research in foreign affairs required sources of information in foreign countries—a fact which distinguished it from other research. But the Advisory Committee chose to deal with this distinction within the larger issue—the relations between social science and the federal government.

The final report of the Advisory Committee thus included a range of recommendations—from measures to strengthen the internal structure of social science research programs in federal agencies to the establishment of a new National Institute for Advanced Research and Public Policy. The report recognized that "the decisions and actions taken by the President, the Congress, and the executive departments and agencies [on complex issues of public policy] must be based on valid social and economic information and involve a high degree of judgment about human behavior." However, there was no presumption that other factors, primarily political, did not enter into the decision-making process or that "knowledge is a substitute for wisdom or common-sense or for decision-making." Indeed, the report was framed in a perspective that accorded politics its place of primacy in governmental decision-making. Nevertheless, the relevance of the behavioral sciences was emphasized as "an important source of information, analysis and explanation about group and individual behavior," an idea that had been expressed as far back as 1932 in

Recent Social Trends and that still remained only imperfectly realized or even understood.

Unlike the authors of *Recent Social Trends*, however, the Academy Advisory Committee could now point to considerable progress in the application of social science to the problems of federal government since the 1930's. Most especially, its report discussed advances, both scientific and institutional, in the fields of statistical services and economic analysis. Learning from these advances, the Committee specified several conditions that were needed for strengthening social science in the government in other fields, "especially those areas of sociology, social psychology, political science, and anthropology that are relevant to new social programs at home and to programs of development assistance in the international field." These conditions "for using the knowledge and methods of the behavioral sciences effectively," were:

(1) an understanding by top administrators of the nature of the behavioral sciences and their relevance to the policies and programs for which they are responsible; (2) a professional environment to attract behavioral scientists into government and to provide incentives and opportunities for their scientific development; and (3) a strategy for research to give cohesion and purpose to behavioral science activities carried on by a department and to relate them to policy processes and program operations.

The report proceeded to suggest several practical steps that could be taken to move toward these goals. These included staffing studies to identify positions for which behavioral science training and experience should be required, in-service training programs in the scope and methods of the behavioral sciences, and methods of organizing and reviewing behavioral science research in any department or agency in terms of a set of strategic goals that related agency missions to developments in the behavioral sciences. The discussion supporting these recommendations gave special attention to the importance of program evaluation and the application of the Planning-Programming-Budgeting System (PPBS). "Program evaluation," it was emphasized:

requires major increases of social and economic information as a basis for measuring the effectiveness of public policies and programs. Increased information brings on increased problems of analysis and of developing conceptual schemes that relate information to the goals and responsibilities of the department or agency. Thus, questions about facts and what they mean become broadened into questions about applying knowledge or finding out something that is not yet known or is little understood. The need for information thus brings with it a need for research, a need for understanding of research by top administrators, and a need for behavioral scientists in government service; a need, in sum, for strengthening the conditions for the effective use of the knowledge and methods of the behavioral sciences.

The Advisory Committee noted that its general recommendations to strengthen social science research applied as much to agencies with foreign affairs and military missions as to domestic agencies. However, two sets of special problems had to be considered when dealing with government-sponsored research abroad. The first involved the connections among the several research programs of foreign affairs and military agencies; the second, the requirements of international collaboration in cross-cultural research.

Project Camelot had raised so much controversy largely because it was sponsored by the Army. Foreign suspicions of American research, while increasingly prevalent, were certainly aggravated by military sponsorship. Yet the military agencies had become by far the largest supporters of social science research overseas. The Committee attributed this to "large total budgets within which to absorb research costs," "a greater receptivity to research than civilian foreign affairs agencies," and the failure of the Department of State to use "research as an instrument of planning" in its own organization and "to provide leadership for government-wide research efforts in international affairs."

"Ultimately," the Committee stated, "the effective use of research in foreign affairs depends on developing in the Department of State and other agencies the kind of staff, working environment, and linkages between research and operations" that the report had already recommended. But the Committee also urged that means be found to coordinate research in international affairs on an inter-agency basis; in effect, to develop a "strategy" for foreign policy research not on an agency by agency basis but on a government-wide basis. Therefore the Committee suggested forming an inter-agency research planning group headed by the State Department. It hoped that this initial step might eventually lead to a better balance in the research effort among agencies with foreign operations, to the determination of "areas of research essential to policy planning," and to instrumentalities to develop "cumulative bodies of knowledge on international problems."

The second set of problems had to do with the need for international cooperation in the behavioral sciences. Again, Project Camelot had been an example *par excellence* of what foreign scholars have called American "academic imperialism" or "unilateralism." The Committee flatly asserted that even if such an attitude was ever justifiable, it simply could not continue: "For both political and scientific reasons, 'unilateralism' will be increasingly resisted and opportunities for research in foreign areas progressively delimited unless research is made a matter of international cooperation." In order to build the bases for such cooperation, the Committee went on to recommend policies that would (1) strengthen the capacity of American universities to engage in international and comparative research and education and (2) assist the developing countries in Asia, Africa, and Latin America to expand their own social science resources so that the manpower and facilities for effective scholarly collaboration would, in fact, be available. Moreover, the burden of carrying out these policies was to be placed on the science and education agencies of the federal government—the National Science Foundation, the National Institutes of Health, or the Office of Education, for example —and not on agencies with foreign or military missions.

In its analysis of the research programs in mission-oriented agencies—in both domestic and foreign affairs—the Committee, while emphasizing the *use* of social science, also urged that *support* for social science range across a spectrum from "broad investigations" of a basic nature to "narrowly applied projects." The Committee here, in effect, adopted the system that had developed in the physical sciences: the creation of pluralistic sources of support for basic research which, from the viewpoint of the government agencies, had the advantage of linking them with important segments of the scientific community. Generally, the universities were to receive support for basic, rather than applied, research. In basic research, the Committee pointed out, "projects should not need to be classified for security reasons" and "findings can be published through normal scientific and professional channels." Such research was "thus consistent with the purposes of institutions of higher education while still contributing to the on-going activities of government."

The recommendations of the Advisory Committee, up to this point, had generally been limited to strengthening the internal organization and staffing of federal departments and agencies for the effective use of social science research. This approach was consistent with an underlying principle expressed in the report: "the use of research requires an integration of the knowledge and methods of the behavioral sciences into the on-going processes of government and not necessarily the creation of new and separate institutions." The expectation that departments and agencies would, in fact, pursue policies that would promote research was another matter. Certainly, any concerted effort to do so would require pressure from the top. Thus the Committee confronted the problem of central organization for social science, and most particularly the organization for scientific affairs within the Executive Office of the President.

In approaching the issue of central organization, the Committee observed that, "for all intents, and purposes, there is no central forum for dealing with common problems of behavioral science or for giving top-level support to policies designed to strengthen the behavioral sciences as an instrument of policy-making and program operations." There were two alternatives: to create a new agency in the Executive Office or to add responsibility for social science policies and programs to an existing agency. Here, the Committee chose the second alternative for two major reasons, one only implicit in its report, the second explicitly stated and fundamental to many of the Committee's conclusions.

The first reason was the practical consideration of limiting the number of top officials reporting directly to the President.

The creation of the Executive Office at the end of Roosevelt's second term was, in the first instance, designed to "help the President" manage the growing federal establishment. More recently, the tendency has been to expand existing staff agencies in the Executive Office when new issues were raised or to push responsibility back into the operating departments and agencies. To establish new agencies—like the Council of Economic Advisers and the Office of Science and Technology—there has had to be a special reason for invoking the authority and prestige of the President or for providing him with a means of accomplishing aims that could not be accomplished through the existing structure. No such reason could realistically be given in the case of social science research.

Moreover, within the Executive Office there already existed, as the Committee indicated, several possible bases for providing a central forum for the problems of social science research, most especially, the Bureau of the Budget, the Council of Economic Advisers, and the Office of Science and Technology. Of the three, the Office of Science and Technology (OST) was most directly concerned with the issues that were involved, that is, policies for social science as part of general science policies. The Committee therefore recommended the expansion of "OST responsibilities to include behavioral science activities" and a reconstitution of the President's Science Advisory Committee to insure a strong (though unspecified) representation from the social sciences. Behind this reasoning there lay two articulated objectives:

In the fields of health, urban rehabilitation, conservation and renewal of resources, and economic and social development, a key objective should be to design programs that utilize and relate knowledge from all disciplines. At the same time, the policies of the federal government for scientific development and educational growth need to be conceived in comprehensive terms, especially as federal support of science becomes increasingly related to federal support for higher education.

The same line of thinking—the need for coherent federal policies that relate to all the sciences—showed itself in the Committee's discussion of the National Science Foundation and the proposal for a separate foundation for the social sciences. The

Committee did not reject the possibility for a separate foundation as proposed by Senator Harris. There was, however, a definite preference expressed in the report for maintaining a single agency responsible for supporting scientific development in all fields—the NSF. Moreover, two lines of action were recommended for the NSF: to exploit the opportunities for greater support for social science which might emerge with the reports of its own Special Commission on the Social Sciences and the Behavioral and Social Science Survey; and to extend its current programs of departmental and institutional grants to the social sciences in order to assist in meeting the needs of large-scale research, the growth of major data sources, and the provision of facilities for research.

The Committee did not ignore the possibility of creating a new institution. But it approached the question from quite another direction than the Harris bill. It saw a need, not for a separate foundation to support the development of the social and behavioral sciences, but for a National Institute for Advanced Research and Public Policy to find effective methods of applying social science to public issues. Endowed by the federal government, but quite independent of it, this institute would have "two major functions: to undertake and sponsor long-range analyses of national policies and problems; and to serve as a forum for continuing interchange between government policy-makers and physical scientists, biological scientists, and behavioral scientists."

The dimensions of the proposed institute were not spelled out in any detail by the Committee; it was presented as an idea rather than a fully drawn-up plan. But the Committee made clear that it was not to be "a substitute for existing research facilities" or "a large holding company for the broad array of specialized organizations already in operation." It was not to take the form of the RAND Corporation or the Urban Institute, or to serve as a contract organization available to government agencies on call. Its "distinctive features" were to be:

> its future-orientation to issues a decade or more ahead, its emphasis on the theoretical and methodological problems of applying knowledge to social action, its concern with the exploitation

of social and economic data, and its educational purpose in serving policy-makers and scientists as a forum for exploring the relevance of knowledge to public policy.

The proposed institute served as a kind of capstone to the total "system" that the Committee report had sought to describe. The Committee's recommendations were consciously interrelated, presumably designed to produce a continual process of action and reaction through which the application of social science research would be strengthened at multiple levels of government and the financing of basic research would be sustained through pluralistic sources of support. The whole process was to be kept under constant surveillance by establishing central responsibility in the Office of Science and Technology. Within this system the institute, it was suggested, would "serve to support the steps [recommended] . . . to strengthen the capacity of the federal government to use the knowledge and methods of the behavioral sciences effectively":

> It could provide a setting for the kind of future-oriented studies that so frequently suffer from the pressures under which the federal departments and agencies are forced to operate. . . . It could facilitate the recruitment of behavioral scientists into the government service by providing grants for innovative research throughout the country and by bringing research scientists working in similar fields together to share their findings with each other and with government officials in areas of potential application. It also could draw its staff, on a short-term or long-term basis, from university departments and from both the executive and legislative branches of the government.

The report of the National Academy's Advisory Committee may be seen as an exercise in consolidation. It brought together, within a single frame of reference, a wide range of political, institutional, and scientific developments and demonstrated their essential connections. It suggested a number of practical first steps—in staffing, training, and organization—which, when taken as a whole, carried more weight than if each were regarded in isolation from the other. The recommendations of the Committee were directed to the federal government and, more specifically, to the

Executive Branch. Their implications, however, went much farther and had considerable relevance for university training in the social sciences and for the role of the Congress in the federal decision-making process.

In its report the Advisory Committee pointed out:

> The capacity for bringing knowledge to bear on practical problems has been given little attention in the education of behavioral scientists. The emphasis has been on teaching and original research. . . . [At the same time] the weaknesses of behavioral science curricula in the . . . professional schools [particularly schools of law] that provide the educational background for many administrators are limiting factors in the use of behavioral science knowledge in government.

What the government needed to do to overcome these weaknesses was summed up in the Committee's recommendations on recruitment, staffing, and training. The response of the universities, however, was left unattended, although it was undoubtedly the kind of question that would be raised more directly and fully in the report of the Behavioral and Social Science Survey group. Only implicit in the Advisory Committee report was the assumption that a serious effort by the federal government to develop the social science "translator" or "professional in application" could have an important influence on university teaching programs. For one thing, the government could stimulate the development of new teaching programs in applied social science through special scholarship assistance and grants for curricula experimentation. For another, distinct career opportunities in applying social science—given value and prestige by government—might be recognized by university departments preparing students with a high preference for careers in government.

Quite explicitly, the Committee acknowledged that its report was "largely devoted to problems in the Executive Branch." It nonetheless recognized, without further elaboration, "the need for a strong analytical capacity, based in the behavioral sciences, in the staff and reference services of the Congress." The more Congress had access to Executive Branch records and reports, the more effective use it could make of the social and behavioral research in executive departments and agencies in order to evaluate public policies and programs. Nonetheless there remained the quite understandable congressional demand for an independent source of knowledge, not only for judgment over executive proposals and actions but also for initiating legislative proposals.

The Advisory Committee may have been correct in limiting its review to the Executive Branch of the federal government. In doing so, it avoided having to deal with complicating issues that have tended to weaken the role of Congress progressively in recent years: the diffusion of power in the Congress, the weaknesses of organization and the procedures that add to institutional fragmentation, and the pressures that electoral politics generate for short-term solutions to persistent and complex social problems.[43] But, in avoiding these issues, the Committee emphasized them all the more. Only in its recommendation for a new National Institute for Advanced Research and Public Policy, did the Committee provide a mechanism through which Congress could tap the resources of the scientific community more systematically and thoroughly than it had in the past. Integrating social science into the processes of congressional deliberation and decision-making remained a problem to be explored.

The Past as Prologue

The report of the National Academy's Advisory Committee was an important reference point in the history of social science in the federal government. The approach of the Committee, with its emphasis on the use of social science research, brought into focus three issues that have run through the evolution of federal relations with social science: whether the knowledge and the methods of the social sciences can contribute effectively to the formation of public policy; whether social scientists should seek federal support for the development of their disciplines; and whether in-

---

[43] For an analysis of contemporary issues of Congress, see David B. Truman (ed.), *The Congress and America's Future* (Englewood Cliffs, N.J.: Prentice-Hall, 1965).

volvement in government and federal support necessarily mean the loss of scientific independence and autonomy. In effect, the Committee responded by defining conditions for the effective use of social science, by recognizing that public support was needed but could not be realistically anticipated without "usefulness" being demonstrated, and by providing a pluralistic system of support and methods of political and professional administration within which scientific independence could be protected.

These issues, however, will continue to be a matter of controversy, as they have been since the early years of the twentieth century. The one incontrovertible point is that there can be no turning back. The relations between social science and the federal government have by now become so complex that they cannot be untangled. Over the years social science has developed a capacity for measuring, evaluating, and predicting social change—though there are still large areas of uncertainty and doubt. At the same time the federal government has shown a growing commitment to serve as a positive force in social change—though there are practical limits to the programs government can effectively manage and constitutional and political limits to the extension of federal authority. These developments, whatever their limits, have drawn social science and the federal government together into a working partnership that will almost certainly grow closer as time goes on.

In *Recent Social Trends*, social scientists had projected a place for "rational intelligence" in government in terms of a concept of planning that would take into account the interrelated determinants of social change. In their report on social science research in *Research—A National Resource*, almost ten years later, they recorded only modest progress toward this broad goal. More practically, they called for increased contact between social scientists and administrative agencies in order to encourage the systematic collection and analysis of social and economic data in government operations and to direct more attention to social problems in university teaching. During the Second World War and the postwar years of international tension, the federal government expanded its programs and, in the 1960's, initiated new programs in response to domestic demands for social change. By the time the PSAC-sponsored report, *Strengthening the Behavioral Sci-*

ences, was published in 1962, important advances had been made in building the theoretical and empirical bases of social science; and the report urged a recognition of the need for sustained federal support for their systematic development. Finally, the National Academy report, *The Behavioral Sciences and the Federal Government,* pushed the process one step further, stressing the connection between the *use* and the *development* of social science and recommending a system of interacting arrangements to reconcile pluralistic bases for research support with coherent policies and central organization.

The National Academy report, moreover, was only one of a series of studies designed to examine the state of the social sciences and to explore their relevance to the problems confronted by American society. And still more studies will have to be undertaken before the terms of the partnership between the federal government and social science can be worked out. The quest for more effective relations between social science research and government policies and programs does not, however, begin with a strong national consensus about either the goals of government or the predictive or analytic capacity of social science. There is often bitter disagreement over the goals of public policy, the increased reliance on "experts" (of any kind), and the limits of objectivity in dealing with social problems; and there is an increased sense of alienation in many groups in the country from the centers of decision-making ruling their lives. In this situation, a deep desire for rationality is mixed with uneasy suspicions about the nature of science and the aims of political power.

In his classic essay, "Science as a Vocation," Max Weber reminded us that "intellectualization and rationalization do *not* . . . indicate an increased and general knowledge of the conditions under which one lives." What they do mean is "the knowledge or belief . . . that there are no mysterious incalculable forces that come into play, but rather that one can, in principle, master all things by calculation. This means that the world is disenchanted."[44]

Few social scientists—and fewer politicians—would assert

---

[44] In H. H. Gerth and C. Wright Mills, *From Max Weber* (London: Kegan Paul, 1947), p. 139.

that the "world" of human relations "is disenchanted" or that "all things" can be mastered by "calculation." Yet there are, in American culture, elements of rationalism and progress which give strength to the application of reason to governing. These come under heavy strain in times of crisis and frustration. But we have suffered too many cruel tragedies in recent history to be satisfied with waiting, as Wesley Mitchell put it many years ago, "for catastrophes to force new ways upon us." The "ways" that we choose will reflect what we believe, what we want, and what we know. Values, aspirations, and knowledge, however, do not exist in isolation from each other. They exist in a process of interaction, each influencing the other. How well knowledge will serve us and how well we serve the growth of knowledge are issues of great complexity that we will continue to face. And, as we do, it is well to understand how we have faced these issues in the past.

APPENDIXES I, II, III, and IV

Extracts from
A Review of Findings by the President's
Research Committee on Social Trends
RECENT SOCIAL TRENDS
IN THE UNITED STATES[1]

Introduction

In September 1929 the Chief Executive of the nation called upon the members of this Committee to examine and to report upon recent social trends in the United States with a view to providing such a review as might supply a basis for the formulation of large national policies looking to the next phase in the nation's development. The summons was unique in our history. . . .

The first third of the twentieth century has been filled with epoch-making events and crowded with problems of great variety and complexity. The World War, the inflation and deflation of agriculture and business, our emergence as a creditor nation, the spectacular increase in efficiency and productivity and the tragic spread of unemployment and business distress, the experiment of prohibition, birth control, race riots, stoppage of immigration, women's suffrage, the struggles of the Progressive and the Farmer Labor parties, governmental corruption, crime and racketeering, the sprawl of great cities, the decadence of rural government, the birth of the League of Nations, the expansion of education, the rise and weakening of organized labor, the growth of spectacular fortunes, the advance of medical science, the emphasis on sports and recreation, the renewed interest in child welfare—these are a few of the many happenings which have marked one of the most eventful periods of our history.

With these events have come national problems urgently demanding attention on many fronts. Even a casual glance at some of these points of tension in our national life reveals a wide range of puzzling questions. Imperialism, peace or war, international relations, urbanism,

---

[1] *Recent Social Trends in the United States,* Report of the President's Research Committee on Social Trends (2 vols.; New York: McGraw-Hill Book Co., 1933), Vol. I, pp. xi–xv and lxx–lxxv.

trusts and mergers, crime and its prevention, taxation, social insurance, the plight of agriculture, foreign and domestic markets, governmental regulation of industry, shifting moral standards, new leadership in business and government, the status of womankind, labor, child training, mental hygiene, the future of democracy and capitalism, the reorganization of our governmental units, the use of leisure time, public and private medicine, better homes and standards of living—all of these and many others, for these are only samples taken from a long series of grave questions, demand attention if we are not to drift into zones of danger. Demagogues, statesmen, savants and propagandists have attacked these problems, but usually from the point of view of some limited interest. Records and information have been and still are incomplete and often inconclusive.

The Committee does not exaggerate the bewildering confusion of problems; it has merely uncovered the situation as it is. Modern life is everywhere complicated, but especially so in the United States, where immigration from many lands, rapid mobility within the country itself, the lack of established classes or castes to act as a brake on social changes, the tendency to seize upon new types of machines, rich natural resources and vast driving power, have hurried us dizzily away from the days of the frontier into a whirl of modernisms which almost passes belief.

Along with this amazing mobility and complexity there has run a marked indifference to the interrelation among the parts of our huge social system. Powerful individuals and groups have gone their own way without realizing the meaning of the old phrase, "No man liveth unto himself."

The result has been that astonishing contrasts in organization and disorganization are to be found side by side in American life: splendid technical proficiency in some incredible skyscraper and monstrous backwardness in some equally incredible slum. The outstanding problem might be stated as that of bringing about a realization of the interdependence of the factors of our complicated social structure, and of interrelating the advancing sections of our forward movement so that agriculture, labor, industry, government, education, religion and science may develop a higher degree of coordination in the next phase of national growth.

In times of war and imminent public calamity it has been possible to achieve a high degree of coordinated action, but in the intervals of which national life is largely made up, coordinated effort relaxes and under the heterogeneous forces of modern life a vast amount of disorganization has been possible in our economic, political and social affairs.

It may indeed be said that the primary value of this report is to be found in the effort to interrelate the disjointed factors and elements in the social life of America, in the attempt to view the situation as a whole rather than as a cluster of parts. The various inquiries which have been conducted by the Committee are subordinated to the main purpose of getting a central view of the American problem as revealed by social trends. Important studies have recently been made in economic changes, in education, in child welfare, in home ownership and home building, in law enforcement, in social training, in medicine. The meaning of the present study of social change is to be found not merely in the analysis of the separate trends, many of which have been examined before, but in their interrelation—in the effort to look at America as a whole, as a national union the parts of which too often are isolated, not only in scientific studies but in everyday affairs.

The Committee's procedure, then, has been to look at recent social trends in the United States as interrelated, to scrutinize the functioning of the social organization as a joint activity. It is the express purpose of this review of findings to unite such problems as those of economics, government, religion, education, in a comprehensive study of social movements and tendencies, to direct attention to the importance of balance among the factors of change. A nation advances not only by dynamic power, but by and through the maintenance of some degree of equilibrium among the moving forces.

There are of course numerous ways to present these divergent questions but it may be useful to consider for the moment that the clue to their understanding as well as the hope for improvement lies in the fact of social change. Not all parts of our organization are changing at the same speed or at the same time. Some are rapidly moving forward and others are lagging. These unequal rates of change in economic life, in government, in education, in science and religion make zones of danger and points of tension. It is almost as if the various functions of the body or the parts of an automobile were operating at unsynchronized speeds. Our capacity to produce goods changes faster than our capacity to purchase; employment does not keep pace with improvement in the machinery of production; interoceanic communication changes more quickly than the reorganization of international relations; the factory takes occupations away from the home before the home can adjust itself to the new conditions. The automobile affects the railroads, the family, size of cities, types of crime, manners and morals.

Scientific discoveries and inventions instigate changes first in the economic organization and social habits which are most closely associated with them. Thus factories and cities, corporations and labor organizations have grown up in response to technological developments.

The next great set of changes occurs in organizations one step further removed, namely in institutions such as the family, the government, the schools and the churches. Somewhat later, as a rule, come changes in social philosophies and codes of behavior, although at times these may precede the others. Not all changes come in this order but sufficient numbers so occur in modern history to make the sequence of value in charting the strains of our civilization. In reality all of these factors act and react upon each other, often in perplexing and unexpected ways.

Of the great social organizations, two, the economic and the governmental, are growing at a rapid rate, while two other historic organizations, the church and the family, have declined in social significance, although not in human values. Many of the problems of society today occur because of the shifting roles of these four major social institutions. Church and family have lost many of their regulatory influences over behavior, while industry and government have assumed a larger degree of control.

Of these four great social institutions, the economic organization, in part at least, has been progressively adjusted to mechanical invention as is shown by the remarkable gains in the records of productivity per worker. Engineers hold out visions of still greater productivity, with consequent increases in the standards of living. But there are many adjustments to be made within other parts of the economic organization. The flow of credit is not synchronized with the flow of production. There are recurring disasters in the business cycle. Employer organizations have changed more rapidly than employee organizations. A special set of economic problems is that occasioned by the transformation in agriculture due to science, to electricity and gasoline, and to the growth of the agencies of communication. Another focus of maladjustments has its center in our ideas of property, the distribution of wealth and poverty—new forms of age-old problems.

The shifting of economic activities has brought innumerable problems to government. It has forced an expansion of governmental functions, creating problems of bureaucracy and inefficiency. The problems of still closer union between government and industry are upon us. It is difficult but vital to determine what type of relationship there shall be, for all types are by no means envisaged by the terms communism and capitalism. The conception of government changes as it undertakes various community activities such as education, recreation and health. Again, the revolutionary developments of communication already have shown the inadequacies of the present boundaries of local governments organized in simpler days, and on a larger scale foreshadow rearrangements in the relations of nations, with the possibility always of that most tragic of human problems, war.

Like government, the family has been slow to change in strengthening its services to its members to meet the new conditions forced upon them. Many of the economic functions of the family have been transferred to the factory; its educational functions to the school; its supervision over sanitation and pure food to government. These changes have necessitated many adaptations to new conditions, not always readily made, and often resulting in serious maladjustments. The diminishing size and increasing instability of the family have contributed to the problem.

The spiritual values of life are among the most profound of those affected by developments in technology and organization. They are the slowest in changing to meet altered conditions. Moral guidance is peculiarly difficult, when the future is markedly different from the past. So we have the anomalies of prohibition and easy divorce; strict censorship and risque plays and literature; scientific research and laws forbidding the teaching of the theory of evolution; contraceptive information legally outlawed but widely utilized. All these are illustrations of varying rates of change and of their effect in raising problems.

If, then, the report reveals, as it must, confusion and complexity in American life during recent years, striking inequality in the rates of change, uneven advances in inventions, institutions, attitudes and ideals, dangerous tensions and torsions in our social arrangements, we may hold steadily to the importance of viewing social situations as a whole in terms of the interrelation and interdependence of our national life, of analyzing and appraising our problems as those of a single society based upon the assumption of the common welfare as the goal of common effort.

Effective coordination of the factors of our evolving society means, where possible and desirable, slowing up the changes which occur too rapidly and speeding up the changes which lag. The Committee does not believe in a moratorium upon research in physical science and invention, such as has sometimes been proposed. On the contrary, it holds that social invention has to be stimulated to keep pace with mechanical invention. What seems a welter of confusion may thus be brought more closely into relationship with the other parts of our national structure, with whatever implications this may hold for ideals and institutions. . . .

Part 4. Policy and Problems

A FORMAL SUMMARY OF PRINCIPLES. What we conceive to be the major problems revealed by our studies of social trends have now been passed in review. By way of summary, a list of these problems in the order of their social importance may be expected. But to draw up such a list requires agreement upon some criterion of social importance, as well as sharp definitions of problems which assume varying forms and meanings as they are viewed from different angles. A summary perhaps more serviceable to future thinking, although less directive of immediate action, can be provided by pointing out in abstract form the general characteristics which social problems have in common.

The fundamental principles are that social problems are products of change, and that social changes are interrelated. Hence, a change in one part of the social structure will affect other parts connected with it. But the effects do not always follow immediately—an induced change may lag years behind the original precipitating change. These varying delays among correlated changes often mean maladjustment. They may arise from vested interests resisting change in self-defense, from the difficulty with which men readjust familiar ideas or ideals, or from various obstacles which obstruct the transmission of impulses from man to man. These interrelated changes which are going forward in such bewildering variety and at such varying speeds threaten grave dangers with one hand, while with the other hand they hold out the promise of further betterment to mankind. The objective of any conscious control over the process is to secure a better adjustment between inherited nature and culture. The means of social control is social discovery and the wider adoption of new knowledge.

THE NEED FOR SOCIAL THINKING. On the principles just stated in bald form it is inevitable that the descriptions of social trends in the following chapters run forward to the series of questions raised but not answered in this summary review of results. If that were not the case, the descriptions would fall lamentably short of thoroughness. The Committee is in the same position as its collaborators. In formulating this general sketch of the complicated social trends which are remoulding American life, it finds its analytic description leading ever and again to a statement of problems which can be solved only by further scientific discoveries and practical inventions.

To make the discoveries which are called for, to design, perfect and apply the inventions is a task which would be far beyond the powers of the Committee and its collaborators, even if we had not been excused in advance from making such an effort. If one considers the enormous mass of detailed work required to achieve the recent decline in American death rates, or to make aviation possible, or to increase per capita production in farming, one realizes that the job of solving the social problems here outlined is a job for cumulative thinking by many minds over years to come. Discovery and invention are themselves social processes made up of countless individual achievements. Nothing short of the combined intelligence of the nation can cope with the predicaments here mentioned. Nor would a magnificent effort which successfully solved all the problems pending today suffice—if such an effort can be imagined. For, if we are right in our conception of the character of cultural trends, the successful solutions would take the form of inventions which would alter our ways of doing things, and thereby produce new difficulties of endless variety. Then a fresh series of efforts to invent solutions for social problems would be needed.

IMPLEMENTING PUBLIC POLICY. In beginning this report, the Committee stated that the major emerging problem is that of closer coordination and more effective integration of the swiftly changing elements in American social life. What are the prerequisites of a successful, long time constructive integration of social effort?

Indispensable among these are the following:

Willingness and determination to undertake important integral changes in the reorganization of social life, including the economic and the political orders, rather than the pursuance of a policy of drift.

Recognition of the role which science must play in such a reorganization of life.

Continuing recognition of the intimate interrelationship between changing scientific techniques, varying social interests and institutions, modes of social education and action and broad social purposes.

Specific ways and means of procedure for continuing research and for the formulation of concrete policies as well as for the successful administration of the lines of action indicated.

If we look at the ways in which the continuing integration of social intelligence may advance, there are many roads leading forward.

1. We may reasonably anticipate a considerable body of con-

structive social thinking in the near future developing in the minds of individual students of social problems, pioneers in social discovery or statesmen in social science. More widely in the future than in the immediate past we may expect the growth of thinking about the meaning of the great masses of social data which we have become so expert and generous in assembling. Is it possible that there is radical inconsistency between the industrious and precise collection of material and the effort to interpret and utilize what has been found out? Or the contrary, is there a compelling urgency that they be brought together both for the sake of science and of society? We may look for important contributions from individual thinkers with a point of view from which the focusing of social problems and their constructive integration is not excluded, but emphasized. Some of these efforts may be widely divergent in conclusions from others, but they should have in common the interrelation of social problems in closer meshed patterns than heretofore. It is also to be anticipated that the initiative in a wide variety of emerging problems will be assumed by research centers, groups, bureaus, institutes and foundations, devoted in some instances to more specialized and in others to more general treatment of social data. A considerable amount of such work is now being done in universities and independent research institutes, and the results are seen in the increasing penetration of social technology into public welfare work, public heath, education, social work and the courts. While some of these inquiries may be fragmentary and often unrelated or inadequately related, there should nevertheless be important findings and inventions of great value to society. It might be said, indeed, that while the most recent phase of American development in the social field has been the recognition of the necessity of fact finding agencies and equipment, and their actual establishment, the next phase of advance may find more emphasis upon interpretation and synthesis than the last.

2. Nor can we fail to observe the interest of government itself, national, state and local alike, in the technical problems of social research and of prevision and planning. A very large amount of planning has already been undertaken, notably by cities and by the federal government, and to a less extent by states and counties. There is reason to anticipate that this form of organization of social intelligence and policy will develop in the future with the increasing complexity of social life and the realization of the significance of social interrelationship. The monumental work of the census alone is an adequate indication of the interest of the organized government in the collection of social data, and there are many other illustrations of the deep concern of the gov-

ernment with the data upon which national policies should rest. The fact-finding work of the executive branch of the government has often been more systematically directed than that of the legislators and the courts, but there are striking examples of the utility of inquiries in all divisions and on all levels of government, in legislative inquiries (especially the interim inquiries) and in judicial proceedings as well as in the undertakings of the more recently developed judicial councils. It is not beyond the bounds of possibility that in dealing with some forms of problems, joint inquiry instituted under the auspices of two or more departments of government might prove to be an effective procedure, in that partisanship and proprietorship in findings would to some extent be minimized.

3. The Social Science Research Council, representative of seven scientific societies, and devoted to the consideration of research in the social field, may prove an instrumentality of great value in the broader view of the complex social problems, in the integration of social knowledge, in the initiative toward social planning on a high level. Important advances have already been made in agricultural research, in industrial and international relations, and striking possibilities lie ahead in the direction of linking together social problems likely otherwise to be left unrelated.

It is within the bounds of possibility that this Council might care to take the initiative in setting up other machinery for the consideration of *ad hoc* problems, and for more and continuous generalized consideration of broader aspects of social integration and planning. It would further be possible for this Council to organize sponsoring groups in which there might be brought together the technical fact finding, the interpretation of data in a broader sense, and the practical judgment of those holding the reins of authority in government, industry and society.

4. Out of these methods of approach it is not impossible that there might in time emerge a National Advisory Council, including scientific, educational, governmental, economic (industrial, agricultural and labor) points of contact, or other appropriate elements, able to contribute to the consideration of the basic social problems of the nation. Such an agency might consider some fundamental questions of the social order, economic, governmental, educational, technical, cultural, always in their interrelation, and in the light of the trends and possibilities of modern science.

In any case, and whatever the approach, it is clear that the type of planning now most urgently required is neither economic planning alone, nor governmental planning alone. The new synthesis must include the scientific, the educational, as well as the economic (including here the industrial and the agricultural) and also the governmental. All these factors are inextricably intertwined in modern life, and it is impossible to make rapid progress under present conditions without drawing them all together.

The Committee does not wish to exaggerate the role of intelligence in social direction, or to underestimate the important parts played by tradition, habit, unintelligence, inertia, indifference, emotions or the raw will to power in various forms. These obvious factors cannot escape observation, and at times they leave only a hopeless resignation to drift with fate. Social action, however, is the resultant of many forces among which in an age of science and education, conscious intelligence may certainly be reckoned as one.

Furthermore, it is important not to overstate the aspect either of integration or concentration in control, or of governmentalism. The unity here presented as essential to rounded social development may be achieved partly within and through the government and partly within other institutions and through other than governmental agencies. In some phases of behavior there are very intimate relationships between science, education, government, industry and culture; and in others the connection may be farther in the background. Some of the centers of integration may be local, others may be national, and still others international in their point of reference. What is here outlined is a way of approach to social problems, with the emphasis on a method rather than on a set of mechanisms. More important than any special type of institution is the attainment of a situation in which economic, governmental, moral and cultural arrangements should not lag too far behind the advance of basic changes.

The alternative to constructive social initiative may conceivably be a prolongation of a policy of drift and some readjustment as time goes on. More definite alternatives, however, are urged by dictatorial systems in which the factors of force and violence may loom large. In such cases the basic decisions are frankly imposed by power groups, and violence may subordinate technical intelligence in social guidance.

Unless there can be a more impressive integration of social skills and fusing of social purposes than is revealed by recent trends, there can be no assurance that these alternatives with their accompaniments of violent revolution, dark periods of serious repression of libertarian and democratic forms, the proscription and loss of many useful elements in the present productive system, can be averted.

Fully realizing its mission, the Committee does not wish to assume an attitude of alarmist irresponsibility, but on the other hand it would be highly negligent to gloss over the stark and bitter realities of the social situation, and to ignore the imminent perils in further advance of our heavy technical machinery over crumbling roads and shaking bridges. There are times when silence is not neutrality, but assent.

Finally, the Committee is not unmindful of the fact that there are important elements in human life not easily stated in terms of efficiency, mechanization, institutions, rates of change or adaptations to change. The immense structure of human culture exists to serve human needs and values not always readily measurable, to promote and expand human happiness, to enable men to live more richly and abundantly. It is a means, not an end in itself. Men cling to ideas, ideals, institutions, blindly perhaps even when outworn, waiting until they are modified and given a new meaning and a new mode of expression more adequate to the realization of the cherished human values. The new tools and the new technique are not readily accepted; they are indeed suspected and resisted until they are reset in a framework of ideas, of emotional and personality values as attractive as those which they replace. So the family, religion, the economic order, the political system, resist the process of change, holding to the older and more familiar symbols, vibrant with the intimacy of life's experience and tenaciously interwoven with the innermost impulses of human action.

The clarification of human values and their reformulation in order to give expression to them in terms of today's life and opportunities is a major task of social thinking. The progressive confusion created in men's minds by the bewildering sweep of events revealed in our recent social trends must find its counterpart in the progressive clarification of men's thinking and feeling, in their reorientation to the meaning of the new trends.

In the formulation of these new and emergent values, in the construction of the new symbols to thrill men's souls, in the contrivance of the new institutions and adaptations useful in the fulfillment of the new aspirations, we trust that this review of recent social trends may prove of value to the American public. We were not commissioned to lead the people into some new land of promise, but to retrace our recent wanderings, to indicate and interpret our ways and rates of change, to provide maps of progress, make observations of danger zones, point out hopeful roads of advance, helpful in finding a more intelligent course in the next phase of our progress. Our information has been laboriously gathered, our interpretations made with every effort toward accuracy and impartiality, our forecasts tentative and alternative rather than dogmatic in form and spirit, and we trust that our endeavors may contribute to the readier growth of the new ideals, ideas and emotional values of the next period, as well as the mechanisms, institutions, skills, techniques and ways of life through which these values will be expressed and fulfilled in the years that are to come.

The President's Research Committee on Social Trends

WESLEY C. MITCHELL, *Chairman*

CHARLES E. MERRIAM, *Vice Chairman*

SHELBY M. HARRISON, *Secretary-Treasurer*

ALICE HAMILTON

HOWARD W. ODUM

WILLIAM F. OGBURN

Executive Staff

WILLIAM F. OGBURN, *Director of Research*

HOWARD W. ODUM, *Assistant Director of Research*

EDWARD EYRE HUNT, *Executive Secretary*

Summary of Memoranda on the Research
of the Federal Government in the Social Sciences
by Charles H. Judd
RESEARCH—A NATIONAL RESOURCE[1]

Introduction

The materials for this report were secured from a number of the bureaus in the executive departments of the Federal Government and from several of the independent agencies of the Government. In each case some representative designated by a Federal department, bureau, or agency prepared a statement with regard to the types of research in which the particular bureau or agency is engaged, the problems encountered in conducting research, and the lines along which conditions for research may in the judgment of the writer of the statement be improved. In most cases some member of the staff of this inquiry had interviews with the representatives of the bureaus or agencies supplying statements and in this way obtained information and suggestions supplementing the written statements.

In addition to the materials collected from governmental agencies which will be summarized in this report, there were prepared as a basis for a more complete treatment of social-science research in the Government three special reports dealing with the following subjects: The Legislative Branch of Government and Research; the Bureau of the Census; the Office of Education and Research. The last mentioned of these reports was prepared for the joint use of the Advisory Committee on Education and the Science Committee of the National Resources Committee. These three special reports were prepared by members of the staff of this inquiry. They treat of research activities and of problems relating to research more fully than do the statements secured directly from governmental agencies. They may be regarded

[1] *Research—A National Resource*, Report of the Science Committee to the National Resources Committee (Washington, D.C., 1938), Part 1, "Relation of the Federal Government to Research," pp. 49–58.

as intensive studies of particular situations. Reference will be made in the course of this report to some of the findings of these intensive studies, but no effort will be made here to cover the ground which those reports cover. For the purposes of the final report of the Science Committee the present summary of statements from governmental agencies is to be recognized as only one of four documents dealing with social science research.

The extent to which there has been increased emphasis on the social sciences in the Federal Government in recent years is shown by Table I, which was supplied by the Civil Service Commission.

The figures reported in Table I do not include social scientists who are in the employ of the Government but are not subject to the Civil Service Classification Act of 1923. Many emergency agencies, notably the large agencies, the Public Works Administration and the Works Progress Administration, have social scientists in their employed personnel who are not included in Table I.

The materials collected from the Federal agencies will not be reviewed in this report with a view to presenting anything like an exhaustive list of the particular research projects on which work is being done. Certain typical research undertakings will be cited by title or will be described very briefly, and the problems on which Federal agencies make comments will be reported for the purpose of showing the scope and character of social-science research in the Federal Government and for the purpose of drawing attention to the problems which such research encounters.

A study of all the statements received from Federal agencies leads to the following generalizations.

Scope of Statistical Data

The fundamental statistical data on which the social sciences depend are, in general, national in scope. The collection of data national in scope is increasingly recognized as a function of the Federal Government. There are, it is true, agencies outside the Federal Government which collect and analyze data national in scope. The American Federation of Labor and the National Industrial Conference Board, to use only two examples, have data on employment and unemployment. The latter has data on national income. Other like examples can be cited, but it is at once evident that the collection of all kinds of census data is so comprehensive an undertaking that only the central Government commands the resources and the authority adequate to the performance

TABLE I

Comparative distribution of permanent full-time, temporary, part-time, vacant, and occupied positions in the departmental service in the District of Columbia, subject to the Classification Act of 1923, and allocated to the professional and scientific service May 15, 1931, and Dec. 1, 1937*

GROUP	MAY 15, 1931		DEC. 1, 1937	
	Number	Percent	Number	Percent
Economic, statistics, and political and social science	683	8.75	2,156	17.28
Education	110	1.41	165	1.32
Anthropology and museum history	26	.33	39	.31
Agricultural and biological science	622	7.96	871	6.98
Physical science	1,175	15.05	1,162	9.31
Medical science	250	3.20	311	2.49
Dental science	8	.10	8	.06
Veterinary science	45	.58	51	.41
Engineering and drafting	2,230	28.56	3,113	24.95
Law	1,515	19.40	3,149	25.24
Patent examining	772	9.89	791	6.34
Art	7	.09	17	.14
Library science	320	4.10	581	4.66
Personnel research and examining	45	.58	63	.51
All groups	7,808	100.00	12,477	100.00

* This table represents a count of the positions under the Classification Act of 1923, recorded in the files of the Personnel Classification Division, U.S. Civil Service Commission. It does not include positions in agencies not under the Classification Act, nor positions in the field service.

of the task. When the census was taken in the early years of the national history of the United States, its purpose was solely to supply the facts necessary for the adjustment of representation in the lower House of the Congress. Gradually the function of collecting data has expanded until today some phase of this activity is an important part of the work of such agencies as the Department of Agriculture, the Department of Labor, the Social Security Board, the Bureau of Internal Revenue, the Office of Education, and the Bureau of Foreign and Domestic Commerce.

It has frequently been assumed that a great deal of duplication existed in the work of the various census-taking agencies and that consultation among the various agencies would reduce this duplication. It is true that some cases of duplication have been found and dealt with. In the main, however, waste due to duplications is insignificant. The advantages which result from cross checking and the necessity in a rapidly moving civilization of securing census figures more frequently than once in 10 years fully justify the collection of statistics by more than one agency.

Examples of the importance of securing data at short intervals are to be found in the information which the Bureau of Labor Statistics collects on such topics as "trends of employment and pay rolls," "hourly earnings, average per-capita weekly earnings, and average hours of work," "labor turn-over," and "building permits"; the estimates made of the national income by the Bureau of Foreign and Domestic Commerce; the various educational statistics collected by the Office of Education; and the statistical materials gathered by the Bureau of Mines.

In many of the cases where information is collected at short intervals the sampling method is employed. The accuracy of the particular sample canvassed is best determined by checking from time to time the sample figures with either over-all census figures or other sampling data collected in related fields.

There is one general problem which arises in connection with census taking which is repeatedly brought up in the statements supplied by Federal agencies. The form in which this problem is commonly presented is a plea for expansion of the facilities for analysis and interpretation of census data. One of the leading statisticians in the employ of the Government put the problem in these terms: "Our Bureau is not interested in mere figures; it is interested in people. I was appointed because of my insistence on interpretation of all statistical data. If we were not to analyze and interpret the statistics which we gather the chiefs of my staff would not be here. Most of them are economists."

On the other hand, it is the expressed belief of certain leading social scientists outside the Government that the chief function of Federal agencies is to collect statistical data. These agencies, it is contended, should perform only a very limited analysis of the data collected, and should leave the interpretation of the data to individuals who are wholly detached from policy-making authorities. The reason for the position thus taken is that association with policy-making authority is believed to bias analysis and interpretation.

It is generally admitted even by those who object to extended analyses and interpretations that the refinement of the data collected requires a certain degree of analysis. The difficulty of drawing a sharp line is evident. There can be very little doubt that, whatever the academic distinctions urged on one side or the other of this discussion, the Federal agencies should go as far in analysis and interpretation as their energy and resources permit. An examination of the publications of the Bureau of Labor Statistics and the Bureau of Agricultural Economics leaves no doubt on this issue.

Authority to Secure Information

The Federal Government has authority, and on occasion exercises its authority, to collect information which is inaccessible to nongovernmental agencies. Striking illustrations of the exercise of authority in the collection of information are found in the researches of the Federal Trade Commission, the Interstate Commerce Commission, and the Bureau of the Census. Each of these agencies is authorized by law to demand information. It is stated by administrators and investigators that in most cases there is no occasion to exercise authority. For example, the industrial and commercial corporations with which the Federal Trade Commission has dealings have in general been willing to open their records to inspection without hesitation. Whether this willingness is due to interest in the outcomes of investigation or to knowledge that authority exists is perhaps an impossible question to answer. Some governmental agencies report that where they have depended on cooperation rather than compulsion they secure more complete returns and more valuable suggestions which aid them in understanding the returns than they secure when compulsion is applied. Governmental agencies have a certain prestige which makes it possible for them to secure information even when they are not specifically granted authority by law to demand access to records.

Whatever the possibility of securing data through cooperation, the fact remains that the Congress has found it desirable to provide in a number of recent enactments creating Federal agencies that these agencies shall have power to summon witnesses and examine records. Provisions of this kind appear in the legislation creating the Federal Reserve Board, the Tariff Commission, the Securities and Exchange Commission, the Communications Commission, and the agencies mentioned in the preceding paragraph.

It is evident that authoritative information on which conclusions with regard to industrial and commercial operations can be based is of the first importance to the social sciences. The natural scientist can usually secure his basic data by direct personal observation of the materials about which he seeks information. The social scientist cannot depend on personal observation. He uses data which are derived from a broader survey of social conditions than he can himself make. Research in the social sciences is therefore always a cooperative enterprise. In many cases the contributions which government alone can make are indispensable. These contributions must be as complete and valid as they can be made, not merely because information is needed by government itself but also because basic data are essential to the development of the social sciences.

Governmental Contact With Social Sciences

Government is in close contact with all the major problems with which the social sciences deal. One statement which is repeatedly made with regard to research in the Federal Government is that it is directed to the solution of urgent and immediate problems. Negatively stated, this comment often takes some such form as the following: Governmental research agencies do not undertake on any large scale fundamental, or pure, research.

It is undoubtedly true that there are many urgent problems of government which occupy the attention of governmental scientists. The anthropologists of the Office of Indian Affairs are constantly called upon to determine who is an Indian. The successive enactments of the Congress give discordant definitions of an Indian, and the financial problems which arise in distributing the wealth belonging to certain tribes involve expert inquiry and consume much time and energy. The appearance of a disease engages the immediate attention of the Public Health Service. The Department of Justice is constantly dealing with emergencies. The Department of State must render prompt decisions on the interpretation of treaties. The Farm Credit Administration, the Reconstruction Finance Corporation, and the Securities and Exchange Commission are in close contact with a great many people and with conditions on which heretofore Government has had little or no information. Whether the inquiries which are involved in meeting the immediate demands of government are to be classified as research or not is a question on which the curious may exercise their dialectic. It is quite certain that, if the action of the Government is to be wise and just, there must be at hand agencies which will give legislators and administrative officials reliable information. The process of securing this information calls for a high grade of trained ability to find materials which are buried in the archives or are obscure because human nature is complex and inaccessible to direct observation. For the purposes of the present discussion it is convenient to use the term "research" rather than some longer and clumsier phrase, such as "scientific inquiry" or "intelligent investigation."

While it is true that there are a great many urgent problems which research workers in the Government have to answer and while some agencies are in fact overwhelmed with such problems, it is true that these very problems ultimately compel the prosecution of fundamental, or pure, research. For example, the Department of State, which is not thought of by the ordinary citizen as a research department, is concerned on a very large scale with fact finding and fact recording, which are certainly as profound as much of the material which appears in the books commonly accepted as examples of political science at its highest level. This Department has divisions which collect information about every section of the world and are prepared to give information to the executive officers of the Government and to legislative committees on conditions in all countries.

The Bureau of Agricultural Economics had for years before the depression been collecting and analyzing statistics on the prices of farm products. When legislation was pending with regard to these prices and later when it became necessary to administer laws affecting prices, it was possible to draw on a large body of factual material in the possession of the Bureau.

The emergency-relief agencies have been obliged in order to direct their own activities to secure data regarding the people of the

United States which have changed the thinking of the people of this country with regard to social conditions and with regard to the responsibility of the Nation for the welfare of its individual citizens.

The Department of Labor in both the Children's Bureau and the Bureau of Labor Statistics has continuous records covering a number of years which must be thought of as fundamental materials in the social sciences. These agencies have analyzed the facts which they have collected far enough so that they can properly be described as scientific agencies, not merely servants of administration.

Commissions and special investigating committees of Congress and of State legislatures, and State constitutional conventions have in a number of conspicuous cases gathered and made available materials which are of a fundamental type. A few conspicuous examples of Congressional commissions which through their inquiries and publications have added largely to the social sciences are the following:

The Industrial Commission created by act of June 18, 1898.

The Immigration Commission created by act of February 20, 1907.

The National Monetary Commission created by act of May 30, 1908.

The Industrial Relations Commission created by act of August 23, 1912.

The Joint Commission on Agricultural Inquiry created by concurrent resolution of June 7, 1921.

Each of these commissions has to its credit a long list of publications which are the results of elaborate inquiries carried on by technical experts who brought to the service of the Government scientific equipment of a superior order and prepared for the Government and for social science reports which can properly be classified as contributions to pure research.

Members of governmental research agencies who have been consulted by members of the staff of this inquiry are convinced that fundamental research in the social sciences is greatly stimulated by contact with administrative agencies. They point out that there is a certain sterility in much of the academic treatment of social problems in courses given in universities because of the lack of contact on the part of students and members of the faculty with the problems which research must solve. It is frequently stated by those who are responsible for the appointment of university graduates in the bureaus of the Government that these graduates are lacking in realistic understanding of the problems of social organization.

Facilities for Collecting Social Science Data

The Federal Government has facilities, many of which are not now fully utilized, for collecting materials useful to the social sciences. The recent Census of Partial Employment, Unemployment, and Occupations utilized the mail carriers of the post offices of the United States to gather information from every family of the Nation. The Department of Agriculture through the county agents and through the land-grant colleges is in direct contact with the rural population of the United States more completely than any other agency, private or public. The Foreign Service of the Government is now used and could be used even more largely in securing various types of information. The Works Progress Administration is in intimate contact throughout the States with industrial and social conditions. The Social Security Board has in its files information about the employed population which is now of unlimited importance and will in the future be even more complete and significant. The Tennessee Valley Authority knows intimately the conditions in the areas which it covers. The Securities and Exchange Commission utilizes the research results of such agencies as the National Bureau of Economic Research and of such private concerns as investment banks. The agents of this Commission frequently have conferences with brokers and others who have knowledge of financial transactions and conditions.

These and other examples which might be cited make it clear that the Federal Government has unparalleled possibilities of collecting information through individuals who are now qualified or with very little training could readily be prepared to bring to the services of social science the information necessary for fundamental studies that are much needed and are quite beyond the reach of any other agency. There is need for a better organization of these potential sources of information. It is altogether conceivable that the decennial census could be taken more efficiently and far more economically than at present if certain of the persons in the field whose services the Federal Government has a right to command were employed in collecting data. The appointment every 10 years of a large number of census enumerators who serve for a short time in a service for which many of them have very limited preparation has opened the way, as history shows with unmistakable clearness, for interference by spoils politics with scientific work to a degree which has rendered the study of population figures difficult and in some important respects invalid. It should be possible, however, to correct most of the defects which the employment of persons of inadequate training introduces into the factual basis for the study of social problems without involving the Government in any additional expense. What is needed is organization.

Status of Governmental Records

The Federal Government has vast collections of records which are in danger of neglect because of lack of proper follow-up analysis. A striking illustration of the truth of this statement is the fact that the Works Progress Administration in its effort to furnish employment to white-collar unemployed individuals contributed through regular Federal agencies to the collection of a great deal of information about the expenditures of families in different parts of the country and in a great variety of typical situations. It is estimated that $5,000,000 was expended in the collection of these data. The question now arises: How are these data to be used? The analysis and the interpretation of the items of information collected were not possible through the field agencies which collected them. Tabulation and expert study had to be provided in order to take full advantage of the investment.

There are in the files of the Government valuable documents which were collected during the life of the National Recovery Administration and were subjected to critical study after that Administration ceased to function. A large sum of money was invested in this critical study, and the information which it gathered is of such value that failure of publication must be regarded as a serious waste.

A more hopeful positive example is to be found in the fact that Congress, becoming aware of the great importance of governmental records, established the National Archives Council and has provided a building and a staff to classify and make available the records of the Government. The housing and cataloging of these materials are steps in the direction of scientific use of data which will be recognized in the future by the whole Nation as highly intelligent. At the present time the significance of what has been done is understood by a comparatively small group of specialists but is not generally appreciated by the people of the country.

Another positive example of the collection of materials for the encouragement and promotion of research is to be found in the Library of Congress. Illustrations may be pointed out to show how the Library of Congress supplies the means for scientific study in special fields. The Library has the largest collection of Chinese literary materials outside Peiping. It has a collection of music scores which attracts scholars from all parts of the world. These and other special collections are being continually increased in value. As an aid to scholarly work, the Library has an inclusive union catalog showing where books can be found in other libraries as well as in its own collection, which is now one of the most extensive and valuable in the world. The example of the Library of Congress has led to the collection and housing in Washington of a number of public and private collections, with the result that Washington is today a center for books second to none.

Congress recognizes the Library as an important adjunct to the legislative branch of the Government because it constantly uses the legislative reference service and its other services for its own purposes. The Library furnishes the documentary materials which are essential as the basis for legislative discussions at the same time that it makes possible through its resources scholarly work in all fields.

If research workers in the social sciences were informed about the rich resources of available raw material in the possession of the Federal agencies, there would be established at once a more intimate relation between scientific workers within and without the Government. There are possibilities of new run-offs from the cards now on file in some of the governmental agencies which would willingly be paid for by research workers and even by business concerns if it were known that such run-offs could be made. It has been suggested that the cards in the files of the Bureau of the Census would be far more extensively used than they now are if means could be devised for making them accessible.

The analogy is not misleading if one states that the Government now has buried in its files as much in the way of intellectual resources as there are natural mineral resources buried beneath the soil of the North American continent. The isolation of social science as cultivated in separate university centers from the actual materials which might be made available results in incalculable waste. To spend millions of dollars in collecting information and then to let it remain inaccessible is altogether unintelligent.

The suggestion has been made from time to time in one form or another that a center be established under governmental auspices where scholars may work in Washington in close contact with the materials which are in the archives of the Government. The Library of

Congress has taken steps in the direction of making provisions of this kind. In the annex to the Library building a series of rooms has been set aside supplementing largely the limited number of rooms now available for scholars in the main building.

Cooperation Between Agencies

The great number of research agencies within the Federal Government is an advantage in that it provides each agency with large possibilities of securing cooperation and a disadvantage in that communication between a given agency and others with which it might cooperate becomes cumbersome. It is quite impossible to give any exact account of the cooperation in research which results from informal personal conferences between members of the bureaus and independent agencies of the Government. Frequent exchanges of information are effected through such conferences, and the ground is often prepared for later, more formal cooperation.

It has been seriously suggested that the Government might very advantageously stimulate interagency associations by helping to organize, in addition to the cafeterias now provided in the various buildings, a central club for employees of the Government where members of different branches of the Government might come in contact with one another.

EXAMPLES OF EFFECTIVE COOPERATION. There are numerous examples of effective cooperation. An extensive study of consumer practices was conducted by the Works Progress Administration in cooperation with the Bureau of Labor Statistics, the Bureau of Home Economics, the Central Statistical Board and the National Resources Committee.

The following paragraph quoted from the statement made by the National Park Service continues the exemplification of the relation between the administrative and scientific activities of the Government which is discussed in preceding paragraphs and at the same time illustrates the advantages which are derived from cooperation between Federal agents.

Other Government agencies which help solve problems for the National Park Service:

Public Health Service details two men to help with sanitary problems.

Bureau of Plant Industry details one man to help with plant disease problems.

Bureau of Entomology studies and makes recommendations on all forest insect matters.

Bureau of Public Roads surveys and builds all major road projects.

Bureau of Fisheries operates fish hatcheries and furnishes fish for planting.

Geological Survey in the past studied and mapped many park areas. Water Resources and Topographic Branches have been most helpful.

Forest Service on occasion has loaned grazing experts and timber-survey experts for special projects.

National Museum has detailed experts to help solve individual archeological and museum problems.

Bureau of Chemistry and Soils.

Weather Bureau.

The United States Tariff Commission makes the following statement:

Under section 334 of the tariff act, the Commission cooperates with other Government departments, in both the giving and receiving of information. Such cooperation has been with the Departments of State, Agriculture, Commerce, and Labor, the Treasury, etc. As explained above, the Tariff Commission cooperates closely with these departments in connection with the trade-agreements program (through Executive Committee on Commercial Policy, the Trade Agreements Committee, and the numerous country committees—all of which are interdepartmental) and informally on numerous occasions in connection with its daily work.

EXAMPLES OF LACK OF COORDINATION. On the other hand there are examples which show that cooperation is not complete. The Bureau of Foreign and Domestic Commerce and the Tariff Commission, both dealing with importation and exportation of commodities, employ different methods of inquiry and appear to have different purposes in mind for their researches. The traditions of the Bureau of Foreign and Domestic Commerce have been largely promotional, and it is only within the last 5 years that the need for and value of basic economic research in both foreign and domestic commerce has been recognized. Of similarly recent origin is the cooperation at present in effect with respect to trade agreement work and foreign trade statistics.

A type of incoordination between Federal agencies which has been commented on of late is that which appears when the activity of some emergency agency seems to invade the established area of operation of one of the regular bureaus of the Government.

The Office of Education and many of the educators of the country were of the opinion that the efforts made by the Government to discover the needs of young people should have been channeled through the Office of Education. The Office of Education was in process of conducting a survey of young people out of school when the relief agencies began to make inquiries in this field for the purpose of adjusting the administrative activities of relief.

It can be argued that relief measures in an emergency should be assigned to a special agency in order to leave the established bureaus of the Government undistracted from their regular duties. The established bureaus, on the other hand, are unduly sensitive with respect to their resources and prestige, and sometimes resent the assignment of funds for research and administration to a temporary agency.

METHODS OF FOSTERING COOPERATION. To one who observes a disagreement with respect to policy such as that described it seems evident that in many cases incoordination is a result of size and lack of proper facilities for communication. The solution of conflicts and the establishment of cooperative relations involve, however, in some cases personal relations which it is extraordinarily difficult to adjust. The method of meeting difficulties of this kind is not easy to prescribe. It is to be hoped that some day research agencies will be able to assume an attitude sufficiently scientific to make cooperation rather than competition universal. In the meantime, the general principle pointed out by the President's Committee on Administrative Management seems to be worth keeping in mind for research agencies as well as for other divisions of the Government:

> Government is a going concern, not a static institution. Each activity therefore has its period of initiation and development, its period of normal operation, and in some cases also its period of decline and liquidation. While this does not change the principles of organization, it does alter profoundly their application in individual cases.

New activities should be organized rather completely on the basis of purpose so that that purpose may be the central driving force of the organization. They should be freed from interference by departments organized on the basis of process. They should also be given virtually complete freedom, or extensive autonomy, within existing departments. In the nature of the case, new purposes cannot be carried out without broad freedom to experiment. To tie a totally new activity either to the regular bureau pattern or to the regular controls may defeat its purpose entirely.

When, however, an activity is organized, its major policies established, its purposes accepted and understood, and its work in the main placed upon a routine basis, then the time has come to bring the activity into the normal structure of organization and under the normal controls. To do so will not endanger the objectives of the organization as such, nor hinder its work, but will rather increase its efficiency, improve not only its own work but also the whole work of government through better coordination, and render it more truly subject to democratic controls.

Particular attention needs to be given to the period of decline and liquidation because departments and bureaus like to keep themselves alive and because they and the pressure groups back of them are incapable of estimating their value. There is among governmental agencies great need for a coroner to pronounce them dead, and for an undertaker to dispose of the remains. Both of these processes are advanced when agencies approaching discontinuance are deprived of their independent status by being brought into large departments and are made subject to the regular controls through the Budget, central accounting, and personnel administration.

In addition to the steps recommended in the foregoing quotation it will undoubtedly be necessary to establish communication between the permanent agencies so that they also will be brought into cooperation. The organization of the Central Statistical Board was a long step in the direction of promoting cooperation. There still remains much to be done in a positive way to initiate cooperative activities rather than merely adjust the undertakings of the various bureaus and independent agencies to one another.

Smithsonian Institution. A unique device for securing coordination of certain lines of research within the Government and also between the Government and outside agencies is to be seen in the Smithsonian

Institution. This Institution has a small endowment and receives funds from Congress. It has a Board of Trustees which manages its affairs and gives it a type of freedom to inaugurate and conduct research in ways that are impossible in most governmental agencies. The latitude in research and in establishment of cooperative relations enjoyed by the Smithsonian Institution is denied to many of the agencies wholly within the Government. There is another reason why research, if it is to be productive in maximum degree, must frequently have the possibility of readjusting itself while in progress. Scientific research often turns up productive leads which could not be anticipated at the time that the particular research project was first planned.

The freedom of the Smithsonian Institution to cultivate all kinds of cooperative relations is indicated by one paragraph from the statement submitted by that Institution. This paragraph is one of several of like kind included in the statement:

In connection with its work the Department of Anthropology of this Institution has been greatly assisted through extensive cooperation with various organizations and has also aided other organizations as indicated by the following few examples:

(1) With the National Geographic Society on the excavation and restoration of Pueblo Bonito in New Mexico.

(2) With the Rockefeller Foundation and the Peking Medical College on the study of the origin of American aborigines.

(3) With the Soil Conservation Service on phases of early Indian agriculture.

(4) With the National Park Service in the historical excavation of Jamestown Island, Va.

(5) With State organizations and the Federal Civil Works Administration in extensive archeological excavations in Florida, Georgia, Tennessee, California, and the Carolinas.

(6) With the Bureau of Indian Affairs on old Indian weaving techniques.

(7) Cooperation with individuals, organizations, and other Government departments on the identification of specimens through their comparison with material now in the national collections. Cooperation of this type is a continuing process reaching to all quarters of the globe. Practically every university and museum in this country has been extended cooperation of this kind.

(8) Close cooperation with numerous Government agencies such as the War Department, National Park Service, Department of Ag-

riculture,[2] the Geological Survey,[3] Bureau of Standards, Bureau of Indian Affairs, Patent Office, and others.

Recruitment and Training of Personnel

The Federal Government has difficulty in securing highly competent research workers with whom to staff its scientific agencies. It seems quite certain in view of the extensive development of research activities within the Government that attention will have to be given to the special training of research workers, especially in the social sciences. The Federal Government has depended in the past on the universities to provide it with properly prepared personnel. The universities have little difficulty in preparing research workers for Government laboratories in the physical and biological sciences and for engineering positions. The natural sciences deal with materials which are the same in Washington and in regions remote from the seat of Government. With respect to some of the fields of applied natural science the situation is different. For this reason the Department of Agriculture has developed a graduate school where its employees are given special educational preparation for the particular duties which they are to perform. The Departments of War and Navy have so many special problems to solve that they have more than any other agencies of the Federal Government established educational courses and institutions of various grades for the preparation of personnel.

Research in the social sciences can be prepared for in some of the courses provided in the universities, but far more than in the natural or applied sciences the novice in social-science research must have experience in close contact with the problems of social organization. The social-science branches of the Federal Government are conscious of the necessity of devoting energy to the preparation of young members of the staff. A system of internship is eagerly desired by many of the agencies. The recent adoption by the Civil Service Commission of the plan of admitting to governmental agencies young people in the rank of junior civil-service appointees has been welcomed in many of the social-science divisions of the Government. The juniors are assigned to regular members of the staff under whom they work and by whom they

---

[2] This Department maintains many research workers in entomology and botany who work continually with the collections of the National Museum.

[3] The Survey has many research workers occupied with the collections of the National Museum.

are trained. One difficulty with the present arrangement, as pointed out by the Bureau of Labor Statistics and other agencies which have undertaken training of juniors, is that, when a well prepared junior presents himself for final classification by the Civil Service Commission, he finds that the experience which he has gained in the service of the Government is not credited as would be study in university classes. The junior candidate is believed by his superiors to have in many cases qualifications far better than those which could be gained anywhere outside the Government service, but this judgment is ineffective in the face of civil-service regulations as they now stand.

Furthermore, there is a universal recognition in the higher branches of governmental services that the exemptions granted to veterans tend to break down completely the merit system which is essential to the procurement of competent research workers. Immediately after the World War, when there could readily be drawn from the ranks of veterans individuals of high or average ability, exemptions were not as calamitous as they are now and will be increasingly later. The longer the period since the war, the poorer the selection of veterans who offer themselves for service in the Government becomes.

Other difficulties frequently mentioned in the statements made by governmental agencies seeking to appoint high-grade research men are the infrequency of civil service examinations, the delays in ranking candidates, and the long-continued standing of registers after they are once established. It is recommended in the statements supplied by governmental agencies that all registers be renewed at frequent intervals, that the requirements be made more severe so that only high-grade men shall secure positions on the registers, and that credit be given for training which juniors have received in governmental offices.

Coordination of Educational Institutions

The Federal Government is handicapped in securing suitable personnel because of lack of knowledge on the part of many academic teachers of the opportunities offered in Government service to research workers of ability. It is a well-known fact that there is little enthusiasm in many American universities and colleges for Government service. It is regarded as true by many teachers of science that Government service is less free than are university and school positions. In the general attitude toward Government, European institutions of education are altogether different from American institutions. The ambition of many of the best students in English and continental schools and universities is to secure positions in Government. The civil service examinations in England and some of the leading continental countries are of the severest type.

The comparative lack of encouragement of students in American institutions to seek places in Government is due in part to a failure on the part of Government and academic institutions to maintain intimate contacts. Academic men frequently do not know the amount or character of highly interesting scholarly study and research going on in the Government. Governmental agencies do not utilize as fully as they might the intellectual resources of the Nation. There is a lack of intercommunication which is deplorable and should be corrected, especially in the fields of the social sciences, where, as pointed out several times in this report, the data for scientific generalizations must be secured in very large measure by the Government.

One area in which intimate relations between the Government and universities have been established far more than elsewhere is in agricultural economics and rural sociology. The long contact between the land-grant colleges and the Department of Agriculture has facilitated an exchange of men and services which has been mutually advantageous and has promoted the interests of rural and national life in a great many ways. There is nothing equally effective in the sphere of business.

Business schools and business research agencies have been established and conducted by private enterprise in this country primarily for the purpose of training managers in practical affairs and of protecting and promoting the interests of business enterprises, especially large businesses. The research which would keep the whole Nation fully informed about business has not been developed to anything like the level reached in agriculture. The members of the staff of this inquiry have sought diligently to discover the reasons for the comparative inadequacy of research in business in the program of the Federal Government. They have been told that the spirit of competition is much stronger in business than in agriculture, that the agencies in Government which might undertake business investigations are much less generously supported by Congressional appropriations than are the agencies which carry on research in agriculture, and that the schools of business are far less mature and far less helpful in promoting researches in business than are the institutions which are responsible for research in agriculture.

It seems clear that research in business requires encouragement and promotion. The small business man can no more support research than can the farmer. It is true that in recent years a number of trade associations have been organized through which business concerns which are too small to conduct researches independently have pooled their interests and secured the advantages of cooperative action in the development of applied science. It seems clear, however, that more will have to be done in the future than has been done up to the present time. The Government of England has subsidized the activities of the trade associations organized in that country.

There is widespread agreement among students of business that elaborate investigations are needed in order that more may be known than is now known about business cycles and the conditions that lead to depressions. There is here an area of research quite as important as the areas which are recognized by everyone as belonging to Government with respect to hurricanes and flood control.

The closer coordination of the educational institutions of the country, including the schools of business, with governmental research, is a matter deserving of the most careful consideration. Advisory committees are organized by many of the governmental agencies. These bring to the seat of governmental activities, usually only for short periods, some of the members of university faculties and leaders in lines of activity other than education. The contacts thus maintained have the double advantage of stimulating activities in the institutions in different parts of the country and of bringing to the service of Government valuable counsel and sympathy. Advisory committees do not seem to suffice. The people of the United States are convinced of the importance and practical usefulness of research in agriculture. This fact is to be explained in part by the existence in each commonwealth of an institution which not only contributes to knowledge about agriculture but keeps the legislature informed about problems of the State and otherwise serves the people of the State. There is at the present time no such popular confidence in research in business.

Appropriations for publication made to many agencies of the Federal Government are inadequate. Not only so, but the skepticism with regard to the propriety of issuing published material, especially published material that is attractive in form, manifests itself in unfavorable comments made in congressional hearings and in congressional debates.

There are examples which can be cited in support of the statements made. The reports which accompany this as partial reports on social science research show beyond the possibility of dispute that the Bureau of the Census and the Office of Education are now in possession of much valuable manuscript material which would be of great use if it could be published. The results of the investigations which were made by a large staff that studied the experience accumulated during the operations of the National Recovery Administration now lie in the files of the Federal Government unavailable alike to legislators and businessmen because there is no money to publish what cost great sums to accumulate. When the officers of the emergency relief agencies brought out an informing and attractive pamphlet, vigorous criticism of the publication was voiced.

Quotations from several of the statements submitted by Federal research agencies are as follows:

Recently, two very important reports of this Commission were made public, but they have not yet been published.

A greater embarrassment by far has been the inadequacy of opportunity to publish manuscripts. There is always a series of worthwhile papers awaiting publication and sometimes 5 or 6 years go by before they can be issued.

Practically no funds for the publication of research findings.

Publication Facilities

The facilities for communication of scientific findings secured by governmental research to the people of the Nation are limited. It is sometimes argued by those who do not regard it as wise to appropriate public funds for publications, that many of the manuscripts prepared by the scientific agencies are obscure in language. That there is ground for this position must be admitted. Scientific men are in the habit of writing for their colleagues rather than for the general public. Furthermore, the refinements of scientific reports often depend on the use of mathematical formulas and technical terminology which are not readily understood by the non-technical reader. The needs of the Nation will not be met nor will the ordinary citizens be satisfied until far more readable information on the social sciences than is now published by the Government is made available. That there is great eagerness for information on all social problems is evidenced by the consumption of reading material in newspapers and magazines and in serious books which far surpasses what was common in earlier periods. The research agencies of the Nation ought to be aware of the demand for popular presentation of social science materials. The social scientists of the country ought to realize that any exclusiveness or aloofness on the part of social scientists is sure to operate to the disadvantage of social science itself.

NEED FOR WIDESPREAD DISSEMINATION OF INFORMATION ON SOCIAL PROBLEMS. Research has always been stimulated by the appearance of conditions that need to be changed. The agricultural investigations which have been referred to several times in this report as extensive and well-supported resulted directly from recognition of the distress in the agricultural areas of the country. There is some indication that investigations in the social fields will be greatly stimulated by the present-day problems of industry, business, and family life. If these indications are accepted at their face value, it follows as an inescapable corollary that this is a period when the social scientists should devote much effort to both the extension of their fields and the rendering of their findings available for general consumption.

The obligation of the Federal Government in the premises is undoubtedly to provide for widespread dissemination of information on all social problems. The distribution of the population, the industrial and population conditions of different parts of the country and the biological facts about human life are as important for the people of this country as the facts with regard to livestock and plant life.

The Works Progress Administration has organized in a number of typical counties of the United States investigations of all the social conditions and possibilities in these counties. A coordinator familiar with the problems of a given area has been appointed. Usually this coordinator has been a member of the faculty of one of the educational institutions in the area. He has been supplied with a plan of operation carefully prepared in the Washington office of the studies. He has also had the assistance of white-collar workers on relief.

The effectiveness of this organization is seen in the discoveries which have been made of unused industrial and recreational facilities in the areas. Above and beyond anything that has issued immediately from the studies, however, is the awakening of a consciousness in the people of the communities in which the studies have been made of the possibility of scientific attack on their social problems. Materials have been accumulated which will be of value during a long period to come.

The National Resources Committee

Advisory Committee

FREDERIC A. DELANO
Chairman

HENRY S. DENNISON

CHARLES E. MERRIAM

BEARDSLEY RUML

Science Committee

CHARLES M. WILTSE
Acting Secretary

WALTER D. COCKING

EDWARD C. ELLIOT

ROSS G. HARRISON

CHARLES H. JUDD

WALDO G. LELAND

JOHN C. MERRIAM

HARRY A. MILLIS

WILLIAM F. OGBURN

EDWIN B. WILSON

Subcommittee on Research

CHARLES H. JUDD
Chairman

WILLIAM F. OGBURN

EDWIN B. WILSON

STRENGTHENING
THE BEHAVIORAL SCIENCES[1]

Introduction

The support and use of modern science in the national interest is recognized today as an important obligation of the federal government. The success of this policy has more than justified the expenditures entailed. Behavioral science has profited from general interest in scientific progress and has received modest but increasing support in recent years. This support, however, has not yet been as effective as it might be, mainly because it has not met certain underlying needs. Yet the general issues studied by behavioral scientists are critically important to our national welfare and security. Ways must be found to strengthen these disciplines and improve their use.

What is the current status of behavioral science? Are there promising developments that need support, or established facts that should be put to work? Are any special measures needed to facilitate the growth of behavioral science or to make its skills and knowledge better known to those who could best exploit them? Such questions are entered into, but not exhausted, in this report, and some key recommendations are made.

The scientific study of behavior has been a relatively recent development. Matter and energy are the domain of the physical sciences. The element of life introduces those complex, transitory features so sensitive to experimental interference that make the biological sciences challenging. When the boundaries of science are pushed back still further to include human behavior and human culture, all the processes of symbolization and self-direction of which the human mind is capable are introduced. The main effort to study behavioral processes scientifically is

[1] *Strengthening the Behavioral Sciences,* Statement by the Behavioral Sciences Subpanel, The Life Sciences Panel, President's Science Advisory Committee (Washington, D.C., 1962).

less than a century old, and most of the work is much more recent. The boundaries are expanding each year to include new behavioral phenomena.

The behavioral sciences have both a fundamental and an applied aspect. As fundamental sciences they are concerned with the careful, dispassionate discovery and analysis of the basic facts of human behavior, individual and social, and with the construction, testing, and revision of theories to explain observed regularities. As applied sciences, they are concerned with the application of facts, tested theories, and developed insight to questions of practice in such areas as education, mental health, personnel utilization, city planning, communications, and the problems of emerging countries. Behavioral scientists use methods common to all sciences: observation, instrumentation, field and laboratory experiments, statistical analysis of data, construction of models and theories, and good, hard thinking.

Perhaps the first impression one has of behavioral science is the enormous scope and variety of its problems and its methods. At one extreme, some psychologists combine biochemical and behavioral techniques to study the brain. At the other, sociologists and anthropologists deal with institutions and cultures. Social psychology studies the relation of the individual to his social and cultural experience. The domain of the behavioral sciences is vast and heterogeneous. The current division into academic fields—psychology, anthropology, sociology, economics, political science, linguistics—is subject to continual revision and amendment.

The general aims and criteria of evidence of the behavioral sciences are the same as they are in other sciences; however, it has so far frequently been necessary to settle for more approximate answers—errors of measurement may be large, and often, where experiments are not yet possible, correlations still substitute for cause-effect relations. The number of variables apparently needed to understand many kinds of human behavior, when combined with random or uncontrolled variations familiar in most of the life sciences, account for imprecision of results. Nevertheless, behavioral scientists are finding ways to develop and test meaningful theories; they have managed to amass a considerable store of tested and useful information.

The impact of the behavioral sciences on our society is far greater than most people realize. At one level they are providing technical solutions for important human problems. But at a deeper level they are changing the conception of human nature—our fundamental ideas about human desires and human possibilities. When such conceptions change, society changes.

In the past few generations, many beliefs about such diverse matters as intelligence, child rearing, delinquency, sex, public opinion, and the management of organizations have been greatly modified by the results of filtering scientific fact and theory through numerous layers of popularizing translation. The casual way in which unproved behavioral hypotheses often find widespread acceptance underscores the importance of strengthening and deepening the behavioral sciences and of securing better public understanding of what they are and what they are not.

The continued progress of the behavioral sciences—and particularly of basic research in these fields—is best assured by applying to them the same policy guidelines that promote growth in any science, and by associating them closely with other sciences. In this connection we note two encouraging steps forward: The National Institutes of Health, a major source of support for basic research in neurophysiology and psychology, are strengthening their programs in sociology, anthropology, and other behavioral sciences; and the National Science Foundation recently established a Division of Social Science.

Development and Present State of Behavioral Science

Many areas of behavioral science have grown rapidly but quite unobtrusively. As a result, it is hard for anyone to get a complete picture of their present scope and depth. This portion of the report offers a sequence of strategically located examples, illustrating, in active areas of behavioral-science research, both successes already attained and challenging problems that can be attacked now or in the near future. These concrete examples may help to suggest the scope and nature of certain of the behavioral sciences, where they stand today, and something of how they got there. Thus, they provide a background for our more general discussion and recommendations.

We have tried to keep this illustrative material as brief as possible. Consequently, many substantial and significant topics, such as mental testing, group behavior, studies of demography, bargaining, and descriptive linguistics, to name but a few, are only mentioned.

Effective experimentation in behavioral science was once thought to be confined to experiments on animals, to the simplest interaction of people with physical stimuli, and to some aspects of human problem solving. One of the advances of recent years has been in our ability to carry out experiments to analyze interactions between people, both in pairs and in groups. As with any experimental technique, an adequate description of what has to be done to make such experiments effective would involve us deeply in detail. So this area, too, is only mentioned.

THE STUDY OF COMMUNICATION. Early studies of "mass communications" were very simply conceived. The "mass media" were thought to provide stimuli to which all the separate individuals in the audience responded in much the same way. This conception had to be discarded, however, once survey techniques were available to measure the impact of such communications on a sample of individuals. It became clear that individuals engage in selective exposure and selective perception. Those least predisposed to change are least likely to allow themselves to be exposed to a persuasive communication, and if they are exposed, are most likely to engage in misperception, a kind of motivated missing-the-point. If a new piece of information would weaken the existing structure of their ideas and emotions, it will be shunned, rejected, or quickly forgotten; if it reinforces the structure, it will be sought out, quickly accepted, and remembered.

This new understanding was soon followed by another development. As evidence accumulated of the strong effects of interpersonal relationships on the acceptance and diffusion of communications, the unit of analysis shifted from the individual to the social network itself. Studies attempted to trace the flow of a new development as it passed through a social network. Thus, a series of researches that began with the study of the impact of mass communication on separate individuals developed into a study of interpersonal networks and the way innovation diffuses through them, with each person using the communications whenever possible to strengthen his existing attitudes and knowledge or to serve his other needs.

Studies of agricultural innovations, such as the introduction of hybrid corn, have shown that different communication media are characteristically used for different functions: Mass media can arouse interest, but interpersonal communication usually determines whether the innovation is adopted or not. Innovation must involve not one but several networks of relations, each able to carry certain kinds of content.

These empirical studies of diffusion were paralleled by the growth of formal, mathematical models. The simplest group of models assumed separate individual exposure either to a constant stream of messages from a central source or to random contacts with already converted individuals who were randomly mixed throughout the population. The need to consider the combination of these two mechanisms of exposure was soon realized, as was the need to assign a limited time during which a newly converted individual could convert others. As more and more such refinements were added, models for the spread of information, innovations, and rumors came to resemble more and more closely the then-current mathematical models for the spread of contagious disease.

An important consequence of models which assumed random complete mixing was a prediction that diffusion would be more complete in larger groups. This consequence was a crucial one for the assumption of random complete mixing, since this assumption must be a poorer and poorer approximation for larger and larger populations. By using aircraft to drop leaflets that asked recipients to pass on a message and then using surveys to chart the spread of the message through the population, experimenters established how the rate of diffusion of the message was affected by the leaflet-to-population ratio, by population density, and by city size. These leaflet experiments showed more complete diffusion in *smaller* towns, and thus indicated that more realistic assumptions about mixing were essential. Two directions were followed, to good effect. The one assumes that contacts between individuals are governed largely by geographic distance, and leads to models for the geographic spread of an innovation. The other takes account of the tendency of social networks to turn back on themselves by giving numerical expression to the degree to which "the friends of my friends are my friends" and leads to models for the spread of an innovation through an acquaintanceship structure.

As field studies proved that more and more details were essential parts of mathematical models for the diffusion of innovations and information, the increasing complexity of these models began to threaten their usefulness. At this point, the availability of electronic computers offered new promise. Instead of solving equations for the average behavior of a diffusion problem, one could use the computing machine to simulate individual instances of diffusion. And this could be done repeatedly, revealing the variability inherent in the model as well as its average behavior. It again seemed possible to study models complex enough to fit the actual phenomena.

Important gaps in our present understanding have been identified through attempts to carry out computer simulations. Knowledge that seems quite satisfactory when presented in verbal form is often found to be inadequate when one tries to write a computer program. Recognition of such gaps is now calling for further empirical research to answer newly formulated explicit questions.

MECHANISMS OF PERSONALITY DEVELOPMENT. The study of personality and the investigation of the stars have something in common. In both instances, one must usually begin with a careful study of the available "natural experiments." Then, once a phenomenon is identified, a mixture of laboratory and natural experiments leads to further understanding. Moreover, even when the ultimate concern is with more commonplace instances, the study of extreme instances often provides important leads to the essentials of the situation.

The study of personality is the study of the more or less enduring mental and emotional characteristics of an individual. Some people are fearful and tense while others are calm and relaxed; some are cheerful and friendly, others pessimistic and depressed, still others hostile; and in such psychiatric disorders as depression, paranoid conditions, or psychoneurotic anxiety one finds extreme personality patterns. What causes different patterns of personality? How do they originate? How are they modified in the course of life? And why are they often resistant to change?

Organic, psychological, and social influences all help to form and change personalities. One kind of mental retardation has been traced to a defective enzyme controlled by a single gene. And studies of mental-health similarities in ordinary and identical twins have indicated that heredity may be an important contributing factor in some of the schizophrenias and other psychoses. The effective use of new drugs has for the first time reduced the population in mental hospitals.

On the psychological side, much of our scientific knowledge of personality has come from two separate areas of research: animal experiments on the one hand and clinical observations of humans on the other. Clinical observations have suggested that the major developments in human personality occur in childhood—that there may be periods of special sensitivity when deprivation of particular pleasures or opportunities may have persistent effects on the developing personality —effects that are extremely difficult to change in adulthood.

Are there really such periods during infancy and childhood? And, if so, do particular types of interference during these periods have predictable results later on? Some studies have compared child-rearing practices in different cultures and have related them to adult personality characteristics. Such cross-cultural studies have indicated rather strongly that the inquiry was on the right track. More specific and conclusive research has been carried out on animals. Studies of animal behavior have demonstrated that there are brief periods in the early life of birds and mammals, including primates, during which the development of certain behavior patterns is especially susceptible to distortion. One example involves the disposition of certain birds to follow. During a short sensitive period the young animal can be induced to follow a particular kind of object. In the normal course of events this object is the mother (or both parents). If, however, no normal object is available during the sensitive period, and if a strange object such as a human being or an effigy or even a flickering light is substituted, the young animal will have strong motivation to follow that object and will later continue to show various consequences of this early exposure.

Systematic observations of natural experiments in our own culture, as when an accident to the mother results in her hospitalization, have convinced many psychologists that there is also a sensitive period in human infancy during which separation from the mother may have serious consequences for adult personality, shifting it toward chronic mistrust, hostility, and delinquency. The convergence of these various lines of evidence is encouraging, but we need to know much more about details, complications, and mechanisms. Why, for instance, does separation from the mother produce such serious after-effects in some cases but not in others?

On the social side, study of the relation of social conditions to personality is just well begun; as a consequence, attention has been centered on psychiatric disorders as extremes of personality, and on the identification of related social phenomena. Although predisposition to psychiatric disorder is in some measure controlled by genes, and although recent advances in biochemistry are demonstrating the role of organic factors, social and cultural influences clearly contribute to the incidence of psychiatric disorders. In one recent community study, for instance, the percentage of psychiatric disorder was found to be more than twice as large where community relations showed distingegration as in neighboring communities where they did not. Experience is showing that it is quite difficult, but possible, to get good data on the incidence of psychiatric disorders, and that the results are worth the effort. The way is now opening up, not only for more extensive and sophisticated surveys, but also for more incisive attempts to identify the psychological links through which social factors have their effects on the individual personality.

MOTIVES AND THE BRAIN. A combination of physiological and behavioral techniques is producing an accelerated output of fruitful research on how injuries to specific parts of the brain affect speech, memory, and problem solving, how the brain selects and analyzes information from the sense organs, and how it controls emotions and drives.

Some studies of hunger provide a typical example. To the layman, hunger usually means an uncomfortable feeling in the stomach, a feeling that is associated with missing meals and that sharpens the pleasure of eating. The behavioral scientist is interested in the effects of hunger on a wide range of behaviors that can be involved in finding and consuming food, and he is interested in the brain mechanisms that control food consumption.

Association of abnormal obesity with certain lesions of the human hypothalamus first suggested that this primitive part of the brain regulates eating. Experiments showed that small bilateral lesions appropriately placed in the brain would cause various species of animals to overeat enormously until they became extremely fat. The first hypothesis was that these lesions intensified hunger by releasing it from inhibition.

Normal hunger can be measured behaviorally, either by the rate at which an animal works at pressing a bar to get food, or by the minimum amount of quinine required to cause the animal to avoid food. Although rats with lesions in the critical areas ate more than normal rats, they pressed the bar less rapidly, and the amount of quinine needed to make them stop eating was smaller. Thus, the behavioral tests showed that the first hypothesis was incorrect; the lesions appeared to interfere with both the maximum level of hunger and the completeness of satiation.

The lesion method has been supplemented by new techniques for stimulating, electrically or chemically, specific areas in the brain. Adrenalin and noradrenalin were first noticed for their effects on the heart and vascular system as parts of the general reaction to stress. When minute crystals of these chemicals are implanted in the "feeding area" of the brain, they cause satiated animals to eat, and to perform specific learned patterns of working for food. But minute quantities of a different class of substances, acetylcholine or carbachol, elicit drinking and working for water, but not eating, when they are implanted in the same place. Injection, into the body, of agents that block the classical responses to each class of substances also differentially blocks the effects of brain implantation of the corresponding crystals, and somewhat reduces differentially normal hunger or thirst. Thus, the brain seems to respond to a chemical code in distinguishing hunger from thirst.

This bird's-eye view of work on hunger and food-seeking behavior could easily be paralleled by similar examples of research on other drives, such as fear. Fear can be learned. We are discovering how fear can be affected by various drugs, how it can be unlearned, and how experimental subjects can be taught to persist in the face of fear. But we need to know much more in order to complete our theoretical understanding of its mechanisms, and of its effects, which may include stomach ulcers and perhaps decreased resistance to infection.

Other motives have been partially explored. There is already experimental evidence that, just as satiation or deprivation affects the way in which an animal works for food, so satisfying a child's need for praise or depriving him of approval can affect the speed with which he works. There is experimental evidence, in both rats and monkeys, that curiosity can produce learning, maintain performance, and be a strong enough motivation to entice a hungry animal away from food. While a promising beginning has been made, most of the important problems lie ahead. We do not know the factors responsible for inhibiting or enhancing either the development of simple curiosity in a cat or the development of intellectual curiosity in a classroom. We know much less about the principles that govern the learning of human social motivation than we do about those governing the learning of information or of skills. But we already have promising ways to attack many such problems and are rapidly finding new ones.

STUDY OF CULTURES AND SOCIETIES. Comparative study of different cultures began in the 19th century, stimulated by interest in human evolution. At first, anthropologists assumed that differences in custom would reflect different levels or steps on an orderly path of evolutionary ascent, with their own European, upper-class, late-Victorian society representing the highest stage. The customs and institutions of the technologically "backward" societies were expected to reveal the steps through which more civilized man had evolved.

As ethnographers began to collect their data, however, these early theories had to be discarded. Data showed clearly that each complex of interrelated customs, however strange and bizarre by Western standards, served the group's needs. It became increasingly evident that customs tend to be internally consistent, to hang together in structured systems.

The interdependence of the parts of such systems is a major determinant of the way innovations are resisted under some conditions and accepted under others. A corollary is, of course, that an imposed change in one custom will usually have widespread effects. For example, chiefs in the Trobriand Islands had many wives, a practice that some of the earlier Western authorities discouraged. In that society, instead of a husband supporting his wife, a brother supports his sister, and if his sister has the honor of being married to a chief, she has to be well supported. Wives were the source of a chief's economic power; they enabled him to supply the food and drink for work parties to accomplish necessary civic projects, such as hollowing out huge logs to produce the ocean-going canoes used in trading. When polygamy was abandoned, the chiefs were too poor to hold work parties, their prestige and authority declined, and certain necessary civic tasks were neglected. Thus, a change in one aspect of the society had unexpected, far-reaching effects.

The study of kinship systems was especially productive in revealing the structure of a strange culture. Kinship terminology proved to be closely associated with forms of family, customs of inheritance, and kin-group organization. If, as in our society, the same behavior is expected toward the mother's sister and the father's sister, they are given the same name "aunt." But if it is important to behave differently toward these sisters, they are given different kinship names. Rigorous methods and concepts which have been developed for the analysis of kinship systems are now being applied to the analysis of other terminological systems—to the native vocabularies for describing animals, plants, colors, and diseases—in order to understand how other peoples organize their perceptions.

More and better ethnological data are raising new questions. For example, do the obvious physiological changes of adolescence inevitably produce emotional disturbances? Many believe this must be so, yet in some societies adolescence occurs without emotional disturbances. Perhaps social conditions play a major role in the problems of adolescence. Ethnographers have discovered many such exceptions to plausible behavioral propositions.

To test any hypothesis on a cross-cultural basis required the accumulation of reliable information for a large sample of the world's societies, a task that often required years of search through the voluminous ethnographic literature and careful evaluation of the reliability of the sources for each society in the sample. In the end, the work was likely to turn up too few well-documented observations of the relevant variables. As a result, the comparative study of culture was largely anecdotal or based on samples too small to provide conclusive answers. Progress was made in solving these problems by the establishment of the Human Relations Area Files. This systematic organization of ethnographic material showed startling gaps in the data, even for societies that had presumably been the most thoroughly studied and described.

These files, which now cover about 200 of the world's societies, provide a valuable but limited basis for comparative studies on a variety of subjects.

STUDIES OF THINKING PROCESSES. "Insight" is a term commonly applied to the achievement of understanding, particularly when it takes place suddenly and dramatically. It is a genuine, if elusive, phenomenon. When people, and even chimpanzees, are faced with certain kinds of novel problem situations, their behavior often makes it appear that solutions occur suddenly and without appreciable connection to previous trial-and-error behavior. Careful studies, however, have shown that in many if not most situations the appearance of solutions is gradual, and is accompanied by much trial-and-error search. Accordingly, it was natural to feel that instances of sudden solution were probably artifacts resulting from crude description. If descriptions were sufficiently refined, would not all solutions be seen to emerge gradually, in ways following simple laws of association?

Experiments on problem solving by animals made important contributions to these questions, partly because animal subjects, which cannot report their introspections, impose a valuable discipline on the experimenter. In general, animal studies corroborated human studies. Problems that were easy for the subject were solved smoothly, undemonstratively, and routinely. At the other extreme, difficult problems generally evoked large amounts of trial-and-error behavior. Insightful problem solving appeared to be more usual with problems of intermediate difficulty.

It was further discovered that so-called trial-and-error behavior was rather complex, even in lower animals. Rats placed in an insoluble maze do not explore it at random but develop patterns of search (taking the right-hand alley, choosing the lighter path), which they shift from time to time, behaving rather as though they held hypotheses. Monkeys can go further, "learning to learn" by developing general and transferable ways of responding to problem situations.

Experiments on human subjects also illuminated the differences between insightful and noninsightful problem-solving behavior. If the basic structure of a problem is shown to a subject, his learning transfers much more readily to new tasks and is retained much longer than it is if he is given detailed and specific instructions for solving each problem. Good teachers have long acted on this principle, but its unequivocal and reproducible demonstration in the laboratory has now opened the way to a study of the detailed mechanism involved.

Further study of insightful problem solving showed that the process of means-end analysis is quite fundamental. People analyze a problem situation in terms of goals and subgoals and, drawing upon their memory of past problem situations, set out to find means for reaching the goal step by step, by solving one subproblem after another. Thus, a chess-player may set up the subgoal of protecting a piece from capture. Associated with this subgoal in his memory might be such means as moving the piece or defending it with an additional piece. Considering one of these means might lead to a new subproblem, such as finding a safe square to move to. Continued observation of problem solving led to more and more adequate description of what is involved in such means-end analysis.

With more detailed observation of the problem-solving process, the jumps of insight became smaller, and more easily explicable by interpolating hypothetical steps, although sudden intuitions still seemed all too numerous to justify full confidence in the detailed correctness of what was interpolated. Certain basic questions remained: To what extent did these descriptions constitute an explanation of mechanism, and not simply a step-by-step narrative of events? Were the processes that had been observed sufficient to account for the problem solving?

A more formal description of problem-solving tasks as mazes or trees in which solutions are scattered, often very sparsely, was an essential tool in answering these questions. Such trees are often very large, the tree for the game of chess, for example, having some 10^{120} branches. Unselective searches of large trees require impractically long times. A successful problem-solver must, even when he employs trial-and-error methods, search in a highly selective way, describable in terms of appropriate rules of thumb. Means-end analysis is but one of the general rules of thumb applied by human problem solvers.

The use of rules of thumb to reduce the effective size of the problem maze provides a plausible explanation for the selectivity that had been observed in trial-and-error search. In every novel situation, the rules of thumb are poor; hence search must be extensive and will appear to an observer as almost random. In familiar situations, the rules of thumb are so good that the solution can be found with hardly any backtracking. Situations of medium difficulty require a modest amount of search, which often appears to be directed rather than blind or random. Thus, solutions of such problems are most likely to appear "insightful."

Applications of these ideas left many of the central problems about problem-solving processes unanswered: What kinds of rules of thumb (in addition to means-end analysis) do human problem solvers employ? How can these rules and their organization be precisely and rigorously described? How can the completeness of a set of rules be tested empirically? What basic symbol-manipulating processes are required to perform the tasks we observe human subjects performing? How must these basic processes be governed and interrelated?

Initial answers to these questions have been found. The key has been nonnumerical simulation of mental processes by the use of digital computer programs and programming systems which focus on combining and modifying symbolized information rather than on doing arithmetic. The resulting models of human mental processes are essentially nonarithmetical and can be tested by presenting identical problems to the computer and to human subjects and then comparing, sentence by sentence, the output that each produces while seeking the solution. One particular information-processing system (the General Problem Solver, which possesses a few basic mechanisms for manipulating symbols and which can carry out means-end analyses and certain abstracting and planning processes) has been able to solve such problems as discovering proofs for conjectured mathematical theorems, solving puzzles, and even writing simple computer programs.

Experience with such information-processing systems shows that the simple processes mentioned above are sufficient to solve certain classes of problems. Moreover, many details of the computer's performance seem to be closely similar to those of a human subject's performance. Computer simulations exhibit most of the phenomena that have been regarded as symptomatic of insight. They sometimes reach solutions suddenly, and they do this under circumstances in which human subjects are likely to have an "aha!" experience. On the average, they spend the most time on the parts of problems on which human subjects spend the most time. They acquire specific patterns of approach to problem solving—patterns which facilitate the solution of certain subsequent problems while impeding that of others—under the same circumstances that cause human subjects to acquire them. Detailed correspondences of this kind provide a severe test for the theory, which is now rigorously stated, partially tested, and able to explain a number of the important processes involved in interesting sorts of human problem solving.

Further comparison of computer simulation with human performance will now lead us to new empirical studies of human behavior and to a steady increase in the predictive power of the theory and the adequacy of its correspondence with human behavior.

CLOSING REMARKS. Anthropological research on changes in primitive societies, sociological research on communication, and psychological research on perception and problem solving are, as we have seen, beginning to fit together to provide an understanding of the conditions under which innovation occurs or fails to occur. This is but one instance of the many ways in which the behavioral sciences are cooperating with one another more frequently, more deeply, and more broadly.

The need of similar cooperation to exploit present opportunities for studying other cultures is now clearly recognized. Social and economic change is a world-wide fact. Western industrialized civilization is spreading explosively. As cultures everywhere become more similar, opportunities are fleeting, especially for the study of societies, and of changes in societies, as varied as these are today. But it has become increasingly clear that decisions as to which aspect of these societies will be most usefully studied must be made with the knowledge and insight of all branches of behavioral science, and that all branches must contribute to the techniques by which such studies are made. For these studies should not only help answer today's questions but should contribute as much as possible to answering those of tomorrow.

Although the particular examples of behavioral study described here are scattered, and thus at best illustrative, they should have delineated a few key points:

(1) Progress in behavioral science has come about by using the scientific processes of observing, experimenting, and extensively following up and correcting working hypotheses. Indeed, all the general attitudes and strategies of physical and biological science have found a place in behavioral science.

(2) The behavioral sciences are diverse in subject matter and state of development, yet ideas and concepts circulate quite freely among them (and techniques circulate steadily, if more slowly).

(3) The division between laboratory experiment on the one hand and observation of what occurs without intervention (often in "natural experiments") on the other is both clear-cut and extremely noticeable in behavioral science, yet neither method can operate at full effectiveness without the other.

(4) Unsolved behavioral-science problems that are clearly solvable, and for which methods of attack are already identified, are no longer minor and trivial. Instead, both their scope and their scientific importance are substantial and steadily increasing.

Recommendations

The continuing development of the scientific study of behavior requires that certain underlying needs be met. This section of the report identifies certain of those needs and makes suggestions for action to meet them.

GENERAL EDUCATION IN BEHAVIORAL SCIENCE. Students should be exposed earlier and more effectively to the possibility of investigating behavioral phenomena by scientific techniques. The scientific approach to behavioral problems would be a valuable part of the general education of all students. This goal might be achieved in the secondary schools by inserting material on behavior in existing courses in biology and by emphasizing newer, empirical approaches in existing courses in social studies. Introductory undergraduate courses should be similarly strengthened.

Outstanding men in the behavioral sciences should follow the lead of their colleagues in physics, mathematics, and biology by devoting special efforts to preparing superior instructional materials for use at the secondary school and introductory undergraduate level.

SPECIFIC TRAINING OF BEHAVIORAL SCIENTISTS. The demand for behavioral scientists, as for all scientists, is outrunning the supply. Shortages exist now in each of the recognized behavioral fields; in each we anticipate an increasing need for well-trained persons in university teaching, in basic research, and in applied research and development. The needs for applied work are especially important in industry and national defense, and in emerging programs such as education and foreign aid. In each of these areas the shortage of trained personnel is likely to set a limit on useful developments. The education of behavioral scientists is such a key problem that a number of different steps should be taken; some of these are needed also in improving the general education of those students who do not go on to specialize.

(1) The recommendations of the Seaborg report are as applicable to the behavioral sciences as they are to other sciences. We agree that the universities need to be strengthened, that first-hand experience with research is an integral part of graduate education, and that it is essential to increase the support for training.

(2) The need for special educational facilities is not as well recog-

nized in the behavioral sciences, perhaps because of their recent emergence as empirical disciplines, as it is in the physical and biological sciences, where educational budgets include the cost of equipping and operating laboratories and field facilities. Both colleges and graduate schools should increase their effort to give students first-hand contact with behavioral-science data and techniques by exposing them to the appropriate clinical material, field trips, or laboratory work. Adequate provision for such work should be made in their budgets.

(3) There is a special need for summer institutes, or other short-term instructional arrangements, to bring research workers and selected teachers up to date in new techniques and experimental procedures. Experience suggests that such arrangements would be more effective if they were set up on a relatively long-term basis and in a suitable research environment. There should be a small core staff to plan during the entire year for the instruction program as well as to work on research. As one specific step in this direction, such a special instructional program should be centered upon the applications of mathematics and computers to the behavioral sciences.

SYSTEMATIC COLLECTION OF BASIC BEHAVIORAL DATA FOR THE UNITED STATES. Both fundamental research in the behavioral sciences and the application of scientific knowledge to human problems could be substantially assisted by making available better and more illuminating basic data about the structure and functioning of American society. We call attention to the great advance over the past generation in the quantity and quality of our information about the economy and to the effective use that is now made of such information in formulating and administering national economic policy. Similar benefits would flow from a corresponding advance in the quantity and quality of information about noneconomic aspects of behavior.

A significant start has been made on the borderlines of economics —the collection of data on family budgets, for example, and on businessmen's expectations—and on the composition, characteristics, and movements of populations. A similar promising start has just been made with the establishment of a National Health Survey. A proposal has been made to establish a special National Family Welfare Survey in the Social Security Administration. But there are many significant aspects of behavior about which systematic data are almost completely lacking. We know something of how people spend their money, but almost nothing of how they spend their time. In addition to uses in basic research, behavioral data will become increasingly important in exploring the problems of the aged, in forecasting the effects of increased leisure on our society, and in many other matters of public policy. There are other areas where good systematic data would be invaluable and where they are now almost wholly lacking: travel and commuting habits, occupational aspirations, the preferences and choices of youth, and the incidence of mental disturbance.

Fortunately, progress has been made in recent years in developing methods for collecting and processing data of these kinds. Available skills in sample design, in survey techniques, in construction of interview schedules, and in electronic data-processing make such data collection feasible and meaningful. The family budget studies already mentioned, and recent surveys of scientific manpower, are examples of what can now be done, and of what needs to be done more often, more systematically, and over a wider range of phenomena. In particular, data that are comparable, systematic, and periodically gathered will be essential for establishing and interpreting trends. Such work should, of course, be planned with definite research purposes in mind. Experience shows that without this, the mere collection of data often proves a fruitless enterprise.

A clear responsibility—already partially recognized in activities of the Census Bureau, Department of Labor, and other agencies—lies with the federal government to exercise leadership in extending and improving the data on which sound behavioral-science knowledge and intelligent application of that knowledge to public affairs rests. The responsibility is enlarging as the need for good behavioral data grows, and as our technical abilities to provide them advance.

There is need for both a re-examination of today's needs and opportunities and continuing careful review of what is being done. Accordingly, we suggest that:

(1) The Social Science Research Council be invited to appoint a standing committee to review and study present practices, needs, and opportunities for gathering information about noneconomic aspects of behavior in American society.

(2) A group broadly representative of relevant government agencies be appointed to follow current and planned activity in this field and to provide appropriate advice in the light of the current possibilities and needs of behavioral science.

COLLECTION AND PROCESSING OF DATA ON OTHER SOCIETIES AND CULTURES. Reliable data systematically collected on the conditions, customs, and patterns of behavior in societies other than our own are indispensable to the behavioral sciences. Comparison across societies provides information which it would be impossible to obtain in our society even by deliberate experiments. Such data are essential for testing the generality of conclusions from studies within a single society and are a fruitful source of hypotheses.

For studies of this kind, comparable data are required on a large sample of the world's societies, representing major cultural differences and all levels of complexity. These data include among other things, ethnographic material, results of statistical surveys, and abstracts of the content of communications. Several partial repositories of such data presently exist—a file of ethnographic materials on a sample of about 200 societies, a file of survey results obtained in various countries, and materials in area institutes at universities. Much of what these repositories contain is neither widely known nor accessible, the collection of data is not well coordinated, and what is collected often fails to meet the developing requirements of behavioral sciences.

Because these data are collected throughout the world by scientists representing many countries, a special study is needed to determine what data about other societies are presently collected by agencies in and out of the government; whether some of the activities just mentioned can be consolidated; what new types of data are most needed to fill in serious gaps; what data of continuing significance will be lost forever if they are not gathered soon; what sorts of data should be collected both systematically and regularly; and how relevant data can best be procured and stored so that they are maximally available.

To answer these questions, a special study group is required, and we suggest consultation with the National Science Foundation, the Smithsonian Institution, the National Research Council, the National Institutes of Health, and the U.S. National Commission for UNESCO in forming it.

THE NEED FOR LARGER UNITS OF SUPPORT FOR BASIC RESEARCH. The scholarly disciplines from which behavioral sciences sprang were in most cases able to carry out their studies without the appurtenances of the empirical sciences. There is little general realization of what special research tools the behavioral sciences now require and insufficient acceptance of the need for providing them. A stage of growth has been reached where some kinds of research cannot be adequately conducted without substantial specialized laboratory equipment or extensive field research organizations.

Furthermore, part of the difficulty lies with behavioral scientists themselves. Feeling that it is almost impossible to secure the really large funding required for a full-scale attack on many basic problems, most behavioral scientists have adapted their ideas and plans to fit available resources. For example, many inquiries that really require national sample surveys, covering people in various strata of society, in fact are based upon a purely local survey or are confined to data from a few haphazardly chosen individuals. Many laboratory experiments which require expensive equipment are not made or are made inadequately. Sufficient funds to make possible the really large-scale support of fundamental projects that are intellectually and scientifically large have been lacking. There has tended to be a relatively lower upper limit on the size of grants for basic research in the behavioral sciences, as compared to those in the physical and biological sciences.

Behavioral scientists can take a first step toward the solution of this problem by making serious and carefully-thought-through proposals for basic research whenever these proposals are justified by research opportunities, whether or not the required scale of support has been traditional. The existence and consideration of good proposals will do much to increase the possibilities of adequate support.

We suggest that a particular effort be made to support basic-research ideas for behavioral science on a scale consistent with their importance and without regard to previous levels of funding.

PROVIDING ADVICE TO GOVERNMENT. In view of the relevance of the findings and methods of behavioral science to a very broad range of governmental operations, the present facilities for providing advice on questions in this area are inadequate. The role taken by the National Academy of Sciences–National Research Council in physical and biological science is unfilled in behavioral science. At present the National Academy of Sciences represents only restricted segments of anthropology and psychology. Most areas of behavioral and social sciences, although relevant to many programs of governmental action, are entirely unrepresented in the National Academy and are included in the National Research Council in only a fragmentary way.

Two courses of action would be highly desirable in order to provide effective sources of behavioral-science advice to government agencies.

(1) The structure of the National Academy of Sciences–National Research Council should be broadened to include the areas of behavioral and social science not now represented.

(2) Federal agencies should make more effective use of the re-

sources of the Social Science Research Council and the other national, professional organizations of the behavioral and social sciences.

RESEARCH AND DEVELOPMENT IN AGENCIES WITH ACTION MISSIONS. Expanding programs at state and national levels in areas of action such as urban renewal and transportation have created a demand for applied research. This demand has been largely unmet, or met in piecemeal, after-the-fact ways. Careful pilot studies have been made in a few instances, as in the introduction of certain new agricultural processes. But in most instances, applied research, if carried out, has been restricted to following after the action and evaluating its effects. Although the few such studies that have been conducted have clearly proved to be valuable, large-scale action programs have seldom been accompanied or preceded by pilot studies which evaluated the several alternative actions that appeared equally attractive. In urban renewal, for example, the data necessary for rational actions in large-scale programs could be provided by the establishment of pilot redevelopment programs of various types and the early comparison of their results. The need is especially great in those areas where an action taken now has consequences that continue far into the future. The establishment of a research and development section of the Agency for International Development is an excellent step. Whenever feasible, agencies whose missions involve actions that will have long-lasting effects should conduct pilot programs incorporating adequate behavioral research prior to the activation of large-scale programs, or at the very least, research on action programs should be undertaken simultaneously with the initiation of action and used to guide further development. This means starting trials now to prepare for the problems of the future.

RESEARCH RELEVANT TO EDUCATION. The behavioral sciences can contribute to many problems of education, such as increasing insightful learning in the classroom and changing those strong influences from fellow students that run counter to the goals of parents and teachers. Basic research has already led to programmed learning, both by programmed texts and teaching machines.

Education has a national budget second only to that of national defense. Yet only a small fraction of 1 percent of this budget has been spent on research and development. This is one obvious reason for the failure of education to make technical advances comparable to those seen in other aspects of our national life. Moreover, for the past 25 years few outstanding research workers in the behavioral sciences have exhibited interest in educational research. Both of these deficiencies are beginning to be corrected, but more remains to be done.

INTERNATIONAL RELATIONS. Some of the most difficult, complex, and vital problems confronting our country are in the area of international relations. Behavioral science is relevant to various aspects of these problems. For example, in dealing with nations whose cultures are radically different from our own, much of the intuitive knowledge which the talented man-of-affairs uses so effectively in dealing with our own society may be irrelevant or actually misleading. Technical knowledge about the detailed nature of the society and the functional interdependence of its components is essential for effective communication, for judging the probable course of events, for leading cooperative efforts, or for giving the proper kind of assistance in the right way.

There are many reasons for the fact that an enormously disproportionate part of the social contacts of a businessman or diplomat in a foreign country is likely to be with the very top social classes. These classes usually represent a minute fraction of the total population; their members lead completely atypical lives and not infrequently have interests and views opposite to those of the majority of the people. Thus, it is easy for the visiting American to be seriously misled, unless he possesses suitable attributes and uses suitable methods of reaching a more adequate sample of people.

Behavioral scientists have no "miracle solutions" to problems of international relations, but they can help. Anthropologists and certain sociologists, for instance, have had much experience with the problems of attitude and methods just mentioned. A study of the practices, special problems, and views of the various government agencies involved must precede any detailed recommendations as to how the principles, facts, and techniques developed in behavioral sciences can be best used in international relations.

Members of the Subpanel

NEAL E. MILLER, *Chairman,* Yale University
KENNETH E. CLARK, University of Colorado
JAMES S. COLEMAN, Johns Hopkins University
LEON FESTINGER, Stanford University
WARD H. GOODENOUGH, University of Pennsylvania
ALEXANDER H. LEIGHTON, Cornell University
GEORGE A. MILLER, Harvard University
HERBERT A. SIMONS, Carnegie Institute of Technology
JOHN W. TUKEY, Princeton University

Consultants to the Subpanel

ELIHU KATZ, University of Chicago
JESSE ORLANSKY, Institute for Defense Analyses
HENRY W. RIECKEN, National Science Foundation

Technical Assistant to the Subpanel

JAMES B. HARTGERING, Office of the Special Assistant
for Science and Technology, The White House

Summary and Recommendations
THE BEHAVIORAL SCIENCES
AND THE FEDERAL GOVERNMENT[1]

The primary purpose of this report is to examine how the knowledge and methods of the behavioral sciences can be brought to bear effectively on the programs and policy processes of the federal government. The federal government faces increasingly complex decisions in foreign affairs, defense strategy and management, urban reconstruction, civil rights, economic growth and stability, public health, social welfare, and education and training. These decisions must be based on all the information that can be made available to administrators and policy-makers. The lack of vital social and economic information on critical issues and the lack of methods for analyzing information and relating it to policies and operations have been constantly emphasized in recent years by a number of public commissions, study panels, and government groups. These have included the National Commission on Technology, Automation, and Economic Progress; the President's Commission on Law Enforcement and Administration of Justice; the Committee on Foreign Affairs Personnel; and the United States Advisory Commission on Information.

In response to the needs of policy-making, there has also been increased support from government departments and agencies for building up the bases of knowledge and information for social and economic programs. The Manpower Training and Development Act of 1962, the Elementary and Secondary Education Act of 1965, the Public Works and Economic Development Act of 1965, and the programs

---

[1] *The Behavioral Sciences and the Federal Government,* Report of the Advisory Committee on Government Programs in the Behavioral Sciences, Publication 1680, National Academy of Sciences–National Research Council (Washington, D.C., 1968).

of the Office of Economic Opportunity and the Department of Housing and Urban Development, together with established programs in the Department of Agriculture and the Department of Defense, all include a range of behavioral science activities from data collection to techniques for program evaluation, as well as support of fundamental research related to agency missions. These activities represent recognition of the pertinence of the behavioral sciences to government affairs. They underscore the need to examine the way behavioral science research is related to planning and management and the methods used for testing research for quality and relevance.

There is no assumption, in this review of the role of the behavioral sciences in the federal government, that knowledge is a substitute for wisdom or common sense or for decision-making. Behavioral science knowledge is a source of understanding about social and individual behavior that has been confirmed by as careful observation, testing, or statistical analysis as is possible. Much of the knowledge of the behavioral sciences is fragmented, much is based on limited verification, and many propositions are only approximate explanations of complex social and behavioral phenomena. The behavioral sciences are, nonetheless, an important source of information, analysis, and explanation about group and individual behavior, and thus an essential and increasingly relevant instrument of modern government. At the same time, there is need to be concerned as much with the development of the behavioral sciences as with their use; indeed, to see both the development and use of the behavioral sciences as parts of a total and continuing problem.

Effective Use of Knowledge

Past experience in the use of the behavioral sciences provides a reference point for examining the organization of research in government. In the field of statistical services, the Bureau of the Census, for example, has contributed to, and relied heavily on, the development of research knowledge and methods. The experience of the Bureau of the Census —with its expertly trained staff, its close ties with the professional communities, its concern with methodologies, and its systematic procedures for substantive review and analysis—provides a pattern of research planning and utilization applicable to research throughout the government. Likewise, there is valuable experience in the application of economic information and analysis to the formation of fiscal and monetary policies. The evolution of the economic advisory system in the federal government has had several results: large-scale participation by professional economists in extending and improving the federal statistical system; employment of trained economists in departments and agencies; creation of high-level advisory agencies, such as the Council of Economic Advisers; and the stimulation of basic research in economics, inside and outside the government, as a result of increasing needs of government for both information and knowledge.

The economic advisory system, like the federal statistical system, is a highly advanced example of applying the knowledge and methods of the behavioral sciences in government. Its development is the result of a good deal of trial and error; increased understanding about the use of the knowledge and methods of economics in the professions and occupations from which many policy-makers come; the accumulation of large and manageable sources of economic data; and increasingly reliable instruments of analysis and projection. Similar developments must be encouraged in other fields of the behavioral sciences, especially in sociology, social psychology, political science, and anthropology, that are relevant to new social programs at home and to programs of development assistance in the international field.

From past experience, three sets of conditions appear necessary for the effective use of the knowledge and methods of the behavioral sciences in government. These conditions are: (1) an understanding by top administrators of the nature of the behavioral sciences and their relevance to the policies and programs for which they are responsible; (2) a professional environment to attract behavioral scientists into government and to provide incentives and opportunities for their scientific development; and (3) a strategy for research to give cohesion and purpose to behavioral science activities carried on by a department or agency and to relate them to policy processes and program operations.

In order to strengthen these conditions throughout the federal government, the Committee recommends:

1. *That each major department and agency, with the support of the Office of Science and Technology and the Civil Service Commission, initiate a staffing study to identify positions for which substantial training and experience in the behavioral sciences should be an increasingly important criterion for appointment, most especially positions involving policy planning, program evaluation and analysis, and research administration and operation.*

2. *That each major department and agency, with the support of the Office of Science and Technology and the Civil Service Commission, initiate a series of continuing programs to strengthen its staff competence in the behavioral sciences, including:*

a. In-service training for planning, evaluation, and research staff in the scope and methods of the behavioral sciences;

b. Opportunities for planning, evaluation, and research staff to gain advanced university training in the behavioral sciences and to participate in professional activities; and

c. Fellowships and internships for university-based behavioral scientists and graduate students to participate in governmental activities involving the behavioral sciences.

3. *That each major department and agency, with the assistance of an advisory panel of behavioral scientists, develop a strategy for the use and support of a the behavioral sciences and maintain under continual review a long-range research program that includes:*

a. A broad spectrum of research activities from applied research to investigations of fundamental behavioral and social processes relevant to department or agency missions;

b. Opportunities through internal staffs and contract and grant arrangements to utilize research resources both inside and outside the government;

c. Continuing programs for the systematic maintenance of historical and operating records as essential sources of research data; and

d. Application of behavioral science knowledge and methods to program evaluation and analysis with provision for experimental projects designed to provide relevant information for future planning.

Foreign Affairs

These recommendations relating to the effective use of the behavioral sciences apply to departments and agencies involved in foreign operations as well as to those chiefly responsible for domestic programs. Nevertheless, research in foreign affairs agencies depends heavily on information sources in foreign countries. This special feature has been complicated by the convergence of three developments since the second world war: the social, political, economic, and technological changes in the world; the increasingly complex international position of the United States; and the growth of the behavioral sciences and their relevance for government planning. This convergence has created two major problems for the government in supporting behavioral science research overseas: the problem of relating the several research programs of foreign affairs and military agencies; and the problem of reconciling the use of research by the government with the requirements for international cooperation in the behavioral sciences.

By and large, the research programs of departments and agencies with foreign operations have developed according to the perception each had of its needs in relation to its own mission. The variety of research programs has encouraged a pluralism in approach to policy issues that is important to retain. But it has reflected the lack of central coordination that has been a constant problem of American foreign policy since the second world war. It has produced pluralism without the counterbalance of central overview and a heavy domination of funding from defense agencies. Generally, research in civilian foreign affairs has been fragmentary, erratic, and weakly defended. Moreover, a low value has been placed on research as an instrument of planning in the Department of State. This has served to limit the Department's role in providing leadership for government-wide research in international affairs and in supporting a place for research in other foreign affairs agencies.

The major mechanism for relating research programs in international affairs on an interagency basis is the Foreign Area Research Coordination Group (FAR). FAR, however, is a voluntary group of some 20 participating agencies with no binding authority over its members and no firm lines to the policy planning process. The Foreign Affairs Research Council in the Department of State serves as another clearinghouse through its function of reviewing research projects for their sensitivity to foreign policy issues. Neither mechanism provides a basis for defining government-wide objectives for research in international affairs. There are no organized means of assuring that areas of research essential to policy planning are supported and that cumulative bodies of knowledge on international problems are developed.

In order to strengthen research in international affairs and achieve balance among the research programs of foreign affairs and military agencies, the Committee recommends:

4. That, in the field of foreign affairs, long-range behavioral science research objectives be drawn up by an interagency planning group headed by the Department of State, with the support of the Office of Science and Technology, and that the research programs of all departments and agencies that operate overseas, including the United States

Information Agency, Agency for International Development, Department of Defense, and the Peace Corps, be continually related to these long-term objectives through the Foreign Area Research Coordination Group and foreign affairs planning mechanisms like the Senior Interdepartmental Group.

International Cooperation in Research

The effective use of research in foreign affairs must be reconciled with the requirements for international cooperation in the behavioral sciences. A lack of financial support threatens the continued growth of international and comparative studies in colleges and universities throughout the country. This situation has been created by the failure to establish the Center for Educational Cooperation authorized under the International Education Act of 1966 and by the decisions of the major private foundations to reduce their support for research and education in international affairs before the government's new program was fully funded.

The level of government support for research and education in international affairs is, however, just one part of the problem. The behavioral sciences have a special need for free and healthy international exchange in research. The important influence of culture on social and human behavior makes it necessary to undertake observations on a cross-cultural basis in order to test general hypotheses. Such research requires, in turn, free access to different national groups and extensive exchange among behavioral scientists from all countries.

From a practical point of view, international and comparative behavioral science research cannot be carried out by Americans without the cooperation of foreign scientists. From both political and scientific perspectives, "unilateralism" will be resisted increasingly and opportunities for research in foreign countries progressively delimited unless research is made a matter of international cooperation. Major responsibility for international cooperation rests with behavioral scientists themselves. A responsibility of the government is to create the most advantageous environment for this development. Such an environment would be enhanced: (1) by placing major governmental responsibility for supporting university-based research overseas in science- and education-based agencies rather than in departments and agencies that have foreign policy or military missions; (2) by strengthening research programs in international organizations; and (3) by programs to assist behavioral science training and education in the developing countries.

The Committee, therefore, recommends:

5. *That primary responsibility for government support for behavioral science research and training conducted in foreign countries by universities in the United States be placed in agencies and programs committed to basic research and research training, particularly the National Science Foundation, the National Institutes of Health, and the proposed Center for Educational Cooperation under the International Education Act.*

6. *That a pattern of programs be developed to strengthen the bases for international cooperation in behavioral science research and to assist in the growth of behavioral sciences in foreign countries, especially in Asia, Africa, and Latin America, through:*

a. Provision in technical and economic assistance programs for the development of faculties and facilities in the behavioral sciences in foreign universities;

b. Special institutional grants to United States universities by the National Science Foundation and the National Institutes of Health to support fellowships for foreign students selected by academic departments and to permit continuing cooperative programs of research and training with foreign universities; and

c. The extension of bilateral and multilateral programs of scientific cooperation in the behavioral sciences and increased support for the behavioral science programs of international organizations like UNESCO and the United Nations Institute for Training and Research.

Science Policies

The development of research strategies and staffing and training policies to strengthen the research component in the government depends on the value attached to the knowledge and methods of the behavioral sciences. This is true, not only within departments and agencies, but also at the highest levels of the government, where policies on the use and support of the sciences are shaped. There is, however, no central forum for dealing with common problems of behavioral science research or for giving top-level support to policies designed to strengthen the behavioral sciences as an instrument of policy-making and program operations.

The science policies of the federal government are the responsibility of the President and the Congress. With the increased relevance of science to public policies, a number of mechanisms, largely stimulated by new advances in the physical sciences, have grown up within the Executive Branch to bring scientific advice to the top level of the government and to support the effective growth of scientific activities throughout the federal establishment. These mechanisms have included the Office of Science and Technology (OST), the President's Science Advisory Committee (PSAC), and the Federal Council on Science and Technology.

In practice, problems presented to OST and PSAC have been discussed mainly in terms of the physical and biological sciences. As a consequence, OST and related organizations have been slow to recognize responsibility for reviewing behavioral science programs or for assessing the impact of behavioral science knowledge on national policies. OST has never developed a staff competence in the behavioral sciences, and only recently was the first behavioral scientist appointed to PSAC. Nevertheless, on a number of occasions, issues of behavioral science research, such as the rights of privacy in relation to research, have been the subject of study by OST- or PSAC-sponsored groups. Also, many technological problems examined by OST, PSAC, and the Federal Council have been infused with economic, social, political, and legal elements. In such cases, OST and PSAC have made use of behavioral science resources, but on a limited *ad hoc* basis.

The question of greater behavioral science capacity in both OST and PSAC gains in importance as behavioral science activities increase in government and as technological problems raise increasingly difficult social and economic issues. There are alternatives to placing responsibility for behavioral science activities in OST. It is possible that such responsibility might be exercised by the Bureau of the Budget, by an expanded and more broadly conceived Council of Economic Advisers, or by a separate office under a new Special Assistant to the President. In the case of the Bureau of the Budget and the Council of Economic Advisers, responsibilities for review of research programs would detract from their primary staff functions. At the same time, it would be unrealistic and mistaken to separate the impact of the behavioral sciences from that of the physical and biological sciences in top-level policy processes by setting up what would be two Special Assistants for Science.

In the fields of public health, urban reconstruction, and economic and social development at home and abroad, a key requirement is the ability to work out comprehensive programs that utilize and relate knowledge from all the sciences. By the same token, the policies of the federal government regarding scientific development and educational growth need to be conceived in comprehensive terms, especially as federal support of science becomes increasingly related to federal support for higher education. The Committee therefore recommends:

7. *That the functions of the Office of Science and Technology be broadened and its resources strengthened in order to assume the same responsibilities for governmental programs in the behavioral sciences as it now exercises for programs in the physical and biological sciences, including the review of government support for the continuing growth of these sciences and special problems with regard to their application to government programs and processes.*

8. *That the President's Science Advisory Committee be organized to include behavioral scientists in its membership in order to deal with the full range of matters brought to its attention, including the social and economic effects of scientific and technological change, the state and needs of American higher education, and the role of the federal government in strengthening scientific developments in all fields, including the behavioral sciences.*

Support for Basic Research

The needs of government departments and agencies for new sources of social and economic information and for new tools of analysis increase the need for a structure within which basic research of a theoretical and methodological nature can be encouraged and supported.

While the federal government finances basic research in the universities and research institutes through a pluralistic system of support, major responsibility for supporting scientific development falls on the National Science Foundation (NSF). The behavioral science program of the NSF has developed in scope and depth in recent years with increased support for the full range of disciplines and methods and with the initial extension of departmental and institutional grants to the behavioral sciences in addition to the more established project grants. The question has arisen, however, whether the patterns of support within the NSF are sufficient to meet the developmental needs of the behavioral sciences or whether there is need for the establishment of a separate National Foundation for the Social Sciences.

The future expansion and direction of government support for the behavioral sciences require a full and balanced assessment of the current state and future needs of these sciences. Such an assessment, together with indications of the ability of the NSF to meet the needs of the behavioral sciences, should emerge as three current reviews are completed: the congressional action amending NSF legislation to specify the social sciences for NSF support and authorizing the Foundation to fund applied as well as basic research; the review of the needs and opportunities for scientific growth being undertaken by the Behavioral and Social Sciences Survey Committee sponsored by the National Academy of Sciences–National Research Council and the Social Science Research Council; and the study of the Special NSF Commission on the Social Sciences on the utilization of the social and behavioral sciences to meet the problems of society.

The combined effect of these reviews could lead to changes in the government system of support for the behavioral sciences within the current structure of the NSF or through new institutional arrangements. Pending completion of these studies, certain general directions and requirements for the development of the behavioral sciences, nonetheless, have become increasingly evident. These were outlined in the report, *Strengthening the Behavioral Sciences,* issued by a special panel sponsored by the PSAC in 1962: the extension of general education in the behavioral sciences; support for graduate training; systematic collection and processing of basic behavioral data for the United States and for other societies; and larger units of support for basic research.

The recommendations of the PSAC-sponsored panel provide guidelines for an expanded NSF program in the behavioral sciences that need not await the result of current studies. Expansion along these lines, moreover, would provide the Foundation with increased operating experience as a base for a larger effort once the direction of these studies becomes clear. The Committee, therefore, recommends:

9. That the National Science Foundation, which has special responsibility for the growth and development of all the sciences and for continuing support of training programs in the sciences, give increased emphasis to institutional and departmental grants in the behavioral sciences and to support of centers that are organized to develop cumulative information and knowledge in the behavioral sciences, and begin to develop an organized base through which to examine and implement the recommendations of current major study groups on the future needs for development and use of the behavioral sciences.

Future-Oriented Research and Public Policies

The recommendations in this report have thus far emphasized strengthening existing instrumentalities in the federal government for the use and support of the behavioral sciences. The report seeks to stress that there are no "instant" answers to the effective use of knowledge. The use of research requires an integration of the knowledge and methods of the behavioral sciences into the on-going processes of government and not necessarily the creation of new and separate institutions. The application of knowledge to public programs and the formation of science and educational policies, moreover, require the combined efforts of all the sciences—physical, biological, and behavioral.

The pluralism of the federal science structure, nevertheless, provides a framework for new and innovating institutions aimed at advanced research and at a continuing examination of the relevance of knowledge to current and future problems of the society. The National Institutes of Health, the national laboratories, the special non-profit research corporations, and the contract method have all served to bring intellectual resources to bear on public policies. They supplement the research, evaluation, and analytical services within the government that, no matter how broadly conceived and administered, are often restricted by pressures of time and by the operating assumptions of existing policies. In a period of rapid and substantial change at home and abroad, the policies and programs of the federal government must become increasingly future-oriented. This orientation will always require new kinds of information, new ways of analyzing data, new collaboration among scientists, new relations between scientists and policy-makers, and new attitudes about the nature of planning.

A new federal institute to sponsor advanced research related to public purposes would serve to strengthen the recommendations for internal review and organization made in this report. It could go farther to provide a kind of lightning rod for future changes as an alternative to the frustrating process of analyzing social and economic crises after they have occurred and taken their toll. It could have important effects, not only on the role of knowledge in federal policy-making, but also on the growth of a deeper sensitivity throughout the society to the problems of applying knowledge to practical issues.

Such an institute would need an independent base of support in order to be free to examine, not only the issues of the society, but also the prevailing premises and perceptions of these issues. Providing this kind of independence would give positive recognition to the place of knowledge in democratic government. The Committee, therefore, recommends:

10. That the President and the Congress create and independently endow a National Institute for Advanced Research and Public Policy in Washington, D.C., to undertake continuing and long-range analyses of national policies and problems, to serve as a center for continuing interchange between government policy-makers and scientists, and to provide a forum in the nation's capital for the full exploration of the growth and application of knowledge from all the sciences to the major issues of the society.

Members of the Advisory Committee on Government Programs in the Behavioral Sciences

DONALD R. YOUNG, *Chairman*
    Visiting Professor, Rockefeller University

HERBERT A. SIMON, *Vice Chairman*
    Professor of Computer Sciences and Psychology,
    Carnegie-Mellon University

FREDERIC N. CLEAVELAND
    Professor of Political Science, University of North Carolina

A. HUNTER DUPREE
    Professor of History, Brown University

GEORGE M. FOSTER, JR.
    Professor of Anthropology, University of California, Berkeley

ALBERT GARRETSON
    Professor of Law, New York University

MORRIS JANOWITZ
    Professor of Sociology, University of Chicago

HERBERT C. KELMAN
Professor of Psychology, University of Michigan

LYLE H. LANIER
Vice President and Professor of Psychology, University of Illinois

WILBERT E. MOORE
Sociologist, Russell Sage Foundation

KARL J. PELZER[2]
Professor of Geography, Yale University

ITHIEL DE SOLA POOL
Professor of Political Science,
Massachusetts Institute of Technology

THOMAS C. SCHELLING
Professor of Economics, Harvard University

JOSEPH J. SPENGLER
Professor of Economics, Duke University

ALEXANDER SPOEHR
Professor of Anthropology, University of Pittsburgh

GEORGE K. TANHAM[3]
Deputy to the Vice President, The RAND Corporation

The Staff

GENE M. LYONS, *Executive Secretary*
Division of Behavioral Sciences, National Research Council

GAY HENDERSON, *Research Assistant*
Division of Behavioral Sciences, National Research Council

---

[2] Because of an overseas assignment, Professor Pelzer was unable to participate in the final drafting of the Committee report.

[3] Dr. Tanham served with the RAND Corporation during the period of the Committee's work; he has since moved to a position with the Department of State.

INDEX

INDEX

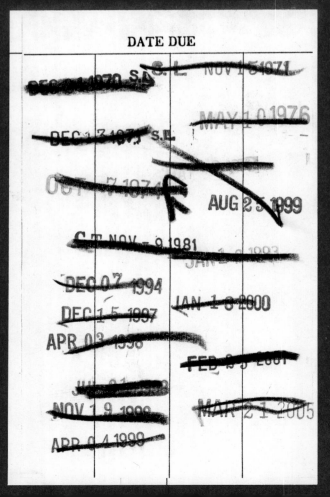

DATE DUE